World Trade and Payments Cycles

WORLD TRADE AND PAYMENTS CYCLES

The Advance and Retreat of the Postwar Order

RICHARD COHEN

Foreword by *NORMAN A. BAILEY*

PRAEGER

New York
Westport, Connecticut
London

Library of Congress Cataloging-in-Publication Data

Cohen, Richard, 1946-
    World trade and payments cycles: the advance and retreat of the
postwar order / Richard Cohen; foreword by Norman A. Bailey.
        p. cm.
    Bibliography: p.
    ISBN 0-275-93251-6 (alk. paper)
    1. International trade—History. 2. East-West trade (1945-)
3. Balance of payments—History. I. Title.
HF1379.C74   1989
382.1'7—dc19   89-3856

Library of Congress Catalog Card Number: 89-3856
ISBN: 0-275-93251-6

First published in 1989

Praeger Publishers, One Madison Avenue, New York, NY 10010
A division of Greenwood Press, Inc.

Printed in the United States of America

∞

The paper used in this book complies with the Permanent
Paper Standard issued by the National Information Standards
Organization (Z39.48-1984).

10 9 8 7 6 5 4 3 2 1

To Laura, my wife and colleague

Contents

Tables, Figures, and Chart   ix

Foreword by Norman A. Bailey   xiii

Acknowledgments   xv

Introduction   xvii

PART I: The Factors Shaping the Postwar Trade and
        Payments Order

     Chapter 1   Forging the Postwar Trade and Payments
                Order: Forces in Conflict   3

PART II: The Advance of the Postwar Trade and Payments
        Order

     Chapter 2   The Period of Postwar Economic
                Reconstruction—1945–52   29

     Chapter 3   The Period of Transition in Trade and
                Payments—1952–58   43

Chapter 4   The Cycle of Rapid Growth in International
            Trade—1959–67   57

PART III: The Emergence of Trade and Payments Cycles and
         the Retreat of the Trade and Payments Order

Chapter 5   Trade and Payments Cycles: Their Structure
            and Differences   81

Chapter 6   The Cycle of Inflationary Growth in World
            Trade—1968–75   123

Chapter 7   The Cycle of Stagflation—1976–82   151

Chapter 8   The Cycle of Disinflation—Phases I–IV:
            1983–86   183

PART IV: The Current Situation and Beyond

Chapter 9   Phase V of the Current Cycle: What's
            Happened to the J-Curve and Inflation   217

Chapter 10 Conclusion: Meeting the Challenge   249

Notes   259

Figure Sources   285

Select Bibliography   287

Index   293

Tables, Figures, and Chart

TABLES

2.1 Average Annual Excess of Dollar Supply Over Dollar Use, Pre-World War II and Post-World War II   32

2.2 Percent of National Trade of Eurasian CPEs with Non-CPEs, CPEs, and USSR in Pre-World War II and Post-World War II Periods   40

3.1 Import and Export Shares and Merchandise Trade Performance of the Developing Sector in the Period of Transition   46

3.2 Developed Sector's Role in World Exports and Imports During Period of Transition   50

3.3 U.S. Balance of Payments, 1952–58   52

4.1 Developing Sector Imports and Primary Commodity Prices in Cycle 1   64

4.2 U.S. Balance of Payments, 1958–67   70

5.1 Domestic Demand Growth Rate Comparison Among the Leading Six Developed Sector Economies in Phase I of the Four Trade and Payments Cycles   97

5.2 U.S. Merchandise Trade Balance and Export and Import Growth Rate in Phases I, III, and V   100

5.3 Developing Sector Merchandise Trade Balance and Export and Import Growth Rate in Phases II, III, V, and VI   104

5.4 Domestic Demand Growth Rates of Key Developed
     Sector Economies in Phase III   105

5.5 Government Fiscal Deficits as a Percentage of GNP in
     Major Developed Sector Economies During Phase V   110

5.6 Major Developed Sector Economy Domestic Demand
     Growth Rates in Phase V   112

5.7 Forces Behind Developing Sector Export Performance
     in Phase V   114

5.8 Developed Sector Domestic Demand Growth Rates in
     Phase VI   119

5.9 Forces Behind Developing Sector Export Performance
     in Phase VI   121

6.1 Changes in Distribution of World Merchandise Trade
     and Current Account Balances in Phases V and VI of
     Cycle 2   139

6.2 Sectoral Shares of Imports and Exports in Cycle 2   142

7.1 Merchandise Trade Balances and Export and Import
     Growth Rates of Major Developed Economies in
     Phases I and III of Cycle 3   155

7.2 National and Sectoral Merchandise Trade Balances and
     Export and Import Growth Rates in Phases V and VI
     of Cycle 3   166

7.3 The Growth of Developing Sector Debt and Net
     Interest and Their Evolving Structure   168

7.4 The Changing Dimensions and Structure of World
     Services Trade   181

8.1 Distribution of World Merchandise Trade Balances and
     Export and Import Growth Rates in Phases I–III of
     Cycle 4   187

8.2 Change in Sectoral Export Shares in Cycle 4   202

9.1 Comparing U.S. Merchandise Trade Balance Recoveries
     in Phase V   223

9.2 Fiscal Stimulus and Domestic Demand Growth in the
     Non-U.S. Developed Sector in Phase V of Cycles 2–4   229

9.3 Import Growth in the Developing Sector From
     Preceding Recession to Phase V   233

9.4 U.S. Agricultural Exports in Phase V and Their Impact
     on U.S. Exports and Merchandise Trade Balance   236

9.5   The U.S. Net Investment Balance and the U.S. Direct
      Investment and Factor Services Income Balance Impact
      on Improvement in the U.S. Current Account Balance
      in Phase V   239

9.6   Consumer Price Inflation in Phase V of the Last Three
      Trade and Payments Cycles   241

FIGURES

Intr.1 Long-Term Trends and Cycles in Postwar Trade and
        Payments   xix

1.1   The Advance and Retreat of World Import and Trade
      Growth, 1952–87   20

1.2   The Rise of Merchandise Trade Imbalances   24

2.1   U.S. Merchandise Exports, Imports, and Trade Balance,
      First Half 1947–Second Half 1952   34

4.1   Growth of Developed Sector Role in World Trade,
      1958–67   59

5.1   The Role of U.S. and Developed Sector Imports in
      World Import Growth in Phase I   99

5.2   Forces Behind Developing Sector Export Recovery in
      Phase II   102

5.3   Changes in Developed Sector Shares of World Imports
      in Phase III   108

5.4   Changes in Developed Sector Economy Net Exports in
      Phase V of the Four Cycles   117

6.1   Dissecting the J-Curve in Cycle 2   135

7.1   Dissecting the J-Curve in Cycle 3   162

8.1   Changes in Developed Sector Net Investment Balances
      and Size of Developing Sector Capital Importer
      Borrowing, 1980–87   211

9.1   Phase V and U.S. Economic Performance   220

9.2   The J-Curve in Phase V of the Last Three Trade and
      Payments Cycles   225

CHART

5.1   The Timing, Characteristics, and Causes of the Six
      Phases of the Trade and Payments Cycles   82

Foreword

In May of 1987 Creditanstalt Bankverein, A.G., of Vienna, Austria, entrusted Norman A. Bailey, Inc., of Washington, D.C., with the preparation of a study of trade and capital movement patterns in the period since the end of World War II.

The study, which forms the basis of this book, was done by analyst Richard Cohen, who responded brilliantly to his assignment. I believe the readers of this work will agree that he has made a major contribution to the economic history of the postwar period, identifying four postwar trade and payment cycles, each consisting of six parallel phases. The analysis is of great descriptive and predictive power and is unlike anything previously done, not invalidating but supplementing established cycle and wave models in a highly useful way.

I would like to thank Creditanstalt and its then-chairman, Dr. Hannes Androsch, for providing the opportunity that resulted in this book.

Norman A. Bailey, Ph.D.
Consulting Economist,
Former Special Assistant to
The President for International
Economic Affairs (1981–83)

Acknowledgments

Several people helped make this book possible. I would like to thank Dr. Norman A. Bailey for his support and encouragement; Creditanstalt Bank of Vienna, Austria, and its former Chairman Dr. Hannes Androsch for sponsoring the study that forms the basis of the book; Frederick Leykam, Chairman of the Washington Defense Research Group, for providing me the opportunity for doing much of the research on the current economic situation that underlies this analysis; Alfred J. Watkins for his valuable and insightful comments on parts of the manuscript; and my wife Laura, without whose collaboration this book would not have come about. I am, of course, solely responsible for any mistakes of fact or judgment.

Introduction

Since 1985 investors, policymakers, and voters have demonstrated un-ease and uncertainty over the state of the United States and world econ-omy. At the center of these concerns have been large imbalances in international trade and payments.

These imbalances have driven government policymakers to concen-trate their attention and energy on remedies. In late 1985 they, supported by many scholars, promoted a traditional prescription centered about dollar depreciation—one anticipated to produce future contraction in the U.S. trade and current account deficits.

From 1985–87 the dollar experienced its largest and longest deprecia-tion in the post-World War II period, yet U.S. external deficits continued to grow. The much heralded "J-curve" failed to mature.[1] The weight of this development caused large movements in the financial markets, the most conspicuous of which was Black Monday.

Today, the markets have been calmed by the belated emergence of the J-curve, but is that calm only temporary? Will the J-curve mature suffi-ciently to correct current imbalances or have policymakers miscalcu-lated? And if they have, what does the future hold in store?

Unfortunately, answers to these questions are neither obvious nor eas-ily attained. They require insight into the complex of forces that have shaped the evolution of world trade and payments in the postwar period. Examination of the historical record has enabled discovery of two interrelated processes in trade and payments—a discovery whose import could not be more timely in helping to address these questions.

First, exploration of the evolution of trade and payments has rendered insight into the existence of distinct cycles in world trade and payments beginning in 1959, cycles whose internal sequential structures are the same. While scholars have long recognized postwar business cycles, none have identified trade and payments cycles. Trade and payments cycles, each with the same six internal phases, have been repeated in the years 1959–67, 1968–75, 1976–82, and 1983–?? (see Figure Intr. 1). But while the structure of each cycle is the same, profound differences distinguish each from the others. It is possible to cull from these inter-cyclical differences trends.

The practical value of this discovery is substantial. By identifying the phase of the trade and payments cycle we are in and applying the trend lines, we can determine where we are, while by projecting both into the future, we can tell where we are headed.

The second conceptual tool useful in understanding the nature of current international imbalances—the concept of long-term trends in world trade and payments—overlaps that of the trade and payments cycles. Indeed, the trend lines defined by the inter-cyclical differences vividly describe a prolonged deterioration in the performance of world trade and payments that has been paralleled by a retreat in national commitment to the goals of the postwar trade and payments order (see Figure Intr. 1). The period of retreat (1968–??) was preceded by a remarkable period of advance in trade and payments performance which was complemented by equally dramatic progress in the commitment of nations to the goals of the postwar order (1945–67).

The modern trade and payments order was predicated on a set of policies and institutions that contended that national macroeconomic (i.e., monetary and fiscal) and commercial (i.e., trade and payments) policies must submit to the requisites of the common good and shun obedience to national economic bias or short-term gain. Macroeconomic policy was to be subservient to international balance of payments adjustment, and commercial policy, to the rules of a liberalized and symmetrical trade order.

Swift balance of payments adjustment assured against a number of evils: large and prolonged merchandise trade and current account imbalances, a rising capital flow to merchandise trade ratio prompted by the financing of larger current account deficits, a rising factor services income to merchandise trade ratio provoked by the cost of maintaining an enlarged stock of international debt, and currency misalignments fostered by a breakdown of the balance of payments adjustment process and growing national macroeconomic policy divergences.

Full commitment to the balance of payments adjustment process ad-

FIGURE Intr.1

LONG-TERM TRENDS AND CYCLES IN POSTWAR TRADE AND PAYMENTS

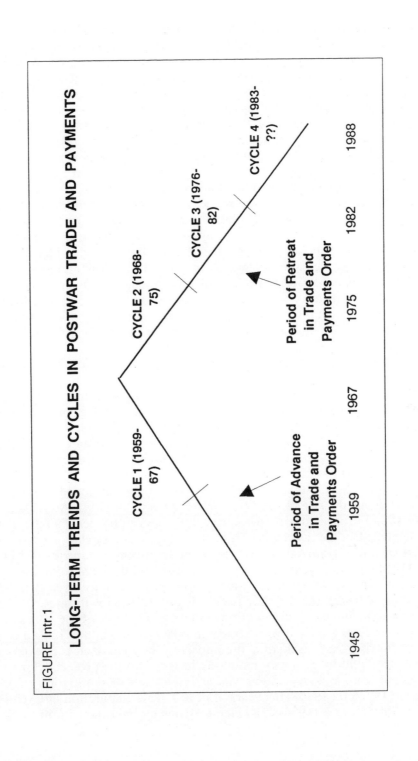

ministered through the new Bretton Woods monetary system spread through fits and starts from the United States to the entirety of the developed sector by Cycle 1 (1959–67), and despite growing pressure to the contrary, merchandise trade and current account imbalances remained small, capital flow and factor services income to merchandise trade ratios were stable, and currency misalignments remained manageable. From Cycle 2 to Cycle 4, however, the Bretton Woods monetary system and a host of more flexible exchange rate regimes replacing it collapsed, while national and sectoral merchandise trade and current account imbalances experienced immense fluctuations which precipitated an expansion in the capital flow to merchandise trade ratio during the 1970s, an expansion that in turn yielded a leap in the factor services income to merchandise trade ratio by the early 1980s. And increasingly in each successive cycle as the balance of payments adjustment process weakened and as macroeconomic policy divergence in the developed sector widened, currency misalignments unimaginable in Cycle 1 (1959–67) arose.

Reduction in barriers to trade (both tariff and nontariff) and adherence to multilateralism in rolling back trade barriers were to induce higher rates of growth in the volume of goods and services trade which it was believed would foster higher rates of growth in the volume of goods and services output.

In the period of advance, trade liberalization—especially in the developed sector—expanded at a rapid pace, climaxing in the creation of large trade-creating "special trade arrangements" in Western Europe and North America during Cycle 1. Not only did the rate of growth in world merchandise trade volume accelerate over this period, but the difference between the rate of world merchandise trade growth and world GDP growth increased, suggesting that world trade was indeed leading world output growth—a cardinal objective of the postwar trade order. But from Cycle 2 to Cycle 4, trade-diverting behavior in the developed sector centered about the rise of the "new protectionism" in North America and Western Europe and widespread resort to nontariff barriers (NTBs) complemented in the developing sector by primary commodity price fixing led by the Organization of Petroleum Exporting Countries (OPEC) trashed the trading rules of the postwar order. While the rate of growth of world merchandise trade volume has been in retreat since Cycle 2, so has the gap between the merchandise trade and GDP growth rates.

An immediately useful application of the discovery of the cycles and the long-term trends in world trade and payments is in providing a context for rigorously evaluating the impact of the J-curve on U.S. external balances, and by doing so, rendering insight into the prospects for correcting contemporary international imbalances. Examination of the years 1973 and 1979—the years of peak J-curve maturation in Cycles 2 (1968–75) and 3 (1976–82)—yields extremely important findings: factors other than dollar depreciation were largely responsible for the improvement in U.S. external balances. These factors were all features of the enormous inflationary pressures that swelled in 1973 and 1979, including huge global food deficits which drove up U.S. agricultural exports, high and accelerating domestic demand growth rates outside of the United States (which also drove up U.S. exports), and a large expansion in nonfood primary commodity prices, which caused unusual advances in the U.S. direct investment income balance.

Today—at a comparable phase in Cycle 4 (1983–??)—these inflationary factors are either not present at all or not present in the same degree they were in 1973 and 1979. This helps to explain why U.S. trade and current account balances began to improve only three to four quarters after dollar depreciation began in the previous two cycles, while it has taken eleven quarters in the current cycle. It also suggests that the relative size of the recovery in U.S. external balances will be smaller in this cycle despite a much larger depreciation of the dollar than in the previous two.

What does this mean for the future? It means that when U.S. domestic demand growth rates converge once again with those of the rest of the world, the United States will be burdened with a structural trade deficit of at least $90 billion and a current account deficit well over $100 billion. These deficits will hang like the sword of Damocles over the world economy—a sword whose cut the world economy got a feel of in October 1987.

A clear understanding of the ramifications of these deficits for the future requires an appreciation of the peculiar evolution of inflationary forces in the current cycle. In Cycles 2 and 3, the onset of recession was hastened and its magnitude aggravated by deflationary macroeconomic policy adjustment taken in response to the surges in goods and services price inflation. Today, in the absence of inflationary explosions akin to those of 1973/74 and 1979–81, many observers have become confused. Some have gone so far as to argue that the failure of an inflationary upsurge to materialize indicates that the modern business cycle has come to an end, while others—still traumatized by the soaring inflation of the 1970s—propose preemptive action against an enemy that has yet to strike forcefully.

Both assessments fail to realize that inflationary forces have not only been weakened in the 1980s, they have also been redistributed. From goods and services prices, these forces have moved to inflate the prices of other assets, at the center of which stands the U.S. dollar. As a result, the challenge to the world economy today is not so much goods and services price inflation as it was at the end of the 1970s, but the expansion of the U.S.'s structural trade and current account deficits which has produced an overvalued dollar.[2]

The proper medicine for this malady is a global adjustment process that infuses the dollar with value by reducing the U.S.'s external deficit. Failing that, the price of the dollar will fall, bringing with it a reduction in the U.S. capital account surplus and higher interest rates—higher interest rates that could provoke a severe contraction in the prices of vulnerable financial assets: Third World foreign debt, farm and energy debt, stocks and bonds, and other U.S. private debt.[3]

Meeting this challenge requires awareness of its existence, knowledge of its nature, and patience in the application of a remedy. Knowledge gathered through examination of the cycles and the long-term trends in trade and payments reveals powerful and entrenched obstacles to success—ones that forbid a "quick fix." Through the remainder of the current cycle, it is essential that governments, led by the Group of Seven (G-7),[4] maintain sufficient credibility in administering the adjustment process that an unmanaged slide in the dollar and other financial asset prices be avoided. With that accomplished, the world economy will face the task of a new Cycle of Adjustment.

The following analysis seeks to contribute to the knowledge required to meet this task and is structured about the impact of two sets of conflicting forces on world trade and payments following World War II. The first array of forces emerges in the immediate postwar period to define the shape of trade and payments from 1945–67—the period of advance. The second contingent of forces surfaces in 1959 to give rise at first to the trade and payments cycles and later, from 1968 to the present, to the reversal in the performance and policy commitment trends that dominated during the period of advance.

Part I—"The Factors Shaping the Postwar Trade and Payments Order" (Chapter 1)—identifies the forces and the interaction among them that have fostered the long-term trends and cycles in contemporary trade and payments. As such, the chapter supplies the conceptual framework for the history that follows.

Part II—"The Advance of the Postwar Trade and Payments Order"— investigates the maturation of the trade and payments order through three distinct stages, stages that reflect the emergence (The Period of Postwar Economic Reconstruction—1945–52, Chapter 2), the establishment (The Period of Transition—1952–58, Chapter 3), and the peaking (The Cycle of Rapid Growth in International Trade—1959–67, Chapter 4) of the ascendance of the world trade and international monetary order. The limitations and vulnerabilities that plague the postwar order during this period are also explored. (The years 1959 through 1967, while spanning the period in which the postwar trade and payments order reaches peak levels of performance, also mark the first appearance of a distinct trade and payments cycle whose internal phases are repeated in the three subsequent cycles.)

Part III—"The Emergence of Trade and Payments Cycles and the Retreat of the Trade and Payments Order"—begins with an analysis of the structure and causes of the trade and payments cycles and includes an examination of the differences among the cycles. The phasal evolution of each of the four cycles and the retreat in the performance of the world market and trade order, and of external balance stability and exchange rate alignment, are examined, as is the consequent impact of these developments on the commitment of nations to the rules and goals of the postwar order. Following a chapter focused on analysis of the structure of and differences among the four cycles (Chapter 5), which includes a review of the phasal evolution of Cycle I, the Cycle of Rapid Growth in International Trade (1959–67), the next three chapters explore the evolution of the subsequent cycles: the Cycle of Inflationary Growth in World Trade (1968–75), the Cycle of Stagflation (1976–82), and the first four phases of the Cycle of Disinflation (1983–86). In addition to a review of the phasal history of the cycles, these chapters include an evaluation of the growing challenges to the postwar trade and payments order.

Part IV—"The Current Situation and Beyond"—explores why the J-curve has not yet and is unlikely in the future to mature during the current cycle (Chapter 9). It then assesses the probable harsh consequences of the failure of policy to reduce external imbalances and offers a set of recommendations for reducing them through a new Cycle of Adjustment (Chapter 10).

Part I

THE FACTORS SHAPING THE POSTWAR TRADE AND PAYMENTS ORDER

1

Forging the Postwar Trade and Payments Order: Forces in Conflict

Behind the long-term trends that define the evolution of postwar trade and payments are powerful and often conflicting forces. The interaction of these forces has produced prolonged periods in which the performance and policy of the postwar trade and payments order advanced (1945–67) and then retreated (1968–present); it has also produced the trade and payments cycles beginning in 1959 and the differences among them.

The ascendance of the postwar trade and payments order was inspired and sustained by two factors:

- National political commitments centered in the developed sector to a liberalized and cooperatively managed trade and payments regime, and
- Global economic conditions conducive to enhanced world trade and supportive of these commitments.

Reactions to the destructive consequences of anarchic trade and exchange rate behavior during the 1930s congealed to foster the creation of a set of transnational institutions in the immediate postwar period which sought to constrict unilateral trade and payments behavior: the Bretton Woods monetary system, the International Monetary Fund (IMF), the International Bank for Reconstruction and Development (IBRD, or World Bank), and the General Agreement on Tariffs and Trade (GATT). The commitment of national governments to the goals and strictures of this institutional framework was reinforced by a series of changes in the postwar world economy and strategic/military balance which served to raise the costs of unilateral trade and payments behavior. Further, the world economy enjoyed a relative abundance of factor inputs—labor, primary commodities, and capital—as well as new civilian technologies, all of which acted to moderate the pressure on national governments to resort to illiberal practices in their international economic behavior, especially by 1948 after immediate postwar shortages had passed.

But even during the period of advance, two forces surfaced whose interplay worked to undermine the stability and effectiveness of the new trade and payments institutions:

- Postwar structural distortions in world trade and payments, and
- National economic policy biases.

The first structural distortion arose from the large postwar U.S. merchandise trade surpluses, which had been built on an unsustainable foundation—temporarily bloated exports and depressed imports. The fixed parity regime of the Bretton Woods monetary system therefore rested on a bed of quicksand. Ultimately, growing dollar overvaluation lay at the center of the process that brought down Bretton Woods. Two additional structural distortions in world trade caused sectoral import growth rate differentials that quickened the pace of crowding in developed sector manufactured goods markets while slowing the rate of development in the developing sector and the centrally planned economies (CPEs).[1] The traumatic postwar reorganization of prewar Eurasian trade and capital flows left nearly one-third of the world's population—that residing in the Eurasian CPEs—all but cut off from trade and capital flows from the other two-thirds, while developing sector import levels were depressed in the wake of prolonged post-Korean War weakness in primary commodity prices. This set of structural distortions constricted the rate of growth in nondeveloped sector markets.

The pressures unleashed by these structural distortions incited a second set of forces, some of which were inherited from the prewar era and some produced by postwar changes in the global economy. As we shall see subsequently, strong national biases in macroeconomic, development, and trade and payments policy borne either from national economic traumas or new postwar economic vulnerabilities (or strengths) were prodded into more forceful expression by the postwar structural distortions. The assertion of these biases first delayed and weakened the power and scope of postwar trade and payments institutions and later helped to undermine them. The first structural distortion and its reinforcement of national economic biases produced ever larger developed sector currency misalignments which eroded the credibility of Bretton Woods, while the second set of structural

distortions incited national economic biases which resulted in a swell of illiberal trade practices that weakened the GATT.

The retreat of the postwar trade and payments order beginning in 1968
was caused by:

- A deterioration in the performance of the world economy, and
- Consequent increased expressions of national economic biases.

Beginning in 1959 labor and primary commodity costs started to rise,
first as a result of the depletion of abundant postwar supplies of both.
This in turn caused a slowdown in the pace of supply-side adjustment beginning in 1968 as growth rates of fixed capital investment declined and
as labor mobility and civilian technological advance slowed. The consequent rise in goods and services price inflation and primary commodity
terms of trade served to aggravate the expression of national economic
biases.

Besides producing a prolonged deterioration in the performance of the
trade and payments order and accelerating the pressure on the postwar
international monetary and trade system, the rising cost of factor inputs
and the economic policy responses to it produced both the structure of
the trade and payments cycles and the inter-cyclical differences.

A REACTION TO THE 1930s: THE INSTITUTIONAL
FRAMEWORK OF THE POSTWAR ORDER

Even prior to the end of World War II a reaction to the negative consequences of the illiberal trade and anarchic exchange rate policies of the
1930s spread through the developed sector. The reaction penetrated the
elites and eventually moved beyond a core of economists to the broader
business and financial communities and to national governments. This
change in attitude had an early impact on the politics of trade policy. In
the world's largest economy, the United States, power to make trade
policy moved from the Congress, where it had resided in the early
1930s—helping to secure the protectionist Smoot-Hawley legislation—
increasingly into the hands of the Executive Branch.[2] The U.S. Congress,
with its numerous constituencies and vulnerability to special interest
pressures, was as a matter of institutional character more prone to press
for illiberal trade policies than was the Executive Branch, which enjoyed
a more national constituency. The transformation in the domestic politics of trade policy started in 1934, when President Franklin D.
Roosevelt's Trade Agreements Act was passed giving the president power
to negotiate bilateral tariffs.

The emerging desire to reverse the 1930s' trends in world trade found expression in the postwar goals of the Anglo-American wartime alliance. In both the 1942 United States-United Kingdom Mutual Aid Agreement and in the Atlantic Charter, the United States and Great Britain committed themselves to a more disciplined monetary system and to free trade following the war's conclusion.

Ultimately, these efforts sought to create an order that ensured that national macroeconomic and commercial policy submit to a regimen that prioritized the most economical global distribution of merchandise goods, services, and financial capital in the belief that such an arrangement would reduce costs and produce stronger economic growth. The trade diversion and inefficient distribution of savings in the 1930s had led to the opposite—weaker economic growth.

The institutional jewel of what emerged from wartime U.S.-U.K. negotiations was the Bretton Woods monetary system.[3] The new system represented a direct reaction to the unstable exchange rates and competitive devaluations which abounded in the 1930s under a regime of floating exchange rates. Following in the path of the earlier gold exchange system, the new monetary system favored coordinated intergovernment management of the process whereby payments imbalances are adjusted, while rejecting the market as the sole mechanism for such adjustment.

At the core of Bretton Woods was the commitment of participating national governments to adjust their domestic macroeconomic policies in order to correct payments imbalances. In practical terms this required non-reserve currency economies to intervene in their national foreign exchange markets to ensure that the value of their currency not deviate beyond one percent on either side of its fixed parity with the reserve currency, the dollar. Thus, surplus economies would be forced to buy dollars with their local currencies, and deficit economies, to sell dollars for their local currencies in order to maintain parity.

These actions altered domestic monetary growth in non-reserve economies. By buying dollars, economies running current account surpluses would accelerate domestic monetary expansion and, as a result, domestic demand and imports. By selling dollars, economies running current account deficits would decelerate domestic monetary expansion and, hence, domestic demand growth and imports. Through this process, non-reserve economies were constrained from adopting balance of payments policies that would result in either excessive surpluses and accumulation of international reserves or excessive deficits and a buildup of foreign debt.

The Bretton Woods system also placed constraints on the behavior of the reserve currency economy. It was restrained from accumulating excessive balance of payments deficits because of the convertibility of its currency to gold. Theoretically, its reserves of gold could be placed at risk if it ran excessive balance of payments deficits. If, on the other hand, the reserve currency economy were to run balance of payments surpluses, it would drain reserves from the rest of the world and undermine world trade growth.

In this way, Bretton Woods imposed powerful pressures on participating economies to behave in ways supportive of stable exchange rates. The system did nonetheless incorporate features aimed at avoiding overburdening deficit economies with the rigors of balance of payments adjustment. Through the creation of the IMF and the IBRD in 1945, means were introduced for redistributing international reserves to economies experiencing short-term balance of payments difficulties or to economies requiring longer-term development assistance. IMF loans to nations experiencing severe balance of payments stress could ease the burden of balance of payments adjustment and thereby encourage national government commitment to such adjustment. In addition, the burden of adjustment could be avoided under certain circumstances through the mechanism of the "adjustable peg": if a national economy reached an undefined point of "fundamental disequilibrium," its exchange rate could be devalued or revalued in relation to the reserve currency, depending on whether it was experiencing balance of payments deficits or surpluses.

Through redistribution of reserves and the "adjustable peg," the new postwar institutions sought to introduce a degree of national macroeconomic policy flexibility into a system whose priority was balance of payments adjustment.

As in the case of the postwar international monetary system, negotiations over the postwar international trade order commenced in 1942 with the Atlantic Charter and Article 7 of the U.S.-U.K. Mutual Aid Agreement. Article 7 stipulated the commitment of both countries to postwar free trade. In Havana in 1948 efforts were made to negotiate the creation of an International Trade Organization (ITO) with significant power to enforce multilateralism in world trade. Following the failure of these negotiations, 23 countries, meeting the following year, agreed to early tariff reduction. Considered an interim agreement to be replaced by a future ITO, the General Agreement on Tariffs and Trade became instead the ITO's permanent substitute. The GATT, which lacks any enforcement mechanism, covered two areas: first, it provided lengthy schedules of tariff concessions for each contracting party; second, it set forth general principles for the conduct of merchandise trade which included the centerpiece of the GATT—the unconditional Most Favored Nation (MFN) principle that made tariff reduction applicable to all contracting parties. GATT trade principles also included the elimination of direct quantitative restrictions (i.e., import quotas), the establishment of uniform customs regulations, and the obligation of members to negotiate tariff remissions at the request of another member.

NEW MOTIVATIONS FOR ADHERENCE: STRATEGIC AND ECONOMIC TRANSFORMATIONS

National commitments to the institutions and goals of the postwar trade and payments order were reinforced by a series of changes in the postwar world. A web of military and economic interdependencies among developed countries, which had existed in the prewar period only at a lower order of intensity, arose in the aftermath of World War II to increase the penalties and reduce the incentives for unilateral trade and payments actions.

Following the Second World War, Germany and Japan lost their independent military power and that of the United Kingdom was downgraded.[4] The developed sector came to rely upon U.S. military power for its ultimate security in a strategic competition with the Soviet Union and the Soviet alliance system. The United States too found itself more dependent on the cohesion of its new alliance system than had been the case during years of relative isolationism prior to the war. The radical change in strategic/military relations within the developed sector increased the pressure on nations to sustain cooperative management in trade and payments. And with even more intensity, the trade and payments policies of the European CPEs were shaped by the new strategic/military environment.

In addition to the postwar breakdown of what had been relative security independence in the prewar period, developed sector nations experienced an erosion of their prewar economic autonomy. Germany and Japan lost their "special trade arrangements" in continental Europe and East Asia, respectively, while British and French "special trade arrangements" with developing sector economies were weakened.[5] The decline in imperial "special trade arrangements" reduced the magnitude of vast protected markets which had existed for developed economies prior to the war. As a result, developed sector economies became more dependent upon developed sector markets, especially the U.S. market, as intra-developed sector trade grew as a proportion of world trade and recoveries in the U.S. market led post-World War II trade expansions.

In addition to market access, the collapse of prewar "special trade arrangements" made access to raw materials for the primary commodity import dependent economies of Western Europe and Japan less secure. Absent guaranteed access to cheap primary commodity resources in colonial empires (and the European CPEs), Western Europe and Japan became dependent upon North American primary commodity exports in the immediate postwar period. In the 1950s, when the principal source of primary commodity imports gradually shifted to the developing sector, secure access came to depend ultimately upon U.S. military and diplomatic assets.

Finally, the postwar world witnessed a greater dependence on cross-border flows of capital. Beginning immediately after the war with large U.S. capital outflows to the developed economies of Eurasia, to the boom in U.S. investment in Western Europe, and then to developed sector direct investment in the developing sector in the 1950s and 1960s, dependence on foreign capital grew.

AN ABUNDANCE OF FACTOR INPUTS

Of equal importance in fostering a period of ascendance for the postwar trade and payments order were the global economic conditions of the time. Absent the sort of shortages that have historically precipitated unilateral action, they also created supply-side circumstances hospitable to an expansion in world trade. By 1948 the extreme shortages of capital and primary commodities experienced immediately after the war had begun to be reversed, and by 1952 there existed a relative abundance of factor inputs.[6] What I have identified as primary inputs—"raw labor" and primary commodities—were in such abundance after the Korean War that supply/demand conditions assured relatively low primary input costs.[7]

The demobilization of military forces in the developed sector and European CPEs after World War II created an enlarged civilian labor pool, a process that occurred again on a smaller scale in the aftermath of the Korean War. The "import substitution" effort in North America during World War II and the postwar economic reconstruction of Eurasia ensured by 1952 greater primary commodity capacity, while the expansion in extractive industry investment in the developing sector in response to the speculative surge in primary commodity prices during the Korean War produced a condition of overcapacity in nonfood primary commodities.

In addition to abundant supplies, the costs of primary inputs were also affected by the relatively high degree of supply-side economic adjustment that took place from 1945–67. What I have identified as the secondary factor input—capital—when subjected to quantitative and/or qualitative improvement can reduce the volume of primary inputs required per unit of output, yielding more favorable supply/demand conditions and thereby lowering primary input costs. Government action in the developed sector during and after World War II worked to drive the quantitative component, measured in the rate of growth of nonresidential fixed investment, above what the market would have determined. The largest investment boom took place in the United States during World War II, and was followed by major investment expansions in the Federal Republic of Germany in the 1950s and in Japan from 1955–64.[8]

The quantitative improvements in capital inputs were supported by qualitative advances. The pace of civilian technological progress escalated in the postwar period as a result of a concentrated science, research, development, and engineering explosion centered in the United States and associated with the Second World War. After the war the fruits of these advances were transferred freely from the defense to the civilian sector and from the United States to Western Europe and Japan. Technological progress was supported by an elevation in the workforce skill level, a development boosted by the high degree of postwar labor mobility in the developed sector. After the war a large rural-urban migration within nations and visible intra-European migration from south to north and east to west served to upgrade sharply the skill level of the developed sector workforce.[9]

The circumstances affecting the costs of factor inputs, primary and secondary, in the postwar period provided for consistent improvement in factor productivity which in turn fueled an acceleration in Gross Domestic Product (GDP) growth rates. The substantial postwar advance in economic output growth served to relieve domestic pressures for illiberal trade and payments behavior and to spur a cross-border transfer of merchandise goods.

POSTWAR STRUCTURAL DISTORTIONS

During this process of ascendance, a series of developments that placed strain on the new trade and payments order surfaced. Indeed, during this period these destructive forces moved to undermine the credibility of the Bretton Woods monetary system and the GATT.

The structural distortions first surfaced in the Period of Postwar Economic Reconstruction (1945–52).

The large U.S. merchandise trade surpluses that emerged in the immediate postwar period to foster a so-called "dollar gap" were predicated on abnormal demand for U.S. exports (especially primary commodity exports) in a reconstructing Eurasia and on reduced U.S. import dependency caused by wartime import substitution.[10] As a result, they were certain to contract as the perturbations which produced them receded. Indeed, directly contradicting signals of dollar undervaluation sent by the "dollar gap," the long-term deterioration in the U.S. merchandise trade balance in the 1950s and 1960s clashed with the regime of Bretton Woods fixed parities to produce an increasingly overvalued dollar.

Further, unusually high nonfood primary commodity prices induced first by the Second World War and more emphatically by the Korean War resulted in significant but temporary spikes in developing sector export earnings. The subsequent spurt of developing sector import growth, especially during the Korean War, brought on an expansion in extractive sector productive capacity. When demand levels driven by Korean War speculative buying subsided, primary commodity prices fell, and because of the expansion in production capacity, nonfood primary commodity prices did not recover until the 1960s—and then only marginally and sporadically. As a result developing sector import growth in the 1950s and 1960s remained weak, retarding both the development process and the rate of expansion of developing sector markets. In the developed sector, relatively cheap primary commodity prices spawned the construction of a manufacturing sector that was excessively raw material and energy intensive, leading to a market whose strength and stability was more vulnerable to primary commodity supply shocks.

The postwar period also experienced enormous distortions in East-West trade that peaked with the Korean War. When measured against prewar performance, the levels of trade between the European CPEs and their traditional trading partners in Western Europe were dramatically lower, while Japan's trade with its principal prewar trading partner, China, had been reduced to a trickle. These prewar trade and capital flows were replaced with less efficient intra-CPE flows, and by trans-Atlantic and trans-Pacific flows.

Developing sector and Eurasian trade and payments structural distortions not only depressed world trade growth, they helped to distort the shape of the global market, a market that became overly dependent upon developed sector import growth because developing sector and CPE hard currency imports were depressed. The increasing dependence on developed sector markets during the period of advance accelerated the pace at which crowding took place in those markets at the same time that their rate of expansion became more vulnerable to surges in primary commodity costs.

THE RESURGENCE OF NATIONAL ECONOMIC BIASES

These postwar structural distortions were not the only factors to place stress on national commitments to the new trade and payments order. Indeed, they interacted with a second set of factors—national economic biases.

After the Second World War, prewar history and postwar conditions produced noticeable macroeconomic, development, and trade and payments biases within developed sector nations. Policies were strongly influenced by differences among nations on key points, including whether prewar (or early postwar) exposure was greatest to unemployment—i.e., the impact of the Great Depression—or inflation, whether import dependency had grown or declined after the war, whether overseas commitments and related defense responsibilities had expanded or receded, and whether a nation's creditor or debtor status had intensified or been reversed.

For the most part, these factors pushed the United States and the second-tier West European economic powers (especially Britain and France) to adopt more expansionist macroeconomic policies and development strategies with low investment and export components, while they persuaded the Federal Republic of Germany and Japan to adopt more conservative macroeconomic policies and development strategies with a high investment and export component.

The United States and the United Kingdom in particular experienced prolonged high unemployment during the Depression, while the Federal Republic was more scarred by its experience with hyperinflation in the 1920s and the immediate post-World War II period.[11] Japan, too, experienced a steep rise in inflation after the war. These different historical experiences were reinforced by postwar economic changes. The U.S.'s import dependency—always relatively low, especially when compared to Western Europe and Japan—decreased further as a result of wartime import substitution. And among developed sector economies, the United States enjoyed one of the lowest levels of primary commodity import dependency, providing it with less exposure to the inflationary consequences of primary commodity supply shocks. While more dependent on imports in general and primary commodity imports in particular than the United States, Britain and France were afforded some relief through the retention of "special trade arrangements" with developing sector primary commodity exporters in the sterling and franc zones, respectively. Japan and the FRG, on the other hand, were stripped of their prewar "special trade arrangements" with primary commodity exporters yet both remained highly import dependent—and dependent especially on primary commodity imports.

The United States and second-tier West European economies continued to bear large defense establishments and overseas military commitments, especially in the wake of the Korean War, while Japan and the FRG were forced to abandon all overseas military commitments and sustain smaller defense establishments.

These conditions provoked differences in developed sector economic strategies which caused differentials in import growth rates and export competitiveness, the results of which helped shake the Bretton Woods parity regime.

During the Great Depression of the 1930s, the developing sector economies experienced a collapse of primary commodity prices which triggered a series of balance of payments crises.[12] After the war, national trade and payments strategies emerged which sought insulation from the vagaries of primary commodity price fluctuations. But these strategies of "import substitution" and of primary commodity "producer cartels" were in sharp conflict with the goals of the new trade and payments order since their success was predicated on trade diversion. "Import substitution" programs were a direct effort to reduce dependency upon goods and services imports by substituting domestically produced goods and services (and by downgrading investment in traditional export sectors), attempting thereby to shield the performance of the domestic economy from the volatility of primary commodity prices and, hence, export earnings.[13] But resort to "import substitution" most often substitutes higher cost, lower quality domestically produced goods and services for lower cost, higher quality imports.

The "producer cartel" represents an even more egregious trade-diverting mechanism. By manipulation of primary commodity supplies, the cartel seeks to sustain prices at levels higher than would be the case if the market were left undisturbed. Also in the postwar period there arose proposals for mechanisms to stabilize primary commodity prices through the trade-diverting option of internationally owned stocks of primary commodities, whose size would be manipulated to influence prices.

The CPEs, now including Eastern Europe and China, emerged from the Korean War with national economies placed on a wartime footing in which near complete "import substitution" was required in order to eliminate dependency on nonsocialist economies.

Since the Korean War, three distinct variations of CPE trade and payments approaches—distinguishable on the basis of the size and duration of trade and capital flows with the nonsocialist sector they countenance—have become discernible. The closed autarkic approach was evident in its most exaggerated form during the Chinese "Great Leap Forward" (1958–60) and the early phase of the Cultural Revolution (1966–68), as well as in the European CPEs during the Korean War.[14]

A more moderate CPE trade and payments approach to the nonsocialist sector appeared in the 1970s with European CPE efforts to secure large volumes of developed sector machinery imports and in 1977/78 when the Chinese "Ten Year Plan" defined a similar objective.[15] In both cases, a "selective" approach to trade with the nonsocialist sector sought large volumes of trade and capital flows but only over a short period. This CPE trade and payments policy serves to secure imports for domestic modernization while avoiding durable integration into the world economy and the dependency on nonsocialist economies that comes with it.

The most "open" CPE trade and payments approach is one in which the desire for modernization in the long term overcomes fear of dependency upon the nonsocialist sector. China's trade and payments integration into the world economy in the 1980s contemplates trade and payments relations with the nonsocialist sector for an indefinite period and involves gradual enlargement of China's import dependency upon that sector. Soviet President Mikhail Gorbachev's proposed domestic and foreign trade reforms imply a shift in Soviet commercial policy toward the "open" approach.[16]

EARLY CHALLENGES TO THE TRADE AND
PAYMENTS ORDER

The interaction of the postwar structural distortions in global trade and payments with national economic biases slowed the progress of the post-war monetary and trade system during the period of advance. Prior to the return of the developed sector to current account convertibility in 1959, only the United States and the economies of Central America operated under the regimen of the Bretton Woods monetary system, despite a 1952 target date set by the IMF in 1947 for such action. The failure to fully implement Bretton Woods in the developed sector until 1959 did not mean there was no progress in the liberalization of international monetary policy during this period. In 1950, the European Payments Union (EPU) was created, and it ushered in current account convertibility within Europe, thereby insulating West European intra-trade from the pressures of the "dollar gap."

But from 1945–59 the structural distortion of a "dollar gap" worked to undermine the implementation of Bretton Woods. Even before the end of World War II the imminence of a postwar "dollar gap" forced the U.S. and Britain to spar over the character of the postwar monetary system.[17] Reflecting the bias of a debtor nation, the British pushed for greater exchange rate flexibility (i.e., greater macroeconomic flexibility) in the new system and the creation of a new currency unit to be managed collectively that would finance postwar current account deficits. But the United States, reflecting the interests of a creditor nation, successfully sought a more disciplined exchange rate regime and avoided a transfer of postwar inflation to the U.S. from the rest of the world by rejecting the British proposal for the creation of new fiat money.

The rejection of the British proposal for the creation of additional international reserves combined with U.S. capital account deficits insufficient to finance the current account deficits of the rest of the world to create a dollar shortage. The emergence of this postwar vulnerability sparked fear over the repercussions of an early return to current account convertibility—fear that was intensified by disaster wrought upon the United Kingdom's balance of payments in 1947 when it took this step.

From 1945 to 1958 the specter of the "dollar gap" reasserted itself intermittently, undermining the establishment of the monetary system agreed to in 1944. The dissolution of the "dollar gap" and the impact of intra-developed sector differentials in macroeconomic and development strategy on trade balances asserted themselves just as Western Europe finally moved to full currency convertibility in 1959. A growing "dollar overhang" buffeted by second-tier West European economy currency overvaluation combined with West German deutsche mark and emerging

Japanese yen undervaluation to threaten the Bretton Woods monetary system.

Dollar overvaluation in the years from 1959 to 1967 exposed two of the technical vulnerabilities of the Bretton Woods system. Balance of payments deficits of the reserve economy at some point in the life of the system would exceed that economy's gold reserves, introducing a question as to the credibility of the reserve currency's gold convertibility. In addition, the system was asymmetric—the reserve currency economy could manufacture its own reserves while non-reserve economies had to accumulate reserves by running balance of payments surpluses. Non-reserve economies were thus vulnerable to the exportation of the reserve economy's domestic inflation.

The postwar international trade order hinged to the principles of the GATT also came under pressure from the combination of postwar structural distortions and the reemergence of national commercial policy biases during the period of advance. But despite an assault on GATT principles, there were significant strides in the liberalization of merchandise trade from 1949–67.

In concert with the establishment of the GATT a liberalization of West European intra-trade evolved in 1949, followed in the mid-1950s by a liberalization of Western Europe's trade with the rest of the world. The momentum carried forward in 1961, when Japan undertook its first significant postwar trade reform. These developed sector initiatives were carried to a new level in the 1960s with an explosion in multilateral trade liberalization. The first set of actions involved the creation of regional "special trade arrangements" in the developed sector, including the European Economic Community (1959–the EEC), the European Free Trade Association (1960—EFTA), and the U.S.-Canadian Automotive Pact (1965). The second wave of multilateral trade liberalization came as a result of the Kennedy Round of the GATT (1964–67)—the first major GATT success.

But just as in the case of the new monetary system, postwar structural distortions and national economic biases worked to slow the momentum of trade liberalization during the period of advance.

Paralleling the negotiations over the postwar monetary order, differences surfaced between the United States and the United Kingdom over the new trade order.[18] The dispute centered about the U.S. desire to eliminate discrimination and preferences in world trade, including imperial preferences such as those reflected in the British Commonwealth. The United States, with the world's strongest economy, with relatively low import dependency, with a strong creditor position, and without "special trade arrangements" of its own, perceived discriminatory trade arrangements as obstacles to its competitive position in world trade. The United Kingdom, on the other hand, with an economy weakened by war, highly dependent on imports, in a new debtor status, and with a "special trade arrangement," opposed elimination of such arrangements.

These U.S.-U.K. differences, exacerbated by tensions over pound sterling current account convertibility, worked to undermine the content of the postwar trade regime as originally proposed in the International Trade Organization. Another force impeding the U.S. goal of a strong international institution to promote multilateralism in trade was developing sector pressure for export preferences, quantitative import restrictions, and controls on international investment.

The balance of payments pressure caused by the "dollar gap" from 1945–52 forced Britain and France to return to forceful import constraints on a number of occasions. Far more important, however, in impeding the expansion of the postwar trade order was the retention of illiberal trade practices in the developing sector and the CPEs—a development exacerbated by the post-Korean War balance of payments stress in developing economies and by the near total import substitution that evolved in the CPE bloc.

Later in the 1950s, developed sector agriculture joined services in being effectively removed from the purview of the GATT. In the 1960s, the weakness of nondeveloped sector markets during the period of advance facilitated early crowding in developed sector markets, leading to the first significant example of the "new protectionism"—the U.S. Long-Term Agreement on Cotton in 1962. From its beginnings in the 1960s when it was focused on textiles, the "new protectionism" spread managed trade—conducted not through multilateral but bilateral agreements—to a broad spectrum of manufactured goods.

THE RISE OF PRIMARY INPUT COSTS

In 1959 a new set of challenges to the ascendance of the postwar trade and payments order emerged when the relative abundance in postwar supplies of primary inputs—primary commodities and labor—began to recede. The depletion of primary input supplies pushed up their costs, provoking, by 1968, a rise in the cost of the third factor input—capital. Rising labor costs in the developed sector, precipitated by near full employment, and rising primary commodity costs, surfacing in the wake of the decline in post-Korean War overcapacity in nonfood primary commodities and the emergence of large CPE food deficits, fostered a shift of resources in the developed sector from economic investment to accounts associated with the social peace, including wages, benefits and government "transfer payments," and from the developed sector to the primary commodity accounts centered in the developing sector. These transformations produced a contraction in the developed sector investment growth rate sufficient to spawn a lower free world investment growth rate by Cycle 2. In addition, by Cycle 2 the high degree of postwar labor mobility had fallen as the pace of change in the rural-urban labor mix in the developed sector slowed to a crawl, as did East-West labor flows, while the productivity of south-north European labor flows declined.[19] Finally, the pace of qualitative improvement in civilian technology weakened as most of the fruits of the World War II boom in science, research, development, and engineering had already been absorbed while new advances in these areas were of a smaller magnitude.

The depletion of primary input supplies and the slowdown in supply-side adjustment caused an acceleration in goods and services price inflation. From 1968 through 1981/82, goods and services price inflation experienced a remarkable escalation.

In addition, the rise in factor input costs produced a decline in the free world economies' Gross National Product (GNP) growth rate, driven by a steady retreat in the factor productivity growth rate. The decline in the GNP growth rate would have been even sharper were it not for the rise in the rate of growth of aggregate domestic and international debt which deferred some of the rising costs of factor inputs, spreading them out over a longer time span.

The European CPEs experienced a similar set of economic circumstances, which arose at approximately the same time as those in the free world economy.[20] However, the decline in European CPE GNP and factor productivity growth rates has been more precipitous. The deeper descent in European CPE economic performance is the result of systemic commitments to the maximization of immediate output—commitments which led to a more rapid depletion of primary input supplies, to historical disinvestment in the primary input sectors of labor (i.e., consumer goods) and primary commodities (i.e., agriculture) which served to make the rise in the costs of both more explosive, and to disincentives to technological changeover—which have suffocated advances in supply-side adjustment.

THE EMERGENCE OF THE TRADE AND PAYMENTS CYCLES...

The rise in primary input costs in the free world economy prompted greater volatility in the expansionary/contractionary makeup of aggregate developed sector macroeconomic and international payments policies as well as in macroeconomic policy differences among developed sector governments than had been experienced from 1945–59.

The interaction of these three variables,

• primary input costs,
• aggregate developed sector macroeconomic and international payments policy, and
• intra-developed sector macroeconomic policy differences,

produced four interrelated developments which have shaped global trade and payments from 1959 to the present:

• the four trade and payments cycles which began in 1959,
• the intercyclical differences,
• the long-term retreat in the performance of world trade and payments since 1968, and
• the decline in national commitments to the postwar international monetary and trade order.

The movements from one phase to the next in the trade and payments cycles are produced by behavioral changes in aggregate developed sector macroeconomic policy as it responds to movement in primary input costs and vice versa, as well as by regular fluctuations in intra-developed sector macroeconomic policy divergences.

The structure of the trade and payments cycles and the causes of their interphasal changes will be examined in depth in Chapter 5, as will the inter-cyclical differences. There, we will explore inter-cyclical differences by measuring the degree of movement in features that characterize each phase of the cycles; here, we will merely identify the broad inter-cyclical differences.

In Cycle 1 (1959–67) and Cycle 2 (1968–75), aggregate developed sector economic policy showed a relatively low sensitivity to goods and services inflation and overindebtedness; in Cycles 3 (1976–82) and 4 (1983–??), sensitivity to both increased.

In Cycle 1 the rise in primary input costs was weak, as was the aggregate developed sector policy response, and the behavior of world trade was therefore still dominated by the positive momentum of the earlier period. Cycle 1 is thus best identified as a Cycle of Rapid Growth in International Trade. In Cycle 2, goods and services price inflation grew dramatically—a development that caused a more rapid rate of growth in trade value compared to trade volume (whereas from 1952–67 the growth rate of trade volume surpassed that of value).[21] Cycle 2 was therefore a Cycle of Inflationary Growth in World Trade. The more restrictive aggregate developed sector macroeconomic policy of Cycle 3 managed to slow the acceleration in goods and services price inflation, but at the cost of lower economic growth—hence, it was a Cycle of Stagflation.[22] And in Cycle 4, an even sharper contractionary turn in aggregate developed sector economic policy resulted in an absolute deflation in primary input prices and a Cycle of Disinflation in goods and services prices.[23]

In addition to the interplay of primary input costs and aggregate developed sector economic policy, inter-cyclical differences reflected ever wider intra-developed sector macroeconomic and development policy divergences. These divergences grew as national economic biases intensified in response to a more costly inflation/unemployment trade-off prompted by the rise in primary input costs. The enlarged intra-developed sector policy differences produced greater inflation, interest rate, overindebtedness and cost of capital differentials, as well as bigger domestic demand growth, import growth, merchandise trade and eventually net investment balance differentials among developed sector economies from Cycle 1 to Cycle 4.

... AND THE RETREAT OF THE TRADE AND PAYMENTS ORDER

Inter-cyclical differences reflect the long-term deterioration in the performance of world trade and payments, and this deterioration has maximized pressure on the postwar trade and payments institutions and on national commitments to their goals. From Cycle 1 through Cycle 4, declining developed sector output growth rates caused at first by rising primary input costs and later by resort to more contractionary economic policies precipitated a parallel erosion in the developed sector import growth rate (in volume) (see Figure 1.1a). This represented a reversal in the trend for developed sector import growth from 1952–67. The negative effect of this development on the world import growth rate was offset to some degree in Cycle 2 by a rise in the nondeveloped sector import growth rate ushered in as a result of an increase in primary commodity prices and by a slow reintegration of the European CPEs into the world economy.[24] Further, in Cycle 2 and during most of Cycle 3, accommodative developed sector international payments policies toward the developing sector and Eurasian CPEs supported the rise in imports. Nevertheless, despite the recovery in the import performance of the developing sector and CPEs from the depressed levels of 1952–67 the world import growth rate fell during Cycles 2 and 3, and in Cycle 4 combined developing sector and CPE import growth came under immense balance of payments pressure, while the developed sector import growth rate continued to drop.

The deceleration in the growth of world imports—a phenomenon centered in the developed sector—had two effects: increased competition for developed sector manufactured goods markets from Cycles 1–4 which incited a surge in the "new protectionism" and a resort to nontariff barriers (NTBs), and a decline in the rate of growth of world trade (export

FIGURE 1.1

THE ADVANCE AND RETREAT OF WORLD IMPORT AND TRADE GROWTH, 1952-87

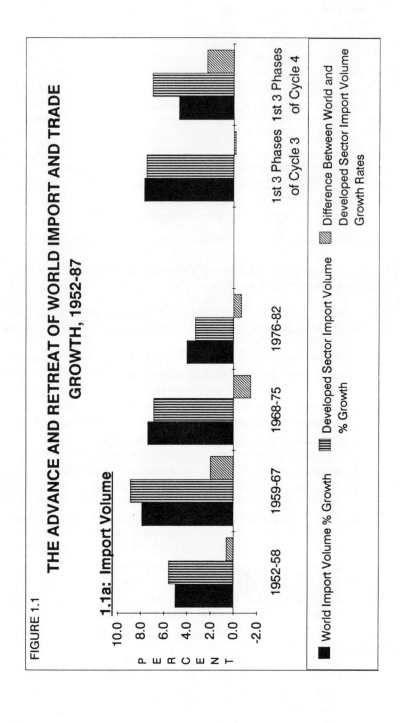

1.1a: Import Volume

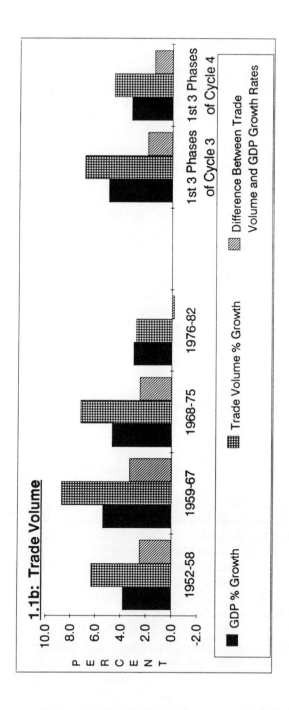

volume). Over the four cycles the percentage of North American and West European merchandise imports receiving protection has increased aggressively, while the slow relaxation in the protection of Japan's merchandise imports has been minuscule in comparison. As a result, the percentage of developed sector merchandise imports under trade protection has grown. Moreover, the number of manufactured good sectors receiving import protection has expanded, with textiles in effect joining agriculture and services outside of the reach of the GATT, and with steel and consumer durable trade becoming heavily managed. At the same time, there has been only a small improvement in developing sector trade practices over the four cycles, with a reversal on this front emerging during Cycle 4 in response to growing balance of payments problems.

In addition to the rise of illiberal trade practices in response to intensified market crowding in the developed sector, the supply/demand conditions that stimulated a steep rise in primary input costs in Cycle 2 provoked ideal conditions for the exertion of primary commodity producer cartel power. The OPEC-induced oil price advances of Cycles 2 and 3 could not have succeeded under the supply/demand conditions of the immediate post-Korean War period. The decline in OPEC power (as well as that of organized labor in the developed sector) in Cycle 4 when supply/demand conditions have forced a drop in primary input costs offers direct evidence on this point.

The decline in the world import volume growth rate from Cycle 1 to Cycle 4 also underwrote a decline in the growth rate of world trade (exports) in volume (see Figure 1.1b). This process reversed the trend in world trade operative from 1952 to 1967. Further, during those earlier years the size of the gap between the rate of growth of world trade volume and world GDP had widened, producing a result that was the explicit objective of the postwar trade and payments order: fostering sufficient trade to lead and therefore enhance economic growth. But from Cycle 1 through Cycle 4 this trend, too, has been reversed as the gap between the two growth rates narrowed (see Figure 1.1b).

Just as the anemic growth in primary input costs and accelerating GDP growth rates from 1945–67 created economic conditions favorable to the ascension of postwar trade policy and performance, the rise in primary input costs and declining GDP growth rates from 1968 to the present have provoked a retreat in policy and performance. Lower GDP growth rates have dragged down import growth rates and have incited trade-diverting behavior (i.e., the "new protectionism" and the OPEC manipulation of oil supplies) large enough to reduce the stimulative impact of world trade on GDP growth.

The reversal in trade and payments trends since 1968 did even more damage to the goals of the postwar monetary order. From Cycle 1 through Cycle 4, the two objectives of the postwar monetary order—minimal merchandise trade and current account imbalances along with stable and aligned exchange rates—have gone increasingly unrealized as trade and current account imbalances and currency misalignments grew forcefully.

From Cycle 1 through the present, the magnitude and volatility of North-South trade imbalances as well as intra-developing sector trade imbalances have shot up, especially when compared to the relatively steady relationships in both which held from 1952–67 (see Figure 1.2a). In Cycles 2 and 3 the developing sector accumulated unprecedented trade surpluses, and the developed sector, large trade deficits predicated on the rise in primary commodity prices. In Cycle 4 developing sector surpluses have stopped growing and would have receded but for a collapse in developing sector imports. Cycles 2 and 3 were also accompanied by a large rift in the merchandise trade balances of developing sector oil exporters compared to importers.

Driven by enlarged macroeconomic policy divergences among the developed nations from Cycles 1–4, the pace of growth of intra-developed sector trade imbalances, marked by Japanese and FRG surpluses and U.S. deficits, quickened (see Figure 1.2b).

The startling growth in sectoral and national merchandise trade imbalances underwrote equally large movements in current account imbalances, producing a rise in the ratio of trade and current account imbalances to world trade. Financing these imbalances, especially in Cycles 2 and 3, prompted the increase in the ratio of capital flows to trade flows, a ratio that had remained relatively steady (aside from the initial turbulence of 1945–52 in the period of the "dollar gap") until 1967. The growing magnitude of cross-border capital flows in Cycles 2 and 3 was enhanced by a rise in intra-developed sector capital flows triggered by the effect of macroeconomic policy differences on inflation, interest rate, and domestic demand growth rate differentials and their impact on national asset values and direct investment opportunities. Along with larger intra-developed sector current account imbalances, these differentials not only prompted greater intra-developed sector capital flows, but more speculative ones.

By the end of Cycle 3, in 1980–82, the growth in intra-developed sector capital flows accelerated. At the same time, the shift to more restrictive developed sector payments policies toward overindebted developing sector economies (and CPEs) prompted a slowdown in North-South capital flows. During Cycle 4 the volume of North-South capital flows has plummeted, while intra-developed sector flows have soared.

As a result, the expansion in the ratio of capital flows to trade flows has continued while the ratio of intra-developed sector to North-South capital flows grew at a mind-boggling pace. The rise in intra-developed sector capital flows has also sparked a growing de-linkage in the relationship between national current account and exchange rate behavior—a

FIGURE 1.2

THE RISE OF MERCHANDISE TRADE IMBALANCES

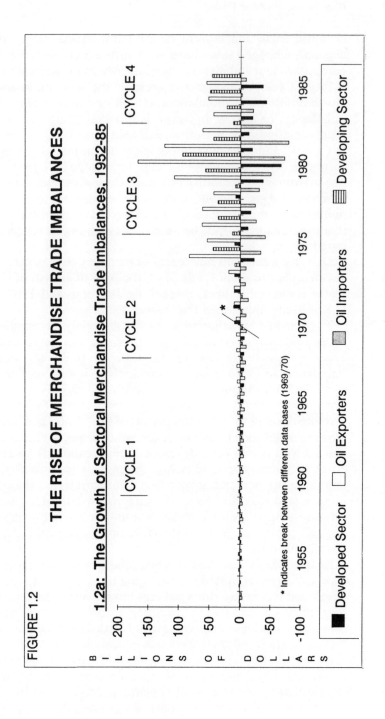

1.2a: The Growth of Sectoral Merchandise Trade Imbalances, 1952-85

24

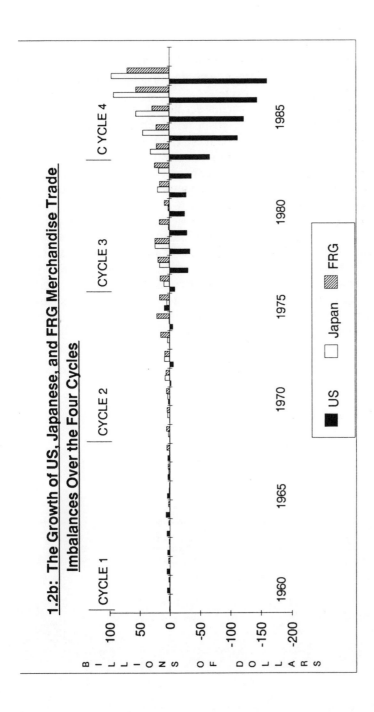

1.2b: The Growth of US, Japanese, and FRG Merchandise Trade Imbalances Over the Four Cycles

development in evidence since the surge of the dollar overhang during Cycle 1 (1959–67), but which took off at a breathtaking pace afterwards. This de-linkage has produced ever larger currency misalignments and exchange rate volatility from cycle to cycle.

Finally, by the end of Cycle 3 the earlier acceleration in cross-border capital flows had begun to weaken the strict relationship between merchandise trade and current account balances. Up until the end of the 1970s, the ratio of services trade to merchandise trade had remained steady. This changed in 1980–82, as a result of a rise in factor services income caused by the much larger stock of international debt and the advance in developed sector interest rates. Indeed, it has been the interest income component of factor services income which has caused the rise in both the services to merchandise trade and the factor services income to non-factor services trade ratios. Because of these changes, large net debtors such as those in the developing sector and, more recently, the United States have failed to see improvements in their current account balances equal in size to the gains in their merchandise trade balances, and this has made the already battered process of international balance of payments adjustment even more difficult.

Part II

THE ADVANCE OF THE POSTWAR TRADE AND PAYMENTS ORDER

2

The Period of Postwar Economic Reconstruction—1945-52

What we identify as the Period of Postwar Economic Reconstruction covers the years 1945–52. It defines a distinct period in global trade and payments; but because of changes in the structure of global demand wrought by the advent of the Korean War, the period can be further divided into two segments: one covering the years from 1945–first half of 1950 during which global demand centered about reconstruction of war-torn Eurasian economies and satisfaction of pent-up World War II demand, and another spanning the period from the second half of 1950 through the first half of 1952, when the focus of global demand shifted toward rearmament, especially in the United States, Western Europe, the Soviet Union and Eastern Europe. During these two phases of the Period of Postwar Economic Reconstruction, three structural distortions in world trade and payments emerged:

- The "dollar gap";
- Overcapacity in world nonfood primary commodity production; and
- An alteration in the structure of post-World War II Eurasian trade and payments sparked by political realignments.

THE RISE OF THE "DOLLAR GAP"

From 1945–48 a so-called "dollar gap" surfaced as a result of an abnormal surge in U.S. merchandise trade and, hence, current account surpluses with the rest of the world, especially Western Europe, predicated on heightened Eurasian demand for U.S. imports needed for postwar reconstruction as well as reduced U.S. import dependence resulting from wartime import substitution.[1]

The dollar gap arose in a postwar world economy that bore little resemblance to that reflected in earlier U.S. and British fears of a return to the depressed conditions of the 1930s. Indeed, rising primary commodity prices and inflation—resulting from insufficient world supplies to meet immediate postwar demand—predominated. In addition to the enormous resource requirements of Eurasian reconstruction, pent-up demand in both developed and developing sectors surged. Postponed consumption, the need to build war-depleted inventories, and a huge demand for new housing in the developed sector combined with demand for capital and consumer imports in the developing sector to put intense pressure on supplies, and this occurred at a time when world output had fallen well below prewar levels (the result of World War II-wrought destruction and disruption of the Eurasian economies).

Early postwar inflation was facilitated by sufficient liquidity to allow for the effective expression of pent-up demand. Unprecedented World War II public deficits in the developed sector resulted in large privately held reserves of liquidity, while in the developing sector current account surpluses, accumulated during the war and sustained by rising postwar primary commodity prices, produced a buildup of reserves, especially in Latin America.

The inflationary pressures of 1945–48 were strongest where the supply-demand mismatch was most extreme—in Eurasia.[2] As a result of abnormal demand and depressed supplies, Western Europe required inordinately large imports, especially of food, raw materials, and capital goods. Depressed domestic output of these resources forced these economies to turn toward the United States and Canada, whose economies had escaped war damage.[3] At the same time widespread import substitution during World War II had made the U.S. economy less import dependent.

Consequently, the non-U.S. developed sector economies, especially Western Europe, ran abnormal merchandise trade deficits while the U.S. ran unusual merchandise trade surpluses.[4]

This development produced a "dollar gap," a situation in which the developed economies of Eurasia, and Western Europe in particular, accumulated large current account deficits with the U.S., Canada, and the developing sector which could not be financed by net private capital inflows from the U.S. or non-U.S. gold production and gold valuation changes.

U.S. merchandise trade surpluses with the rest of the world were not a new development. Since the late 19th century the U.S. economy had run persistent merchandise trade surpluses.[5] However, until World War I,

U.S. services trade deficits (caused primarily by large factor services income deficits) and private transfers in the form of immigrant wage remittances to countries of origin had been even larger, producing current account deficits. Cumulative financing of U.S. current account deficits had fostered a U.S. net investment deficit with the rest of the world.

But in the 1920s persistent U.S. current account surpluses caused by merchandise trade surpluses large enough to overcome services trade and private transfer deficits laid the foundation for the appearance of a U.S. net investment surplus with the rest of the world. The U.S. net investment surplus was built on U.S. private capital outflow.

During the 1930s, the non-U.S. current account deficit was financed by the continued strong outflow of U.S. private capital and increased transfers of gold to the U.S. (supported by a rise in the volume and price of monetary gold in the 1930s). But in the immediate post-World War II period when U.S. current account surpluses rose in response to larger U.S. merchandise trade surpluses, there was no improvement in either the volume or price of monetary gold, and U.S. private capital outflows were well below prewar levels (see Table 2.1). As a result, the rest of the world—and especially Western Europe—was forced to draw down reserves and liquidate overseas assets in order to finance their current account deficits. Because those efforts would ultimately have been insufficient, the dollar gap would have undermined Eurasian reconstruction as well as world output and trade growth had an alternative means of financing it not been created.

The Underlying Decline of the "Dollar Gap"—While Fears of Its Expansion Persist

The pressures of the "dollar gap" from 1945–48 sensitized developed sector economies in particular to the problem. These sensitivities were later exacerbated by transitory surges in the "dollar gap" in 1949 as a result of a U.S. recession and in 1951 due to a contraction in U.S. imports following the peak of the Korean War. Awareness of the underlying retreat of the "dollar gap" and its inevitable demise brought on by reduced developed sector import dependence on the U.S. as well as the eventual dissipation of unusually low U.S. import dependence was therefore diluted.

Until 1952, the "dollar gap" was largely financed by means of unusual capital outflows from the U.S. to Western Europe and Japan in the form of loans and grants. From 1945–52 these capital outflows, the largest portion of which were the result of the Marshall Plan, amounted to $35 billion, or the equivalent of 10 percent of world trade.[6] The United States became the primary exporter of capital and the developed sector nations of Eurasia, especially Western Europe, became the primary importers.

TABLE 2.1

AVERAGE ANNUAL EXCESS OF DOLLAR SUPPLY OVER DOLLAR USE, PRE-WORLD WAR II AND POST-WORLD WAR II ($Millions)

	Payments on Current Account and Long-Term Net Capital Supply of Dollars to Rest of World	Use of Dollars by Rest of World	Excess of Supply Relative to Demand	World Output of Gold	Excess of Supply Over Use
1926-29	7,011	-6,962	49	309	358
1934-36	2,876	-3,212	-336	808	472
1938	3,062	-4,018	-956	976	20
1948	11,433	-17,339	-5,906	613	-5,291

SOURCE: UN World Economic Report 1949-50.

Moreover, U.S. transfers of dollars to these nations were in excess of their current account deficits with the U.S. The net dollar inflow to Western Europe and Japan above what was required to service current account deficits with the U.S. was essential to finance their current account deficits with the rest of the world. Hence, U.S. financing of current account deficits of Eurasian developed sector economies resulted in a contraction of U.S. reserves. Indeed, from 1945–52 the rest of the world accumulated reserves at U.S. expense.

Although world imports were constrained by insufficient dollars, world output approached prewar levels in 1948 and reached those levels the following year. The improvement in world output relieved inflationary pressures. This return to more normal economic conditions was also reflected in the first signs that the growth rates in West European demand for U.S. imports were beginning to abate—a development which, combined with large official U.S. capital outflow, suggested that the "dollar gap" of the first years of the postwar period might be easing.

This trend was first interrupted in 1949 with the onset of a U.S. recession precipitated by the easing of pent-up postwar demand. The recession that commenced at the end of 1948 with inventory liquidation was over by the end of the first half of 1949, and was moderated by strong domestic demand for housing and motor vehicles as well as by the impact of countercyclical income insurance programs. Nevertheless, the 1949 recession caused a drop in U.S. imports while at the same time sustained economic growth in the rest of the world supported improvement in U.S. exports, a combination that resulted in visible growth in the U.S. merchandise trade and current account surpluses (see Figure 2.1).

In addition, the decline in U.S. imports provoked by the inventory liquidation undermined developing sector export volume and prompted a softening of primary commodity prices. During the 1940s and 1950s the two developing sector primary commodity exporters most sensitive to developments in the U.S. economy were Latin America and the overseas sterling area. In 1949, the worsening of the external balances of the overseas sterling area combined with similar though less severe deterioration in U.K. balances to foster the first large speculative currency movements of the postwar period out of the pound sterling. This aggravated the sterling area's payments difficulties, forcing it to engineer efforts to slow dollar imports. Ultimately, in September 1949, the pressure against the pound sterling forced its devaluation, along with 23 other currencies including other West European currencies, against the dollar.[7]

The trauma of these 1949 upheavals, coming in the aftermath of the failed 1947 British return to current account convertibility, riveted global attention on the "dollar gap" and the dollar's apparent undervaluation, and weakened appreciation of the underlying trend which had begun to reveal itself in 1948—the erosion of dollar merchandise trade and cur-

FIGURE 2.1

US MERCHANDISE EXPORTS, IMPORTS, AND TRADE BALANCE, FIRST HALF 1947 - SECOND HALF 1952

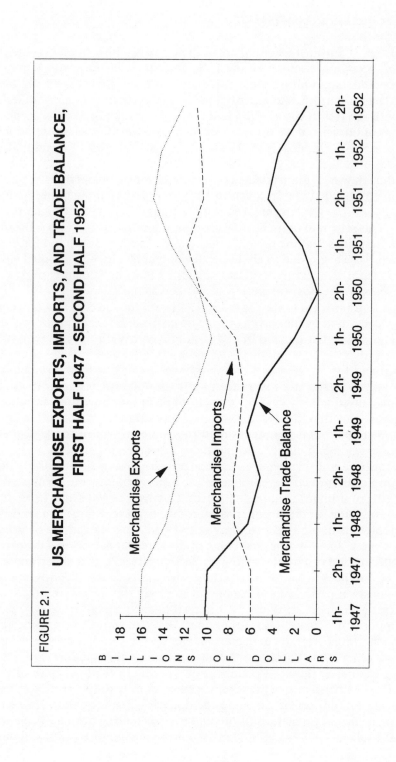

rent account surpluses and the eventual overvaluation of the dollar (see Figure 2.1).

The underlying trend reasserted itself in the second half of 1949 with the advent of a U.S. economic recovery. The easing of the "dollar gap" in the second half of 1949 was aided by continuation of constraints on dollar imports, especially in the U.K., further softening of primary commodity prices (a large share of Western Europe's imports from the U.S. continued to be primary commodities), and a reflux of flight capital to Western Europe which had gone to the U.S. in early 1949.

But the development that provided clearest insight into the certain future deterioration of the U.S. merchandise trade surplus and the "dollar gap" was the recovery in West European intra-trade that commenced in 1949—a recovery that provided for substitution of European for U.S. exports.

In 1949, the economies of Western Europe, after having developed some cross-border organization in 1948 as the result of the creation of the Organization for European Economic Cooperation (OEEC) to administer U.S. aid, enacted significant intra-trade liberalization which had an important trade-creating impact.[8] Hence, even while the U.S. was in recession for half of 1949 and its imports fell, world trade in volume for the entire year grew by a hefty 9.0 percent, led by a surge in West European intra-trade which grew by 20.0 percent (the other sector of the world economy witnessing such dynamic trade growth in 1949 was European CPE intra-trade).

In 1950, the basis for accelerated West European intra-trade was enhanced with the creation of a liberalized payments regime—the European Payments Union (EPU) which permitted convertibility of West European currencies, thereby freeing West European intra-trade from the constraints of the "dollar gap." Indeed, the West European liberalization of internal trade and payments represented the most prominent advance of the post-World War II objective of trade and payments policy reform up to that point, and its results in greater economic and trade growth were evident. These policies contributed to one of the crucial developments that would persistently erode the dollar gap—declining West European dependence on U.S. exports.[9]

The Korean War Distorts the "Dollar Gap"

In the middle of 1950, a new development erupted to distort the evolution of the dollar gap. With the onset of the Korean War, the focus of global demand shifted toward rearmament. At the initiation of the war neither its duration nor its geographical limits were certain. Laboring under this uncertainty, the markets overestimated the degree of rearmament. The demand for nonfood primary commodities anticipated by the markets as necessary to stock strategic reserves and facilitate production of defense machinery fueled a speculative surge in their prices. This price rise combined with the unusual U.S. demand for such commodities to spark a large expansion in U.S. imports. At the same time, the greater domestic demand for capital goods in the form of defense machinery undermined U.S. capital goods exports, especially to Western Europe.

These developments brought on an abnormal acceleration in the decline of the "dollar gap" as U.S. merchandise trade and current account surpluses plummeted (see Figure 2.1).

But just as the early phase of the Korean War accelerated the decline of the "dollar gap," the latter stages of the war provoked an expansion of it. The failure of the Korean War to widen induced the U.S. to make cuts in its strategic stockpile beginning in the second half of 1951, while at the same time the scope of U.S. rearmament reached its upper limits. These developments lowered U.S. and world demand for nonfood primary commodities, undermining their prices. While the volume and prices of U.S. primary commodity imports were contracting, U.S. exports of capital goods to a newly enriched developing sector spurred renewed growth in U.S. merchandise exports.

These two factors combined to reverse the decline of the "dollar gap." Its renewed expansion from the second half of 1951 through the first half of 1952 was predicated on a big improvement in the U.S. merchandise trade surplus, while U.S. private capital outflow in the form of direct investment followed nonfood primary commodity prices down (see Figure 2.1). As a result, in 1951 U.S. reserves actually grew.

Dollar surpluses rose at the expense of the developing sector, whose deficits increased. In addition, in the second half of 1951 British and French merchandise trade balances deteriorated as the U.K. and France were forced to increase imports of nonfood primary commodities while other developed sector economies were reducing such imports.[10] The U.K. and France had earlier decided to deplete stocks and defer imports of high priced primary commodities; but in the second half of 1951 they were forced to restock. Their deteriorating trade and current account balances coincided with rising external deficits in the overseas sterling and franc zones.

The subsequent fall of British and French reserves precipitated a new round of speculative capital movements out of the pound sterling and the franc. Both London and Paris, as well as their overseas affiliates, were forced to reimpose controls on dollar imports and soon thereafter to adopt restrictive domestic economic policies.

Although the 1951/52 resurgence of the "dollar gap" did not provoke the degree of financial instability generated by its 1949 expansion because non-U.S. economies, especially those in Western Europe, were now stronger, it hindered appreciation of the underlying decline of the "dollar gap" which had first surfaced in 1948 and then reasserted itself in 1949/50.

Early Signs of FRG and Japanese Export Power

During the Korean War period of 1951/52, the first indications of other forces that would accelerate the reduction of the "dollar gap" appeared.

While Britain and France suffered under balance of payments stress, reserve losses, and speculative assaults on their currencies, the Federal Republic of Germany emerged from the Korean War a European economic power. The absorption of U.S. capital goods output in domestic rearmament and later, in 1951/52, in satisfying developing sector demand resulted in a capital goods shortage in a Western Europe still recovering from World War II and simultaneously rearming. The FRG stepped in to fill the capital goods gap, exploiting its historical comparative advantage in this sector.[11]

Consequently, the Federal Republic ran huge merchandise trade surpluses with the EPU throughout the Korean War period, experiencing its first post-World War II export boom while at the same time rebuilding its reserves. Indeed, FRG merchandise trade surpluses and reserves continued to grow even in the face of the renewed expansion of the "dollar gap" from the second half of 1951 through the first half of 1952.[12]

Japan also experienced its first post-World War II economic boom during the Korean War and like that of the FRG, it too was export-led. Unlike the FRG, however, Japan's export expansion of 1951/52 was not with its traditional trading partner—China—but with the United States. The "procurement boom" of 1951/52 was predicated on U.S. military-related expenditures in Japan linked to the war effort in Korea. While unsustainable, the "procurement boom" sensitized Japan to the prospects for rapid development centered about exports.[13]

Following the Korean War, Bonn and Tokyo would pursue policies to accelerate the export-centered growth experienced in the early 1950s. The rise of FRG and later Japanese export power would, in the 1950s and 1960s, increase the momentum of deteriorating U.S. merchandise trade balances.

THE EMERGENCE OF PRIMARY COMMODITY OVERCAPACITY

The second structural distortion to emerge during the 1945–52 Period of Postwar Economic Reconstruction was excess capacity in developing sector nonfood primary commodity production. The longer term result of extractive sector overcapacity was prolonged weakness in developing sector terms of trade in the 1950s and 1960s which translated into slower rates of import growth and, hence, development than otherwise would have been the case.

The combination of large developed sector World War II military expenditures in the developing sector and rising wartime primary commodity prices increased developing sector and especially Latin American reserves. (Latin America was the principal developing sector primary commodity supplier of the U.S.)[14] Continued gains in primary commodity prices in the immediate postwar period combined with enlarged reserves to permit a significant advance in imports—imports that had been suppressed during World War II as a result of near full developed sector absorption of its own capital goods output.

The inflow of capital goods to the developing sector went principally to extend extractive sector capacity, although some went to support early "import substitution" efforts. In addition, especially in Latin America, pent-up demand for consumer good imports grew.

The early postwar boom in primary commodity prices which helped finance the developing sector import expansion began to weaken in late 1948 as a recovery in Eurasian primary commodity output had by then begun. In 1949 the U.S. inventory liquidation further undermined primary commodity prices, resulting in the first serious postwar balance of payments difficulties in the developing sector. The faltering export earnings quickly led to import retrenchment, a rundown of reserves, and a buildup of foreign debt.

From the subsequent U.S. recovery beginning in the second half of 1949 to the commencement of the Korean War in the second half of 1950, primary commodity prices stabilized but did not recover. It was the advent of the Korean War which undermined the stability of primary commodity prices and eventually fostered a supply-demand mismatch in nonfood primary commodities.

The uncertainty over the Korean War's size and duration created the foundation for the speculative rise in primary commodity prices in the second half of 1950. During that half-year raw material prices rose by 18.0 percent, and in the first half of 1951 they rose by another 24.1 percent.[15] The enormous rise in nonfood primary commodity prices resulted in a large improvement in developing sector terms of trade. Moreover, while developing sector exports rose precipitously in value in the second half of 1950, imports remained constrained as a result of the continuation of policies launched to offset earlier balance of payments stress. The consequent improvement in merchandise trade and current account balances in the second half of 1950 created the foundation for a boom in capital goods imports in 1951.

By the second half of 1951 the failure of U.S. rearmament to meet market projections relaxed the growth of demand for capital goods in the developed sector and this created the opportunity for a surge in developing sector capital goods imports. For the most part, these imports were devoted to expanding extractive sector productive capacity—a process aided by a burst in direct foreign investment. Both domestic and foreign investment were attracted by the rising prices of nonfood primary commodities.

In the second half of 1951 the speculative boom in nonfood primary commodity prices began to fall as the war failed to expand and the U.S. reduced its strategic stockpile, unleashing a wave of inventory liquidation. As a consequence, demand weakened in early 1952, creating profound downward pressure on nonfood primary commodity prices. In the second half of 1951, raw material prices fell by 11.3 percent, and in the first half of 1952, by another 7.3 percent.[16]

While these prices tumbled the developing sector sustained its import boom, provoking a big deterioration in its merchandise trade and current account balances beginning in the second half of 1951 with the sterling area suffering the earliest erosion.[17]

Developing sector trade and development patterns during the Korean War underwrote two phenomena that would have prolonged influence— soft nonfood primary commodity prices and relatively weak developing sector import growth. Overcapacity in the nonfood primary commodity sectors caused by the unusual investment in extractive industries during the Korean War served to suppress prices, which in turn weakened developing sector export earnings and consequently import growth. This latter development would have a lasting impact on the shape of the world market in the aftermath of the Korean War.

THE RESTRUCTURING OF EURASIAN TRADE AND PAYMENTS

The final structural distortion in global trade and payments to take root in the 1945–52 period involved a major contraction in East-West trade and capital flows when measured against pre-World War II levels. In addition to the decline in these flows between Western Europe and the new CPEs of Eastern Europe, faltering trade and capital flows between Western Europe and the Soviet Union and between Japan and mainland East Asia, especially China, combined to radically alter the face of intra-Eurasian trade and capital flows (see Table 2.2).

Prior to World War II, Western Europe had been the primary importer of East European food exports (indeed, loss of these food sources was in part responsible for Western Europe's excessive postwar dependence on U.S. and Canadian food supplies), while traditional West European exports of manufactured goods and financial capital to Eastern Europe collapsed. At the same time, Japan's trade with China and its trade links with the northern sector of Korea crumbled in the years from 1945–52.

TABLE 2.2

PERCENT OF NATIONAL TRADE OF EURASIAN CPEs WITH NON-CPEs, CPEs, AND USSR IN PRE-WORLD WAR II AND POST-WORLD WAR II PERIODS (Percent)

	1937		1948			1950		
	CPE	Non-CPE	USSR	Other CPE	Non-CPE	USSR	Other CPE	Non-CPE
China			2		98	46	15	39
USSR	4	96		67	33		80	20
Hungary	13	87	17	17	60	29	38	33
Czech.	11	89	16	15	69	28	32	40
Poland	7	93	23	17	60	25	33	42

SOURCE: UN World Economic Survey 1955.

The momentum of the transition in intra-Eurasian trade and payments flows escalated in the immediate postwar period, reaching an apex during the Korean War (see Table 2.2).[18] By 1951, trade between Western Europe and the European CPEs was down 25–30 percent from its already historically low 1948 level. Prior to the Korean War, the dislocation in mainland East Asia continued after World War II as civil strife dominated China, Korea, and Indochina. Although China's civil war came to a halt in 1949, from 1950–52 China's trade with the nonsocialist world fell precipitously and the intensification of Sino-American tensions springing from the Korean War extinguished any remaining hope in Tokyo for a revival of Sino-Japanese trade.

During the Period of Postwar Economic Reconstruction, Eurasian developed sector trade and capital flows with socialist Eurasia shrank, while those with North America increased. The Eurasian CPEs replaced their losses on current and capital account transactions with the developed economies of Europe and Japan with a massive improvement in intra-CPE trade and capital flows. Eastern Europe redirected its food and manufactured goods exports to the Soviet Union and received in turn Soviet raw material and energy exports. From 1946–55, Eastern Europe under Soviet pressure ran merchandise trade and current account surpluses with the Soviet Union. It is estimated that the cumulative East European flow of unrequited transfers to the USSR during this period was $14 billion—the equivalent of the U.S. Marshall Plan for Western Europe.[19]

But intra-trade among the East European CPEs was not enhanced or encouraged. Each East European development program was similar and this distortion in economic development undercut traditional trade flows within Eastern Europe.[20] Import dependency within Eastern Europe shifted to the Soviet Union, not other East European economies. In addition, from 1950–52 China and North Korea were slowly integrated into the European CPE network of trade and payments, a development that accelerated in 1953.

There is little doubt that these Eurasian trade and payments distortions worked to weaken the rate of postwar output growth. In addition, they served in the post-Korean War period to alter profoundly the potential configuration of the world market. Absent integration of non-CPE and CPE markets and with depressed rates of developing sector import growth, post-Korean War world trade became more reliant on the vitality and character of developed sector markets than otherwise would have been the case.

3

The Period of Transition in Trade and Payments—1952–58

The period from the second half of 1952 through 1958 marked a transition in world trade and payments. During this Period of Transition, the postwar structural distortions which took hold from 1945 to 1952 conspired to help produce two developments with lasting implications.

First, the post-Korean War world market—a market whose configuration has persisted to the present—was shaped. Although the parameters of the world market underwent transitory modifications in the 1970s, the fundamental configuration remained. Two forces combined to determine the boundaries of the world market in merchandise goods, one positive, one negative.

The positive force was unleashed as a result of the change in developed sector domestic demand patterns in the aftermath of the Korean War and by the intensification of trade and payments reform. The center of developed sector demand shifted from Eurasian recovery (predominant during the 1945–50 period) and armaments (key in the Korean War years of 1950–52) to civilian demand that would, over time, increasingly be weighted toward consumer goods. These developments worked to buttress developed sector intra-trade.

The negative force stemmed from two of the structural distortions afflicting world trade and payments in the period of reconstruction— overcapacity in nonfood primary commodities and disengagement of the Eurasian CPEs from traditional trade and payments relations with the rest of the world. These developments depressed both North-South and

East-West trade, as well as the vitality of developing sector and CPE hard currency markets.

The second transformation in world trade and payments which unfolded from 1952–58 also had its roots in the preceding period. During the period of transition the "dollar gap" increasingly dissipated, as the abnormally large U.S. merchandise trade surpluses of the early postwar years continued their long-term downward march. By the end of 1958, the "dollar gap," which had been the primary concern in the postwar period, was being rapidly replaced by a "dollar overhang." In addition, intra-West European external imbalances began to surface as the Federal Republic of Germany sustained current account surpluses and reserve growth while second-tier West European economies (i.e., the United Kingdom, France, and Italy) saw the performance of their external sectors weaken.

The emerging "dollar overhang" combined with intra-West European trade and payments imbalances to produce international monetary instability which escalated in the 1960s.

THE NEGATIVE FORCES SHAPING THE CONTEMPORARY WORLD MARKET

The boundaries of the contemporary world market were in part shaped by two postwar structural distortions: overcapacity in nonfood primary commodity production and postwar changes in the structure of Eurasian CPE trade and payments with the rest of the world. They served to depress developed sector manufactured exports to the rest of the world. With immense development requirements in both the developing sector and the CPEs, robust imports by these regions would have resulted in larger volumes of developed sector capital goods exports.

Instead, the weakness of developing sector imports and CPE hard currency imports increasingly concentrated world trade flows in the developed sector. The import weakness of the developing sector and the CPEs also meant that their pace of economic development would be slower and therefore that the speed at which competitive challenges to the developed sector from alternative manufacturing centers arose would be impaired.

The Developing Sector: Constrained Import Growth

From the second half of 1952 through 1958, the developing sector's share of world imports fell (see Table 3.1). Import weakness was the result of softness in export earnings. When the developing sector's export volume did improve during this period its terms of trade did not, as nonfood primary commodity prices showed little response to surges in foreign demand—a direct result of production overcapacity. Consequently, whenever developing economies moved to relax restraints on imports during the 1952–58 period, they encountered balance of payments difficulties.

But while nonfood primary commodity prices showed reduced sensitivity to foreign demand growth, they were extremely sensitive to falling foreign demand and this was forcefully evident during the 1958 recession. The deep drop in export earnings that year prompted an equally sharp reduction in imports (see Table 3.1).

The oversupply in nonfood primary commodities was in evidence immediately after the Korean War. From the second half of 1952 through the first half of 1953, demand for primary commodities picked up as deteriorating economic activity caused by a lull in West European growth (itself generated by low Korean War levels of personal consumption and British and French domestic deflationary programs) gave way to economic recovery. However, because of overcapacity the rise in nonfood primary commodity export volume was not accompanied by a price recovery. The failure of prices to recover was especially marked in Latin America and the overseas sterling area, but because import restrictions remained in place, there was some improvement in current account balances.[1]

By the second half of 1953, many developing sector governments felt secure enough to reduce import restraints. But the resulting improvement in imports precipitated new balance of payments disequilibria, most notably in Latin America. In 1953 Brazil, facing a deterioration in its current account balance and beset by capital flight, required a $300 million U.S. Export-Import Bank loan, and in 1954 Mexico, Brazil, and Chile were forced to devalue their currencies in league with most of Latin America.[2] Relaxation of constraints on imports had propelled the developing sector aggregate trade surplus of 1953 into deficit in 1954 (see Table 3.1).

By 1955, further growth in export volume to the developed sector and renewed restraints on imports slowed the deterioration in the developing sector's merchandise trade balance. The sector's payments balances were also helped by capital inflow, principally in the form of direct investment—increasingly from the United States.

The year 1955 marked the peak of the first post-Korean War trade recovery, and although the world trade volume growth rate slowed in 1956, developing sector export volume continued to advance. This, however, was not accompanied by an improvement in nonfood primary commodity prices.[3] Nevertheless, after several years of import restraint, developing sector economies were encouraged by the gains in export volume to pursue an expansion of imports. While its import growth rate increased in 1957, the developing sector export growth rate dropped as developed

TABLE 3.1

IMPORT AND EXPORT SHARES AND MERCHANDISE TRADE PERFORMANCE OF THE DEVELOPING SECTOR IN THE PERIOD OF TRANSITION

	1952	1953	1954	1955	1956	1957	1958
Import Share (CIF)	27.9%	25.5%	25.5%	25.0%	24.2%	24.8%	24.4%
Export Share (FOB)	25.9%	25.5%	25.7%	25.2%	24.0%	22.6%	22.9%
Exports (FOB)*		$25.27	$26.34	$28.17	$29.73	$30.82	$29.23
Imports (CIF)*		-$24.45	-$26.50	-$28.63	-$31.03	-$34.56	-$32.94
Balance*		$0.82	-$0.16	-$0.46	-$1.30	-$3.74	-$3.71

SOURCE: Import and Export Share - UNCTAD Handbook 1972; Exports, Imports, and Merchandise Trade Balances - GATT International Trade 1957/58.

* Billions of Dollars

sector domestic demand weakened, world trade growth faltered, and primary commodity prices fell.[4]

Worsening trade and current account balances in 1957 were eased by improved inflows of capital, especially in the form of direct investment. U.S. long-term investment in the developing sector, primarily Latin America, was up one-sixth in 1957, West European foreign investment increased, and the Soviet Union's and Czechoslovakia's capital exports to the developing sector grew in concert with new Soviet efforts to contest the West politically in the Third World.[5]

Nonetheless, developing sector reserves fell by 4 percent in 1957 after growing by 2 percent the year before. In 1956, 9 percent of developing sector economies had reserves sufficient to support only two months of imports, while the following year the percentage doubled to 18 percent. The onset of a deep developed sector recession in late 1957, which lasted through much of 1958, further weakened developing sector terms of trade as primary commodity prices collapsed while manufactured goods prices continued to rise. Terms of trade losses alone cost the developing sector $2 billion in 1958.[6]

The decline in the developing sector's exports began in the middle of 1957 but it was not until early 1958 that its imports began to contract. That year, export value declined by 5.2 percent, while import value dropped by 4.7 percent—enough to bring a halt to the sizable expansion of the aggregate developing sector trade deficit. With capital inflow insufficient to finance current account deficits in 1958, developing economies were forced to endure stiff import restraint, to draw down further on reserves, and to turn to the World Bank and IMF whose activity escalated during 1957/58.

Minimal Improvement in East-West Trade and Payments Flows

Developed sector exports to the CPEs grew only marginally from 1952 to 1958. Brought to a virtual halt during the Korean War, East-West trade and developed sector trade with China underwent some improvement during those years; nevertheless, CPE hard currency import growth from 1952–58 equaled only 21.7 percent of the depressed growth of developing sector imports.[7] Indeed, the major developments in CPE trade and payments during this period continued to be in the dimensions and direction of CPE intra-trade and capital flows.

With the death of Stalin in 1953, the tight, centralized administration of the Soviet economy was eased slightly. Historical disinvestment in agriculture and the consumer sector was reduced somewhat at the expense of heavy industry and defense.[8] But while Soviet economic growth rates improved following the Korean War, the previous disinvestment in agriculture placed absolute limits on agricultural output which, in turn, put a brake on overall Soviet economic development. Nonetheless, from 1952–58 the Soviet Union was not yet in food deficit and thus not in need of non-CPE food imports on a sizable scale.

The 1953 relaxation of the Stalinist economic model brought change to USSR trade and payments relations with Eastern Europe. Eastern Europe's current account surplus with the USSR dissipated and its capital outflows to the USSR ended. Beginning in 1955 the Soviet Union began to run trade surpluses with Eastern Europe, which grew significantly in the late 1960s and 1970s. In addition, the 1952–58 period was marked by a sizable growth in Sino-Soviet trade. The advance in Sino-Soviet and Sino-East European trade was paralleled by heightened intra-CPE capital flows in the form of loans and grants to China.[9]

The other discernible shift in European CPE trade flows during this period related to the developing sector as the Soviet Union and some East European nations opened trade relations with politically important Third World nations, especially in North Africa and West Asia. In concert with these trade relations, the European CPEs began to export capital to the developing sector.

DEVELOPED SECTOR DEMAND PATTERNS—THE POSITIVE CONTRIBUTION

Depressed developing sector and CPE hard currency import growth represented only one set of forces defining the shape of the post-Korean War world market. The other feature of the world economy to affect the boundaries of the world market was the change in developed sector demand patterns away from armaments to civilian goods. The Korean War's end not only relieved pressure on personal consumption in the U.S. and Western Europe caused by high wartime taxation, it reduced the volume of investment resources diverted to the national defense sector.[10] This latter development combined with lackluster developing sector imports of capital goods to permit the developed sector to invest sufficient resources in new productive capacity to satisfy the post-Korean War demand for consumer goods.

Thus, during the 1952–58 period a powerful investment component in the developed sector expansion persisted, as the building of capacity needed to satisfy growing consumer demand overlapped the initiation of huge investment drives in the FRG and Japan.

During the Period of Transition in World Trade and Payments, the developed sector market in consumer goods led by that of the U.S. began to exhibit real dynamism. The blossoming of this market in the United States was the driving force behind the gradual elimination of its artificially low post-World War II import dependence. In addition, the larger volumes of energy and raw materials consumed by this market ultimately propelled the United States into greater reliance on nonfood primary commodity imports. Symptomatic of the vitality of the U.S. consumer market, in the 1958 recession when the remainder of the developed sector experienced a contraction in imports, those of the U.S. declined only marginally because consumer durables imports remained robust.

Notwithstanding the perturbation in the 1970s resulting from the rise in primary commodity prices and the consequent improvement in developing sector imports, the developed sector market has been at the center of world import growth, and this was the case from 1952–58 (see Table 3.2).

As a result of the vitality of the developed sector manufactured goods market, intra-developed sector trade's share of world trade persistently grew, and at the same time manufactured goods' share of world merchandise trade increased while primary commodities' share fell. Moreover, early signs that developed sector regional intra-trade would lead world trade surfaced as it grew marginally faster than developed sector intra-trade as a whole. The 1952–58 period also revealed the critical role that West European intra-trade would play in world trade.

The emerging role of regional intra-trade was muted, however, during the 1952–58 period as a result of West European trade liberalization with the rest of the world and, especially, the dollar area.[11] While full current account convertibility of West European currencies was delayed until January 1, 1959, Western Europe reduced trade restraints on dollar and other non-West European imports. Since Western Europe had enjoyed substantial intra-trade liberalization in 1949 and regional currency convertibility in 1950, the benefits of intra-trade and payments liberalization had made its mark there before 1953. As a result, West European trade liberalization with the rest of the world in the 1950s enhanced the rate of developed sector intra-trade but not regional intra-trade growth.

THE EVAPORATION OF THE "DOLLAR GAP"

A second notable change in world trade and payments during the 1952–58 Period of Transition was the dissipation of the dollar gap. In the 1960s, when the "dollar gap" had given way to a "dollar overhang," attention was focused upon large capital outflows from the United States as the primary culprit. As a result, many observers have failed to recognize the principal source of the "dollar overhang"—the inevitable decline of U.S. trade and, hence, current account surpluses which first began in 1948. It was the fall of U.S. merchandise trade surpluses which—although often blurred by transitory developments from 1952–58—drove the process that resulted in growing dollar overvaluation in the 1960s.

During the 1952–58 period, several factors worked to undermine the

TABLE 3.2

DEVELOPED SECTOR'S ROLE IN WORLD EXPORTS
AND IMPORTS DURING PERIOD OF TRANSITION
(Percent Share of World Imports)

	1952	1953	1954	1955	1956	1957	1958
Developed Sector Exports	62.4	61.9	62.4	63.2	64.7	65.9	65.6
Intra-Developed Sector Exports	36.3	37.3	37.1	38.5	40.1	40.3	39.6
Manufactured Goods Exports	43.0	43.2	43.5	45.2	47.5	47.7	48.6
Developed Sector Imports	64.1	65.2	64.7	66.0	66.5	65.6	64.7

SOURCE: Developed Sector and Intra-Developed Sector Exports - GATT International Trade 1959;
Manufactured Goods Exports - GATT International Trade 1985/86; Developed Sector Imports -
UNCTAD Handbook 1972.

bloated U.S. trade surpluses of the postwar period. Abnormal postwar dependence on U.S. exports, especially in Western Europe, declined. U.S. import dependence, which had been depressed immediately following the Second World War, revived as developed sector manufactured exports, especially consumer goods, penetrated the U.S. market.[12] In addition, U.S. exports suffered from the weakness of developing sector markets which had been more dynamic in the period of postwar reconstruction and from the low level of CPE hard currency imports. Finally, stronger investment in the export sectors of the FRG and Japan from 1952–58 improved their competitiveness relative to the United States. (In the case of Japan, intensive export sector investment did not show up in improved competitiveness until the 1960s.)

But the underlying contraction of U.S. merchandise trade surpluses from 1952–58 was often blurred by transitory developments that produced temporary results akin to the 1949 U.S. recession and the drop of U.S. imports in the aftermath of the Korean War peak.

The fall of the U.S. merchandise trade surplus from 1952–58 was intermittently disrupted by a series of special circumstances. Because the 1954 U.S. recession had little impact on the economic activity of the rest of the world, U.S. exports were permitted the luxury of expanding while imports weakened. This served to temporarily enlarge the U.S. trade surplus, as did the mid-1950s institution of a "surplus disposal program" which facilitated U.S. government overseas sales of excess cotton and food products purchased from U.S. producers at higher subsidized prices but sold abroad at the lower world market prices.

A second stimulant to exports was the linkage of U.S. private capital outflow in the form of direct investment to exports of U.S. goods and services used to construct, operate, and maintain overseas U.S. enterprises. U.S. exports were also temporarily enhanced when Western Europe reduced import restrictions on U.S. products. Poor West European harvests in 1956 created a temporary bulge in U.S. exports, and in 1957 the Suez crisis forced Western Europe to turn from West Asia to the United States (as well as North Africa) for its petroleum imports.

While in the absence of such special circumstances the U.S. merchandise trade surplus would have been certain to contract, after the Korean War U.S. capital outflow not only grew but underwent a change in character. By 1953, U.S. official aid and loans which had financed global current account deficits during the period of reconstruction dropped. Financing of European and Asian dollar current account deficits became increasingly dependent upon U.S. overseas military purchases (which grew in response to the post-Korean War forward positioning of U.S. military forces, especially in Western Europe) and upon larger long-term U.S. private capital outflows, principally in the form of direct investment (see Table 3.3—military expenditures and U.S. private capital).

TABLE 3.3   **US BALANCE OF PAYMENTS, 1952-58 ($Billions)**

	1952	1953	1954	1955	1956	1957	1958
Merchandise Trade Balance	2.5	1.3	2.4	2.8	4.5	6.1	3.3
Current Account Balance	2.9	0.3	1.9	2.4	4.1	6.3	3.3
Government Transactions	-5.4	-4.5	-4.3	-4.9	-5.2	-5.6	-5.2
Military Expenditures	-2.0	-2.3	-2.4	-2.6	-2.8	-2.8	-3.4
US Private Capital	-1.2	-0.4	-1.6	-1.2	-3.0	-3.2	-2.8
Overall Balance	-1.7	-2.6	-2.0	-1.7	-2.3	-0.7	-3.9
Total Gold & Foreign Reserves	1.2	2.3	1.7	1.4	1.5	-0.2	3.4
Errors & Omissions	0.5	0.3	0.2	0.4	0.7	0.7	0.4

SOURCE: UN World Economic Survey 1959.

The reserves of the rest of the world grew in the immediate post-Korean War period as the "dollar gap" eased. The decline of the gap was attributable to marginal growth of U.S. goods and services exports while U.S. imports of goods and services rose sharply; as a result, the U.S. goods and services trade surplus shrank from $7.3 billion in 1948 to $2.3 billion in 1953.

But in 1954, the pace of decline of the "dollar gap" weakened as the U.S. trade surplus improved due to a recession-induced drop in imports.

Between 1955 and 1957 two contending forces influenced dollar balances. First, U.S. import dependency increased. From 1953–57, U.S. imports grew faster than GNP. But U.S. exports grew even more rapidly from 1955–57.

A driving force behind U.S. export dynamism in 1954/55 was the initiation of the "surplus disposal program" which, when combined with Western Europe's poor harvest in 1956, produced renewed health in U.S. primary commodity exports.[13] Further, by 1955/56 the rapidly growing West European economies had reached capacity limits and thus required larger imports of U.S. intermediate and machinery goods.

At the same time that U.S. exports showed renewed vigor, U.S. import growth began to soften in response to restrictive demand management programs promoted by an Eisenhower Administration fearing the rebirth of inflation—and as a result, by the second half of 1956 the "dollar gap" was back with renewed force. The developments of the first half of 1957 were even more persuasive on this score. The Suez crisis had cut West European trade links to West Asian oil and Western Europe was forced to turn to the United States for petroleum.

Consequently, the U.S. current account surplus grew in 1957 sufficient to permit growth in U.S. reserves for the first time since 1951 (see Table 3.3—current account and reserves)—even while U.S. long-term capital outflow, led by direct investment, was peaking.

But the export boom, predicated as it was on special circumstances, was unsustainable. By mid-1957, the Suez crisis was over and petroleum once again flowed to Western Europe from West Asia, the "surplus disposal program" had come to an end, and West European demand for U.S. exports began to weaken.

In 1958, heightened U.S. import dependence and the evaporation of the 1957 export boom resulted in an unprecedented decline in U.S. reserves and substantial gold outflow to Western Europe. U.S. imports only fell marginally as imports of consumer durables continued to grow right through the 1958 recession. At the same time West European imports from the United States fell sharply, precipitating a 16.5 percent decline in total U.S. exports. West European and Japanese exports only fell by 2.0 percent.

Consequently, in 1958 the "dollar gap" collapsed even in the face of sizable retrenchment in private U.S. capital outflow.

The Emerging Challenge of FRG and Japanese Export-Centered Growth

An important subplot in the weakening of dollar surpluses was the simultaneous strengthening of the surpluses of the Federal Republic of Germany, fueled by its enormous trade gains with the EPU. Indeed, the flip side of the FRG's rise to surplus status in the 1952–58 period of transition was the beginning of the relative decline of second-tier European trading powers—the United Kingdom, France, and Italy.[14]

By the end of the Korean War, the FRG had supplanted the U.S. as Western Europe's leading capital goods supplier, and from 1952–58 its economy was guided by government policies committed to the enhancement of its recently won trade advantage.

What lay behind the FRG's long-term success in sustaining trade surpluses and strong reserve growth were huge investments with a large export component undertaken during the post-Korean War 1950s.[15] Although the FRG sustained very high rates of investment in the 1960s and up until 1973, this investment was increasingly less productive than it had been in the earlier decade. The 1950s investment program represented a successful application of "supply-side" economics: tax cuts targeted to stimulate investment and reduce the cost of capital by improving savings rates were matched with persistent government fiscal surpluses resulting from highly constrained government outlays.[16] The government fiscal surpluses ensured that the enlarged volume of domestic savings would result in a reduction in the cost of capital.

From the second half of 1952, when French and British balance of payments constraints were eased, to 1955, Western Europe experienced an unrestrained economic expansion which was unaffected by the 1954 U.S. recession. However, by 1955 some West European economies were again faced with balance of payments stress, and by 1956, as the U.S. recovery weakened, a number of West European countries registered growing external deficits.

During the period from the second half of 1952 through 1956, the Federal Republic of Germany ran large merchandise trade surpluses with continental Western Europe while also sustaining merchandise trade surpluses with the U.S. In 1957, when the U.S. trade surplus improved significantly, the FRG ran a massive surplus with the EPU while French and British current account balances faltered.

By the second half of 1957, short-term capital movements out of France and the United Kingdom (as well as another deficit economy, the Netherlands) into the Federal Republic of Germany had erupted and were followed by broad-based anticipation of a West European currency realignment. In the middle of the year, Paris was forced to reimpose import restraints which, when combined with a better agricultural harvest, served to improve its trade balance. After Paris' adoption of yet stiffer import restraints in the fall of 1957 and following import contraction in second-tier West European economies, speculative capital returned to France and the U.K. from the FRG in early 1958. The British balance of payments position was enhanced by an improvement in its trade balance and by capital inflow from the United States caused by higher U.K. real interest rates.

FRG export volume continued to grow through the 1958 recession and it was only as the result of long-term capital outflow from the FRG that Bonn's reserves fell. However, the future would reveal that the more reliable trends in West European trade and payments were those that preceded the 1958 recession. FRG merchandise trade surpluses were on the rise with the rest of Western Europe where second-tier economies were turning toward trade deficits.

The first second-tier West European currency to suffer as a result of the above trends was the French franc. As the 1958 recession came to a close, France's trade balance worsened, prompting a large speculative move against the franc (short-term capital left France for the FRG). Failing to stem the speculative assault by intervention with borrowing from the EPU, Paris was forced to devalue the franc in December 1958. The franc devaluation represented the opening shot in a series of West European currency devaluations and revaluations which persisted through the 1960s.

Far smaller than the economies of Western Europe during the period of transition and crippled by the absence of sufficient reserves to avoid balance of payments problems, the Japanese economy—which, like the FRG, had tasted export-centered growth during the Korean War "procurement boom"—moved, like the FRG, to foster investment growth rates above the developed sector average with emphasis on modernizing and expanding its export sector.[17]

In the aftermath of the "procurement boom" Japan had settled into recession, sparked by balance of payments deficits which forced Tokyo to borrow from the IMF on three occasions in 1953. So-called "window guidance" or tight money policy which was used as the means for restraining imports in 1954 also produced a recession. Nevertheless, a post-procurement boom consensus among business and government leaders crystallized, centered about the objective of "catching up with the West" in economic terms. This consensus was spelled out in a 1955 government White Paper which promoted a major restructuring of the Japanese economy predicated on investment with a powerful export component.[18] At that time Japan's GNP was equivalent to Argentina's, half that of the

FRG, and one-fiftieth that of the United States. By 1968, its GNP surpassed that of the FRG and, by the early 1980s, it approached half the size of the U.S. GNP.

Japan's recovery from the 1954 recession (which coincided with the U.S. recession) commenced in 1955 and was led by a boom in investment that was guided by an industrial policy implemented through the Ministry of International Trade and Industry (MITI), which selected heavy industry as the priority investment target.[19] Japan's export growth during this period was, however, based on the output of its old industrial base (concentrated in light industry consumer goods). This would change in the 1960s as investments during the "Jimmu boom" years from 1955–57 produced a more competitive manufacturing sector. But in the second half of the 1950s—before these investments bore fruit—the weakness of Japan's economy was evident as the country ran an excessive trade deficit in 1956 and consequently stumbled anew into severe balance of payments difficulties in 1957. A heavy dose of "window guidance" produced another large recession in 1958.

4

The Cycle of Rapid Growth In International Trade—1959-67

While the first postwar trade and payments cycle appears in the 1959–67 period, world trade and payments remains dominated by the momentum of trends that evolved from 1945–58. Indeed, it is in the 1959–67 period that these earlier trends fully mature. We turn our attention first to the maturation process before examining the phasal character of Cycle 1 in the following chapter.

From 1959–67 the world market configuration that had emerged in the earlier period fully blossomed, and with ever more vigor world trade growth was led by developed sector intra-trade, which itself was significantly enhanced by the emergence of regional "special trade arrangements," including the European Economic Community (EEC), the European Free Trade Association (EFTA) and the U.S.-Canadian Automotive Pact.

Another important feature of the maturation of the post-Korean War world market was the emergence of clear differentiation among developing sector economies. The trade performance of two groups of developing sector economies with special links to the developed sector manufactured goods market became clearly distinguished by their trade performance: developing sector manufactured goods exporters, or Newly Industrializing Economies (NIEs), who compete in developed sector manufactured goods markets; and developing sector oil exporters who supply the energy resources required to sustain developed sector manufacturing.

While aggregate developing sector imports and CPE hard-currency imports remained soft, the strength of developed sector import growth and

the derivative network of trade flows among developing sector manufac̄-
turing and oil exporters produced the most intense period of growth in
world trade in modern times.

The second development—beyond the maturation of the post-Korean
War world market—that dominated the 1959–67 trade and payments
landscape also represented an extension of trends evident from 1952–58.
From 1959–67, the "dollar gap" of the 1940s and 1950s swung around to
become a "dollar overhang." There were two causes: the long-term contraction in U.S. merchandise trade and, hence, current account surpluses,
and the insufficiency of U.S. savings to finance private domestic investment and growing government fiscal deficits as well as foreign investment and overseas military expenditures. Larger government fiscal
deficits not only exacerbated the investment squeeze; they abused the
dollar's reserve currency status, bolstering the overvaluation of the currency. Also during this period the deutsche mark, already undervalued by
the second half of the 1950s, became increasingly so. The desire of U.S.
authorities to sustain an overvalued dollar and Bonn's preference for an
undervalued mark contributed to the gradual unraveling of the Bretton
Woods monetary system.

THE MATURATION OF THE POST-KOREAN
WAR WORLD MARKET

During the 1959–67 period, world trade growth accelerated. In volume, it advanced at an average annual rate of 8.7 percent, visibly higher
than the 1952–58 average of 6.3 percent. The 1959–67 span of world
trade growth was the longest and most robust in the 20th century, challenged only by equally dynamic but shorter periods in the 19th century.
When the volume of world trade growth from 1968 to 1973 is added to
that from 1959–67, the result is by far the longest and most dynamic period of world trade in modern times as it grew at an annual rate of 9.2 percent from 1959–73.[1]

Equally impressive was the stimulative impact of world trade on world
GDP growth as the world GDP growth rate peaked in Cycle 1, when the
difference between the rate of growth of world trade and world GDP was
the greatest of any postwar period.[2]

What was responsible for this unprecedented surge in world trade?
The primary cause was an intensification of the market trends discernible from 1952–58. Developed sector trade continued to lead world trade
as its share grew every year from 1959–67. The dynamism of developed
sector intra-trade was reflected in the persistent rise in the share of
world merchandise trade accounted for by manufactured goods (see
Figure 4.1).

Manufactured goods trade was itself increasingly comprised of con-

FIGURE 4.1

GROWTH OF DEVELOPED SECTOR ROLE IN WORLD TRADE, 1958 - 67 (Percent Share)

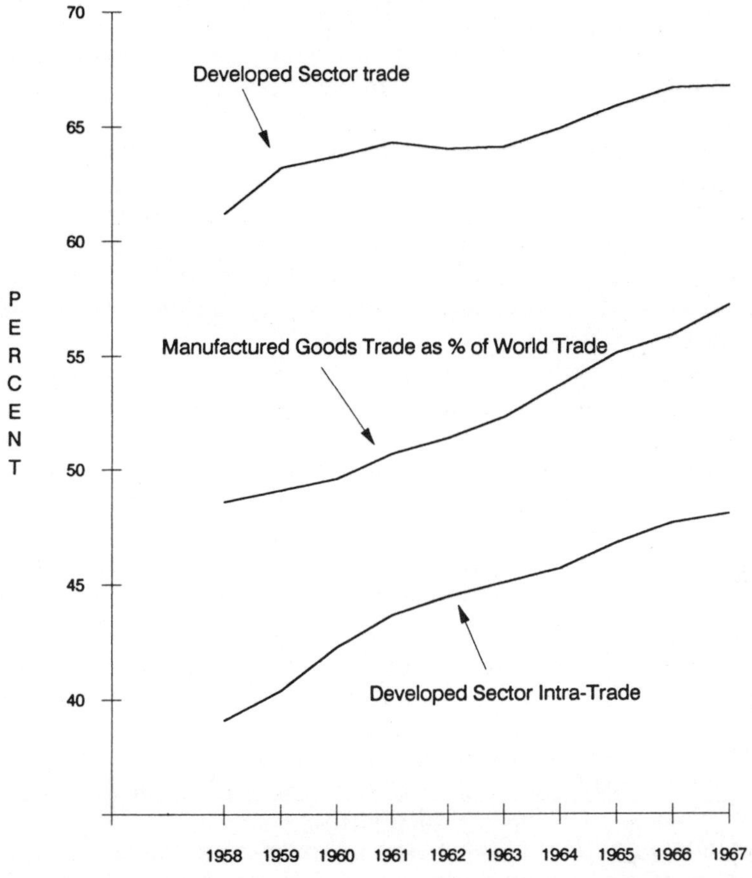

sumer goods, as the share of capital goods in manufactured goods trade fell. In absolute terms, however, trade in capital goods rose at a healthy pace. High FRG and Japanese investment growth rates persisted through the 1959–67 period and, while other developed sector investment growth rates slowed through most of this period, there was a short, sector-wide investment boom in 1964.[3] The explosion in demand throughout the developed sector for consumer goods—especially durables, led by autos—spread rapidly from the U.S. throughout most of Western Europe following the 1958 recession. And in the aftermath of the 1965 Japanese recession, personal consumption growth played a larger role in sustaining Japan's economic growth than was the case in the 1950s and early 1960s.[4]

In addition, the maturation of the post-Korean War market was further enhanced by a development that, while in evidence from 1952–58, was muted as a result of West European trade liberalization with the rest of the world—namely, regionalization of developed sector intra-trade. From 1959 to 1967, this regionalization was enhanced by the creation of "special trade arrangements."

The Treaty of Rome was concluded in 1957 but was not operational until January 1, 1959.[5] That year, EEC member nations' tariffs with one another were reduced by 10 percent. While philosophically at odds with the GATT Most Favored Nation (MFN) principle, there is little doubt that the EEC created more trade than it diverted.[6] In July 1960, most of the remaining West European economies forged the European Free Trade Association (EFTA), modeled on the EEC. Later, in 1965, the U.S. Canadian Automotive Pact was concluded. While a host of other "special trade arrangements," old and new, proliferated—most of which were intra-developing sector, such as the Latin American Free Trade Association (LAFTA)—the EEC, the EFTA, and the U.S. Canadian Automotive Pact were most critical in furthering the expansion of world trade.

While these "arrangements" did not represent the ideal of liberalized trade and, indeed, in principle contradicted such a regime, in aggregate they fostered a more liberalized world trade order.

The most important of these "special trade arrangements" was the European Economic Community, centered about three continental West European trading powers—the FRG, France, and Italy. For most of the 1959–67 period, EEC intra-trade growth rates surpassed those of developed sector intra-trade. The EEC intra-trade growth rate from 1960–68 averaged 13.5 percent a year, well above the developed sector intra-trade average yearly growth rate over the same period of 10.1 percent.[7] EFTA, comprising most non-EEC West European economies including Great Britain, barely failed to average intra-trade growth rates higher than the developed sector as a whole from 1960–68. The average EFTA intra-trade growth rate over this period was 9.6 percent.[8] With the rise of automobile trade—which soared during this period, especially after 1962—the U.S.-

Canadian Automotive Pact took on importance as U.S.-Canada trade growth rates often surpassed those of developed sector intra-trade from 1960–68. The average North American intra-trade growth rate from 1960–68 was 11.5 percent.[9]

During the 1959–67 period, the shares of world trade accounted for by both developed sector intra-trade and trade falling under "special arrangement" increased. But the most rapid rate of developed sector trade growth during this period was registered by U.S.-Japanese bilateral trade and not regional "special arrangement" trade, with Japanese exports to the U.S. showing particular strength. U.S.-Japan trade from 1960–68 grew by 14.2 percent a year.[10]

At the beginning of the 1960s, the high-speed growth of EEC intra-trade and GNP combined with the transformation of the "dollar gap" into a "dollar overhang" to profoundly concern the newly inaugurated Kennedy Administration in Washington. The regional trade and GNP growth boom in Western Europe inspired U.S. fears of a bifurcation of the developed sector into two trading zones.[11] The EEC's Common Agricultural Policy (CAP) became the symbol of this threat. In part, concern over excessive trade regionalization precipitated the most successful GATT round up to that point—the Kennedy Round (1964–67). While the EEC's CAP emerged unharmed, the Kennedy Round did succeed in securing the first across-the-board (nonmanufacturing industry specific) tariff reduction among all member nations. On average, such tariffs were slashed by one-third, the largest of any single GATT negotiating round.

But beyond the impressive trade and payments reform of this period—including the move to full currency convertibility among the developed economies of Western Europe in 1959, significant Japanese trade liberalization in 1961, and Japanese payments liberalization in 1966—early signs of limitations to future trade liberalization, including threats of a rollback of reforms already made, surfaced during these years.

The consolidation of the EEC CAP, when combined with U.S. agricultural subsidies and protection policies launched in the 1950s, ensured that an important component of world merchandise trade—agriculture—would be outside of the reach of the GATT, in effect limiting GATT applicability to trade in manufactured goods.[12]

Moreover, the initial signs of crowding in developed sector manufactured goods markets exacerbated by the increased export competitiveness at the low-tech, labor-intensive end of the manufactured goods spectrum represented by Japan (in the second half of the 1950s) and the NIEs (in the first half of the 1960s) prompted a response from the U.S. Congress in 1962. The price the Kennedy Administration paid for the enhanced presidential negotiation authority of the Trade Expansion Act (which included authorization for the GATT negotiations) was the Long-Term Agreement on Cotton, which sought U.S. import quotas on cotton products.[13] The legislation represented the first substantial evidence of a "new protectionism" centered in the developed sector and, in particular, in the U.S. and Western Europe—a new protectionism that was aimed at shielding increasingly crowded domestic manufactured goods markets from foreign competition. This 1962 action was the godfather of the international Multi-Fibre Arrangement (MFA) of 1974 which, for practical purposes, placed trade in textiles beyond the GATT reach.

While a backlash against "excessive" imports first surfaced in the developed sector in Cycle 1, a reaction against "insufficient" imports in the developing sector emerged. The export weakness of the developing sector caused by poor terms of trade not only forced an extension of the 1950s practice of intermittent resort to import controls; it also prompted more assertive developing sector efforts to circumvent the impact of depressed primary commodity prices on economic development.[14] At the first gathering of the United Nations Conference on Trade and Development (UNCTAD) in 1964, the outlines of a so-called New World Economic Order (NWEO) were defined, as the developing sector argued for a transfer of resources from developed nations to compensate for the impact of primary commodity price fluctuations on development. In addition to aid and technology transfer, the NWEO encompassed two trade-diverting initiatives: the creation of primary commodity buffer stocks to be used to manipulate primary commodity prices and trade preferences for developing sector manufactured exports.

While the primary commodity buffer stock proposal failed to be realized, managed prices for some primary commodities—including coffee, tin, and rubber—*did* materialize, and in the first half of the 1970s the developed sector gradually implemented a Generalized System of Preferences (GSP) for developing sector manufactured exports.[15]

But the most important initiative to reverse the plight of the primary commodity producer in Cycle 1 in light of future events was the creation of the Organization of Petroleum Exporting Countries (OPEC) in September 1960.[16]

THE DEVELOPING SECTOR: NEW THEMES FAIL TO OVERCOME OLD TRENDS

While the pattern of developing sector import growth sustained 1952–58 trends constricting the dimensions of the world market, three new themes surfaced in developing sector trade and payments which would later have a profound impact.

First, in 1963 primary commodity prices surged, suggesting the ultimate demise of the oversupply in nonfood primary commodities endured since the early Korean War period. This in turn helped fuel a short-lived but relatively strong advance in developing sector imports in 1964.

Second, in 1966 developing sector nations resorted to accelerated foreign borrowing, including commercial bank borrowing, to sustain imports in the face of falling terms of trade. This signaled a shift of capital inflow to the developing sector away from direct investment, which had proceeded vigorously in the 1950s and 1960s, to medium- and long-term loans. As a result of this transformation, a smaller percentage of foreign capital flows to the developing sector was devoted to fixed investment, while a larger percentage went to prop up short-term growth and consumption (i.e., balance of payments debt with a large government component).

Finally, two groups of developing nations clearly distinguished themselves from the others on the basis of their trade performance. The first group, the Newly Industrializing Economies, penetrated developed sector markets with manufactured goods exports at the low-tech, labor-intensive end of the spectrum (textiles, nonferrous metals and light industry products). The majority of these economies were located in East Asia and included Taiwan, Hong Kong, South Korea, and Singapore; they were joined by several Latin American economies, especially Brazil and Mexico. The second group of developing sector exporters, the petroleum exporters concentrated in OPEC, supplied energy no longer sufficient from domestic developed sector sources.

But despite the emergence of these new themes in developing sector trade and payments, deteriorating primary commodity prices and import weakness—problems that had plagued the sector since the Korean War—continued to dominate. Although developed sector economic activity and imports rebounded in 1959, primary commodity prices still declined, albeit at a slower pace than in the 1958 recession. Since developing sector nations' import constraints had been maintained through 1959, their reserves improved. Nevertheless, while their external finances progressed, imports—especially imports of capital goods—did not (see Table 4.1).

The year 1960 began with a West European import boom, centered in the EEC, stimulating greater developing sector primary commodity exports. The advance in foreign earnings allowed for relaxed domestic demand management policies which in turn resulted in a mini-import boom. But by the second half of 1960, the U.S. economy was descending into a short recession which led to renewed weakening in primary commodity prices. The result was a rise in developing sector external deficits by the end of 1960, a resurgence of flight capital, a drawdown of reserves, and a ratchet up in borrowings from the IMF.

Exacerbated by weaker West European industrial production, 1961 saw a new contraction in nonfuel primary commodity prices, and in

TABLE 4.1

DEVELOPING SECTOR IMPORTS AND PRIMARY COMMODITY PRICES IN CYCLE 1 (Percent)

	1959	1960	1961	1962	1963	1964	1965	1966	1967
PERCENT SHARE:									
Developing Sector Imports as Share of World Imports (CIF)	22.6	22.9	21.9	20.9	20.0	19.6	19.0	18.8	18.4
PERCENT GROWTH:									
Developing Sector Import Growth Rate (CIF)	-1.4	10.2	3.0	1.0	4.5	9.2	5.3	8.3	3.0
Nonfuel Primary Commodity Prices	-1.6	0.0	-0.3	0.0	1.6	6.0	3.0	5.6	-3.6
Food Prices	-0.6	-1.5	2.2	2.1	5.1	2.8	-2.5	6.5	-0.3
Oil Prices (Average Posted Price)	-4.9	0.4	0.7	-0.4	-0.4	1.1	-3.7	1.5	0.0

SOURCES: For Developing Sector Import Growth Rate and Share of World Imports: 1959-60 - UNCTAD Handbook 1972, 1961-67 - Handbook 1983; for Percent Growth: Nonfuel and Food Prices - IMF IFS Yearbook 1986, Oil Prices - Morris Adelman, The World Petroleum Market, Baltimore, Md.: Johns Hopkins Press, 1972, p. 342.

order to halt the expansion of external deficits, the developing sector was forced to enact strict import constraints and to continue borrowing from the IMF. This process extended into 1962.

The years 1963–65 saw the first major improvement in primary commodity prices since the Korean War. Large food deficits opened up in the European CPEs in 1962/63 which provoked new demand for free world food supplies. In addition, the oversupply of nonfood primary commodities in evidence since the 1950s ended. Developing sector exports (value) rose in both 1963 and 1964 at visibly higher growth rates than at any time since the Korean War, in good part the result of higher primary commodity prices. Indeed, primary commodity export prices, which rose by 4.3 percent in 1963, surpassed the price improvement of manufactured exports. The advance in developing sector export earnings in 1963/64 led to a new import expansion in 1964.

In 1965 the developing sector's trade balance did not worsen, even though its export growth rate declined, as its import growth rate also fell. But in 1966, as export growth continued to weaken, the import growth rate expanded, sparking a wider aggregate developing sector trade deficit. The bigger deficit was financed by enlarged foreign debt, and when the sector's payments situation worsened in 1967 due to recession conditions in the developed sector and weaker primary commodity prices, external deficits were reduced through a lowering of the import growth rate (see Table 4.1).

While overall developing sector import growth remained relatively weak from 1959–67, two groups within the developing sector began to distinguish themselves clearly with respect to trade performance.

Centered in East Asia, developing sector manufacturing exporters' exports grew faster than developing sector exports. Manufacturing exports increased as a share of developing sector exports from 17.2 percent in 1961 to 19.3 percent in 1967.[17]

During the Cycle of Rapid Growth in International Trade, developed sector imports of developing sector fuels rose vigorously, especially as the more energy-dependent West European and Japanese economies expanded. In Cycle 1, the volume of developing sector petroleum exporters' exports grew more rapidly than did developing sector export volume. From 1960–67 developing sector export volume grew by 46 percent, but oil exporter export volume grew even faster—by 85.1 percent.[18] Because oil prices failed to correspond to volume growth in the 1960s (in part the result of developed sector oil company policy), petroleum exporters' exports in value only grew apace with aggregate developing sector export value. From 1960–67 developing sector export value grew by 46.3 percent, almost equivalent to its rate of volume growth. However, oil exporter export value only grew by 54.9 percent, far below its export volume growth rate.[19]

Early Convulsions in CPE Trade and Payments

In the 1959–67 period internal economic and political conditions within the CPEs produced some improvement in hard currency trade and even more dramatic changes in the direction of intra-CPE trade. But enlarged CPE hard currency imports, like the brief advance in developing sector imports in 1964, were not sufficient to alter the world market configuration.

In the early 1960s, the Khrushchev regime ran up against rising primary input costs in the Soviet economy—a development that caused all leading economic indicators to decline over the 1961–65 period.[20] The descent of the Soviet economy from its performance levels of the late 1950s was accompanied by the first large post-World War II sectoral recession in Soviet agriculture, which forced the Soviets to turn to the nonsocialist economies for enlarged volumes of imports in order to close domestic food deficits. After virtually no growth in Soviet imports from the developed sector from 1959–62, such imports grew by 71.7 percent in 1963 and 86.9 percent in 1964. After the food deficit closed, Soviet imports from the developed sector dropped 48.2 percent from their 1964 peak by 1967.[21] In the 1970s, sectoral recessions in Soviet agriculture would generate renewed food deficits and the need for substantial agricultural imports from nonsocialist producers.

Following Khrushchev's erratic efforts to contest the decline in Soviet economic performance by reallocating investment resources, and after his ouster, the new Soviet regime launched a series of economic reforms designed to revitalize the economy. In 1966/67 the reform process seemed to slowly open the door to greater trade with the developed sector. A similar process unfolded in the East European CPEs, as several countries (in particular, Czechoslovakia and later Hungary) went beyond the Soviet Union's economic reforms. Nonetheless, the resulting small improvement in European CPE hard currency imports was insufficient to make a dent in the market configuration that had evolved from 1952–58.

European CPE trade and payments relations with the developing sector were expanded during the 1959–67 period. The Soviet Union and East European CPEs ran persistent trade surpluses with the developing sector and remained net capital exporters to it. During this period, European CPE trade and payments relations with Latin America grew as a result of exports and capital flows to Cuba. At the same time, European CPE trade and payments flows spread more broadly throughout the developing sector to sub-Saharan Africa and South and Southeast Asia (S/SEA) from their earlier stronghold in North Africa and West Asia.

China, too, made its initial trade and aid forays into the developing sector, moving beyond its traditional regional trading partners of North Korea and North Vietnam to concentrate on sub-Saharan Africa.

The major alteration in CPE intra-trade during this period stemmed from the Sino-Soviet political rupture. In 1960, Soviet aid programs to China were slashed. Sino-Soviet trade had already begun to falter as a result of China's economic strategy during the "Great Leap Forward" (1958–60), but following the 1960 aid cut Sino-Soviet and Sino-East European trade and capital flows fell precipitously. As a result, from 1959–62 Soviet exports to the Asian CPEs dropped by 56.2 percent and East European CPE exports to the same sector dropped 58.8 percent. All of the decline was due to an even deeper drop in European CPE exports to China.[22]

As its post-Great Leap economic "Readjustment" (1961–66) unfolded, China slowly and cautiously turned elsewhere for needed imports—to Japan and Western Europe. Thus, while the European CPEs' trade with the developed sector progressed, so did that of the People's Republic of China. But in principle and as a matter of strategy, CPE trade and payments remained autarkic in orientation during Cycle 1.

THE SURGE OF THE DOLLAR OVERHANG

In addition to the maturation of the world market configuration, the 1959–67 period witnessed a transformation of the "dollar gap" into a "dollar overhang."

The principal cause of this turn of events was the unsustainability of U.S. merchandise trade surpluses in Cycle 1. The decline of U.S. merchandise trade and, hence, current account surpluses within the context of the Bretton Woods fixed parity regime caused the dollar to become increasingly overvalued.

It also meant that if the United States were to avoid exposure of the internal vulnerabilities of the Bretton Woods system (the "credibility" and "asymmetry" problems), it would have to either reduce capital outflows or improve its merchandise trade balance. To accomplish the former, the U.S. would have to effectively limit its economic and military power abroad (by containing official and private capital outflows). Alternatively, the U.S. could try to revive its merchandise trade performance by revitalizing merchandise exports and/or trimming the growth of merchandise imports.

Accomplishing the latter objective would be especially difficult. In addition to the dissipation of the postwar structural distortions that had bolstered the U.S. trade balance after World War II, U.S. trade performance in Cycle 1 suffered from the impact of three additional factors.

First, the United States was increasingly challenged for market share by the export power of the Federal Republic of Germany and Japan, both of which had specifically adopted investment-intensive development strategies geared to improving merchandise trade competitiveness, while the United States had not.

In addition, after the macroeconomic conservatism of the Eisenhower years Washington introduced expansionist policies that tended to accelerate domestic demand growth at the cost of public sector deficits, while among the U.S.'s principal competitors, the FRG's macroeconomic conservatism held firm. In the FRG the Bundesbank as well as conservative governments used macroeconomic policy primarily to fight the prospect of inflation. As a result, macroeconomic policy differences between the United States and the FRG tended to increase domestic demand growth and inflation differentials between the two, differentials detrimental to U.S. external balances.

Finally, the 1959–67 period represented one in which demand for and, hence, prices of primary commodities grew less rapidly than prices of manufactured goods. A higher proportion of primary commodities was represented in U.S. exports and a higher proportion of manufactured goods in U.S. imports compared to Western Europe and Japan. Thus, the commodity composition of U.S. trade also hampered its competitiveness relative to its developed sector trading partners whose aggregate imports included a larger share of primary commodities and aggregate exports, a larger share of manufactured goods than the U.S.

Nevertheless, just as in the 1952–58 period, special circumstances of a transient nature arose to intermittently imply a revitalization of the U.S. merchandise trade balance.

The Evolution of the Dollar Dilemma, 1959–67

The period from 1959 through 1961 appeared to demonstrate that the only development that could ease the deterioration in the status of U.S. balance of payments would be a U.S. recession—provided the rest of the developed sector continued to enjoy robust growth. The year 1958 saw a huge outflow of reserves from the U.S. to the tune of $2.3 billion. In 1959 reserve losses continued, as $1.0 billion left the United States. The deterioration in the U.S. balance of payments in 1959 was the by-product of an economic recovery in the United States, a development that would be repeated with greater vigor in the first stages of every subsequent trade and payments cycle. In 1959, U.S. imports rose 16.3 percent (developed sector imports grew by 7.6 percent), fueled by inventory rebuilding and an outburst of pent-up consumer demand following the 1958 recession. The rise in U.S. imports led to a further drop in the U.S. merchandise trade surplus and this represented the largest contribution to the worsening U.S. payments balance in 1959. The worsening of the U.S. payments balance in 1959 was also aggravated by increased U.S. capital outflows resulting from the renewal of strong long-term private investment abroad. Cycle I marked the period of mammoth expansion for U.S. corporations abroad, drawn especially by the growth of investment opportunities in Western Europe.

The U.S. merchandise trade balance improved in 1960. In the second half of that year, the United States once again entered into a recession which caused a contraction in imports (see Table 4.2). At the same time, Western Europe, led by the EEC, was experiencing an enormous import boom which stimulated growth in U.S. exports. Nevertheless, the sharp deterioration in the U.S. payments balance in 1958 and 1959 combined with the emergence of interest rate differentials unfavorable to the U.S. as Washington was forced to lower interest rates in an effort to revive the U.S. economy from recession while Bonn and London raised interest rates (the former to contest the threat of inflation and the latter to reverse growing capital account deterioration) to provoke a surge of "hot money" flows from the United States to Western Europe which were greater than the improvement in the U.S. merchandise trade surplus.

Speculative capital flows out of the United States continued into early 1961. In response, the first concerted trans-Atlantic defense of the dollar commenced. During the 1960s this defense machinery would expand into a complicated web of central bank and government arrangements. In early 1961, the FRG, the target of "hot money" flows, tried to reduce net capital inflow by accelerating its debt repayments to and increasing its military purchases from the U.S. while making large contributions to the United Nations. FRG efforts to stem capital inflow and avoid the pressures for revaluation of the deutsche mark—a development warranted by prolonged mark undervaluation—were unsuccessful and the mark was revalued by 5.0 percent that year.

Simultaneously, the newly installed Kennedy Administration entered office mindful of the country's balance of payments deterioration and weakening international competitiveness. In 1961 it took initial steps to reverse the trends. Short of undermining U.S. foreign economic and military objectives, the Kennedy Administration initiatives required that traditional overseas U.S. military purchases be made in the United States, while incentives for overseas investment be reduced. In addition, as a means of increasing U.S. merchandise trade competitiveness and to further restrict capital outflow, the Kennedy Administration early introduced supply-side tax cuts aimed at improving domestic investment. To increase exports, the Administration also launched a number of export enhancement efforts, including stricter linkages between U.S. foreign aid and purchase of U.S. goods.

The Kennedy Administration policy mix sought to combine a revival of the U.S. merchandise trade performance with constraints on capital outflows. However, the latter effort was careful to avoid any meaningful weak-

TABLE 4.2

US BALANCE OF PAYMENTS, 1958-67 ($Billions)

	1958	1959	1960	1961	1962	1963	1964	1965	1966	1967
Merchandise Exports	16.26	16.30	19.65	20.11	20.78	22.27	25.50	26.46	29.31	30.67
Merchandise Imports	-12.95	-15.31	-14.76	-14.54	-16.26	-17.05	-18.70	-21.51	-25.49	-26.87
Balance	3.31	0.99	4.89	5.57	4.52	5.22	6.80	4.95	3.82	3.80
Official Unrequited Transfers	-1.90	-1.96	-1.99	-2.36	-2.37	-2.33	-2.40	-2.77	-2.41	-2.38
Current Account	0.77	-1.36	2.83	3.83	3.38	4.41	6.81	5.41	3.03	2.59
Net Capital Other Than Reserves	-3.17	-0.41	-5.21	-4.18	-4.92	-5.99	-7.43	-6.21	-3.42	-5.80
Errors & Omissions	-0.41	-0.52	-1.02	-1.00	-1.11	-0.36	-0.91	-0.42	-0.63	-0.22
Change in Reserves	2.29	1.04	2.14	0.61	1.53	0.38	0.17	1.22	0.57	0.05

SOURCE: IMF IFS Yearbook 1986.

ening of U.S. global military and economic power. Further, the entire
Kennedy approach dodged the alternative of realigning the Bretton Woods
parities in the direction of devaluing the dollar. Not only would U.S. developed sector trading partners object to such a realignment, but such a move
would undermine the credibility of the fixed rate monetary system and reduce the purchasing power of the dollar. The U.S. government had no interest in seeing the latter two developments materialize.

The second period in the 1959–67 evolution of the "dollar overhang"
was characterized by an unsustainable stabilization of the U.S. balance of
payments.

In 1962, the U.S. payments balance experienced some improvement,
largely in response to the set of Kennedy Administration programs
launched in 1961 and maintained in 1962. Most effective in easing U.S.
balance of payments difficulties were export enhancement programs and
the reduction in U.S. military purchases overseas. In addition, international measures to build confidence in the dollar were expanded, including an IMF agreement to provide the U.S. with standby credits and
central bank agreement on swap arrangements.

In early 1963, more efforts were made to help curb U.S. capital outflow. A new tax on foreign investment—the so-called "interest equalization tax"—was proposed and in January, the U.S. Federal Reserve raised
the discount rate, making U.S. interest rates competitive with other developed sector interest rates, thereby inhibiting U.S. capital outflow.
These moves were complemented by the Bundesbank, which launched
new efforts to deter FRG capital inflow.

In 1963 U.S. balance of payments problems were further eased by a
series of developments that would play a similarly important role in
1973 and 1979 in causing improvement in the U.S. merchandise trade
and current account balances (see Table 4.2). The first was the emergence of large food deficits centered in the USSR and stretching through
most of Eurasia. Heightened demand for food had a strong impact on
the trade balances of food surplus in North America (especially Canada,
which exported food without restraint to the Eurasian CPEs in 1963/
64). Both the volume and price of U.S. food exports surged, and fully 40
percent of the 1963 improvement in U.S. exports came from agricultural products. While the growth in U.S. agricultural exports to Western
Europe was strongest, U.S. exports to the European CPEs grew by 100
percent.

A second element propping up the U.S. merchandise trade balance
emerged in 1964 (and would recur in 1973, 1975, and 1979)—the relatively high level of developing sector imports. For the U.S. and Japan, exports to the developing sector represented a higher proportion of total
exports than was the case for Western Europe. Following the 1963 primary commodity price boom, developing sector imports increased vigor-

ously. In 1964 U.S. exports to all regions of the world rose, including another 100 percent increase in exports to European CPEs. Most important, however, was a boom in exports to the developing sector. U.S. exports to neighboring Latin America grew by 16.6 percent, and to oil-exporting West Asia, by 16.6 percent.

But while the U.S. experienced current account balance progress in 1964, its capital account balance deteriorated even more sharply with a new wave of capital outflow, sparking a period of heightened U.S. government countermeasures. In early 1965 the "interest equalization tax" was implemented and was followed by actions to limit bank lending to nonresidents and to reduce outflows from corporations and businesses (especially multinationals.)

The final period in the evolution of the "dollar overhang" commenced in 1965. While the capital account deficit was contained that year, the underlying deterioration of the U.S. merchandise trade balance resurfaced with force as global food deficits receded and developing sector terms of trade worsened, thus fostering a slowdown in U.S. exports (see Table 4.2). The only developing sector area to sustain its previous year's gains in imports from the U.S. was West Asia (i.e., oil exporters). Moreover, the proclivity of the U.S. to stimulate domestic demand by means of larger public deficits spurred higher import growth. In 1966, when the U.S. fiscal deficit ratcheted up in order to finance an escalation of the military effort in Southeast Asia and the first phase of "Great Society" domestic programs, U.S. imports grew substantially.

During the same period, the FRG under Bundesbank leadership moved to constrain domestic demand growth out of fear of inflation and concern over a swing into current account deficit in 1965. Most of the other key West European economies, aside from France, were also constraining domestic demand for balance of payments reasons. But U.S. imports jumped 18.5 percent in 1966, while export growth was only sustained through improved developing sector imports made affordable by an acceleration in foreign indebtedness. The 1966 weakening in the U.S. balance of payments, like that of the previous year, was caused by a declining merchandise trade surplus aided by growing U.S. military expenditures overseas.

The U.S. balance of payments deficit moved sharply upward in the second half of 1966 and continued to worsen, albeit very moderately, in 1967, as the U.S. entered a growth recession triggered by Fed efforts to check inflation which helped slow import growth. But ominously signaling a new phase in U.S. merchandise trade flows that would unfold in the next trade and payments cycle, the U.S. merchandise trade balance with Japan plunged into deficit in 1967.

THE ESCALATION IN INTRA-WEST EUROPEAN IMBALANCES AND THE RISE OF JAPAN

Another destabilizing series of trade and payments imbalances rumbled through the developed sector in the years from 1959 to 1967. Dissolution of the structural distortions in U.S. trade in the immediate postwar period not only ensured a deterioration in the U.S. merchandise trade surplus, but also that the merchandise trade deficit of the rest of the world would fall.

From 1952–67 nonfood primary commodity prices were depressed, undermining improvement in aggregate developing sector merchandise trade balances (subsectors of the developing sector most closely linked to the post-Korean War world market configuration—the energy and manufacturing exporters—did enjoy some improvement). In addition, the continuation of highly constrained CPE trade with the rest of the world ensured that the CPEs would not be the beneficiaries of declining U.S. merchandise trade surpluses.

The group of nations that saw its merchandise trade balance improve in the wake of the faltering U.S. trade performance was the remainder of the developed sector. But trade balance performances in the non-U.S. developed sector were highly uneven from 1952–1967. Commercial, development, and macroeconomic policy differences among developed nations played a crucial role in determining relative trade performance during this period. Already evident from 1952–58, the combined impact of conservative macroeconomic policy and an export centered development strategy in the FRG and the more activist macroeconomic policies and weak export development orientation of second-tier West European economic powers, especially the U.K. and France, yielded growing trade and payments imbalances in Western Europe. By 1958 these intra-West European imbalances produced their first victim, the French franc.

Throughout the 1959–67 period (despite a revaluation in 1961) the deutsche mark remained undervalued while the dollar and second-tier West European currencies had become overvalued. Paralleling the experience of the dollar, a vast network arose in the 1960s to defend West European currency parities, but by 1967 it was evident that these measures were not sufficient.

In addition, another challenge to the stability of the Bretton Woods parity regime began to surface in 1965 when Japan started to run large and growing merchandise trade surpluses.

FRG Trade Dominance in Western Europe and the Decline of the Second-Tier Powers

By the middle of the 1950s, the deutsche mark had already become undervalued. After joining the British pound sterling in the devaluation of

1949, the mark was further devalued in 1950 in response to another FRG balance of payments deficit.

In 1951, however, the FRG, based on its booming capital goods exports to Western Europe, ran a merchandise trade surplus and started to rebuild its inadequate reserves. By 1957, persistent trade and current account surpluses and reserve improvement forced Bonn to consider revaluation of the mark. But fear that the imminent West European return to current account convertibility in 1959 would lead to outflows of capital and a decline in reserves (i.e., fear of a renewed dollar gap) forced abandonment of early mark revaluation plans.[23] Nonetheless, pressure for a mark revaluation was building in 1957/58 and it overlapped the December 1958 franc devaluation.

From the second half of 1959 this pressure shifted onto the pound sterling. The United Kingdom and the overseas sterling area had emerged from the post-World War II reconstruction in a weakened condition.[24] During the early stages of World War II Britain had to pay $6 billion for badly needed U.S. imports since the U.S. Neutrality Act only permitted exports to the European belligerents on a cash-and-carry basis. This crippled U.K. finances as virtually all of the nation's foreign exchange reserves had evaporated by 1942. With U.S. entry into the war a Mutual Aid Agreement was signed in 1942, and through Lend-Lease the U.K. received $27 billion in supplies from the U.S. during the remainder of the war while paying only $6 billion in exchange. U.S. assistance kept British international payments balanced during the war years.

But in August 1945—shortly after Japan's surrender—the U.S. abandoned Lend-Lease, thereby exposing the enormous war-aggravated vulnerabilities of the U.K. economy. In the absence of a sizable British retrenchment in domestic and foreign investment and a resort to a siege economy, London was forced to seek a large postwar loan from Washington. In December 1945 the Anglo-American Loan Agreement was signed, supplying the U.K. with up to $3.75 billion until 1951. But the politics of the loan agreement committed the badly weakened British economy to current account convertibility within one year. The subsequent collapse of the U.K.'s reserves in 1947 in the wake of its temporary return to current account convertibility showed the weakness of the postwar British economy. Although a major recipient of Marshall Plan aid, the U.K. and the sterling area once again revealed their underlying weakness during the 1949 U.S. recession.

Britain's export growth rate was far inferior to that of continental Europe, especially the FRG, from 1948 to 1960 (as was that of the U.S.), and the rate of growth of FRG and Japanese industrial production was perhaps ten times as great as that of the U.K. over that same period.[25] For the United States, a much larger economy than the British and with a smaller ratio of trade to GNP, such trade and industrial growth differentials could be absorbed with less threat to its reserve currency status than was the case for the United Kingdom, especially since sterling area merchandise trade and payments balances underwent such erratic swings in the late 1940s and 1950s. At the end of the 1948–60 period—from 1957–60—Britain ran recurrent balance of payments deficits while the Federal Republic persistently accumulated reserves.

The U.K. balance of payments performance was hampered by an expensive overseas security and administrative apparatus, deteriorating export competitiveness and domestic macroeconomic policies which stimulated import growth. These factors increasingly undermined confidence in the pound sterling and its gold convertibility.

In the aftermath of the recovery of the French trade balance in 1959, the British trade deficit expanded, the result of rising imports provoked by restocking of inventories drawn down during the 1958 recession. The deteriorating British trade balance once combined with net capital outflows weakened the U.K. payments balance, causing an early exodus of short-term capital from Britain to the FRG and the U.S. This induced London to raise interest rates to halt the outflow of capital in late 1959—a policy that continued into 1960, when these higher rates attracted short-term capital inflows which temporarily stopped the bleeding in the British payments balance.

But in the first half of 1961 the dam broke: huge volumes of short-term capital left the U.K. both before and after the early-year mark revaluation. British reserves fell sharply as London fought to stabilize the pound. Western Europe's central banks were soon forced to come to Britain's aid as the developed sector moved in a coordinated fashion to meet the challenge to the pound. The FRG launched a series of measures to reduce capital inflow, the West European central banks advanced London a large short-term loan, while the U.K. launched efforts to control capital outflow. British interest rates were raised, non-sterling area investment was restricted, overseas administrative costs were reduced, and borrowing from the IMF commenced to contest this major challenge to the Bretton Woods parities. Further, ten countries agreed to lend the IMF $6 billion to construct a war chest to meet the threat and the U.K. immediately drew from it. Finally, London took action to slow imports and in the second half of 1961, the assault on the pound sterling came to a halt.

Even in these early currency upheavals, Bonn found itself in a policy quandary. Sustaining an undervalued mark meant running persistent current account surpluses, and since long-term FRG capital outflow, while growing, was insufficient to offset current account surpluses, the FRG was accumulating reserves. The balance of payments surplus translated into faster growth in domestic money supply, while the undervalued mark served to raise the domestic merchandise price floor and exacerbate pressure on FRG industrial capacity and labor supply, producing inflationary pressures. Stimulation of unwanted but implicit inflationary forces caused by prolonged external surpluses prompted efforts to reduce domestic money supply growth which, in turn, eventually resulted in higher FRG interest rates. The latter development would then attract foreign capital inflow, which would induce new growth in money supply.

If the Federal Republic of Germany chose to maintain both an undervalued currency and a domestic priority of fighting inflation, its policies would have a deflationary impact on its domestic demand growth (suppressing its imports and expanding its trade surpluses), while its trading partners would be forced under balance of payments stress to adopt more deflationary macroeconomic policies.

Indeed, such a process was important in precipitating the FRG recession of 1967. But this occurred only after leading West European trading partners of the FRG—France, Italy, and the U.K.—had been forced to introduce more contractionary measures beginning in 1964.

In 1962, calm settled in after the currency instability of the preceding year. The huge ad hoc apparatus constructed by developed sector monetary authorities and governments had seemingly worked. But the following year the challenge to monetary stability erupted anew. The immediate precipitant was the Eurasian agricultural recession of 1963 and the rise in primary commodity prices. Food deficits and rising primary commodity prices caused a 16 percent advance in French and 25 percent advance in Italian imports. French and Italian macroeconomic policy accommodated the inflationary pressures of rising import costs, while the FRG moved to contest them. Widening West European inflation differentials joined merchandise trade imbalances to provoke a speculative assault on the Italian lira.

In response, Bonn enhanced efforts to slow capital inflow—efforts that were successful enough to cause a decline in FRG reserves in 1963 despite a huge merchandise trade surplus. Washington, West European central banks and the IMF opened credit lines to Italy to help it contest the challenge to the lira. More conservative domestic economic policies were put in place in Italy and France and, once combined with a European agricultural recovery in 1964/65, resulted in improved payments balances for both countries. Although France avoided a recession, Italy entered one in 1965, while both economies had to accept zero growth in imports.

No sooner had the assault on the lira quieted than renewed pressure amassed against the pound sterling, as outflows of capital from the United Kingdom accelerated in 1964. In response London took steps to further curb the outflow of capital and to restrain imports by means of a new import surcharge tax. These British efforts yielded a large reduction in the U.K. current account and capital account deficits in 1965. While generating impressive balance of payments results in 1965, the U.K.'s deflationary policy package faltered in the first half of 1966 as the country's merchandise trade deficit grew—the result of a rise in imports. This surprising development sparked a new period of speculation against the pound sterling which was only calmed by extraordinary deflationary measures that reduced the country's "long-term basic balance" deficit by 50 percent.

In 1966, the weakening pound sterling was joined by worsening French trade balances as Paris relaxed domestic austerity measures, permitting imports to rise twice as fast as exports. The French current account balance moved into deficit in the second half of 1966, but balance of payments stress was temporarily mitigated by continued strong capital inflow.

While U.K. external balances were not improving sufficiently and French balances were deteriorating anew, the FRG launched measures in 1966 to constrain domestic demand growth. In 1965, FRG imports had grown by 20.7 percent, prompting a current account deficit. While current account losses were offset by large capital inflows, Bonn adopted domestic deflationary policies in order to restore a current account surplus and to attack inflation.

In 1967, the FRG recession strengthened the country's trade balance while the British and French trade balances faltered. This turn of events brought unbearable speculative pressure on the pound sterling, forcing it and currencies closely linked to it to devalue. The first major currency realignment since the 1958 franc devaluation and the 1961 mark revaluation, the 1967 sterling devaluation effectively eliminated the currency's reserve status and left the dollar standing alone to bear the fallout from later trade and payments imbalances.

The Assertion of Japanese Export Power

To add to the growing intra-developed sector trade and payments imbalances, beginning in 1965/66 Japan entered the realm of strong and continuous trade surpluses, except for several years when Japan's economic expansion continued while the rest of the developed sector sank into recession or primary commodity prices rose dramatically. Of equal importance, Japan's bilateral merchandise trade balance with the U.S. moved into surplus.

After the 1958 recession, Japan's economy recovered as it had during the early 1950s—on the foundation of exports facilitated by a rebound in the U.S. market. From 1959–61, a boom at first sparked by exports and pent-up consumer demand was eventually led by investment. But in late 1961 the economy, again inhibited by balance of payments difficulties, moved into recession—albeit one that was much milder than the balance of payments-induced recessions of the 1950s. As the U.S. and West European economies moved into a new boom phase in 1963, Japan's economy, again led by exports, was pulled into an economic expansion that was sustained until 1965 by investment and construction driven by the 1964 Olympic Games in Tokyo.

The 1965 recession was the deepest in Japan's postwar history up to that point, and for the first time it was not a result of balance of payments stress but rather of overcapacity. Through high rates of investment in the 1950s and first half of the 1960s, Japan had overbuilt.[26]

In 1965, however, the recession served to swing Japan's merchandise trade and current account balance into surplus as imports weakened while exports continued to grow. But the following year imports were back up as the Japanese economy recovered. What is of most interest is that Japan continued to run steady external surpluses as the result of a more powerful expansion in exports. Indeed, Japan's robust export expansion eliminated the threat of balance of payments-induced recession, a threat that had plagued it until 1963. From 1966 to 1971 Japan's exports expanded twice as fast as world exports, demonstrating the competitive edge that Tokyo's long-term investment strategy had won. The Japanese economy moved forcefully into a leadership position in world exports of trucks, transistor radios, automobiles, and ships, as well as capital goods.

By 1966 Japan had managed to attain the same share of world exports that it had enjoyed in 1938. What was different, however, was the momentum behind its export drive and the fact that its leading trading partner was no longer China, as in 1938, but the United States. The expansion of Japan's bilateral merchandise trade surplus with the U.S. in 1968 and beyond would emerge as a critical feature of trade and payments imbalances in the 1970s and 1980s.

Part III

THE EMERGENCE OF TRADE AND PAYMENTS CYCLES AND THE RETREAT OF THE TRADE AND PAYMENTS ORDER

5

Trade and Payments Cycles:
Their Structure and Differences

While 1959–67 represents the peak period of acceleration in world trade growth in the postwar period, it is also one in which a discernible cycle in trade and payments appears, a cycle whose internal sequential structure is later repeated—in 1968–75, 1976–82, and 1983–??. Discovery of these trade and payments cycles and their differences offers a powerful tool for explaining the evolution of trade and payments performance since 1959 and for identifying the forces that will influence it in the future.

THE STRUCTURE OF THE TRADE AND PAYMENTS CYCLES

Since 1959, four successive trade and payments cycles have evolved, each with the same six phases (see Chart 5.1).

Phase I. Phase I of each trade and payments cycle begins with economic recoveries in the developed nations and a revitalization of world trade based upon developed sector import growth. The center of developed sector import growth has consistently been the United States. Higher U.S. import growth rates than those of the remainder of the developed sector in each Phase I was caused by domestic demand growth rate differentials between the U.S. and other developed nations. As a result, during each Phase I U.S. external balances deteriorated, and because the dollar failed to depreciate—indeed, in the last two Phase Is the dollar has appreciated—the dollar became increasingly overvalued.[1]

CHART 5.1

THE TIMING, CHARACTERISTICS, AND CAUSES
OF THE SIX PHASES OF THE TRADE AND
PAYMENTS CYCLES

	Characteristics of Phase	Causes of Phase
PHASE I: CYCLE 1 - 1959 CYCLE 2 - 1968 CYCLE 3 - 1976 CYCLE 4 - 1983/84	● Aggregate developed sector domestic demand and import growth rates surge. ● US domestic demand and import growth rates accelerate faster than those of the rest of the world. ● US merchandise trade and current account balances deteriorate. ● The dollar becomes more overvalued as its exchange rate fails to depreciate.	● *Aggregate developed sector macroeconomic policy turns more expansionist.* ● *US macroeconomic policy turns even more expansionist than that of the rest of the developed sector.*
	* * *	* * *
PHASE II: CYCLE 1 - 1959/60 CYCLE 2 - 1968-70 CYCLE 3 - 1976/77 CYCLE 4 - 1983/84	● Developing sector export volume and unit value grow. ● The advance in developing sector exports prompts an early improvement in the sector's external balances.	● *A tighter primary input market places upward pressure on goods and services prices; the recovery in primary input costs is led by primary commodities.*
	* * *	* * *
PHASE III: CYCLE 1 - 1960-62 CYCLE 2 - 1969-71 CYCLE 3 - 1977/78 CYCLE 4 - 1985/86	● Aggregate developed sector domestic demand and import growth rates contract. ● Growth rates of developing sector export volume and unit value decline in response. ● The developing sector export value growth rate recedes, producing deterioration in the sector's external balance. ● In the first two cycles, US external balance deterioration in Phase I is reversed; in the last two, US external balances continue to deteriorate, at a slower pace.	● *Aggregate developed sector macroeconomic policy retrenches in response to the threat of goods and services price inflation.* ● *The primary commodity price recovery weakens in response to this retrenchment.* ● *In the first two cycles, US macroeconomic policy adjustment leads to the retrenchment; in the last two cycles, US macroeconomic policy fails to adjust.*

	Characteristics of Phase	**Causes of Phase**
	* * *	* * *

PHASE IV:
CYCLE 1 - 1961/62
CYCLE 2 - 1971
CYCLE 3 - 1977
CYCLE 4 - 1985

● Exchange rate turbulence breaks out.

● In the last three cycles the policy response featured US depreciation of the dollar and adoption of reflationary economic policies by surplus US developed sector trading partners.

● The US responds to declining US and world output growth rates and to US external imbalances accumulated in the first half of the cycle.

* * *   * * *

PHASE V:
CYCLE 1 - 1963-65
CYCLE 2 - 1972-74
CYCLE 3 - 1978-80
CYCLE 4 - 1986-??

● Aggregate developed sector domestic demand and import growth rates accelerate.

● Developing sector export volume and unit values recover.

● Developing sector export value advances, prompting a recovery in that sector's external balances and a deterioration in developed sector external balances.

● US external balances recover based on an expansion in US exports.

● Second-tier West European economies lead a retreat of external balances in the remainder of the developed sector.

● In the last three cycles there were efforts to halt dollar depreciation and shift the burden of adjustment to macroeconomic policy.

● Aggregate developed sector macroeconomic policy becomes more expansionist.

● Primary input markets tighten in response, leading to a recovery in primary commodity prices.

● The macroeconomic policy of US developed sector trading partners becomes more expansionist than that of the US.

* * *   * * *

PHASE VI:
CYCLE 1 - 1966/67
CYCLE 2 - 1974/75
CYCLE 3 - 1980-82

● Developed sector domestic demand and import growth rates contract.

● Developing sector export volume and unit value growth rates deteriorate.

● Developing sector export value falters, fostering deterioration in the sector's external balances while developed sector external balances improve.

● Aggregate developed sector macroeconomic policy retrenches in response to the Phase V rise in goods and services prices.

● In Cycle 3, the retrenchment was extended to developed sector payments policy toward the developing sector.

● Primary input markets soften and costs weaken.

83

Phase II. During Phase II in each cycle, the boom in developed sector imports that emerged in Phase I inspired growth in the volume of developing sector primary commodity exports. With the oversupply in nonfood primary commodities having weakened by the late 1950s, the rise in demand that brought increases in export volume also either prompted an expansion or slowed the decline in developing sector export unit value and primary commodity prices. This phenomenon emerged at some point during Phase II of each cycle (1959/60, 1968–70, 1976/77, and 1983/84). The consequent recovery in developing sector exports (value) and the maintenance of constrained imports early in Phase II in response to merchandise trade balance losses in the previous recession yielded progress in the sector's external balances early in Phase II. Phase II primary commodity price increases coincided with tighter labor markets in the developed sector prompted by the rise in domestic demand, and this resulted in higher labor costs.

Phase III. Phase III commenced with a ratcheting down of economic growth rates in the developed nations, producing a fall in their import growth rates. Phase III unfolded in 1960–62, 1969–71, 1977/78, and 1985/86. In the first two cycles, Phase III began with U.S. deflationary macroeconomic policies launched to fight inflation and improve external balances. In the first year of Phase III—1960 and 1969—the contraction in the U.S. import growth rate was offset by dynamic West European import growth and the developed sector import growth rate therefore continued to expand. However, in the second year—1961 and 1970—the West European import growth rate deteriorated. The result was a reduction in the aggregate developed sector import growth rate and because of the earlier decline in the U.S. import growth rate, Phase III in the first two cycles also involved some improvement in U.S. merchandise trade and current account balances.

In Phase III of the last two trade and payments cycles—1977/78 and 1985/86—the decline in the developed sector domestic demand and import growth rates was not led by a contractionary U.S. macroeconomic policy. While U.S. domestic demand and import growth declined less decisively than in Phase III of Cycles 1 and 2, Western Europe's import growth rate, reflecting a less accommodative West European macroeconomic policy, failed to accelerate as it had in 1960 and 1969. As a result, U.S. and West European domestic demand growth rates did not experience a reversal in relative performance as in Cycles 1 and 2 and the U.S. merchandise trade and current account balances not only failed to improve but continued to deteriorate.

In each Phase III, the decline in the developed sector import growth rate served to weaken the expansion in developing sector primary commodity export volume, and this coincided with a slowdown and, in some cases, a reversal in the advance in primary commodity prices and developing sector export unit value. The developing sector also underwent a lagged recovery in imports in each Phase III in response to improved external balances in Phase II, which, in concert with faltering export (value) growth, worsened its merchandise trade and current account balances.

Phase IV. Phase IV of each cycle was marked by U.S. policy initiatives whose objective was to revitalize the withering economic expansion and reverse the deterioration in U.S. external balances accumulated in the first half of the cycle. The first such initiative was introduced by the Kennedy Administration in 1961–62. U.S. economic growth was stimulated by means of a more accommodative government macroeconomic policy and the primary component of that policy—supply-side tax cuts— were charged with enhancing U.S. international competitiveness. To induce a recovery in external balances, the Kennedy Administration also enacted a series of export promotion programs and instigated a new GATT round with the primary objective of opening West European markets to U.S. agricultural exports.

While the Kennedy Administration program worked within and indeed sought to secure the Bretton Woods monetary system, the subsequent U.S. initiative launched at the same point in the next cycle, 1971, required a profound alteration of the postwar monetary system. The formula proposed by the Nixon Administration—dollar depreciation, reflation in surplus trading partners' economies, and promises to restrain U.S. domestic demand growth—were reemployed at similar points in subsequent cycles. The goals of the Carter Administration policy of 1977/78 and the Reagan Administration-initiated Plaza Accords of September 1985 represent the functional equivalents of the Nixon Administration's objectives when it abandoned the Bretton Woods system in August 1971.

Each Phase IV also witnessed significant exchange rate volatility spawned by three factors: U.S. external imbalances accumulated in earlier phases of the cycle, U.S. policy initiatives launched in this phase of the cycle, and intra-West European trade imbalances—thus, the deutsche mark revaluation of 1961, the float of the mark and Dutch guilder and the revaluation of the Swiss franc and Austrian schilling in 1971 preceding the August 15 Nixon policy initiative, the dollar depreciation and yen/mark appreciation of 1977/78, and the dollar depreciation and yen/mark-led currency appreciations of 1985–87. (In the latter two cases, exchange rate turbulence again began prior to the U.S. Phase IV initiative.)

Phase V. The next phase of the cycle, Phase V, was dominated by two developments: an inflationary upsurge in goods and services prices and the appearance of improvement in U.S. merchandise trade and current account balances. In Cycle 1, by 1963/64 the reflationary component of the U.S. Phase IV policy initiative launched in 1961/62 (several second-tier West European economies, notably France and Italy, also adopted reflationary programs) revived the developed sector domestic demand growth rate, and this in turn provoked a recovery in nonfood primary commodity prices. In subsequent cycles in 1971–73, 1978/79, and 1986/ 87, large-scale currency intervention by West European governments (especially Bonn) and Tokyo to contest dollar depreciation led to an expansion in their domestic money supplies, and in some cases monetary expansion was accompanied by government fiscal expansion. The resulting acceleration in West European and Japanese domestic demand growth rates combined with sustained U.S. domestic demand growth to spark recoveries in nonfood primary commodity prices.

Importantly, the opening of large food deficits in the European CPEs which first emerged in 1962/63 occurred at the same point in the two subsequent cycles, in 1972/73 and in 1978/79, and the entrance of the CPEs as buyers in nonsocialist markets drove up food prices. In 1988 strain on world food supplies, this time based on agricultural production losses in North America, also drove world food prices up.

The primary commodity price recovery of 1963/64 was repeated in 1972–74, 1979–81, and from the second half of 1986 through 1988. At the same time a higher degree of resource utilization (i.e., lower unemployment rates and higher industrial capacity utilization rates) in the developed sector, especially the U.S., put additional pressure on goods and services prices.

The second development that surfaced during Phase V of all cycles was the appearance of improvement in U.S. trade and current account balances. A crucial point to be learned from examination of U.S. merchandise trade and current account performances in 1973, 1979, and 1988 is that their improvement was only partly the result of the J-curve phenomenon. Progress in U.S. trade performance in 1963/64 was in no way a reflection of the J-curve since the dollar had not previously depreciated.

Indeed, in both 1973 and 1979 U.S. trade and current account improvement was more the result of nonfood primary commodity price increases and CPE/developing sector food deficits than of the maturation of the J-curve. In 1973 a large proportion of U.S. export growth was attributable to the advance in agricultural exports, which almost equaled the entire gain in the merchandise trade balance, and in 1979 agricultural exports again played a role in the recovery of the U.S. trade balance. Further, in 1973, 30 percent of the improvement in the U.S. current account balance was due to a larger factor services income surplus predicated on increased U.S. direct investment income, and in 1979 a larger factor services income surplus accounted for over 75 percent of the current account improvement.[2] In both cases, the growth of U.S. direct investment income was driven by a rise in primary commodity prices and the strong position of U.S. overseas direct investment in extractive sector industries.

Phase V in the last three cycles has included agreements to halt dollar depreciation and shift the burden for intra-developed sector balance of payments adjustment more to macroeconomic policy—the Smithsonian Agreement of 1971, the Bonn Summit of 1978, and the Louvre Accords of 1987. And in all cases, the new exchange rate regimes associated with these agreements collapsed prior to the end of Phase V.

Phase V has also been marked by recoveries in developing sector exports and, as a result, in developing sector merchandise trade and current account balances. At the same time, rising primary commodity import prices produced deterioration in the merchandise trade balance of the developed sector, especially second-tier West European economies.

Phase VI. Phase VI, the final phase of the cycle, was driven by developed sector government deflationary macroeconomic policies taken in response to rising goods and services price inflation and growing balance of payments difficulties. In Cycle 1 Bundesbank efforts in 1966 complemented by U.S. Fed tightening precipitated an FRG recession and U.S. growth recession in 1967.

In Cycle 2, after being freed from having to defend the Smithsonian parities, the Bundesbank moved forcefully in 1973 to constrain FRG money supply growth, and a year later Japanese Finance Minister Takeo Fukuda introduced a harsh deflationary policy to contest Japanese inflation.[3] At the same time, the second-tier economies of Europe were forced to adopt more deflationary macroeconomic policies in response to balance of payments stress and inflation. This prompted the appearance of recession conditions in 1974/75. In Cycle 3 the deflationary turn in aggregate developed sector macroeconomic policy first introduced at the end of 1979 was more forceful than in Phase VI of the previous cycle, and compounding this, developed sector international payments policy took an increasingly restrictive turn.

The economic recessions which followed these developed sector economic policy measures in 1967, 1974/75, and 1981/82 resulted in weaker primary commodity prices and deterioration in developing sector external balances. The subsequent recoveries started the cyclical process all over again.

THE CAUSES OF THE TRADE AND
PAYMENTS CYCLES

The phases of the trade and payments cycles are the result of regular fluctuations in three variables: primary input costs, aggregate developed sector macroeconomic and international payments policies, and intra-developed sector macroeconomic policy differences.

The foundation for the regular and visible movement in these variables was created by the tightening of primary input markets—i.e., primary commodity and developed sector "raw labor" markets—toward the end of the 1950s. The consequent rise in primary input costs instigated a more profound economic policy dilemma: if accommodated by economic policy, these costs would yield higher rates of goods and services price inflation; if not accommodated, they would constrain the growth of goods and services output. The strength of the increase in primary input costs made the policy choices surrounding the traditional inflation/ unemployment trade-off more difficult than had been the case after World War II when labor supplies were plentiful and after 1952 when nonfood primary commodity supplies were in abundance. Movement from one phase to the next within the trade and payments cycles is in part produced by the fluctuation in aggregate developed sector macroeconomic and international payments policy as it reacts to the rise in goods and services price inflation or to the contraction in the goods and services output growth rate, and by the fluctuation in primary input costs, especially primary commodity prices, as they react to the expansionary or contractionary tilt in developed sector macroeconomic and international payments policy.

The heightened policy dilemma surrounding the inflation/unemployment trade-off also incited historical macroeconomic policy biases within developed nations. These biases in turn produced regular interphasal fluctuations in the differences among these governments' macroeconomic policies: in some phases their policies diverge sharply, in others, they converge (see Chart 5.1).

The movement of these variables which produce the six phases of the trade and payments cycle can be seen clearly in the evolution of Cycle 1 (1959–67).

Phase I. Phase I of Cycle 1—which appeared in 1959—was the result of a developed sector recovery from the 1958 recession, a recovery spurred in part by a more accommodative macroeconomic policy. This policy led in 1959 to an increase in the developed sector's domestic demand growth rate strong enough to prompt a 7.6 percent rise in its import growth, following minimal growth the preceding year.

The developed sector resort to a more expansionist macroeconomic policy in Phase I of Cycle 1 was not evenly distributed throughout the sector. The United States, reflecting its historical biases, experienced a more dramatic domestic demand growth rate recovery than did the remainder of the developed sector, and as a result the U.S. import growth rate soared above that of the entire sector, reaching 16.3 percent. These large intra-developed sector import growth rate differentials fostered a deterioration in the U.S. merchandise trade and current account balances and an early hint of dollar overvaluation.

Phase II. The expansionist tilt in aggregate developed sector macroeconomic policy in Phase I provoked tighter supply conditions for primary inputs, inducing a small rise in their cost and the beginning of a short-lived Phase II at the end of 1959, which lasted through the first half of 1960. Most important, by the end of 1959 the condition of oversupply in the nonfood primary commodity sector operative since the Korean War was briefly reversed, producing a small rise in nonfood primary commodity prices. The jump in developed sector domestic demand in 1959 had prompted an increase in developing sector export volume which, together with the rise in primary commodity prices, produced an improvement in developing sector exports (value) and a recovery in the sector's merchandise trade balance.

Phase III. Phase III of Cycle 1, which began in 1960, sprang from an aggregate developed sector macroeconomic policy reaction to the advance in primary input costs and the consequent threat of goods and services price inflation. This reaction produced a contraction in the growth rate of developed sector domestic demand which in turn relaxed pressures on supplies of primary inputs in 1961/62. The result was a softening in primary input costs, reflected in weaker primary commodity prices, and a receding inflation threat. Developing sector export volume growth slowed and export unit value declined in response to the drop in demand. The latter two developments undermined developing nations' exports (value) and, because their imports had risen at the beginning of Phase III in 1960 in response to Phase II export growth, their external balances worsened, forcing an eventual weakening of developing sector imports which surfaced in 1961/62.

The contraction in the aggregate developed sector domestic demand growth rate in Phase III of Cycle 1 was led by the United States, which because of its behavior relative to the remainder of the developed sector during Phase I had suffered a deterioration in its external balances and greater inflationary pressures. Western Europe's policy reaction to the threat of goods and services price inflation emerged later, in 1961. The later decline in Western Europe's domestic demand growth rate allowed for a reversal of the 1959 domestic demand growth rate differential between the U.S. and the rest of the developed sector in 1960, and this was reflected in an improvement in U.S. external balances.

Phase IV. Phase IV was marked by a U.S. policy response to the decline in the U.S. and global GNP growth rates in Phase III, as well as to the deterioration in U.S. external balances in the first half of the cycle. Phase III began in 1960 with a U.S. economic recession, and was followed by a decline in the West European and developing sector domestic demand growth rate in 1961/62. In addition, the improvement of U.S. external balances in Phase III rested heavily upon import compression produced through a mechanism to which the U.S. economic policy bias was hostile—recession. More acceptable would have been an export-led recovery in U.S. external balances that would permit higher levels of U.S. domestic demand growth. Indeed, in successive trade and payments cycles U.S. economic biases would become more assertive in both Phases III and IV. But in Phase IV of Cycle 1, the United States was not yet prepared to sacrifice an overvalued dollar in order to improve its trade competitiveness. As a result the Kennedy Administration was restricted to supply-side adjustment through its tax plan and to export enhancement efforts, including market opening initiatives to boost trade competitiveness.

Phase V. In response to the decline of world economic output in Phase III, the developed sector resorted to a more expansionist aggregate macroeconomic policy led by U.S. Phase IV initiatives which in turn produced an acceleration in the developed sector domestic demand growth rate beginning in 1963. The advance in the developed sector domestic demand growth rate resulted in a Phase V tightening of primary input markets which fueled a sharp recovery in primary commodity prices in 1963/64 and an acceleration of goods and services price inflation. In addition to a rise in nonfood primary commodity prices, food deficits erupted in the European CPEs in 1962/63, prompting a steep rise in food prices.

The increase in developed sector domestic demand growth also prompted an expansion in developing sector export volume which, when joined with the unit value gains, produced a sizable jump in developing sector exports (value) in 1963/64—a jump substantial enough to produce a recovery in that sector's merchandise trade balance and to facilitate renewed growth in its imports.

The flip side of this process was a deterioration in the developed sector's merchandise trade balance due to the rising unit value and volume of primary commodity imports, and this traumatized the external balances of the most exposed of the larger developed sector economies— the second-tier West European economies, which, in Cycle 1, were Italy and France.

Ironically, while aggregate developed sector external balances deteriorated due to rising imports, those of the United States improved due to rising exports. In Phase V of Cycle 1, this development was almost entirely the result of the commodity composition of U.S. exports, which was more weighted to primary commodities and food in particular than was that of Western Europe or Japan. Phase V saw a large volume and unit value expansion in these exports. A second reason for the U.S. export improvement was also related to the recovery in primary commodity prices. Their revival facilitated an expansion in the developing sector domestic demand and import growth rate, and the developing sector accounted for a larger share of U.S. exports than was the case for the remainder of the developed sector.

Phase VI. The rise in primary input costs and the subsequent escalation of goods and services prices in Phase V precipitated a macroeconomic policy reaction within the developed sector. The shift to a more contractionary macroeconomic policy began with Bundesbank moves in 1966 to constrict money supply growth.[4] From the Federal Republic, where the subjective fear of inflation was greatest, the transformation in developed sector macroeconomic policy moved to the United States, where the objective threat of inflation was greatest. In 1966 the Fed tightened monetary policy, sparking a rise in interest rates. Second-tier West European economies had been forced to adopt a deflationary monetary and fiscal policy mix even before FRG and U.S. actions in response to Phase V balance of payments stress (i.e., France and Italy) and, following the Bundesbank initiatives of 1966, began to experience renewed balance of payments stress (i.e., the United Kingdom and France).

Finally, the drop in the aggregate developed sector domestic demand growth rate unleashed supply-demand conditions that undermined the pace of primary commodity price growth and developing sector external balances.

INTER-CYCLICAL DIFFERENCES: THEIR CAUSES AND DIMENSIONS

While each cycle contained the same sequence of phases, there were nevertheless important differences between the cycles. What caused each cycle to differ from the others? The differences among the cycles stem from differences in the degree of interphasal fluctuation from one cycle to the next in the values on the three variables—primary input costs, aggregate developed sector macroeconomic and international payments policy, and intra-developed sector macroeconomic policy differences— whose interaction produced the structure of the cycles.

The Growing Complexity of the Policy Dilemma

Before assessing inter-cyclical differences, it is important to understand that the inflation/unemployment dilemma prompted by the tightening of primary input markets beginning in the late 1950s increased in complexity over the course of the four cycles. In addition to goods and services price inflation, accommodation of rising primary input costs produced two related economic ills by Cycle 2—overindebtedness and underinvestment.

An acceleration in both domestic and foreign overindebtedness in some sectors of the free world economy began during Cycle 2 as a result of the widespread resort to financial deficits as a means for accommodating rising primary input costs. Overindebtedness set in when financial deficits began to grow more rapidly than nominal GNP, eventually producing—by Cycle 3—a further complication as the costs of maintaining the stock of debt (i.e., interest) also began to grow more rapidly than nominal GNP in some sectors.[5]

In addition to deficits, rising primary input costs have been accommodated by diversion of resources to primary input sectors. In the case of "raw labor," this has meant accelerated growth in wages, benefits, and government transfer payments to individuals which in the developed sector has, beginning in Cycle 2, led to an increase in the ratio of personal consumption and broader social peace accounts (i.e., government transfer payments) to GNP.[6] At the same time, the rate of growth of economic investment in the developed sector and free world economy has declined over the cycles.[7]

In addition to diversion of resources to meet rising labor costs, there was a parallel transfer of resources to the primary commodity sector in Cycles 2 and 3 which produced a change in the composition of economic investment in the free world economy. Investment growth rates for mining and agriculture (and real estate) rose more rapidly than those for manufacturing, reversing a trend that had unfolded from 1952 to 1967.[8] This development weakened the pace of qualitative advance in capital as lower technology capital (requiring less advanced labor skills) associated with extractive sector investment gained favor at the expense of higher technology investment associated with the manufacturing sector.

Interestingly, the European CPEs experienced the same pressures on economic investment over the course of the four cycles. Although resource concessions to labor were far weaker—a development that avoided raising capital costs but at the expense of weaker labor productivity—European CPE national defense spending rose as a percentage of GNP, forcing economic investment's share of GNP to falter.[9] And because of historical disinvestment in the primary commodities sector, especially agriculture, and a subsequent more rapid rise in the costs of inputs from this sector than in the free world economy, the diversion of resources to investment in lower quality capital in the European CPEs occurred earlier and evolved with greater intensity than in the developed sector. Indeed, beginning in 1976 at the start of Cycle 3, the USSR has undergone a process that can only be characterized as economic "primitivization" in which the percentage of investment resources accounted for by manufacturing has declined while that for primary commodities (agriculture and energy) has surged.[10]

The result of resource diversion to primary input sectors in the free world economy was underinvestment, revealed in the decline in the developed sector and aggregate free world economy fixed investment growth rate commencing at the end of Cycle 2 (this was complemented by growing underdevelopment marked by larger shares of investment devoted to primary commodity sectors and smaller shares to manufacturing). Underinvestment (and underdevelopment) contributed to a slow-down in the supply-side adjustment process.

The Changing Inter-Cyclical Relationship of Developed Sector Economic Policy and Primary Input Costs

Over the course of the four trade and payments cycles, the inflation/unemployment dilemma increased in dimension and complexity. Efforts beginning at the end of the 1950s to avert faltering short-term output growth ushered in goods and services price inflation, overindebtedness, and underinvestment—all of which imply weaker long-term output growth. This contradiction between the consequences of short-term efforts and long-term prospects provoked greater inter-cyclical shifts in aggregate developed sector macroeconomic and international payments policy and incited ever wider divergences in economic approach among the developed sector economic powers.

In Cycle 2 as the costs of primary inputs rose more vigorously than in the previous cycle, aggregate developed sector macroeconomic and international payments policy became more accommodative as fear of output contraction overrode concern with goods and services price inflation and related economic ills. In Cycles 1 and 2 the rise in primary input costs assumed a dominant position, acting as the catalyst in its relationship with aggregate developed sector economic policy, which assumed a reactive posture.

The dynamic and direction of this relationship began to shift at the end of Cycle 2 when concern over goods and services price inflation precipitated a more contractionary aggregate developed sector economic policy. In Cycle 3, and particularly in its later stages, concern over goods and services price inflation intensified, and this concern extended to developing nation and East European CPE overindebtedness and to government overindebtedness and underinvestment in the developed sector. Aggregate developed sector macroeconomic policy therefore became less accommodative toward the end of Cycle 3 and developed sector payments policy toward the developing sector and European CPEs turned decidedly deflationary. As a result, the pace of acceleration in primary input costs began to slow, as did goods and services price inflation and related economic ills.

The projection of late Cycle 3 developed sector macroeconomic and international payments policy into Cycle 4 prompted a contraction in primary input costs, disinflation in goods and services prices, and a slowdown in the growth of free world overindebtedness due to a reduction in the ratio of non-U.S. developed sector government deficits to GNP and to the failure of developing sector capital importers' current account deficits to continue to grow as a percentage of GDP.[11]

The Inter-Cyclical Growth of Policy Divergences
in the Developed Sector

At the same time, macroeconomic policy and development strategies among developed nations over the cycles have increasingly diverged as the dimensions and complexity of the inflation/unemployment trade-off provoked a more vigorous assertion of national economic biases.

Greater U.S. fear of output contraction than of goods and services price inflation inspired Phase IV U.S. policy initiatives beginning in Cycle 2 predicated on a more accommodative aggregate developed sector economic policy involving dollar depreciation and reflationary economic policies in Western Europe and Japan (in Cycles 2–4). In each successive trade and payments cycle following Cycle 2, U.S. Phase IV initiatives have countenanced greater reflationary adjustment (i.e., larger dollar depreciation and more expansionary macroeconomic policy adjustment abroad). And beginning with Phase III of Cycle 3 (1977) the U.S. abandoned the contractionary macroeconomic policy responses to inflation and external imbalances that it had adopted in Phase III of Cycles 1 and 2.

This behavior reflected a lower U.S. sensitivity to inflation and related ills compared to the remainder of the developed sector. Even in Cycle 4 the United States has been able to support its aversion to output compression—this time at no expense in inflation—though at the cost of mammoth acceleration in its government and foreign overindebtedness, reflected in the enormous advance of the U.S. government fiscal, merchandise trade, and current account deficits as percentages of GNP in Cycle 4 compared to earlier cycles.[12]

The explosive growth of U.S. government fiscal and external deficits during Cycle 4 also reflected the failure of U.S. policy to reverse the growing underinvestment of the preceding two cycles. The Cycle 4 effort to do so centered about large supply-side tax cuts, the greatest portion of which came from an income tax rate reduction aimed at bolstering the U.S. savings rate and thereby reducing the cost of capital. However, the U.S. savings rate has fallen over the course of Cycle 4, indicating that the income tax cuts have led to increased personal consumption, not to savings.[13] At the same time the ratio of national defense spending to GNP has grown and this, once combined with the tax cuts, has produced a large expansion in the U.S. government fiscal deficit and continued high capital costs.[14]

While U.S. economic policy has tended toward greater accommodation over the cycles, the trend has been the reverse for the other major developed sector economies. Those economies with historical biases similar to those of the U.S.—the second-tier West European economies—have, because of their smaller size and greater dependence on imports, been forced to adopt a more contractionary policy over the course of the cycles. In Phases I and V of Cycles 2 and 3 (that is, 1968/69 and 1973/74 in Cycle 2 and 1976/77 and 1979/80 in Cycle 3), the expansionary phases in developed sector economic policy, these economies were subjected to severe balance of payments stress and consequent currency depreciations which compelled them to adopt more conservative economic policies.

With the first resounding burst in primary commodity prices in 1973, the Federal Republic of Germany, responding to its historical fear of inflation, resorted to a more contractionary macroeconomic policy from which, among the major economic powers, it has been the least willing to depart. At the end of Cycle 3 Bonn launched initiatives to reduce its government fiscal overindebtedness but, like the second-tier West European economies, it was compelled to support high labor and social peace costs which undermined corporate profits and diverted investment resources to government transfer payments to individuals.[15] Hence, FRG efforts to arrest underinvestment have lacked vigor.

Tokyo responded somewhat later than Bonn to the primary commodity price explosion in Cycle 2, reflecting a less severe historical fear of inflation. Nevertheless, Japanese exposure to the vulnerabilities of primary commodity price-induced inflation made it more sensitive to inflation than the U.S. Toward the end of Cycle 3 Tokyo, like Bonn, committed itself to reduction of its government fiscal overindebtedness in the 1980s. But in comparison to the remainder of the developed sector, Japan enjoyed a higher personal savings rate and lower social peace costs which have resulted in lower capital costs and a more forceful supply-side adjustment process than in the other developed nations.[16]

These intra-developed sector economic policy divergences have caused growing domestic demand and import growth rate differentials between the U.S. and the remainder of the developed sector over the four cycles, and this has been one of the principal reasons for the deterioration in U.S. external balances. These divergences also suggest why the growth of FRG external surpluses have come to depend more on lower import growth and Japan's, on sustained export vigor.

MEASURING INTER-CYCLICAL DIFFERENCES

Inter-cyclical changes in the magnitude of interphasal fluctuations in the three variables have produced major transformations in the behavior of trade and payments. While the magnitude of the fluctuations in the three variables is often difficult to quantify, the changes in trade and payments they have produced are easily measured.

Precise measurement of inter-cyclical differences—one that compares the dimension of the features characterizing each phase of the trade and payments cycle (features that, as we have seen, were produced by the regular interphasal fluctuations in the three variables)—not only provides the most concrete evidence of the existence of the trade and payments cycles but also permits insight into long-term inter-cyclical trends.

Phase I. Comparison of domestic demand growth rates among the leading developed sector economies in Phase I of the four cycles indicates that the turn to a more expansionist macroeconomic policy in this phase is more vigorous in the United States than in the rest of the developed sector (see Table 5.1—domestic demand growth in Phase I minus previous cycle average). The domestic demand growth rate performance of the leading developed sector economies in Phase I of Cycle 2 shows the greatest convergence of any of the four Phase Is. Greater divergence reappears in Phase I of Cycle 3 and expands in Phase I of Cycle 4 (see Table 5.1).

In Cycle 1, the U.S. domestic demand growth rate in 1959 was 3.9 percentage points higher than its average from 1955–58 (before the cycles appeared), while the FRG's was only 0.9 percentage points higher, the combined second-tier West European domestic demand growth rate (i.e., the average of the U.K., France, and Italy) was equal to its 1955–58 average, and Japan's was only 2.5 percentage points higher than its 1955–58 average.

In Cycle 2 the U.S. domestic demand growth rate in 1968 was 0.2 percentage points higher than its average in Cycle 1, while the FRG's was also 0.2 percentage points higher. But the second-tier West European economies' domestic demand growth rate in 1968 was 0.4 percentage points lower than its Cycle 1 average. Only Japan did better than the U.S. on this score in 1968. Its domestic demand growth rate was 1.1 percentage points higher than its Cycle 1 average.

In Phase I of Cycle 3 the differences between the U.S. and the remainder of the developed sector became more stark. The U.S. domestic demand growth rate in 1976 was 4.0 percentage points higher than its Cycle 2 average, while the combined FRG/Japan average was 0.6 percentage points lower than its Cycle 2 average. The second-tier West European economies' domestic demand growth rate in 1976 was 2.0 percentage points higher than it averaged in Cycle 2.

Finally, in Cycle 4 the differences between the U.S. and the rest of the developed sector intensified. In Phase I of Cycle 4 (in 1983/84) the domestic demand growth rate of the U.S. averaged 3.5 percentage points higher than it did in Cycle 3, while the average for the FRG/Japan over those two years was 0.9 percentage points lower than the average for Cycle 3, as was the combined average domestic demand growth rate of the second-tier West European economies.

The evolution of domestic demand growth rates in Phase I of each cycle among the leading developed sector economies also reveals a revitalization of these rates from the recession years of 1958, 1967, 1975, and 1982. It was these advances that underwrote recoveries in world trade as developed sector imports in Phase I of all cycles grew as a share of world

TABLE 5.1

DOMESTIC DEMAND GROWTH RATE COMPARISON AMONG THE LEADING SIX DEVELOPED SECTOR ECONOMIES IN PHASE I OF THE FOUR TRADE AND PAYMENTS CYCLES (Percent Growth)

	Average 1955-1958	CYCLE 1: 1958/	1959	1959 Minus 55-58 Avg.*	CYCLE 2: C.1 Avg.	1967/	1968	1968 Minus C.1 Avg.*
US	2.8	0.3	6.7	3.9	4.5	3.0	4.7	0.2
FRG	7.1	4.6	8.0	0.9	5.3	-1.7	5.5	0.2
Japan	6.8	4.0	9.3	2.5	10.6	12.2	11.7	1.1
UK	1.6	0.6	4.6 ⎫		3.6	4.2	3.3 ⎫	
France	5.3	1.9	1.6 ⎭ 0.0		5.3	4.8	4.6 ⎭ -0.4	
Italy	4.9	4.0	5.9		5.7	7.9	5.4	

	CYCLE 3: C.II Avg.	1975/	1976	1976 Minus C.II Avg.*	CYCLE 4: C.III Avg.	1982/	1983/84	83/84 Minus C.III Avg.*
US	2.0	-1.9	6.0	4.0	3.4	-1.9	6.9	3.5
FRG	3.8	0.2	5.7 ⎫		2.3	-2.0	2.2 ⎫	
Japan	6.8	0.7	3.7 ⎭ -0.6		4.4	2.8	2.8 ⎭ -0.9	
UK	2.0	-1.8	2.6		1.3	2.2	3.6	
France	4.5	-1.0	7.1 ⎫		3.4	3.5	-0.1 ⎫	
Italy	3.7	-5.9	6.4 ⎭ 2.0		3.5	0.3	2.0 ⎭ -0.9	

SOURCE: Cycle 1 - OECD National Account Statistics, 1986; Cycles 1-4 - OECD Economic Outlook, Dec. 1987.

/ - Separates last year of preceding cycle.   *Percentage Points

imports (value) (see Figure 5.1a). This process accelerated in Phase I of Cycle 4 despite a decline in the developed sector import growth rate compared to earlier Phase Is (see Figure 5.1b), as the combined imports of the developing sector and the CPEs fell.

The greater advance of the U.S. domestic demand growth rate compared to other developed nations and the world ensured that U.S. import growth in Phase I would lead developed sector and world import growth (see Figure 5.1a). The differentials between the U.S. import growth rate and the developed sector and world import growth rates were highly visible in Phase I of all cycles, but in Cycle 4 they widened substantially (see Figure 5.1b) because of the larger domestic demand growth rate differentials between the U.S. and the rest of the developed sector and the negative combined developing sector and CPE import growth rate.

The surge of U.S. imports in Phase I underwrote an expansion of the U.S.'s share of world import and developed sector import growth (see Figure 5.1c). Again, this process noticeably accelerated in Cycle 4.

The large expansion in U.S. import growth relative to the rest of the world caused a deterioration in U.S. merchandise trade and current account balances in Phase I of all cycles—a development that worsened in the third and fourth cycles, when the U.S. domestic demand and import growth rate differentials with the rest of the world widened (see Table 5.2).

During Phase I of each cycle the dollar became overvalued, a process that accelerated in Cycles 3 and 4. In Cycles 1 and 2, Phase I took place under the fixed exchange rate regime of Bretton Woods; hence, the dollar's exchange rate remained firm in both 1959 and 1968 as no major currency realignments within Bretton Woods took place. It should be noted, however, that in December 1958 and especially in November 1967, substantial realignments took place that had the effect of appreciating the dollar (i.e., the French franc devaluation of 1958 and the British pound-led devaluations of 1967). But under any circumstances, U.S. trade and current account balances faltered in 1959 and 1968 in the wake of a longer-term underlying weakening in both balances, while the dollar's value did not depreciate, indicating overvaluation. In 1976 and 1983/84 under a floating exchange rate monetary system, when U.S. external balances deteriorated more sharply (especially in 1983/84), the dollar appreciated, suggesting greater overvaluation than had occurred in Phase I of earlier cycles. In 1976 the dollar appreciated by 5.2 percent according to the IMF-measured effective exchange rate and in 1983/84 it appreciated even more strongly, by 14.1 percent.[17]

Phase II. In response to the acceleration of developed sector import growth in Phase I of all four cycles, developing sector export volume has risen in Phase II of each cycle. The expansionary turn in aggregate developed sector macroeconomic policy and its impact on the developed

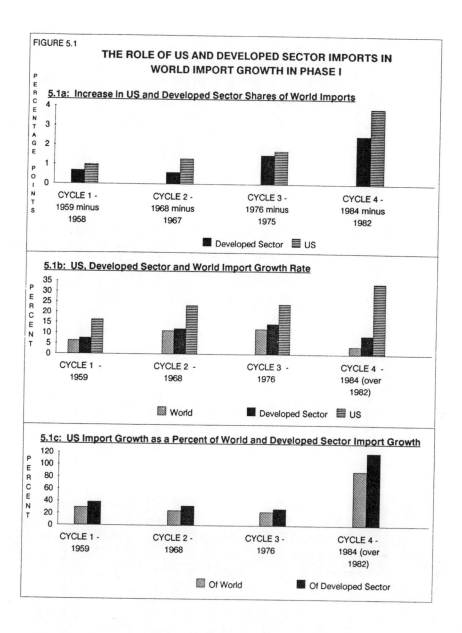

FIGURE 5.1

THE ROLE OF US AND DEVELOPED SECTOR IMPORTS IN WORLD IMPORT GROWTH IN PHASE I

5.1a: Increase in US and Developed Sector Shares of World Imports

PERCENTAGE POINTS

| | CYCLE 1 - 1959 minus 1958 | CYCLE 2 - 1968 minus 1967 | CYCLE 3 - 1976 minus 1975 | CYCLE 4 - 1984 minus 1982 |

■ Developed Sector   ☰ US

5.1b: US, Developed Sector and World Import Growth Rate

PERCENT

| | CYCLE 1 - 1959 | CYCLE 2 - 1968 | CYCLE 3 - 1976 | CYCLE 4 - 1984 (over 1982) |

▨ World   ■ Developed Sector   ☰ US

5.1c: US Import Growth as a Percent of World and Developed Sector Import Growth

PERCENT

| | CYCLE 1 - 1959 | CYCLE 2 - 1968 | CYCLE 3 - 1976 | CYCLE 4 - 1984 (over 1982) |

▨ Of World   ■ Of Developed Sector

TABLE 5.2

US MERCHANDISE TRADE BALANCE AND EXPORT AND IMPORT GROWTH RATE IN PHASES I, III, AND V

(Merchandise Trade Balance - $Billions; Exports and Imports (FOB) - Percent Growth)

PHASE I:

	CYCLE 1:		CYCLE 2:		CYCLE 3:		CYCLE 4:		
	1958/	1959	1967/	1968	1975/	1976	1982/	1983	1984
Merchandise Trade Balance	$3.3	$1.0	$3.8	$0.6	$8.9	-$9.5	-$36.3	-$67.3	-$112.5
Export Growth Rate	0.0%		4.8%	9.4%	9.0%	7.1%	-10.9%	-4.5%	9.0%
Import Growth Rate	17.7%		5.5%	22.7%	-5.4%	26.5%	-6.6%	8.6%	23.6%

PHASE III:

	CYCLE 1:			CYCLE 2:			CYCLE 3:		CYCLE 4:		
	1959/	1960	1961	1968/	1969	1970	1976/	1977	1984/	1985	1986
Merchandise Trade Balance	$1.0	$4.9	$5.6	$0.6	$0.6	$2.6	-$9.5	-$31.1	-$112.5	-$122.2	-$144.5
Export Growth Rate	0.0%	20.9%	2.0%	9.4%	8.3%	16.8%	7.1%	5.3%	9.0%	-1.9%	3.8%
Import Growth Rate	17.7%	-3.3%	-1.4%	22.7%	8.5%	11.5%	26.5%	22.3%	23.6%	1.7%	9.0%

PHASE V

	CYCLE 1:			CYCLE 2:			CYCLE 3:			CYCLE 4:		
	1962/	1963	1964	1971/	1972	1973	1977/	1978	1979	1986/	1987	1988*
Merchandise Trade Balance	$4.5	$5.2	$6.8	-$2.3	-$6.4	$0.9	-$31.1	-$34.0	-$27.5	-$144.5	-$160.3	-$125.2
Export Growth Rate	3.5%	7.2%	14.3%	1.9%	14.1%	44.5%	5.3%	17.6%	29.8%	3.8%	11.4%	26.7%
Import Growth Rate	12.4%	4.9%	9.4%	14.3%	22.4%	26.3%	22.3%	15.7%	20.5%	9.0%	11.2%	7.7%

SOURCE: IMF IFS Yearbook 1986 and Nov. 1988; and US Merchandise Trade Balance, 3rd Quarter 1988 (Preliminary), US Department of Commerce, Nov. 28, 1988.

/- Separates last year of previous phase.   * First three quarters 1988.

sector import growth rate in Phase I has had a direct influence on the size and duration of the expansion in developing sector export volume in Phase II of all cycles. The length of the developing sector export volume expansion has also depended upon the timing of developed sector macroeconomic policy adjustment in Phase III (see Figure 5.2a). In the first two cycles, the dynamism of West European domestic demand growth in 1960 and 1969 (at the beginning of Phase III) was sufficient to sustain the acceleration in developing sector export volume, which had begun in 1959 and 1968, even while U.S. domestic demand growth rates fell.

In 1976 the acceleration in developing sector export volume growth was more pronounced than in 1959 or 1968, because the contraction in developing sector export volume was very sharp in the 1975 recession while it had continued to grow in the 1958 and 1967 recessions. But in 1977 developing sector export volume growth collapsed, marking a radical departure from its 1960 and 1969 performance. This was due to West European and, secondarily, Japanese adoption of more deflationary macroeconomic policies in Phase III of Cycle 3 than in earlier Phase IIIs. In Cycle 4 the Phase II recovery in developing sector export volume was relatively small, a fact that can be attributed to weaker Phase I domestic demand and, therefore, import growth rates in the developed sector (due entirely to lower non-U.S. developed sector domestic demand and import growth rates) than in earlier cycles.

Developing sector export volume growth rates in Phase II of the four cycles travel on a long-term trend line which rises from Cycle 1 to Cycle 2 and from Cycle 2 to Cycle 3 before declining markedly from Cycle 3 to Cycle 4. Developing sector export unit value, nonfuel primary commodity prices, oil prices, and developing sector exports (value) express a similar long-term trend. Growth rates in all four rise from Cycle 1 to Cycle 2 and then again from Cycle 2 to Cycle 3 before plunging in Cycle 4 (see Figure 5.2b, c, d, and e).

The rise of the developed sector domestic demand growth rate in Phase I not only prompted increases in the developing sector export volume growth rate, but as the oversupply in nonfood primary commodities that characterized the post-Korean War period dissipated, the developing sector export unit value growth rate also improved (see Figure 5.2b). By 1968–70 when the oversupply in nonfood primary commodities had been eliminated, the rise in the developing sector export volume growth rate was accompanied by a prolonged advance in nonfood primary commodity prices—a development that had failed to materialize in Phase II of Cycle 1.

In Cycle 3, the inflationary momentum carried over from Phase V of Cycle 2 (1972–74) resulted in larger improvements in primary commodity prices and in developing sector export unit value in 1976/77 than had

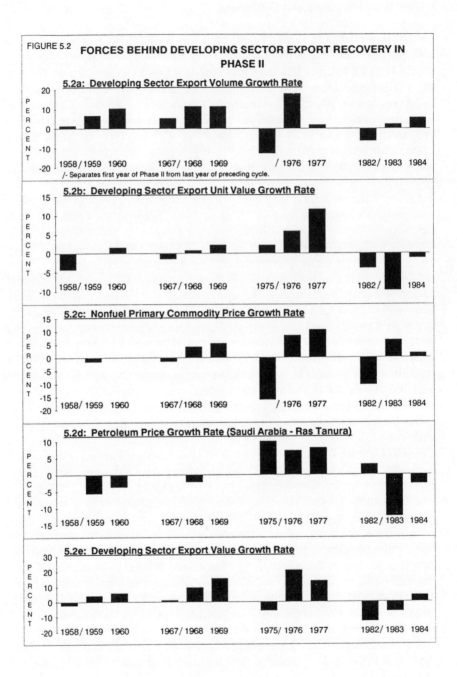

FIGURE 5.2 **FORCES BEHIND DEVELOPING SECTOR EXPORT RECOVERY IN PHASE II**

5.2a: Developing Sector Export Volume Growth Rate

1958 / 1959 1960   1967 / 1968 1969   / 1976 1977   1982 / 1983 1984
/- Separates first year of Phase II from last year of preceding cycle.

5.2b: Developing Sector Export Unit Value Growth Rate

1958 / 1959 1960   1967 / 1968 1969   1975 / 1976 1977   1982 / 1984

5.2c: Nonfuel Primary Commodity Price Growth Rate

1958 / 1959 1960   1967 / 1968 1969   / 1976 1977   1982 / 1983 1984

5.2d: Petroleum Price Growth Rate (Saudi Arabia - Ras Tanura)

1958 / 1959 1960   1967 / 1968 1969   1975 / 1976 1977   1982 / 1983 1984

5.2e: Developing Sector Export Value Growth Rate

1958 / 1959 1960   1967 / 1968 1969   1975 / 1976 1977   1982 / 1983 1984

occurred in 1968/69. The greater deflationary tilt in developed sector macroeconomic and payments policy during Phase I of Cycle 4 produced conditions during Phase II—1983/84—in which nonfuel primary commodity prices, which had dropped in the 1981/82 recession, showed only minimal recovery, oil prices faltered, and developing sector export unit value continued to contract. (In 1984 the rate of contraction in developing sector export unit value declined.)

The improved volume and unit value growth rate of developing sector exports in Phase II has resulted in growth in developing sector exports (value) (see Figure 5.2e). But while in the first three cycles developing sector exports (value) moved from negative or marginally positive growth rates in the recession years of 1958, 1967, and 1975 to healthy positive growth rates in Phase II, in the fourth cycle the developing sector export growth rate continued negative in 1983, albeit less strongly than in the recession year of 1982, before turning marginally positive in 1984.

The recovery in the developing sector's export value in Phase II of all cycles provided the foundation for improvement in its merchandise trade balance (see Table 5.3) The export value expansion was accompanied early in Phase II by low import growth, reflecting continuation of recession period efforts to restrict imports. Combined, these forces produced advances in the sector's merchandise trade balance. But at the beginning of Phase II of Cycle 4 (in 1983) the merchandise trade balance improvement was due to continued negative import growth, as the export decline of the recession years only slowed. And at the peak of Phase II of Cycle 4 (in 1984), the improvement in the developing sector merchandise trade balance resulted from virtually zero import growth and marginal export growth.

Phase III. Phase III of all cycles commenced with a weakening of the aggregate developed sector domestic demand growth rate and a consequent decline in the sector's import growth rate. In the first two cycles Phase III was initiated by a contraction in the U.S. domestic demand growth rate, while in Cycle 3 it began with a fall in the West European domestic demand growth rate (see Table 5.4). The initial decline in the U.S. domestic demand growth rate in Cycles 1 and 2 was induced by Washington's shift to a more deflationary macroeconomic policy—a development whose impact on the aggregate developed sector domestic demand growth rate was offset by an acceleration in these rates in other developed economies (especially in Western Europe) from their Phase I levels.

But in Cycle 3 the U.S. domestic demand growth rate in Phase III continued at a strong pace, in part neutralizing the fall in the rate for Western Europe. Hence, in Cycles 1 and 2 Phase III began with a rapid convergence of developed sector domestic demand growth rates, while in Phase III of Cycle 3 it began in 1977 with an exacerbation of Phase I divergences, before some convergence set in in 1978 (see Table 5.4).

TABLE 5.3

DEVELOPING SECTOR MERCHANDISE TRADE BALANCE AND EXPORT AND IMPORT GROWTH RATE IN PHASES II, III, V AND VI
(Merchandise Trade Balance - $Billions; Exports and Imports - Percent Growth)

PHASE II:

	CYCLE 1:			CYCLE 2:			CYCLE 3:			CYCLE 4:		
	1958/	1959	1960	1967/	1968	1969	1975/	1976	1977	1982/	1983	1984
Merchandise Trade Balance	-$3.2	$2.0	-$3.0	-$2.2	-$2.1	-$1.2	$26.5	$46.2	$46.2	$17.8	$24.2	$54.2
Export Growth Rate*		4.6%	7.0%	3.3%	8.0%	12.1%	-4.4%	1.0%	14.0%	-11.7%	-7.3%	3.5%
Import Growth Rate**		0.3%	11.7%	3.9%	7.8%	10.9%	15.6%	7.2%	19.7%	-6.0%	-7.1%	-0.4%

PHASE III:

	1960/	1961	1962	1969/	1970	1971	1977/	1978		1984/	1985	1986
Merchandise Trade Balance	-$3.0	-$3.4	-$2.6	-$1.2	-$1.5	-$2.1	$46.2	$22.4		$54.2	$57.2	$19.6
Export Growth Rate*	7.0%	1.3%	3.4%	12.1%	11.2%	10.8%	14.0%	5.1%		3.5%	-4.2%	-4.5%
Import Growth Rate**	11.7%	3.8%	0.3%	10.9%	14.5%	13.1%	19.7%	16.8%		-0.4%	-3.1%	-0.7%

PHASE V:

	1962/	1963	1964	1971/	1972	1973	1974	1978/	1979	1980
Merchandise Trade Balance	-$2.6	-$1.2	-$1.2	-$2.1	$3.8	$11.3	$64.5	$22.4	$68.1	$107.2
Export Growth Rate*	3.4%	11.1%	7.3%	10.8%	17.7%	48.7%	94.8%	5.1%	38.1%	33.6%
Import Growth Rate*	0.3%	6.5%	10.2%	13.1%	11.0%	38.4%	59.0%	16.8%	19.8%	32.8%

PHASE VI:

	1965/	1966	1967	1974/	1975	1980/	1981	1982
Merchandise Trade Balance	-1.8	-2.1	-2.2	64.5	26.5	107.2	50.5	17.4
Export Growth Rate*	6.3	8.3	3.3	94.8	-4.4	33.6	-2.0	-11.7
Import Growth Rate*	5.3	8.4	3.9	59.0	15.6	32.8	10.7	-6.0

SOURCE: Cycles 1 and 2 - Yearly Reports in IMF IFS Yearbooks of 1960s and 1970s; Cycles 3 and 4 - UNCTAD Handbook 1987.
/ - Separates last year of previous phase.   * FOB   ** CIF
NOTE: Cycles 1 and 2 are not directly comparable to Cycles 3 and 4 due to different data bases, but patterns hold.

TABLE 5.4

DOMESTIC DEMAND GROWTH RATES OF KEY DEVELOPED SECTOR ECONOMIES IN PHASE III OF THE FOUR CYCLES (Percent Growth)

	CYCLE 1:			CYCLE 2:				CYCLE 3:			CYCLE 4:		
	1959/	1960	1961	1968/	1969	1970	1971	1976/	1977	1978	1984/	1985	1986
US	6.7	1.4	2.7	4.7	2.6	-0.5	3.2	6.0	5.5	4.9	8.7	3.6	3.9
FRG	8.0	9.4	3.2	5.5	8.7	6.9	3.8	5.7	2.7	3.6	2.0	0.9	3.8
Japan	9.3	13.4	16.1	11.7	11.6	10.3	3.5	3.7	4.3	6.0	3.8	4.0	4.0
UK	4.6	6.4	2.7	3.3	-0.1	2.2	2.3	2.6	-0.4	4.1	2.7	3.0	3.8
France	1.6	6.1	5.7	4.6	8.0	4.7	5.0	7.1	1.9	2.8	0.5	2.2	3.8
Italy	5.9	7.9	8.1	5.4	7.2	6.9	1.0	6.4	0.6	2.4	4.4	3.1	3.2

SOURCE: Cycle 1 - OECD National Account Statistics 1986; Cycles 2-4 - OECD Economic Outlook, June 1988.
/- Separates Phase I from Phase III.

In Cycle 4, Phase III started with convergence in developed sector domestic demand growth rates, but the process of convergence was not as rapid as in Phase III of Cycles 1 and 2. Further, the convergence relied almost completely upon a drop in the U.S. domestic demand growth rate since there was virtually no improvement in the domestic demand growth rates of other large developed sector economies. Moreover, intra-developed sector domestic demand growth rate differentials in Phase I of Cycle 4 were greater than in previous cycles. Hence, at the beginning of Phase III in 1985, convergence, while substantial, was incomplete, although by the following year, at the end of the Phase, it was nearly full.

The developed sector import growth rate in Phase III declined from its Phase I level in 1961, 1971, 1977, and 1985 (see Figure 5.3a). In 1960 and 1969/70 this development was delayed due to the surge in West European imports. In Cycle 3 it was hardly visible because of the sustained rate of U.S. domestic demand growth. In Cycle 4 the fall in the developed sector import growth rate began at the start of Phase III and was large.

The convergence of developed sector domestic demand growth rates in Phase III of all cycles was reflected in changing patterns of major developed economy import growth rates (see Figure 5.3a). In Cycles 1 and 2, the reversal in the direction of intra-developed sector import growth rate differentials from Phase I was radical and swift. The U.S. import growth rate, after surpassing the developed sector import growth rate in Phase I, fell sharply below it in Phase III. But in Cycle 3, following the pattern of domestic demand growth rates, there was no change in developed sector import growth rate divergence in 1977 compared to 1976 before a more moderate convergence in 1978. And throughout Phase III of Cycle 3, the U.S. import growth rate remained higher than that of the developed sector as a whole.

In Phase III of Cycle 4, intra-developed sector import growth rate differentials followed the behavior of domestic demand growth rate differentials. In 1985, the U.S. import growth rate fell precipitously but other developed sector import growth rates failed to advance, yielding a situation in which the U.S. import growth rate did not fall below that of the developed sector. In 1986 the rise in West European import growth pulled the developed sector import growth rate above that of the United States.

The U.S. decision to reverse course at the onset of Phase III of Cycles 3 and 4 and abandon resort to a more deflationary policy mix and Western Europe's simultaneous moves toward a less accommodative policy mix produced interesting trends in their relative contributions to import growth. In the first two cycles, Phase III was marked by growth in Western Europe's share of world imports and a drop in the U.S. share (see Figure 5.3b). But in Phase III of Cycle 3, the U.S. share continued to grow and the West European share of world imports actually fell. In Cycle 4, the U.S.'s share continued to grow in 1985 before declining in 1986, while Western Europe's share increased as it had in Cycles 1 and 2.

The changing patterns of intra-developed sector import growth in Phase III of successive cycles paralleled enormous changes in the behavior of the U.S. merchandise trade and current account balances (see Table 5.2). In the first two cycles, these balances improved during Phase III as a result of constrained U.S. import growth and strong export growth in 1960 and 1970 related to the powerful West European import expansions. In Phase III of Cycle 3, the U.S. merchandise trade and current account deficits increased—the result of a sustained high U.S. import growth rate and a weaker U.S. export growth rate that lasted until 1978, when Western Europe's domestic demand growth rate accelerated. In Phase III of Cycle 4, the U.S. merchandise trade and current account balances also continued to expand, because of negative U.S. export growth in 1985 reflecting weak domestic demand growth rates outside of the U.S. and because of revived U.S. import growth in 1986.

The slowdown in the developed sector import growth rate in each Phase III had a negative impact on the pace of expansion of developing sector export volume and export unit value.[18] In Cycle 1 the growth rate of developing sector export unit value fell back to zero in 1961, in Cycle 3 to barely positive growth in 1978, and in Cycle 4 it contracted in 1985 and 1986. Only in Cycle 2 did a deterioration in the developing sector export unit value growth rate fail to materialize. The behavior of developing sector export unit value and primary commodity prices during Phase III evolved along trend lines strikingly similar to those of Phase II. Both showed the greatest strength in Phase III of Cycles 2 and 3 and the greatest weakness in Phase III of Cycle 4.[19]

While developing sector export unit value growth has tended to weaken in Phase III, especially towards the end of the phase, developing sector import growth rates have tended to advance, especially at the beginning of the phase in response to that sector's trade balance improvement in Phase II. A higher developing sector export growth rate in Phase II has traditionally encouraged it to increase import growth in the early stages of Phase III (see Table 5.3). This was the case in Cycles 1, 2, and 3 (1960, 1969, and 1977). However, this failed to occur in Cycle 4—in part because the developing sector's export recovery during Phase II was extremely weak and its export unit value growth rate turned increasingly negative at the very beginning of Phase III, as well as because of the existence of deflationary developed sector payments policies toward the developing sector (a phenomenon absent at similar stages in the earlier three cycles). Despite developing sector efforts to restrain import growth at the end of all Phase IIIs, earlier Phase III import growth and declining export growth have conspired to compel its merchandise trade balance to worsen (see Table 5.3).

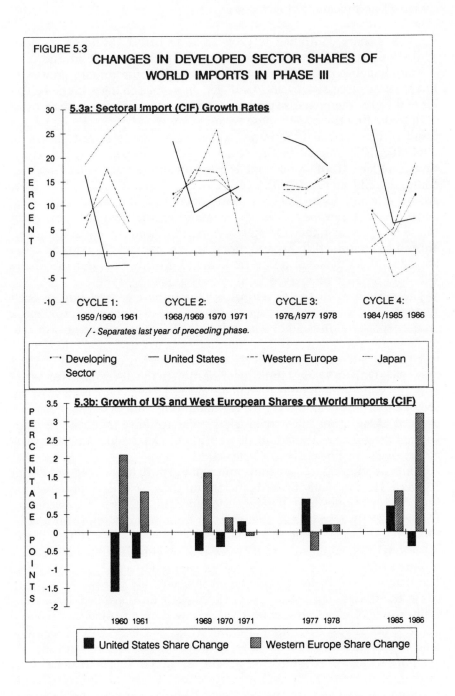

FIGURE 5.3

CHANGES IN DEVELOPED SECTOR SHARES OF WORLD IMPORTS IN PHASE III

5.3a: Sectoral Import (CIF) Growth Rates

PERCENT

CYCLE 1: 1959/1960 1961
CYCLE 2: 1968/1969 1970 1971
CYCLE 3: 1976/1977 1978
CYCLE 4: 1984/1985 1986

/ - Separates last year of preceding phase.

···· Developing Sector ⎯ United States --- Western Europe ···· Japan

5.3b: Growth of US and West European Shares of World Imports (CIF)

PERCENTAGE POINTS

1960 1961   1969 1970 1971   1977 1978   1985 1986

■ United States Share Change   ▨ Western Europe Share Change

Phase IV. It is difficult to measure the reflationary force of Phase IV U.S. policy initiatives. In the first two cycles, U.S. macroeconomic policy tilted toward a deflationary mix in Phase III. But this was not the case in Cycles 3 and 4. Hence, in Cycles 1 and 2, Phase IV U.S. policy initiatives were more explicitly charged with avoiding domestic recession than was the case in Phase IV of Cycles 3 and 4. Because in Phase III of Cycles 3 and 4 the U.S. economy did not sink into recession, U.S. macroeconomic policy in Phase IV of these two cycles did not involve a new fiscal or monetary expansion. Therefore, in 1961/62 and in 1971 U.S. domestic demand growth rates accelerated, while in 1978/79 they decelerated moderately and, on the whole, they decelerated in 1987/88 (compared to 1985/86). Also, in Cycle 1 U.S. Phase IV initiatives did *not* include dollar depreciation, but *did* in Cycles 2, 3, and 4; and in Cycle 4 the magnitude of dollar depreciation was far greater than in Cycles 2 and 3.

Phase V. A principal objective of U.S. policy initiatives in Phase IV has been to encourage higher rates of import growth among the country's developed sector trading partners while reducing the rate of growth of U.S. domestic demand. To some degree, this has been achieved in all four cycles.

In each cycle the fiscal and monetary policy differentials among the developed nations were transformed in Phase V compared to earlier phases. The average U.S. government fiscal deficit as a percentage of GNP declined from its Phase III peak in Phase V (see Table 5.5). At the same time, from Cycle 1 to Cycle 3 this ratio rose from Phase III levels in Phase V for major U.S. developed sector trading partners. But in Cycle 4, while the U.S. government deficit to GNP ratio fell in Phase V from its Phase III peak, those of its leading trading partners also dropped (aside from the FRG, whose government deficit to GNP ratio has risen slightly in Phase V of Cycle 4 from Phase III levels).

In addition, while the ratio of U.S. government deficit to GNP declined in Phase V from its Phase III peak, in each Cycle, the Phase V ratio itself has differed sharply from cycle to cycle. Because Phase III ratios are higher in each successive cycle, the Phase V ratio is also higher in each successive cycle.

This same pattern afflicted the status of the government deficits of leading U.S. trading partners in Phase VI of Cycles 1–3. Through Phase V of Cycle 3, each successive Phase V witnessed an increase in the government fiscal deficit as a percentage of GNP for major developed sector economies other than the U.S. (save for the FRG from Cycle 1 to Cycle 2). But in Phase V of Cycle 4, the average government fiscal deficit as a percentage of GNP for major developed economies other than the U.S. dropped from that of Phase V of Cycle 3. This occurred while the U.S. fiscal deficit to GNP ratio grew substantially in Phase V of Cycle 4 over that of Phase V of Cycle 3.

TABLE 5.5

GOVERNMENT FISCAL DEFICITS AS A PERCENTAGE OF GNP IN MAJOR DEVELOPED SECTOR ECONOMIES DURING PHASE V OF THE FOUR CYCLES (Percent)

	CYCLE 1: 1962/	1963	1964	1965	Phase V Avg.	CYCLE 2: 1971/	1972	1973	Phase V Avg.
US	-1.3	-0.8	-0.9	-0.2	-0.6	-2.2	-1.5	-1.3	-1.4
FRG	-0.4	-0.7	-0.2	-0.4	-0.4	0.3	0.7	1.3	1.0 } -0.3
Japan	-0.3	-0.8	-1.1	-1.6	-1.2	-0.2	-1.6	-1.6	-1.6 } avg.
UK	0.3	-0.5	-1.2	-1.6	-1.1 }	-1.1	-2.4	-3.0	-2.7
France	-1.7	-2.0	-0.4	0.0	-0.6 } -1.5	-0.4	0.7	0.4	0.6 } -3.5
Italy	-1.7	-2.4	-2.2	-3.9	-2.8 } avg.	-6.9	-7.8	-8.9	-8.4 } avg.

	CYCLE 3: 1977/	1978	1979	Phase V Avg.	CYCLE 4: 1985/	1986	1987	Phase V Avg.
US	-2.6	-2.6	-1.4	-2.0	-4.9	-4.8	-3.4	-4.1
FRG	-3.4	-4.2	-3.3	-3.8 } -4.9	-0.9	-1.0	-1.3	-1.2 } -2.2
Japan	-6.1	-6.6	-5.3	-6.0 } avg.	-3.7	-3.1	-3.0	-3.1 } avg.
UK	-3.0	-4.9	-5.2	-5.1 }	-2.4	-2.2	-1.2	-1.6
France	-1.2	-1.4	-1.5	-1.5 } -6.6	-3.3	-2.8	-2.5	-2.7 } -5.6
Italy	-11.9	-15.4	-11.2	-13.3 } avg.	-13.5	-12.7	-12.2	-12.5 } avg.

SOURCE: Cycles 1-3 - IMF IFS Yearbook 1986; Cycle 4 - OECD Economic Outlook, June 1988.

/- Separates last year of previous phase.

NOTE: Cycle 4 is not directly comparable to others because of different data base, but patterns hold.

In addition to the rise in U.S. developed sector trading partner fiscal deficits as a percentage of GNP in Phase V from Phase III levels (aside from Cycle 4), major U.S. developed sector trading partners have adopted more expansionist monetary policies. During Phase V of Cycles 2, 3, and 4, in efforts to contain dollar depreciation, Japanese and West European governments (Tokyo and Bonn especially) have ushered in huge growth in domestic money supply. Japan and FRG Phase V monetary expansions were more vigorous in Cycles 2 and 4 than in Cycle 3.

The pattern of Phase V macroeconomic policy adjustments has been paralleled by the evolution of domestic demand growth patterns (see Table 5.6). In all cycles except Cycle 2, the average U.S. domestic demand growth rate during Phase V was lower than the previous peak growth rate in Phase III. At the same time, other leading developed economies have for the most part experienced the opposite trend so that their average Phase V domestic demand growth rate was higher than its peak in Phase III.

But the gap between the U.S. domestic demand growth rate and those of the other leading developed nations in Phase V has differed in each cycle. This gap was wider in Cycle 2 compared to Cycle 1, was equivalent in Cycle 3 to Cycle 2, but narrowed in Cycle 4 compared to Cycle 3 (see Table 5.6).

The initiatives engineered in Phase IV by the United States caused two important developments which have dominated every Phase V: an increase in the aggregate developed sector domestic demand growth rate and intra-developed sector domestic demand growth rate differentials more favorable to U.S. external balances.

The first development fostered an advance in the developed sector import (volume) growth rate (see Figure 5.7). Its pace of growth in Phase V over the year prior to the beginning of Phase V was significantly greater in Cycle 2 than in Cycle 1. The pace of improvement slowed somewhat in Cycles 3 and 4.

The increase in the developed sector import growth rate in Phase V prompted an expansion in the developing sector export volume growth rate (see Figure 5.7). The rate of improvement in developing sector export volume growth followed the cyclical pattern of the developed sector import growth rate in Cycles 1 and 2. But in 1979 the developing sector export volume growth rate failed to accelerate in response to the acceleration in the developed sector import volume growth rate. This suggests that the rise in developed sector import volume growth was concentrated in manufactured imports and that the advance in primary commodity prices that year suppressed the dimension of the developing sector export volume recovery. In 1987 the close relationship between the recovery in the developed sector import and developing sector export volume growth rates returned.

TABLE 5.6

MAJOR DEVELOPED SECTOR ECONOMY DOMESTIC DEMAND GROWTH RATES IN PHASE V OF FOUR CYCLES (Percent Growth)

CYCLE 1:	1962/ 1963	1964	1965	Phase V Avg.		CYCLE 2:	1971/ 1972	1973	Phase V Avg.
US	5.6 4.0	5.0	6.4	5.1		US	3.2 5.3	4.4	4.9
FRG	5.2 2.3	6.8	6.7	5.3 } 7.5		FRG	3.8 4.0	3.3	3.7 } 6.7
Japan	5.8 11.4	12.9	4.4	9.7 } avg.		Japan	3.5 9.0	10.3	9.7 } avg.
UK	1.2 3.9	6.6	1.7	4.1		UK	2.3 4.1	7.8	6.0
France	7.2 6.0	7.3	3.7	5.7 } 4.2		France	5.0 6.5	6.0	6.3 } 6.1
Italy	6.5 7.1	0.3	0.9	2.8 } avg.		Italy	1.0 3.5	8.2	5.9 } avg.

CYCLE 3:	1977/ 1978	1979	Phase V Avg.		CYCLE 4:	1985/ 1986	1987	Phase V Avg.
US	5.5 4.9	1.5	3.2		US	3.6 3.9	2.5	3.2
FRG	2.7 3.6	5.5	4.6 } 5.5		FRG	0.9 3.8	2.9	3.4 } 4.1
Japan	4.3 6.0	6.5	6.3 } avg.		Japan	4.0 4.0	5.1	4.6 } avg.
UK	-0.4 4.1	3.6	3.9		UK	3.0 3.8	4.2	4.0
France	1.9 2.8	3.8	3.3 } 3.8		France	2.2 3.8	3.1	3.5 } 3.8
Italy	0.6 2.4	5.9	4.2 } avg.		Italy	3.1 3.2	4.6	3.9 } avg.

SOURCE: Cycle 1 - OECD National Account Statistics 1986; Cycles 2-4 - OECD Economic Outlook, June 1988.

/- Separates last year of Phase III from first year of Phase V.

The rise in the developing sector export volume growth rate has been accompanied by a recovery in primary commodity prices in Phase V of all cycles (see Table 5.7). It is crucial to note that more than advances in developed sector import growth rates were involved in driving primary commodity prices up. Phase V of Cycles 1, 2, and 3 intersected large food deficits and consequent unusual demand for food imports, especially among the CPEs; in Phase V of Cycle 4 pressure on world food supplies has risen again, but this time as a result of agricultural output deficits centered in North America.[20] And in Phase V of Cycles 2 and 3, political/military instability in the Middle East/Persian Gulf region and the assertion of OPEC power combined to drive up petroleum prices.

Both oil and nonfuel primary commodity price movements in Phase V generally reflect the cyclical evolution of the developed sector import growth rate and developing sector export volume growth rate and parallel the long-term trends in primary commodity price movement of Phases II and III, experiencing the strongest advances in Phase V of Cycles 2 and 3 and weakening significantly in Cycle 4. The rate of growth of both oil and non-oil primary commodity prices in Phase V of Cycle 2 was far steeper than in Cycle 1, the result in part of greater acceleration in the developed sector domestic demand growth rate and, hence, import growth rate in Phase V of Cycle 2 compared to Cycle 1 and the complete elimination of the Korean War-generated supply/demand mismatch in nonfood primary commodities by the beginning of Cycle 2.

The other element that explains the dramatic rise in primary commodity prices in Phase V of Cycle 2 compared to Cycle 1 was the organizational strength of the OPEC cartel and its willingness and ability to exercise its power in the early 1970s.

The strength of primary commodity price growth in Phase V of Cycle 3 does not seem to have been warranted by the pace of improvement in the developed sector import growth rate. Instead, food deficits followed by OPEC exercise of its power and market overreaction to the fall of the Shah of Iran and the onset of the Iran-Iraq War appear to have been more responsible for the huge dimensions of the primary commodity price rise. The more anemic recovery of primary commodity prices in Phase V of Cycle 4 is in line with the relatively weak advance in the developed sector import growth rate. The less severe food deficits and the deterioration of the market foundation for the exercise of OPEC power also explain why primary commodity prices in Phase V of Cycle 4 have not risen more rapidly.

The recovery of primary commodity prices in Phase V of all cycles has encouraged accelerated growth in developing sector export unit value (see Figure 5.7). The inter-cyclical evolution of the developing sector export unit value growth rate in Phase V follows the inter-cyclical patterns of primary commodity prices.

TABLE 5.7

FORCES BEHIND DEVELOPING SECTOR EXPORT PERFORMANCE IN PHASE V (Percent Growth)

	CYCLE 1:			CYCLE 2:				CYCLE 3:			CYCLE 4:	
	1962/	1963	1964	1971/	1972	1973	1974	1978/	1979	1980	1986/	1987
Developed Sector Import Volume Growth Rate	8.2	8.7	10.0	4.8	9.1	12.5	1.2	3.4	9.9	0.0	8.6	4.0
Developing Sector Export Volume Growth Rate	7.5	3.5	10.2	1.0	7.8	19.1	-22.1	2.8	2.7	-5.7	22.3	4.4
Developing Sector Export Unit Value Growth Rate	-1.1	2.3	2.2	10.0	9.1	25.0	160.0	2.1	34.7	51.5	-24.7	10.9
Nonfuel Primary Commodity Prices	0.0	1.6	6.0	-2.4	7.5	62.2	21.1	1.2	21.3	6.2	-3.8	8.2
Food Prices	2.1	5.1	2.8	3.1	8.1	80.4	23.6	13.2	16.7	8.6	-12.0	2.3
Oil Prices	-2.0	-2.0	-6.1	28.8	13.8	42.4	261.7	2.3	35.9	66.1	-40.7	12.9
Developing Sector Import Value Growth Rate	6.1	8.6	8.7	13.3	17.7	45.5	108.9	4.5	38.5	34.2	-7.4	15.1

SOURCE: Developed Sector Import Volume and Developing Sector Export Volume, Export Unit Value, and Export Value - UNCTAD Handbook 1979, 1983, 1987; Nonfuel Primary Commodity and Food Prices - IMF IFS Yearbook 1986 and IFS, Nov. 1988; Oil Prices, First 3 Cycles - IFS Yearbook 1988 (Saudi Arabia - Ras Tanura), Cycle 4 - OECD Economic Outlook, June 1988 (spot prices).

/- Separates Phase IV from Phase V.

The advances in developing sector export volume and unit value in Phase V resulted in merchandise trade balance gains (see Table 5.3). The progress in developing nations' external balances was also helped early in Phase V by slow growth in their imports caused by efforts to constrain imports in response to Phase III merchandise trade balance losses. Phase V of Cycle 4 is not only noteworthy because of the poor developing sector export growth rate and, hence, merchandise trade balance gain but also because of the weak developing sector import growth rate recovery.

The improvement in the developing sector merchandise trade balance in Phase V of each cycle was paralleled by the worsening of the developed sector merchandise trade balance, a development generated by swelling import volume and unit value. In Cycle 4, however, the worsening of the developed sector merchandise trade balance has been minimal, as has the rise in primary commodity prices.[21]

The second result of U.S. initiatives in Phase IV was a series of directional changes in merchandise trade, current account, and net export balances within the developed sector. The causes of these changes are numerous. In part they are attributable to developed sector currency realignments and changed differentials in domestic demand growth rates. Indeed, it is through these vehicles that the Phase IV U.S. policy initiatives in Cycles 2–4 hoped to generate a recovery in U.S. external balances.

But also important in bringing about these changes have been the inflationary aftershocks of Phase IV U.S. initiatives, CPE centered food deficits, and OPEC-driven oil price increases, all of which contributed to increases in primary commodity prices. The commodity composition of trade for each developed country and the size and character of its net investment balance with the rest of the world have significantly impacted its national merchandise trade and current account performance in Phase V.

Phase V has seen improvement in U.S. merchandise trade and current account performance in all cycles (see Table 5.2). That such improvement was almost as pronounced in Cycle 1 as in Cycle 2 and more pronounced in Cycle 1 than in Cycles 3 and 4 is suggestive of the limited role dollar depreciation has played in the recovery in the U.S. merchandise trade balance. (The basis for this judgment is examined in Chapter 9.)

The long-delayed and less robust U.S. merchandise trade recovery in Phase V of Cycle 4 is due to weaker recovery in non-U.S. developed sector domestic demand growth rates than in Phase V of Cycles 2 and 3, a less vigorous recovery in primary commodity prices which has slowed the advance in developing sector imports compared to earlier Phase Vs, and the absence of large European-centered food deficits which has reduced the pace of advance in U.S. agricultural exports compared to earlier Phase Vs. The intensity of the Phase V primary commodity price recovery and the status of the U.S. net investment balance have had an even more profound impact on U.S. current account performance than changes in the U.S. merchandise trade balance. The U.S. factor services income balance is strongly affected by both variables. In Cycles 2 and 3 in particular, the dimensions of U.S. overseas direct investment in the primary commodity sector, especially petroleum, fattened the U.S. factor services income surplus. Also, in the first three cycles the U.S. was a net creditor. During Phase V of these cycles the U.S. factor services income surplus improved. In Phase III of Cycle 4 the U.S. became a net debtor and the Phase V primary commodity price recovery has been weak. As a result, the U.S. factor services income surplus has fallen in Phase V of Cycle 4.

Dollar depreciation appears to have had a more profound impact on real net exports than on nominal trade balances. However, the strong improvement in U.S. net exports (in constant dollars) in Phase V of Cycle 1 suggests that dollar depreciation alone cannot be the cause (see Figure 5.4). Developed sector domestic demand differentials more favorable to the U.S., strengthened developing sector import growth rates, and the surge in U.S. agricultural exports have been crucial to U.S. net export recoveries in Phase V. That all of these factors have been weaker in Phase V of Cycle 4 compared to Cycles 2 and 3 helps explain the less robust recovery in U.S. net exports.

In addition, in Cycles 2 and 3 the more impressive advance in U.S. net export volume came at the beginning of Phase VI—1974 and 1980 (see Figure 5.4). But in 1974 while U.S. net exports were undergoing a huge advance, the U.S. merchandise trade balance was deteriorating, and in 1980, when U.S. net exports made another surge, the pace of improvement in the U.S. merchandise trade balance slowed. Why? The reason for this development was the rise in primary commodity prices, especially for petroleum, which drove up import prices. Hence, import volume fell while import value grew.

Although FRG and Japanese merchandise trade balances and real net exports showed little coherence with anticipated Phase V patterns in Cycle 1, those patterns began to emerge in subsequent cycles, especially the contraction in Japan's net export volume (see Table 5.4). In Cycles 2, 3, and 4, Japan's net exports (in constant yen) fell during Phase V. A major contributor to this development, Japan's currency appreciated in each Phase V against the U.S. dollar, and Japan's two-way trade with the U.S. represented a higher proportion of its total trade than was the case for the FRG, whose currency also appreciated against the dollar. This is one reason why while Japan's net exports fell in Phase V of Cycles 2, 3, and 4, FRG net exports in volume fell only in Phase V of Cycles 3 and 4.

Also, in Cycle 2 the FRG's merchandise trade balance improved while Japan's deteriorated.[22] Its advance after the mark had appreciated

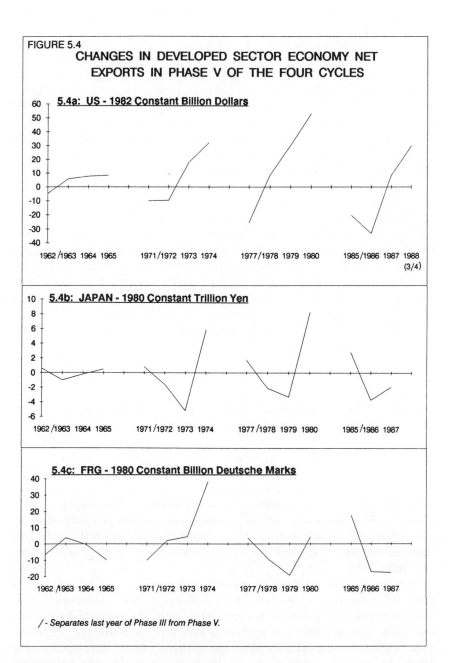

FIGURE 5.4

CHANGES IN DEVELOPED SECTOR ECONOMY NET EXPORTS IN PHASE V OF THE FOUR CYCLES

5.4a: US - 1982 Constant Billion Dollars

(3/4)

5.4b: JAPAN - 1980 Constant Trillion Yen

5.4c: FRG - 1980 Constant Billion Deutsche Marks

/ - Separates last year of Phase III from Phase V.

against the dollar is only partly explained by the relatively lower dependency of FRG trade on U.S. markets and on primary commodity imports compared to Japan. More important was Bonn's ability to contain domestic inflation during Phase V of Cycle 2, thereby enhancing trade competitiveness. In Cycle 3, both the FRG's and Japan's merchandise trade balances worsened during Phase V.[23] The decline was exacerbated in 1979 by unusual FRG and Japanese imports of primary commodities as a hedge against future price rises. While the U.S. merchandise trade balance has belatedly begun to improve in Phase V of Cycle 4 and Japan's has begun to deteriorate, the FRG's merchandise trade balance has not.[24]

The largest proportion of the losses to the developed sector merchandise trade and current account balances in Phase V was borne by the smaller economies, especially the second-tier West European economies —those that encountered substantial balance of payments stress in Phase V of the first three cycles.[25] In Cycle 4 this stress has been less intense because the primary commodity price recovery has been minimal and the acceleration in second-tier West European economies' domestic demand growth rates has been more moderate, although in 1987/88 the United Kingdom began to suffer severe merchandise trade and current account losses.

Phase VI. The impact of rising inflation and growing developed sector government indebtedness in Phase V of all cycles prompted a policy response within the developed sector that brought an end to this phase. In Cycle 1 inflation and overindebtedness were marginal compared to Cycles 2 and 3 and therefore the total developed sector policy response was not as forceful as it would be later. In Cycle 2 the Phase VI deflationary policy response was broader, beginning in the FRG in 1973 and spreading to Japan in 1974 and to the second-tier West European economies. In Cycle 3, the Phase VI deflationary policy response was deeper and more uniform in the developed sector and, commencing at the end of 1979, it spread from macroeconomic to international payments policy. The decline of developed sector domestic demand growth rates in Phase VI has followed the pattern established in macroeconomic policy adjustment (see Table 5.8).

The reduction in the developed sector domestic demand growth rate in Phase VI of the first three cycles prompted a decline in its import growth rate. The lower developed sector import growth rate in Phase VI has followed the cyclical pattern of its domestic demand growth rate (see Table 5.9). In Cycle 1—the cycle in which the reduction in the developed sector domestic demand growth rate was the most moderate—the drop in its import growth rate was also the smallest.

In Cycle 2, the Phase VI drop in both the domestic demand growth and import growth rates was much greater. In Cycle 3, contraction in the developed sector domestic demand and import growth rates was as deep as

TABLE 5.8

DEVELOPED SECTOR DOMESTIC DEMAND GROWTH RATES IN PHASE VI OF THE THREE CYCLES (Percent Growth)

	CYCLE 1:			CYCLE 2:			CYCLE 3:			
	1965/	1966	1967	1973/	1974	1975	1979/	1980	1981	1982
US	6.4	6.1	3.0	4.4	-1.7	-1.9	1.5	-1.8	2.2	-1.9
FRG	6.7	1.7	-1.7	3.3	-2.2	0.2	5.5	1.1	-2.6	-2.0
Japan	4.4	10.3	12.2	10.3	-2.4	0.7	6.5	0.8	2.1	2.8
UK	1.7	1.6	4.1	7.8	-2.2	-1.8	3.6	-2.9	-1.7	2.2
France	3.7	5.6	4.8	6.0	2.5	-1.0	3.8	1.6	-0.1	2.2
Italy	0.9	6.1	8.1	8.2	2.9	-5.9	5.9	6.7	-1.2	0.3

SOURCE: Cycle 1 - OECD National Accounts Statistics 1986; Cycles 2 and 3 - OECD Economic Outlook, Dec. 1987.

/- Separates Phase V from Phase VI.

in Cycle 2 and was spread out over a longer period. The Phase VI fall in the developed sector import growth rate had a direct impact on the developing sector export volume growth rate (see Table 5.9), which followed the same pattern of decline as the developed sector import growth rate.

The decline in the developed sector domestic demand and import growth rate in Phase VI resulted in looser markets and significant downward pressure on prices for primary commodities (see Table 5.9). Nonfuel primary commodity prices have been most vulnerable to this pressure, lacking producer cartels effective enough to administratively reduce supply. The pattern in these primary commodity prices in Phase VI followed the inter-cyclical pattern of developed sector import growth rates. The credibility of OPEC's threat to administer supply and the advent of the Iran-Iraq War during Phase VI of Cycle 3 tended to protect the price of oil, although petroleum's terms of trade worsened.

The decline of primary commodity prices in Phase VI was reflected in worsening developing sector export unit value growth (see Figure 5.9). Here again, the pattern closely followed the inter-cyclical evolution of primary commodity prices.

In Phase VI of Cycles 1–3, the growth rate of developing sector export value also declined and it followed the inter-cyclical patterns of developing sector export volume and unit value growth rates (see Table 5.9).

A falling developing sector export growth rate in Phase VI combined with continued high rates of import growth carried over from the end of Phase V to foster severe losses in the developing sector merchandise trade balance in the first three cycles: the depth of this deterioration followed the inter-cyclical pattern of the declining developing sector export growth rate in Phase VI (see Table 5.3).

The deterioration of the developing sector merchandise trade balance was reflected in improvement in the developed sector trade balance in Phase VI. Declining import and primary commodity price growth produced improvement in the developed sector merchandise trade balance and the pattern of developed sector merchandise trade balance advance in Phase VI paralleled the inter-cyclical pattern of developing sector merchandise trade balance losses in Phase VI of Cycles 1–3.[26]

TABLE 5.9

FORCES BEHIND DEVELOPING SECTOR EXPORT PERFORMANCE IN PHASE VI (Percent Growth)

	CYCLE 1:			CYCLE 2:			CYCLE 3:			
	1965/	1966	1967	1973/	1974	1975	1979/	1980	1981	1982
Developed Sector Import Volume Growth Rate	5.6	13.2	4.7	12.5	1.2	-9.8	9.9	0.0	-2.0	-1.0
Developing Sector Export Volume Growth Rate	6.5	7.6	1.4	19.1	-22.1	-12.7	2.7	-11.5	-6.0	-6.4
Developing Sector Unit Value Growth Rate	1.1	3.4	0.0	25.0	160.0	7.7	34.7	50.5	5.0	-7.6
Nontuel Primary Commodity Prices	0.3	5.6	-3.6	62.2	21.1	-16.2	21.2	5.9	-10.6	-10.5
Oil Prices (Ras Tanura)	0.0	0.0	0.0	42.4	261.7	10.0	13.4	7.8	0.9	-7.2
Developing Sector Import Value Growth Rate	5.9	7.4	2.0	45.5	108.9	-6.0	38.5	34.2	-1.3	-13.1

SOURCES: Developed Sector Import Volume and Developing Sector Export Volume, Export Unit Value and Export Value - UNCTAD Handbook 1987; Non-Fuel Primary Commodity Prices and Oil Prices (Ras Tanura) - IMF IFS Yearbook 1986.
/- Separates Phase V from Phase VI.

6

The Cycle of Inflationary Growth in World Trade—1968-75

Spanning the years from 1968 to 1975, Cycle 2 was notable for an inflationary expansion in world trade. During the cycle the stable relationship between growth rates of world trade in value and volume that had characterized the 1952–67 period was altered, as the growth rate of export value rose in relation to export volume.[1] While the growth rate of export volume declined from its peak in Cycle 1, the growth rate of export value experienced a huge advance over its Cycle 1 performance.

This development resulted from the combined impact of a shift in aggregate developed sector macroeconomic and international payments policy to a more inflationary mix and the complete elimination of post-Korean War production overcapacity in nonfood primary commodities.

A comparison of the phases in Cycles 1 and 2 brings the inflationary momentum that marked the latter cycle into stark relief. In Phase I of Cycle 2, aggregate developed sector macroeconomic policy took on a greater expansionist character in order to kick-start an economic recovery out of the 1967 recession. The scale of developed sector fiscal and monetary stimulus in 1968 dwarfed that employed in Phase I of Cycle 1 (1959). In Phase V of Cycle 2 (1972–74), aggregate developed sector macroeconomic policy was even more permissive when compared to Phase V of Cycle 1 (1963–65), and during this period developed sector international payments policy became more accommodative than was the case from 1963–65.

The rise in primary commodity prices was much more forceful in both

Phase II (1968–70) and Phase V (1972–74) of Cycle 2 than during these phases of the previous cycle (1959/60 and 1963–65).

Finally, because of the greater goods and services price inflation in Phases II and V of Cycle 2, the shift in aggregate developed sector macroeconomic policy to a more deflationary mix in Phase III (1969–71) and Phase VI (1974/75) had a sharper recessionary impact than did similar policy turns in Phase III (1960–62) and Phase VI (1966/67) of Cycle 1.

PHASES I AND II—RESORT TO EXPANSIONIST FISCAL POLICY AND THE EARLY SURGE IN PRIMARY COMMODITY PRICES

The first two phases of Cycle 2 produced enormous pressures—in the form of goods and services price inflation and enlarged intra-developed sector trade imbalances—for a retrenchment in developed sector macroeconomic policy.

The developed sector in aggregate was persuaded to resort to a higher order of government fiscal deficits in 1968 because failure to do so would have produced a weaker and more fragile economic recovery. Rising primary input costs and insufficient advances in investment and civilian technology to offset those rising costs during Cycle 1 was having a demonstrable impact by the beginning of Cycle 2. Further, the growing government fiscal deficits of the developed sector elevated that sector's domestic demand growth rate in 1968, triggering a second development—a surge in primary commodity prices and higher goods and services price inflation.

Finally, intra-developed sector macroeconomic policy differences over the inflation/unemployment trade-off produced larger trade imbalances at the beginning of Cycle 2, with FRG and Japanese balances showing marked improvement and U.S. and second-tier West European balances undergoing aggravated deterioration. Both intra-developed sector trade imbalances and the pressure they placed on the fixed parity regime of Bretton Woods had already become evident in Cycle 1. In Phase I of Cycle 2, this pressure increased.

With even greater intensity than in the 1959–67 cycle, Phase I of the 1968–75 cycle commenced with a strong developed sector recovery centered in the United States. The vigor of the 1968 U.S. economic expansion was reflected in a 23.3 percent advance in U.S. imports, greater than the 16.3 percent growth of 1959.

Underwriting U.S. import growth in 1968 was strong domestic demand growth, fueled by an acceleration in the U.S. government fiscal deficit caused by increased outlays to finance the Vietnam War and Great Society programs.[2]

In addition, the other major developed sector economies increasingly resorted to government fiscal deficits to prop up domestic demand growth. In 1966, Japan made use of government fiscal deficits to support economic growth following the 1965 recession and this continued in 1968, while the FRG government turned to deficit spending for the first time since its founding in order to escape the 1967 recession.[3]

Despite the adoption of reflationary policies throughout the developed sector in 1968, both the expansion of the U.S. government fiscal deficit and the acceleration of the U.S. domestic demand growth rate exceeded those of its major developed sector trading partners.[4] A higher U.S. domestic demand growth rate helped to push the U.S. merchandise trade balance close to deficit in 1968.[5] At the same time Japan's bilateral merchandise trade surplus with the U.S. shot up from $0.4 billion in 1967 to $1.2 billion, while the FRG's merchandise trade surplus expanded, fueled by growing gains at the expense of the rest of Western Europe, especially France, whose payments balance along with that of the United Kingdom worsened.[6]

With more vigor than in 1959, the growth in developed sector domestic demand pushed the limits of primary commodity and labor supplies. This development had a more profound impact on the supply-demand status of nonfood primary commodities than did a similar surge in developed sector domestic demand in 1959, and it also precipitated a greater advance in labor costs.

Phase II of the 1968–75 cycle commenced when primary commodity prices began to climb in late 1968, a process that spread through the spectrum of primary commodities until the middle of 1970, when the price advance was calmed by a recession in the developed sector.[7] In late 1968 and early 1969 metals and minerals prices began to rise, followed by food and then tropical beverage prices in 1969, culminating in rising oil prices in the middle of 1970. During this first primary commodity price advance of the 1968–75 cycle, several changes suggesting future developments appeared.

First, an enormous increase in demand for petroleum further distinguished oil producers from other developing sector exporters as the volume of developing sector petroleum exports from 1967–70 grew ever more rapidly than non-oil developing sector export volume. During these years oil exporter export volume grew by 41.4 percent, while the export volume of non-oil exporters grew by 22.9 percent.[8]

Second, the recovery in developing sector export earnings resulted in strong growth in that sector's imports, especially in 1970/71. In 1971, developing sector imports grew as a percentage of world imports more strongly than at any time since the Korean War.

Third, the advance in primary commodity prices incited a process which undermined the price stability in traded goods that had been in effect since 1953. While price stability in traded goods continued in 1968 as world trade volume grew by 10.8 percent and world trade value by 10.7 percent, by 1970 world trade value grew by 14.2 percent, far surpassing trade volume growth which registered 8.7 percent.[9]

At the same time labor costs in the developed sector began to grow as a result of tight labor markets. In Western Europe labor discipline showed a marked decline as a strike wave, which began in France in 1968, spread to Italy and the Federal Republic of Germany. As a West European "wage explosion" erupted in 1969, in Washington the Johnson Administration's Great Society reinforced New Deal countercyclical programs.[10] And in the Federal Republic with the Social Democrats ascending to power in 1969, broadbased pro-labor legislation was passed, insuring incomes.[11]

Thus increasingly, developed sector governments—with the exception of Japan, which was able to withstand political pressure from its more disciplined workforce—undertook to absorb the cost to personal incomes of inflation resulting from earlier fiscal deficits and concurrent primary commodity price rises. This meant larger fiscal deficits and higher inflation which, when added to rising wages and benefits, resulted in lower corporate profits, higher capital costs, and lower rates of investment. It also meant higher prices for manufactured goods—a development that exacerbated the rise in the prices of traded goods already under way as a result of growing primary commodity prices.

PHASE III—A FINAL EFFORT TO SALVAGE BRETTON WOODS WHILE FIGHTING INFLATION

The U.S. response to its worsening balance of payments position and to the rise in inflation was to adopt, as it had in 1960, a deflationary macroeconomic package.

It is probable that after the surge in U.S. GNP growth in 1968 the U.S. economic growth rate would have tempered in 1969/70 in any event; but as a result of the U.S. government turn to a deflationary fiscal and monetary policy course, the U.S. economy found itself in a recession by the fourth quarter of 1969—a recession that continued deep into 1970.

The deterioration in the U.S. merchandise trade balance in 1968 was not only greater than in 1959 but, because the country's trade balance had gone through a cycle of decline from 1959 to 1967, its trade surpluses had all but vanished by the end of 1968.[12]

The U.S. policy response to its predicament continued to be built around respect for the regime of Bretton Woods parities, even though by 1968 the overvaluation of the dollar had become palpable. The size of dollar obligations accumulated outside the U.S.—exacerbated through the emergence of an offshore market in dollars, the so-called Eurodollar market—had long surpassed U.S. gold reserves.[13] Confidence in the dollar had been decreasing throughout the 1960s and after the pound devaluation of 1967 and, with the deterioration in the U.S. merchandise trade balance in 1968, pressure on the dollar grew, reflecting itself in a speculative rise in gold prices. In 1968, the developed sector central banks moved to contest the threat to the dollar implied in rising free market gold prices by creating a two-tier gold pricing structure in which central banks pledged to retain the lower fixed price of gold in their transactions.

Temporary stability was won only by Washington's resort to a deflationary macroeconomic package which in 1968 led to a rise in U.S. real interest rates, bringing new inflows of capital sufficient to produce a balance of payments surplus in that year even while the U.S. merchandise trade surplus contracted. Further, the U.S. government undertook to reduce its fiscal deficit. As a result of tax rate increases, revenues rose while outlays were cut in Fiscal Year 1969, when the U.S. government produced its last fiscal surplus.

But two developments that were not crucial in the first three phases of Cycle 1 asserted themselves at the beginning of Cycle 2 to complicate intra-developed sector trade imbalances: Japanese export power and intra-developed sector inflation differentials favorable to the FRG.

While the U.S. trade balance stopped deteriorating in 1969, its bilateral trade balance with Japan continued to worsen. Even though Japan enjoyed robust economic growth in 1969, its imports from the developed sector hardly grew. Its imports from the developing sector grew substantially, however, revealing Japan's uneven import links to the world economy. The result was large Japanese trade surpluses with the developed sector, especially the United States. Further, in 1970 while the Organization for Economic Cooperation and Development (OECD) as a whole ran a trade surplus of $3.8 billion, Japan's trade surplus was $2.0 billion, and in 1971 when the OECD surplus reached $7.9 billion, Japan's was $5.8 billion. Hence, Japan's trade surplus was substantial enough to account for over half of the entire OECD trade surplus. Underlying this development was the full maturation of Japan's export power.

The intra-developed sector trade imbalances of 1968/69 were accompanied by wider intra-developed sector inflation differentials than had been the case in the previous cycle, as the U.S., U.K., France, Italy, and Japan ran higher inflation rates than the FRG (Bonn's monetary policy remained more aggressive in containing inflation than those of the other major developed sector economies). The wider inflation differentials enhanced the trade competitiveness and, as a result, the external surpluses of the FRG. The FRG's inflation-induced trade advantages and the inflation differentials themselves triggered larger and more volatile short-term speculative capital flows to the FRG, adding to the challenge to the Bretton Woods parity regime.

Efforts to rectify escalating trade imbalances in the developed sector and to contain inflation led to a deceleration in the aggregate developed sector domestic demand growth rate in 1970/71.

In 1969, with slower economic growth at home and a continued economic expansion abroad, especially in Western Europe—the same conditions that had produced an improvement in the U.S. merchandise trade balance in 1960—the United States averted further losses to its merchandise trade surplus while high U.S. real interest rates sustained capital inflow. But the price of stabilizing the dollar and the Bretton Woods parity regime while simultaneously fighting inflation was an economic recession of length and intensity greater than that of 1960.

Under greater balance of payments stress than in 1959–61, the second-tier West European trading powers in 1968/69 gradually introduced a regime of deflationary programs which severely depressed domestic demand by 1970/71.[14] And in an effort to contest inflation Bonn and Tokyo followed with their own resort to a more deflationary policy posture.

As in Cycle 1, the earlier U.S. adoption of deflationary macroeconomic measures produced an earlier deceleration in the U.S. domestic demand growth rate than in the remainder of the developed sector. While the U.S. entered into recession in late 1969, the second-tier West European economies only began to slow in 1970 and the FRG and Japan saw their economies slow even later. Hence, while the U.S. domestic demand growth rate was most depressed in 1970, the domestic demand growth rate of the remainder of the developed sector was weakest in 1971.

But in 1970 U.S. imports behaved as they did in the 1958 recession, not the 1960 recession, as U.S. consumers continued strong purchases of foreign goods.[15] Further, the absence of significant improvement in the U.S. trade balance in 1970 was unlikely to be rectified in 1971, when the domestic demand growth rate of the remainder of the developed sector would drop.[16]

As in Cycle 1 the slowdown in aggregate developed sector domestic demand growth in Phase III (1970/71) undermined the growth rate of developing sector export volume. But the deterioration in the developed sector import growth rate in 1970/71 caused less weakness in primary commodity prices than it had in 1961/62, reflecting the impact of the long-term tightening of primary commodity markets.[17]

In Phase III, the less severe damage to primary commodity prices and the sharper rise in developing sector exports in Phase II of Cycle 2 (1968–70) compared to 1959/60 permitted a larger and more extended recovery in developing sector imports.[18]

PHASES IV AND V—THE NIXON SHOCK AND THE INFLATION EXPLOSION

As Phase III matured in 1970, the U.S. government faced two increasingly troubling developments—an economic recession and only marginal improvement in the U.S. merchandise trade and current account balances. Since the Great Depression, U.S. macroeconomic policy had been traditionally biased toward recession avoidance; but to escape recession in 1970, the U.S. government would have to swallow two bitter pills—renewed advances in goods and services price inflation and the termination of the Bretton Woods parity regime.

Late in 1970 Washington gave an early signal as to what its decision would be as interest rates were lowered. The relaxation in monetary policy was quickly complemented by a more expansionist fiscal policy.

As a result of the reversal in monetary policy, perceptible interest rate differentials were generated between the U.S. and other developed sector economies still under Phase III deflationary policy discipline, especially the FRG, Switzerland, Japan, and the U.K.

Consequently, the U.S. capital account balance, which had been bolstered by high real interest rates in 1968/69, began to worsen in 1970. Capital outflows swelled in the first half of 1971 to the tune of $12.5 billion. At the same time, U.S. imports grew as a result of fiscal and monetary stimulus, while other developed economies remained under the dictates of deflationary policies and depressed domestic demand growth rates offering little encouragement to U.S. exports. The worsening U.S. trade balance in 1971 caused further trouble for the U.S. payments balance.

With speculative pressure against the dollar building, the FRG and the Netherlands acted in the spring of 1971 by allowing their currencies to float. Switzerland and Austria revalued their currencies. But these actions were inadequate to stem the bleeding of the dollar as, in the first week of August 1971, large capital outflows from the U.S. erupted.

Then, on August 15, President Nixon announced a series of unilateral U.S. actions. First, dollar convertibility to gold was suspended. In addition, the U.S. imposed a 10 percent surcharge on what amounted to about 60 percent of its imports (the vast majority of these imports were from other developed economies). At the same time, the U.S. acted to check the inflationary implications of the August 15 program and its already enacted monetary and fiscal complements with wage and price controls.

The suspension of gold convertibility removed the discipline of the Bretton Woods monetary system from U.S. macroeconomic policy, while holding out the option to U.S. trading partners that it might be reinstated under certain conditions. One of the objectives of the August 15 announcement was to eliminate dollar overvaluation by means of a currency realignment in which the dollar would be devalued. The August 15 package sought to put pressure on U.S. trading partners to agree to such a realignment under penalty of having to endure the alternative—abandonment of dollar-gold convertibility (the absence of any systemic discipline on U.S. macroeconomic policy) and the protectionist 10 percent surcharge on U.S. imports.

In essence the August 15, 1971 U.S. policy initiatives introduced a set of U.S. trade and payments objectives predicated on serving U.S. desires to avoid recession and to reverse the deterioration of external imbalances.

- It called for a devaluation of the dollar.
- It put pressure on U.S. trading partners, especially those enjoying balance of payments surpluses, to accelerate domestic demand growth as a means of replacing economic growth lost in net exports because of the lower dollar. Overseas reflation would advance the rate of U.S. export growth.
- It announced a U.S. commitment to contain the inflationary effect of its reflationary fiscal, monetary, and commercial policy by means of wage and price controls (i.e., by means other than macroeconomic policy).

This recipe, with only minor modifications, was later repeated by the U.S. government at precisely the same point in subsequent trade and payments cycles, under the Carter Administration in 1977/78 and under the Reagan Administration through the September 1985 Plaza Accords. The substance of the policy represented a direct challenge to FRG and Japanese export-centered economic development and to FRG deflationary biases.

In all three cases, the U.S. secured its first objective—dollar depreciation. But in each successive cycle, U.S. success in obtaining its second objective—FRG and Japanese reflation—has weakened as both Bonn and Tokyo became increasingly unwilling to adopt expansionary macroeconomic policies.

In Cycle 2, after an initial period of uncertainty in which Japan at first contested the U.S. policy with large-scale intervention in currency markets in support of the dollar and internal dissension arose in Western Europe over how to respond to the U.S. initiatives, a developed sector policy consensus was forged with the conclusion of the Smithsonian Agreement in December 1971. The dollar was devalued 12 percent against developed sector currencies and 7 percent against all currencies. The yen and the deutsche mark were significantly revalued. The realignment of developed sector currencies did not, however, include a reintroduction of the dollar's convertibility to gold. This development shifted pressure for maintaining the Smithsonian parity regime away from U.S. macroeconomic policy and onto U.S. trading partners' macroeconomic policies and onto their ability and willingness to directly intervene in the markets to support the Smithsonian parities.

By means of the August 15, 1971, Smithsonian Agreement process, the dollar was devalued and the second U.S. objective of obtaining trading partner reflation was secured. Throughout 1972, open-ended intervention in the currency markets to support the Smithsonian parities, especially by Bonn and Tokyo, prompted a large expansion in their domestic money supplies.[19]

In addition, in Japan government outlays grew by 25.0 percent in 1972 as Tokyo tried to sustain its high-speed growth of the 1960s by offsetting anticipated deterioration in its net export volume.[20] Losses in export-centered economic growth were to be neutralized by increased domestic demand growth fueled by government public works projects and tax cuts for businesses to stimulate investment. In late 1971 the Sato government engineered a tax cut and followed it with a 1972 budget featuring huge increases in outlays. In June 1972, Prime Minister Hideo Sato was replaced by former MITI Minister Kakuei Tanaka who encouraged further growth in government outlays under a plan to relocate Japanese industry to the country's west coast.

In the FRG, government outlay expansion was ushered in by the Social Democratic Party (SPD) in 1970 and continued in 1971 and 1972, supported by accelerated money supply growth. FRG inflation consequently surged in 1971/72 well above recent historic rates.

The combination of dollar devaluation and developed sector expansionist macroeconomic policies had three consequences that would be repeated in subsequent cycles at precisely the same point.

- First, the agreement among developed sector economies to restabilize exchange rates—which in the 1968–75 cycle resulted from the Smithsonian Agreement, in the 1976–82 cycle from the Bonn Summit and in the 1983–?? cycle from the Louvre Accords—unraveled.
- Second, the reflationary policy mix pursued by the developed sector was succeeded by a surge in goods and services prices resulting from a recovery in primary commodity prices and labor costs.
- Finally, a transitory improvement in U.S. merchandise trade and current account balances, most often attributed to the appearance of a J-curve, occurred. In the 1968–75 cycle, U.S. merchandise trade and current account balances improved in 1973.

The Unraveling of the Smithsonian Agreement

The inflationary wave which swelled in the developed sector in 1972 ultimately toppled the Smithsonian parities in March 1973. Removal of fiscal and monetary discipline sent Canada's trade balance into deficit and turned the U.K.'s 1971 current account surplus into a deficit by mid–1972. These developments quickly sparked a speculative challenge to the Canadian dollar and British pound. In June 1972, the Canadian dollar was devalued and the pound was permitted to float. But the full unraveling of Smithsonian parities was postponed in the second half of 1972 by massive currency intervention by Bonn and Tokyo to ward off speculative pressure against the Italian lira and the U.S. dollar.

The dollar's predicament was the result of a worsening in the U.S. trade balance caused by a surge in merchandise imports in 1972. A principal cause of this development was the December 1971 dollar devaluation which drove up the price of U.S. imports. Thus, while U.S. import volume continued to grow in 1972—in part because of reflationary macroeconomic policies in the U.S.—the value of those imports grew even more.

This twist in U.S. merchandise trade performance resulting from dollar depreciation is anticipated in the J-curve, but was not expected by the markets. The weakening of the U.S. trade balance forced the U.S. to again raise interest rates (while its trading partners were lowering theirs)—an action that provoked large capital inflows which helped moderate the deterioration in the U.S. balance of payments.

Despite these last-minute efforts, by early 1973 the Smithsonian parities were set to collapse. The process began with an exodus of capital from Italy to Switzerland and was followed by flows of "hot money" to the FRG. With Bonn unable to stem the inflow, the dollar was devalued by 10 percent in March. Subsequently, the European exchange markets were closed in the face of inordinate speculative flows. When they reopened, an intra-EEC parity regime was announced under which EEC currencies were to float jointly within a new global regime of floating exchange rates.

The Burst in Primary Commodity Prices

A second consequence of expansionary developed sector fiscal and monetary policies was unusual acceleration of global demand. This served to alter the supply-demand match for nonfood primary commodities, a development that in turn sparked and sustained the most prolonged and strongest rise in primary commodity prices in the postwar period.[21]

In its early stages the escalation in primary commodity prices was exacerbated by new food deficits in the CPEs, just as had been the case in 1963. This time, Soviet food deficits were complemented by those in China and India.[22]

The escalation in primary commodity prices in fact began in the middle of 1972 with the announcement of U.S.-USSR wheat negotiations. Through the remainder of that year, wheat prices shot up 20 percent, leading a broad rise in food prices. Lagging behind food prices, metals and minerals prices soon began to take off.

Following an agreement between OPEC and developed sector distributors of crude oil in Teheran in 1971, world oil prices began to rise.[23] By the third quarter of 1972, the petroleum price rise surpassed those for wheat and sugar. By the end of the fourth quarter of 1972, the jump in oil prices had surpassed those registered for the whole of cereals.

Primary commodity prices rose rapidly and across a broad spectrum in 1973. For the year, the terms of trade of primary commodities leaped 20 percent. Then in the fourth quarter, in the wake of the Arab-Israeli War, the Arab members of OPEC used the occasion to launch an embargo on oil shipments to much of the developed sector, which in turn prompted a series of unprecedented petroleum price increases. As a result, in 1974 the terms of trade of developing sector petroleum exporters rose an incredible 300 percent while developing sector terms of trade as a whole grew by 42 percent.

The more rapid rise in petroleum prices compared to nonfuel primary commodity prices in 1974 was in large part due to the market distorting advent of a producer cartel—OPEC—the sort of organization that did not exist in effective form for producers of other primary commodities. The differentials in 1974 for fuel and nonfuel primary commodity price growth accelerated the differentiation of developing sector oil exporters from oil importers, a process which had been evolving since the early 1960s when differentials in export volume growth between the two groups had become noticeable.

A Closer Look at the J-Curve In Phase V of Cycle 2

Because much has been said of the success of the policy mix promoted by the U.S. in 1971 (and repeated in 1977/78) in generating improvement in U.S. trade and current account balances in 1973 (and later from the second quarter of 1978 into 1980), it is important to examine more closely the causes of the improvement.

Most striking in examination of the progress in U.S. merchandise trade and current account balances that stretched from the end of the third quarter of 1972 to the end of the fourth quarter of 1973 are the limits of the role of the so-called J-curve in accounting for it. Indeed, study of this period and the period from the end of the first quarter of 1978 through the end of the third quarter of 1980 when similar progress unfolded reveals that *other* variables unrelated to dollar depreciation played a crucial role.

First, it is critical to note that in 1973 when the U.S. merchandise trade balance improved by $7.3 billion and the current account balance by $12.9 billion, U.S. imports grew at a very rapid pace.[24] Indeed, in 1971

U.S. imports only grew by 14.3 percent, but in 1972, after the Smithsonian dollar devaluation, they grew by 22.4 percent and, in the year in which the U.S. trade and current account balances underwent improvement, 1973, U.S. imports grew by 26.3 percent. Importantly, in 1979—the other year of U.S. merchandise trade balance progress often attributed to the J-curve—U.S. imports also grew at a rapid pace.

There is little question that the rise in the U.S. import growth rate in 1972 was in part the result of higher import prices caused by the Smithsonian devaluation. Compared to 1971 the U.S. merchandise trade balance of 1972 deteriorated by $4.1 billion. Thus, the real gain in the U.S. merchandise trade balance caused by the J-curve is not accurately reflected in the 1973 improvement, since dollar devaluation facilitated deterioration in the balance in 1972.

If we now look at U.S. merchandise trade performance for the two years in which the Smithsonian dollar devaluation had an impact—1972 and 1973—a different picture emerges. Compared to 1971, the 1973 merchandise trade improvement is only $3.2 billion, not $7.3 billion (as it is when compared to 1972) (see Figure 6.1).

In this last exercise, our intention is not to identify the precise impact of the J-curve on U.S. external balances but to put into perspective the impact it may have had. On this basis it is evident that during the full period in which the J-curve was at work, the U.S. merchandise trade balance did not improve as much as is often advertised.

More important is the fact that since the progress in the U.S. merchandise trade balance was not caused by a contraction in the rate of growth of imports, all of the advance in 1973 was the result of U.S. export growth. And indeed, U.S. exports grew at a rate of 44.5 percent in 1973, compared to only 14.1 percent in 1972.

Was all of the gain in U.S. export growth in 1973 the result of the J-curve phenomenon? It can be said without question that it was not. A critical factor driving U.S. export growth in 1973 was a special circumstance caused by food deficits in the USSR, China, and India, beginning in 1972, which forced up both the volume and unit value of U.S. agricultural exports. While it is difficult to be precise about the impact of global food deficits on U.S. agricultural exports in 1973, its role can be estimated by looking at U.S. agricultural export growth for the previous two years in order to arrive at a sense of what the average growth in U.S. agricultural exports would be under normal conditions. By doing so we judge that approximately 32.7 percent of total U.S. export growth in 1973 was attributable to special circumstances that increased foreign demand for U.S. agricultural products. If these special circumstances had not emerged, U.S. exports would have grown by 30.0 percent, not 44.5 percent. Perhaps more important, export growth in 1973 attributable to these special circumstances was equivalent to 98.6 percent of the total

FIGURE 6.1

DISSECTING THE J-CURVE IN CYCLE 2

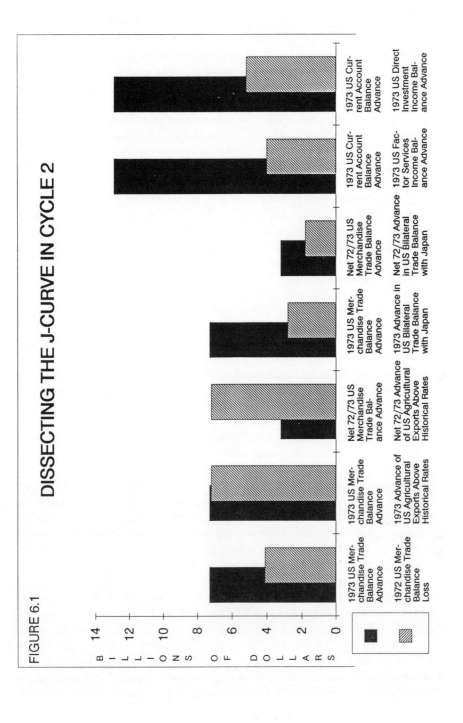

improvement in the U.S. merchandise trade balance (see Figure 6.1). In short, if the food deficits had not surfaced, the U.S. merchandise trade balance would have only improved by $0.1 billion, not $7.3 billion.

Actually, the increment to U.S. exports caused by food deficits is exaggerated in our example since a certain portion of the improvement in their growth in 1973 over previous years no doubt did come from the Smithsonian and March 1973 dollar devaluations; but it is difficult to be precise about this impact. What is clear is that special circumstances accounted for a substantial part of the gain in U.S. agricultural exports.

The food deficits not only affected U.S. agricultural exports in 1973. Because the shortages erupted in 1972, they had a significant impact on the volume and unit value of U.S. agricultural exports in 1972 as well. By applying the same methodology used to ascertain the expansion of U.S. exports above recent historical rates for 1973 to the two years 1972–73—a period coinciding with the evolution of the J-curve—we see that the expansion in U.S. agricultural exports above historical rates is more than double the size of the advance in the U.S. merchandise trade balance (see Figure 6.1).

That the J-curve did have an impact on the U.S. merchandise trade balance in 1972/73 is certain. Perhaps the most impressive example of the J-curve at work was the transformation in the U.S.-Japanese bilateral merchandise trade balance in 1973, when the U.S. merchandise trade deficit with Japan contracted by $2.8 billion (see Figure 6.1). It would be difficult to accept the full magnitude of this improvement as solely the reflection of the J-curve. In 1972, after the dollar devaluation of the preceding year, the U.S. merchandise trade balance with Japan deteriorated by $1.0 billion (see Figure 6.1). Hence, the improvement over two years was $1.8 billion, not $2.8 billion. In addition, it is certain that a portion of the advance in U.S. exports to Japan came not from the J-curve but from rising primary commodity prices (especially food prices).

The greater impact on the progress of the U.S. merchandise trade balance over the 1972/73 period generated by the unusual expansion of U.S. agricultural exports compared to the improvement in the U.S.-Japan bilateral merchandise trade balance suggests that factors other than dollar devaluation had at least as much and probably more effect on advances in the U.S. merchandise trade balance than did the J-curve.

The limits to the J-curve's influence were also evident in the 1973 merchandise trade performance of the FRG. While the mark had appreciated significantly against the dollar, FRG external surpluses were up substantially in 1973. In the spring of that year—as soon as it was freed from the discipline of defending the Smithsonian parities—the Bundesbank moved to attack inflation through a restrictive monetary policy which tended to exacerbate inflation differentials between the FRG and the remainder of the developed sector, making FRG exports more competitive.[25] In 1973, FRG exports grew by 45.5 percent (slightly higher than those of the U.S.). In addition, the tight money policy tempered domestic demand and, hence, import growth.

If the improvement in the U.S. merchandise trade balance attributable to the J-curve was smaller than generally believed, the improvement in the U.S. current account balance attributable to the J-curve would also be smaller. Of the total current account balance improvement of $12.9 billion, 30.1 percent was the result of an advance in the U.S. factor services income surplus, a development unrelated to the J-curve (see Figure 6.1). The equivalent of 40.1 percent of the total current account improvement in 1973 was the result of an advance in U.S. net direct investment income (U.S. net interest income fell in 1973). The gains in U.S. net direct investment income were the result of an advance in gross direct investment income (equivalent to 49.6 percent of the 1973 current account gain). The growth in gross direct investment income was the result of the full recovery in primary commodity prices—U.S. direct investment overseas in the 1950s and 1960s held a strong position in the extractive sectors—and of West European economic growth.

The commodity composition of U.S. trade and its behavior in an inflationary environment such as existed in 1973, special circumstances that may amplify the benefits of an inflationary environment for U.S. external balances, and the sensitivity of factor services income to primary commodity prices all had a profound impact on the behavior of the U.S. merchandise trade and current account balances.

It is also noteworthy that U.S. imports grew vigorously in 1973. It is certain that under circumstances of sustained import growth, durable improvement in the external balances of a nation is unlikely. U.S. merchandise trade and current account performance in 1974 proves the point. That year, the U.S. merchandise trade balance deteriorated by $6.4 billion, offsetting much of the 1973 gain. [26]

PHASE VI—RECESSION: THE ANTIDOTE TO INFLATION

The rise in primary input costs led to a radical change in trade and current account balances among developed sector economies from 1972–75.

By the end of 1973 a number of them—the U.K., France, and Italy, as well as Canada—were under severe balance of payments pressure (see Table 6.1). Further, the impact of rising primary commodity prices compounded by growing labor costs and accommodated by ever larger public deficits had underwritten levels of inflation not seen since the early stages of the Korean War.[27]

The Federal Republic, led by the Bundesbank, reacted in the spring of 1973 to meet the inflationary challenge.[28] A year later, in February 1974,

Tokyo launched a concerted assault on inflation by raising its discount rate and sharply cutting public works expenditures. Through draconian use of monetary and fiscal tools, Japan's inflation rate was brought down by the end of 1974.

The 1974 development that exacerbated already deteriorating developed sector trade and current account balances and propelled inflation up to yet higher rates of growth was the unprecedented rise in petroleum prices, a residual development of Phase V. Because of its early resort to a deflationary policy mix, the FRG was the only developed economy to post a trade surplus in 1974—and a huge one at that—due again to its inflation differential-determined export advantage and to new foreign demand for capital goods, especially in West Asia and the European CPEs (see Table 6.1). But the total EEC trade deficit grew 300 percent in 1974, with the United Kingdom registering the largest deficit of $12.5 billion and Italy second at $8.5 billion. France, too, swung into merchandise trade deficit in 1974. Tremendous balance of payments pressure was placed on those economies, which forced stiff deflationary programs and resort to import controls.

With the FRG and Japan adopting contractionary programs and with other developed sector nations forced by balance of payments stress to turn to deflationary policies, the developed sector was drawn into recession.

While the landing in the 1974/75 recession was softened by growing domestic and international debt, it was nonetheless the deepest recession to that point in the post-World War II period.

Recession conditions in the developed sector depressed imports, and because the developing sector and CPEs were sheltered by developed sector payments policies and continued to enjoy strong import growth, the developed sector trade and current account deficits of 1974 withered in 1975.

The 1974 British and Italian merchandise trade deficits shrank significantly in 1975 (see Table 6.1). France climbed back into trade and current account surplus while Japan's trade surplus expanded as it approached current account balance. The FRG's large trade surplus of 1974 was nearly equaled in 1975.

However, the largest trade and current account balance swing in 1975 was that experienced by the United States. Demonstrating the fragility of the country's 1973 trade performance, the U.S. trade balance had swung back into deficit in 1974 as the agricultural export boom of the previous year subsided and as the rest of the developed sector took stronger and earlier steps to attack inflation and external imbalances than did Washington.

But the later fall in U.S. economic growth compared to the rest of the developed sector ensured that its 1975 trade and current account im-

TABLE 6.1

CHANGES IN DISTRIBUTION OF WORLD MERCHANDISE TRADE AND CURRENT ACCOUNT BALANCES IN PHASES V AND VI OF CYCLE 2 ($Billions)

	Merchandise Trade Balance				Current Account Balance			
	1972	1973	1974	1975	1972	1973	1974	1975
US	-6.4	0.9	-5.5	8.9	-5.8	7.1	1.9	18.1
Japan	8.9	3.6	1.4	4.9	6.7	-0.1	-4.7	-0.7
FRG	8.3	15.5	21.6	16.8	0.8	4.7	10.3	4.1
UK	-1.9	-6.3	-12.5	-7.5	0.5	-2.5	-7.8	-3.6
France	1.0	0.4	-4.8	1.1	-0.4	1.4	-3.9	2.7
Italy	-0.1	-4.0	-8.5	-1.2	2.0	-2.5	-8.0	-0.6
Developed Sector	6.8	3.6	-32.2	-0.8	15.2	16.6	-17.4	10.4
Developing Sector	3.8	11.3	64.5	26.5	-8.2	-4.5	36.4	-3.0
Oil Exporters	9.2	15.5	84.4	52.5	2.2	5.3	64.0	31.7
Oil Importers	-5.3	-4.2	-19.9	-26.4	-10.0	-9.8	-27.6	-34.7
Manufacturing Exporters	-1.1	-0.1	-9.4	-8.4	-2.0	-3.0	-11.9	-11.7

SOURCE: US, Japan, FRG, UK, France, and Italy - IMF IFS Yearbook 1986; Developed, Developing, Oil Exporters, Oil Importers, and Manufacturing Exporters - UNCTAD Handbook 1979.

provement would be stronger than that of other developed economies, as its imports deteriorated more sharply. In addition, the U.S., like Japan, sent a larger proportion of total exports to the developing sector than did the West European economies and thus saw its export growth supported by the continuation of developing sector import vigor.

The rise in oil prices played a key role in U.S. current and capital account balances from 1973–75. Not only did it facilitate an expansion of U.S. exports to developing sector oil exporters; it continued to generate large profits for U.S. petroleum companies abroad which fattened the U.S. factor services income surplus, and because oil exporters invested a portion of their windfall in the United States, the U.S. capital account was also bolstered. These advantages were unlike any others in the developed sector in helping to offset the negative impact of higher oil prices on payments balances.

In 1974 the entire developed sector outside of the FRG required capital account surpluses in order to balance payments. The situation was particularly bad in the United Kingdom, Italy, and Japan. Indeed, Italian imbalances precipitated a new assault on the lira which, while ultimately leading to a depreciation of the currency, had to be fought with large borrowings from a new IMF Oil Facility and the Bundesbank. The U.K. was also forced to tap the IMF Oil Facility and received a large long-term credit from Saudi Arabia, while Japan too had to rely heavily on short-term borrowings. In 1975, as developed sector trade and current account deficits retreated, such activity receded.

In 1975 the developing sector trade surplus shrank as the decline in developed sector import growth blunted the acceleration in primary commodity prices and forced a large decline in developing sector export volume. Even prior to 1975, the majority of developing nations' external balances were shattered by the rise in petroleum prices. While the developing sector as a whole ran large trade and current account surpluses in 1974/75, developing sector oil importers accumulated larger trade and current account deficits.

Nevertheless, oil importers were able to sustain import growth as a result of new foreign loans increasingly issued by commercial banks. The increase in foreign indebtedness of the developing sector in 1974/75 was much greater than it had been at a similar point in Cycle 1.

THE WORLD MARKET: CHALLENGES TO GROWTH AND CHANGES IN STRUCTURE

In Cycle 2 the rate of growth of world import volume fell from its postwar peak in Cycle 1.[29] The reduced pace of expansion in the world market was accompanied by a modification in its structure. In Cycle 2 the developed sector import growth rate (in volume) also declined from its postwar peak reached in Cycle 1 but, unlike trends that characterized the 1952–67 period, the import growth rate of the developed sector lagged behind that of the world as a whole. Further, by the end of Cycle 2 developing sector imports (value) grew and developed sector imports declined as percentages of world imports from what they were at the end of Cycle 1, reversing another trend that had endured from 1952–67 (see Table 6.2).

The decline in the rate of expansion in the world market produced two additional developments—a contraction in the growth rate of world trade (export volume) from its postwar peak in Cycle 1, and once combined with a steeper drop in the growth rate of the developed sector market, it induced more intense crowding in the manufactured goods markets of that sector.

The source of the slowdown in the world and developed sector market expansion was the sharp rise of primary commodity prices in Cycle 2. Not only did it precipitate market conditions in the developed sector that fed an aggravation of trade-diverting behavior—the "new protectionism"—it did so in the developing sector as well. The complete elimination of post-Korean War production overcapacity in nonfood primary commodities created conditions conducive to successful exploitation by a primary commodity producer cartel—OPEC.

The World Market Expansion: Changes in Pace and Structure

Despite continued acceleration in the world import (volume) growth rate from 1968–73, a hint of a dramatic future decline did surface in Phase III of Cycle 2 when the degree of reduction in the developed sector domestic demand and import growth rates (volume) was larger than in Phase III of Cycle 1. Then in Phase VI of Cycle 2 the contraction in the developed sector import growth rate (volume) was far steeper than it had been in Phase VI of the preceding cycle. This decline was substantial enough to produce a large drop in the world import growth rate and it was this drop, occurring in 1974/75, that was responsible for dragging the Cycle 2 average below that of Cycle 1 (see Table 6.2).

Like the decline in the world import growth rate, the modified configuration of the world market was the result of a steeper rise in primary commodity prices in Phases II and V and deeper recessions in the developed sector as a result of macroeconomic policy adjustment in Phases III and VI of Cycle 2 compared to Cycle 1. These conditions produced an expansion of the developing sector's share of world imports (in value) (see Table 6.2). The rise in primary commodity prices from 1968–70 had produced sufficient export earnings to support a larger jump in developing sector imports than had been the case in Phase II of Cycle 1. And of equal importance, the harsher effects of aggregate developed sector macroeconomic policy adjustment in Phase III of Cycle 2 compared to the same

TABLE 6.2

SECTORAL SHARES OF IMPORTS AND EXPORTS IN CYCLE 2 (Percent Share)

	1967	1968	1969	1970	1971	1972	1973	1974	1975
IMPORT SHARES (CIF) --									
Developed Sector	70.2	71.1	72.0	72.3	72.3	72.7	72.7	71.5	67.6
Developing Sector	18.4	18.0	17.4	17.1	17.3	16.5	16.7	19.1	20.9
CPEs	11.3	11.0	10.6	10.6	10.3	10.8	10.6	9.4	11.2
EXPORT SHARES --									
Developed Sector		67.6	NA	69.2	69.2	69.0	68.0	62.8	63.8
Intra-developed Sector		49.5	NA	51.6	51.8	52.5	51.0	44.5	43.3
Developing Sector		18.3	NA	17.8	18.1	18.2	19.4	26.4	24.3
Manufactured Goods		59.2	60.4	60.9	62.0	62.6	60.6	54.9	57.3

SOURCE: Import Shares (CIF) - Handbook 1983; Export Shares of Developed, Intra-developed, Developing Sectors - GATT International Trade 1976/77; Manufactured Goods Export Share - GATT International Trade 1985/86.

phase in Cycle 1 served to aggravate the slowdown in developed sector import growth (in value) in 1971. This dynamic in sectoral import growth rates would be played out with more intensity in Phase VI of Cycle 2.

The developing sector's transition to trade surplus and its buildup of foreign reserves in 1972 combined to facilitate a major expansion in that sector's imports in 1973. That year, developing sector imports grew three times as fast as they had during the preceding year. But they still grew more slowly than developed sector imports.

In 1974/75 the post-Korean War world market was visibly transformed: the developing sector market began to grow more rapidly than that of the developed sector. In 1974 developed sector imports grew by 44.1 percent while developing sector imports grew by 65.6 percent. In 1975 developed sector imports suffered their first contraction in the post-World War II period, falling by 0.2 percent, while developing sector imports grew by 16.3 percent.

A disproportionate share of the import growth in the developing sector during 1974/75 was accounted for by oil exporters. But liberal developed sector payments policies permitted non-oil exporters to sustain import growth while accumulating larger trade deficits.

In addition to dynamic growth in developing sector imports in 1974/75, European CPE hard currency imports also vigorously advanced. A new "selective" trade strategy toward the West calling for large machinery imports combined with bigger food import requirements underwrote the increase. Like the developing sector oil exporters, the Soviet Union was comfortably situated to execute its import strategy, having gained a hard currency windfall from its oil and gold exports.[30] And like the non-oil exporting developing sector, the East European CPEs were permitted to accumulate greater hard currency trade deficits and sustain their hard currency import drives through the auspices of a liberal developed sector international payments policy.

World Trade Growth Slows

Both the pace and structure of world trade growth in volume and value followed the pattern of world import growth in Cycle 2. From 1968 to 1973 the growth rate of world trade (in volume) accelerated beyond its Cycle 1 annual average. However, for the entirety of Cycle 2 it was lower than for Cycle 1 because in 1974/75 the growth rate of world trade volume tumbled under the weight of rising primary commodity prices (see Table 6.3).

Manufactured goods continued to account for a growing portion of total world trade (in value) at the beginning of Cycle 2, reaching 59.2 percent in 1968, up from 49.1 percent at the beginning of Cycle 1 in 1959. From the end of the Korean War in 1953 manufactured goods' share of world trade had grown each year, and this continued until 1973 when the boom in primary commodity prices forced the share of manufactured goods down (see Table 6.3). The rise in oil prices in 1974 accelerated the retreat of manufactured goods in world trade before depressed developed sector and healthy developing sector imports reversed the process in 1975.

The changing shares of manufactured goods and primary commodities in world trade paralleled changes in the shares of the developed and developing sector in world trade (see Table 6.2). From 1953 the developed sector's share of world trade had increased each year while that of the developing sector had declined. This rested upon the prolonged weakness in primary commodity prices following the Korean War and the assertion of dynamic developed sector intra-trade. From 1968 to 1972 this pattern continued, despite the strongest surge in primary commodity prices since the Korean War in 1969–70. Later, however, the 1973/74 boom in primary commodity prices forced the developed sector's share of world trade to decline while the developing sector's increased.

The weakening of developed sector export growth in Cycle 2 was led by the same forces that had fueled its ascendance from 1952 through 1967— intra-developed sector and "special arrangement" trade (see Table 6.2). In 1968 developed sector intra-trade again led world trade, while developed sector special arrangement trade (led by rapidly growing intra-EEC trade) continued to lead developed sector intra-trade. The dynamism of developed sector intra-trade and special arrangement trade was brought to a temporary halt in 1971 when recession conditions in parts of the developed sector slowed import growth.

In 1973/74 developed sector intra-trade gave way to North-South trade as the most dynamic. The primary commodity price explosion boosted developing sector exports and created the basis for a major expansion of developing sector imports, In 1975 North-South trade once again led world trade even though developing sector exports to the developed sector weakened. From 1973 to 1975 the rate of growth of developed sector "special arrangement" trade faltered as the EEC (now expanded to include the United Kingdom) saw its intra-trade growth rate decline.

The severe recessionary impact of the developed sector's turn toward a less accommodative macroeconomic policy caused the developed sector import growth rate to decelerate in 1974/75. And the fact that a much larger portion of its imports was accounted for by higher priced primary commodities suggests the degree to which the value of developed sector manufactured goods imports had dropped in 1974/75. This served to exacerbate crowding in the developed sector manufactured goods markets in the second half of Cycle 2—crowding that was only partially relieved by the expansion in developing sector and CPE hard currency markets.

An Escalation in Illiberal Trade Practices

Illiberal trade policy reactions to crowded developed sector manufactured goods markets first surfaced in 1962 with the U.S. action on textiles. In 1968, with crowding in U.S. markets more pronounced, pressures built for a surge in the "new protectionism." Suffering from the burden of an overvalued dollar—reinforced by commitment to the Bretton Woods parities—and from a surge in imports from modern manufacturing centers in Asia, the U.S. Executive and Congress put their feet to the protectionist pedal from 1969–71 with Japan emerging as the principal target (in the early 1960s the EEC had been viewed by the U.S. as the major competitive threat). New means for protecting markets through forced management of bilateral trade in the form of Orderly Marketing Agreements (OMAs) and later Voluntary Restraint Agreements (VRAs) emerged to frontally assault GATT trade principles. The U.S. sought such arrangements on Japanese steel and synthetic textile exports in 1969. In 1971, soon after having launched a 10 percent surcharge on the majority of its imports, the U.S. successfully leveraged an OMA on Japanese synthetic textiles.

The intensity of the "new protectionism" abated in Phase V of Cycle 2, as it would consistently do in succeeding cycles, only to return with more vigor in Phase VI. With recession and high rates of unemployment in the developed sector in 1974/75, the momentum of the "new protectionism" grew. In 1974 it featured the signing of the Multi-Fibre Arrangement (MFA) involving bilateral trade quotas on textile products. In effect, the MFA placed textile and clothing trade outside the reach of the GATT, a status shared by agricultural and services trade. The U.S. and Western Europe emerged as the centers of the "new protectionism" and the targets were Japan and the Newly Industrializing Economies (NIEs).

In addition, the market conditions that gave rise to the Cycle 2 expansion in primary input costs created an opportunity for the exploitation of trade-diverting practices in the developing sector, and the result of these actions created new market conditions by the end of Cycle 2 which prompted a second wave of pressure for illiberal trade practices in the developing sector. The former materialized in the OPEC-induced oil price rise of 1974 and the latter, in the form of a push from oil-importing developing nations for management of primary commodity prices and preferences for developing sector manufactured exports as means for relieving new and more extreme balance of payments stress.

THE GROWTH OF TRADE IMBALANCES AND THE RISE OF CAPITAL FLOWS

While world trade and the world market experienced substantial alterations in Cycle 2, especially in the second half, so did the size and structure of merchandise trade imbalances.

Compared to Cycle 1, both sectoral and national merchandise trade imbalances endured much larger interphasal changes in Cycle 2, and by the end of the cycle huge trade imbalances had amassed which were not present at the end of Cycle 1. Developing sector merchandise trade balances enjoyed enormous improvement while those of the developed sector deteriorated, oil exporter balances experienced a remarkable advance while those of oil importers declined, and FRG and Japanese trade surpluses grew while U.S. and second-tier West European economy trade balances faltered.

The most violent swings occurred in the merchandise trade balances of the developed and developing sectors. After seeing its trade surplus expand in the recession environment of 1971, the developed sector found its merchandise trade balance deteriorating sharply in 1973/74, before recovering in 1975 (see Table 6.1). The developing sector's merchandise trade balance followed the opposite path. After having its merchandise trade deficit grow in 1971, the developing sector merchandise trade balance improved dramatically from 1972–74, before deteriorating in the 1975 recession (see Table 6.1). By the end of Cycle 2 the developing sector had accumulated a trade surplus. Both the advance of developing sector and the deterioration of developed sector merchandise trade balances followed the movement of primary commodity prices.

By 1974 the rates of growth of different primary commodity prices diverged, and this fostered radical changes in merchandise trade balances within the developing sector. The terms of trade of developing sector manufacturing exporters worsened from 1972–74 in the face of a rise in the broad spectrum of primary commodity prices and these nations' aggregate merchandise trade balance followed their terms of trade down (see Table 6.1). In 1974 the merchandise trade balance of all developing sector non-oil exporters underwent profound deterioration as non-oil primary commodity prices flattened while oil prices shot up (see Table 6.1). In 1975 the merchandise trade balance of both non-oil and oil exporters weakened as primary commodity prices plateaued while imports to both sectors continued to rise. Exiting Cycle 2, developing sector oil exporters had accumulated large merchandise trade surpluses while both developing sector manufacturing exporters and non-oil primary commodity exporters faced substantial merchandise trade deficits.

Like those within the developing sector, merchandise trade balances within the developed sector were subject to divergences. Three factors determined the trade performance of individual developed sector economies in Cycle 2: the commodity composition of their trade, their national attitude toward inflation, and the competitiveness of their manufacturing sector.

Clearly, those countries worst off on these three counts were the second-tier West European economic powers which were highly dependent on primary commodity imports and were weak in primary commodity exports while they enjoyed only moderate strength in overseas extractive sector investments (West European overseas investment was heavily concentrated in debt instruments). In addition, these economies historically tended toward macroeconomic expansionism and lacked a concentrated investment effort in their manufacturing export sectors, especially compared to the FRG or Japan. As a result, they found themselves under extreme balance of payments stress in Phases I and V of Cycle 2 and came out of the cycle with weaker merchandise trade balances than they had upon entering it.

The United States enjoyed the greatest advantage in the commodity composition of its trade. Compared to Japan, the FRG, and the second-tier West European economies, the percentage of primary commodities in U.S. imports was far smaller while the percentage in its exports was much larger. Of critical importance was the portion of agricultural goods in U.S. exports and oil in U.S. overseas direct investment. Together they were the largest contributors to the U.S. merchandise trade and current account balance improvement of 1973.

The United States, however, retained an expansionist macroeconomic policy and lacked a concerted investment strategy for its manufacturing sector. As a result, during the primary commodity price rise of 1968–70 the U.S. merchandise trade balance continued to falter. It faired much better in the inflationary environment of 1973. Indeed, relative to GNP the U.S. merchandise trade and current account improvement in 1973 was stronger than in any other Phase V. In addition to food exports and direct investment income, the U.S. enjoyed other benefits of an inflationary environment, including peak domestic demand growth rates among its developed sector trading partners and much enlarged developing sector imports.

In 1974 the U.S.'s merchandise trade balance worsened because its macroeconomic policy adjusted more slowly than did the rest of the developed sector's, food deficits abroad closed, and its oil import bill rose. But in 1974 the U.S. current account balance declined by less than the U.S. merchandise trade balance because its services surplus continued to grow and it did so as a result of further increases in direct investment income.

In 1975, U.S. macroeconomic policy was forced onto a more deflationary course, and this served to depress U.S. imports. Lower imports plus continued strong exports to the developing sector, especially OPEC, pushed the U.S. merchandise trade balance back into surplus.

FRG trade was more dependent upon primary commodity imports and less on primary commodity exports than was U.S. trade. The differentials were even more egregious for Japan, who suffered from the highest primary commodity import dependency of the leading developed

sector economic powers. In addition, FRG and Japanese direct investment positions in overseas extractive sectors were even weaker than were
those of the second-tier European economies.

Nevertheless, the Federal Republic and Japan experienced an improvement in their external balances at revealing points in Cycle 2 as a result of
traditional macroeconomic biases against inflation and superior manufacturing sector competitiveness.

By Cycle 2 the performance of the FRG's external balances had already
become more reliant upon its macroeconomic policy bias than its investment strategy. Starting in the 1960s FRG investment, while sustaining
1950s rates of growth, was nonetheless less productive.[31] It was from
1973–75 when the boom in primary commodity prices unfolded that the
FRG made its strongest gains in its merchandise trade and current account surpluses in Cycle 2. FRG manufactured goods exports gained a
large competitive edge during this period as a result of the country's lower
inflation rate, which stemmed from Bonn's resort earlier than other developed nations to deflationary macroeconomic measures, especially
monetary measures. The FRG's tighter monetary policy also served to
weaken its imports, and, indeed, in Cycles 3 and 4 it would be low import
growth derivative of anemic domestic demand and not export growth
that would secure larger FRG external surpluses.

Japan, on the other hand, had seen its macroeconomic policy grow
more expansionary as its earlier export investment drive had, by 1966,
produced sufficient export growth to eliminate the chronic balance of
payments stress which had guided Japanese macroeconomic policy onto
a more deflationary course from 1952–64. The big improvement in
Japan's external balances from 1968–72 was entirely the result of its export dynamism as its export growth rate exceeded that of all developed
sector economies. After suffering a severe setback in 1974 due to an enlarged oil import bill, Japan's external balances quickly recovered. Tempered by the reminder of its trade balance vulnerability, especially to
surges in primary commodity prices, Japan's macroeconomic policy has
become more restrained in Cycles 3 and 4. Nevertheless, it has been
Japan's export advantages built on vigorous supply-side adjustment that
have driven up its external surpluses in these two cycles.

The Rise of Capital Flows

The transformations in merchandise trade and current account patterns in Cycle 2 prompted changes in capital flow patterns. During Cycle
2, the ratio of cross-border capital flows to goods and services trade began
to grow, propelled by severe current account shocks produced by the
boom in primary commodity and, in particular, oil prices and by the im-

pact on national asset values of growing interest rate, inflation, and current account balance differentials within the developed sector.

The former development derived from the rise in primary input costs which dominated Cycle 2 and the latter development from the growing divergences in intra-developed sector macroeconomic policy response to the rise in primary input costs. Macroeconomic policy differentials within the developed sector were further encouraged by the U.S. abandonment of the dollar's gold convertibility in 1971 and by the termination of fixed exchange rates in favor of a floating rate regime in 1973. The first event removed the discipline of the Bretton Woods system from the macroeconomic policy of the reserve currency economy—the United States—while the second event removed the discipline of the Smithsonian fixed parities from non-reserve currency economy macroeconomic policy.

The most dramatic change in capital flows during Cycle 2 came in the volume of North-South flows, and in particular the volume of private capital flows from North to South.[32] As a result of the uneven rise in primary commodity prices in 1974, the current account balance of non-oil exporting developing sector economies fell into deep deficit and private commercial banks in the developed sector stepped in to play a larger role in financing current account deficits. The Eurodollar banks which had emerged in the 1960s flourished in the 1974/75 recession. Large flows of developing sector oil exporter surpluses moved into these banks and were recycled to deficit oil importers in both the developing and developed sector on a scale that permitted continued growth in international reserves and in the imports of developing sector oil importers. In 1975 the Eurodollar market alone was responsible for $68 billion in balance of payments related bank loans.

In addition to the "petrodollar recycling" process, the volume of cross-border capital flows was boosted by larger official flows from international lending institutions as well as from developed sector and OPEC governments to economies in both the developed and developing sector experiencing severe balance of payments stress.[33] These included an extraordinary IMF, U.S., and Bundesbank loan to Italy to support the lira, direct Saudi Arabian loans to the United Kingdom and Japan, and the creation of an IMF Oil Facility which was heavily tapped by Italy and the U.K.

The increase in cross-border capital flows to finance current account deficits was supplemented by a rise in intra-developed sector capital movements reflected largely in short-term capital flows and "errors and omissions." As current account performance, interest rate, and inflation rate differentials within the developed sector grew in Cycle 2, "hot money" flows swelled. In 1968 the FRG experienced large capital inflows from France and the U.K. and these were followed by an equally large reflux of capital to France and the U.K. in 1969. In 1970/71, the U.S. resort to a more expansionist monetary policy precipitated large short-term capital outflows. And during the life of the Smithsonian Agreement, "hot money" flows sustained vigor, ultimately undermining the Smithsonian parity regime.

The rise in short-term capital flows provoked greater government currency intervention, at first in the fall of 1971 to stabilize the dollar and then in the second half of 1972 to protect the Smithsonian parity regime. This produced larger intra-developed sector official capital flows.

Through the auspices of private commercial bank lending and official currency intervention the higher rates of growth in world reserves that began in 1970 were sustained through the remainder of Cycle 2. From 1961–69 international reserves grew at a 2.1 percent annual rate while from 1970–73 they grew at a 23.9 percent rate.

7

The Cycle of Stagflation—1976–82

In Cycle 2, two of the factors that shaped both the structure of the trade and payments cycles and the inter-cyclical differences interacted in a particular manner. The huge advance in primary input costs—the first factor—precipitated a response in the second—aggregate developed sector macroeconomic and international payments policy. But in Cycle 3 this dynamic was reversed as aggregate developed sector economic policy assumed a more proactive role while the behavior of primary input costs became more reactive.

In addition to the change in the relationship between the two variables, there arose a change in the behavior of the variables themselves. In Phases I, III, V, and VI of Cycle 3 aggregate developed sector macroeconomic and international payments policy increasingly retreated from the degree of inflationary tilt it exhibited in Cycle 2. The less inflationary developed sector economic policy mix of Cycle 3 produced a less vigorous acceleration in primary input costs during Phase V and a sharper deceleration of such costs in Phases III and VI when compared to the same phases in Cycle 2.

The result of policy retrenchment was a slower paced rise in primary input costs, accomplished at the price of a lower rate of GNP growth. Cycle 3 is thus marked by "stagflation"—continued but slower advances in goods and services price inflation coupled with lower economic growth rates.[1]

The economic adjustment process in the free world economy that emerged in Cycle 3 was disproportionately weighted toward the "demand side." Policies aimed at constraining demand were not complemented by supply-side initiatives equal in scope.[2] Successful supply-side adjustment would have permitted reduction in the demand for primary inputs without the negative demand-side adjustment effect on economic growth.

Symptomatic of insufficient supply-side adjustment, the investment growth rate in the manufacturing sector deteriorated in this cycle, as it had during the previous one. This declining rate of growth was the result of four developments. From the supply side, such investment was constrained by lower rates of output growth; from the demand side, it was constrained by increased resource diversion to personal consumption and government transfers to individuals, to financing the costs of maintaining larger stocks of domestic and foreign debt, and to investment in primary commodity productive capacity and inventory accumulation.

A similar set of circumstances confronted the European CPEs at the beginning of Cycle 3. A more egregious contraction in the GNP growth rate than encountered in the free world economy struck these countries beginning in 1976, and this combined with severe shortages in extractive sector output (agriculture in 1975, energy in 1976/77) to foster a deceleration in manufacturing sector investment growth rates, especially in the Soviet Union.[3] Unlike the developed sector, the Soviet Union avoided large transfers of resources to social peace accounts (i.e., personal consumption) in order to contain the rise in capital costs, but only at the expense of a deep erosion in labor productivity. In addition, the Soviet Union increased its subsidies to social peace in the East European economies by accepting bigger trade surpluses with Eastern Europe.[4] Added to the strain on Soviet investment resources prompted by the ratchet down in the GNP and labor productivity growth rates and by bigger trade surpluses with Eastern Europe, Moscow diverted ever larger proportions of investment resources to the lower-tech extractive sector.

Within the developed sector, the leading exporters—the United States, Japan, and the Federal Republic of Germany—experienced the constraints on investment that arose in Cycle 3 differently, and these differentials worked to enhance the export competitiveness of Japan while weakening that of the FRG and the U.S.[5] Despite suffering the highest degree of dependency on primary commodity imports of all the developed sector export powers, Japan enjoyed substantially lower social peace costs and a higher personal savings rate, which caused capital costs to rise more slowly than in the U.S. and the FRG. This allowed Japan to undertake more vigorous efforts to neutralize its greater vulnerability—primary commodity import dependency—through supply-side adjustment.

Capital costs rose more rapidly in the Federal Republic of Germany and the United States, where the process of supply-side adjustment was relatively weak. Like the rest of Western Europe, the Federal Republic suffered from social peace costs higher even than those in the U.S., while its personal savings rate was lower than that of Japan. In the U.S. the savings rate was the lowest of all, while social peace costs were palpably higher than in Japan.

As a result, with ever greater intensity in Cycles 3 and 4, Japan's trade and current account surpluses came to rest upon its export dynamism.

The wider differentials in intra-developed sector trade competitiveness that emerged in Cycle 3 overlapped a second development that distinguished this cycle from its two predecessors: greater differentials in demand-side adjustment. In Cycle 3 the combined effect of the FRG's historical sensitivity to inflation and of the severity of second-tier West European economies' balance of payments problems fostered a collective West European macroeconomic policy retreat that outstripped that of Japan, who also moved to a less inflationary policy mix. Unlike Japan, the growth of FRG trade and current account surpluses in Cycles 3 and 4 has not come from export dynamism but from lower import growth.

The decline in the domestic demand growth rate of the non-U.S. developed sector in Cycle 3 was unmatched in the United States, which continued to pursue an economic strategy driven by its historical fear of recession and unemployment. As a result, the deterioration in U.S. trade and current account balances accelerated.

PHASES I AND II—ECONOMIC POLICY DIVERGENCE IN THE DEVELOPED SECTOR AND A MODERATE EXPANSION IN PRIMARY INPUT COSTS

In 1976, the first year of Cycle 3, greater differences emerged in developed sector macroeconomic policies and domestic demand growth rates than had been the case in Phase I of the first two cycles. During that year, the revival in world import growth was centered in the United States, just as it had been in 1968 and 1959. In 1968 U.S. imports had grown by 23.2 percent (in 1959, by 16.3 percent), while in 1976 they grew by 24.1 percent. And the principal beneficiaries of the 1976 U.S. import boom were developing sector oil exporters and Japan, the world's two most dynamic exporters during Cycle 2. That year, U.S. imports from developing sector oil exporters grew by 42.0 percent, and from Japan, by 41.0 percent.

But unlike 1968, import growth throughout the remainder of the developed sector was demonstrably weak. Aside from those which ran external surpluses, most West European economies—including the second-tier economies—came out of the 1974/75 recession with larger trade and current account deficits than they had coming out of the 1967 recession. France and Italy suffered a substantial rise in their trade deficits in 1976 as a result of renewed import growth. And the United Kingdom, returning to an austere economic policy, was only able to reduce its trade deficit by holding down imports (see Table 7.1—the U.K., France, and Italy).

Developed sector economies with external deficits were thus under greater balance of payments stress in Phase I of the 1976–82 cycle than they had been in Phase I of the previous two cycles, and they would have been forced to constrain import growth even more if they had not borrowed $31 billion from abroad and, in some cases (London and Paris), run down reserves to finance imports. The fragile payments balances inherited by second-tier West European economies from Cycle 2 and the threat posed to them by Phase I import growth provoked a major attack on the lira in 1976 and a prolonged assault on the pound, which carried over into 1977.

Other differences had evolved among developed economies by the beginning of Cycle 3 which not only affected those with external deficits, but those with surpluses as well. Developed economies exited the 1974/75 recession with higher inflation rates than had existed at the beginning of Phase I of the previous cycles.[6] On top of this, the developed sector emerged from the recession with larger stocks of domestic debt and aggregate domestic deficits, especially public sector deficits. In 1976 Italy's public deficit was 10 percent of GNP, for the U.K. the figure was 6 percent, for the FRG, 5 percent, for Japan, 4 percent, the U.S., 3 percent, and for France, 2 percent.

While developed sector economies with external deficits were thus under double-barreled pressure to resort to a more deflationary macroeconomic policy mix, the FRG and Japan, the principal developed economies with external surpluses, had accumulated substantial government fiscal deficits during Cycle 2 and were highly exposed to rising primary input costs. Further, the Japanese economy experienced a sudden erosion of its external surpluses in 1973/74. These developments, once combined with the national economic and trade and payments biases of the two nations, pressed the governments of both to adopt a less accommodative fiscal and monetary policy mix in 1976 than they had at the beginning of Cycle 2.

In 1971, the Japanese government's dependency on government bonds was 9.4 percent. By 1975 it had grown to 26.3 percent, and in both Japan and the FRG the government deficit as a percentage of GNP rose in the recession. In addition to the specter of government overindebtedness, reaction to inflation had already locked Bonn, under Bundesbank guidance, into a more deflationary domestic monetary policy as early as 1973, while in reaction to rising inflation Japan had followed a contractionary domestic fiscal and monetary path in early 1974.

As a result, in Phase 1 of the 1976–82 cycle domestic demand growth rate differentials between the U.S. and the remainder of the developed sector had widened from what they were in 1968 and 1959—a develop-

TABLE 7.1

MERCHANDISE TRADE BALANCES AND
EXPORT AND IMPORT GROWTH RATES OF MAJOR
DEVELOPED ECONOMIES IN PHASES I AND III OF CYCLE 3

	Merchandise Trade Balance ($Billions)				Export Growth Rate (Percent Growth)			Import Growth Rate (Percent Growth)		
	1975/	1976	1977	1978	1976	1977	1978	1976	1977	1978
US	8.9	-9.5	-31.1	-34.0	7.1	5.3	17.6	26.5	22.3	15.9
Japan	4.9	9.8	17.2	24.3	20.5	20.2	20.3	12.9	10.5	14.5
FRG	16.8	16.1	19.5	24.6	12.4	14.9	20.4	16.4	13.7	19.2
UK	-7.5	-7.0	-3.9	-3.0	5.6	22.3	21.3	3.8	13.6	18.4
France	1.1	-5.0	-3.3	0.1	8.0	13.5	21.9	20.7	9.2	15.5
Italy	-1.1	-4.2	-0.1	2.9	6.7	21.7	23.9	15.1	9.2	17.1

SOURCE: IMF IFS Yearbook 1986.

/- Separates last year of preceding cycle.

ment that had a strong impact on the U.S.'s merchandise trade and current account performance.[7] From the trade and current account surpluses of 1975, U.S. external balances swung into deficit in 1976. U.S. bilateral balances with Japan and with oil exporters suffered acute deterioration. The U.S. merchandise trade deficit with Japan, which stood at $1.7 billion in 1975, grew to $5.4 billion the following year. And unlike Phase I of Cycles 1 and 2 when the dollar's value remained fixed, in Phase I of Cycle 3, dollar overvaluation was exacerbated by a 5.2 percent dollar appreciation.

While U.S. external balances faltered in 1976, Japan and the FRG combined accumulated a larger merchandise trade surplus (see Table 7.1).

Despite heavy balance of payments and inflationary burdens in the developed sector, 1976 world output and trade (in volume) growth rates resembled those of the 1960s and early 1970s and, as in 1968 and 1959, the recovery in developed sector imports fueled a rise in developing sector export volume. The rise in developed sector demand also sparked a recovery in primary commodity prices and developing sector export unit value. While nonfuel primary commodity and oil prices rose more vigorously in Phase II of Cycle 3 than they had in Phase II of earlier cycles, the improvement paled in comparison to the primary commodity price surge in Phase V of Cycle 2.[8]

During Phase II, the developing sector merchandise trade and current account balances improved, but the duration and size of the improvement were smaller than in Phase V of Cycle 2.[9] In 1976, both developing sector oil exporters and importers enjoyed improved merchandise trade and current account balances. But in 1977 this came to an abrupt halt as the developing sector's export growth rate contracted while its import growth rate picked up.

PHASE III—THE ABSENCE OF U.S. RETRENCHMENT AND WEST EUROPEAN TRADE RECOVERY

Unlike in previous cycles, Phase III in the 1976–82 cycle did not commence with U.S. resort to deflationary policies to combat a worsening payments balance and the threat of inflation, even though in 1976 U.S. merchandise trade and current account balances had faltered and U.S. inflation was high relative to post-World War II performance and to contemporary inflation among leading U.S. developed sector trading partners. As a result, the decline in the U.S. GNP growth rate in 1977 was small compared to the descent of the U.S. economy into recession in 1960 and 1969/70, and imports continued to grow briskly—albeit more slowly than the previous year—aided by the 1976 dollar appreciation and the need for petroleum imports to stock the new U.S. Strategic Petroleum Reserve.[10]

In addition, unlike in 1960 and 1969, Western Europe failed to offset the slower 1977 U.S. import growth rate. Indeed, in 1977 both West European domestic demand and import growth rates declined from their 1976 levels.[11] By 1977, second-tier West European economies were under immense balance of payments pressure to slash imports. France constrained import growth while Italy came close to trade balance by means of deep cuts in its import growth rate. The United Kingdom, however, found enough breathing space as a result of the beginning of North Sea oil production to relax its deflationary macroeconomic policy and allow imports to grow at a healthy pace.

Fearing renewed inflation, the West European economies enjoying external surpluses, led by the FRG, sustained their less accommodative policy mix into 1977. And after a sputtering economic recovery in 1976, Japan renewed expansion of the government fiscal deficit in order to stimulate domestic demand growth—but did so cautiously to avoid rekindling inflation.[12]

The changed policy mix in the U.S. and the remainder of the developed sector caused domestic demand growth rates, which had converged rather rapidly in Phase III of the previous cycles, to continue to diverge in 1977. Once combined with dollar appreciation in Phase I, the wider domestic demand growth rate differentials resulted in the continued expansion of U.S. merchandise trade and current account deficits in 1977—a process that extended through the first quarter of 1978. In Cycles 1 and 2, U.S. external balances had improved at comparable stages, in 1960/61 and 1969/70. Symptomatic of the deterioration in U.S. external balances, the bilateral merchandise trade deficit with Japan, which had grown from $1.7 billion in 1975 to $5.4 billion in 1976, shot up to $8.0 billion in 1977.

While the U.S. trade and current account balances faltered in Phase III, those of the FRG and Japan continued to grow.

Despite the absence of U.S. resort to deflationary policies at the beginning of Phase III, the world output and trade growth rate visibly declined in 1977, whereas in 1960 and 1969 no such decline had occurred. The most important cause of this change was the drop in the West European domestic demand growth rate and Western Europe's reduced role in world trade growth.

The extremely poor performance of primary commodity prices in 1978 was a reflection of the fact that the aggregate developed sector domestic demand growth rate suffered an earlier slide than it had in Phase III of the first two cycles. As a result, in 1978 the terms of trade of developing sector primary commodity exporters turned negative and developing sector merchandise trade and current account balances worsened.[13]

PHASES IV AND V—THE CARTER SHOCK AND A WEAKER RECOVERY IN PRIMARY COMMODITY PRICES AND U.S. EXTERNAL BALANCES

One of the most alarming developments during the first three phases of the 1976–82 cycle was the undaunted deterioration in U.S. merchandise trade and current account balances—a circumstance which had not occurred in Phase III of Cycles 1 and 2.

The floating exchange rate monetary system which was, according to its proponents, to facilitate corrective capital flows in response to emerging current account imbalances did not work in 1976. As U.S. trade and current account balances faltered, the dollar appreciated. After some dollar depreciation in early 1977, U.S. merchandise trade and current account deficits continued to expand. Under U.S. government instigation, the dollar ultimately underwent a prolonged depreciation from late 1977 through 1978.

That the dollar did not depreciate in Phase I is testament to the fact that short-term speculative capital movements will not always act to restore balance of payments equilibrium in a floating exchange rate regime. Indeed, two other factors gain increased influence over exchange rates. First, in a market regulated only by the threat that major developed sector governments may act in concert to influence exchange rates, market psychology and speculative momentum play a large role. Second and more important, differentials in the real value of assets from one economy to another provoked by wider inflation or interest rate differentials and bigger external imbalances can incite greater cross-border capital flows and, consequently, movement in exchange rates. Growing differences in national inflation, interest rate, and external balance performances are prompted by expanding macroeconomic policy divergences among nations—divergences that are given greater latitude to express themselves in a floating rate regime.

The decline in U.S. external balances in 1976/77 and the ratcheting down of U.S. economic growth in 1977 compelled the incoming Carter Administration to act, as had the Kennedy and Nixon governments.

In 1977, the Carter Administration adopted a version of the Nixon program of 1971. The differences between the Carter and Nixon initiatives are marginal and were the result of the different circumstances in which they were employed. The August 15, 1971, policy was pursued when a fixed exchange rate regime was still in place and its principal objective was therefore to engineer a dollar devaluation and remove the constraints on U.S. economic policy generated by the Bretton Woods monetary system, constraints that called for a more deflationary U.S. macroeconomic approach in 1971. The Carter Administration initiative was promoted under a regime of floating exchange rates. Its objective, like Nixon's, was to reduce the price of the dollar so as to generate improvement in the U.S. merchandise trade balance. But the Carter Administration could more easily pursue this objective by coaxing the market into recognition of the dollar's overvaluation. It could therefore more specifically and publicly identify the second objective of prodding its trading partners to adopt reflationary macroeconomic policies as its top priority.

The central goal of the Carter program, aside from easily gotten dollar depreciation, was to win FRG and Japanese commitments to reflate their economies and thereby reduce the domestic demand growth rate differentials between them and the U.S. Systematic pressure was applied on Bonn and Tokyo from early 1977 to reflate—with the club of further dollar depreciation and yen/mark appreciation being held over their heads.

In the summer of 1978, after prolonged dollar depreciation, an accord was reached among leading developed sector economies at the Bonn Summit.[14] The functional equivalent of Cycle 2's Smithsonian Agreement, the Bonn Summit agreement created an intervention pool of $30 billion to be used to stabilize the dollar (while the Smithsonian Agreement established fixed and publicly declared parities, the Bonn Summit reached agreement on a looser set of reference zones for key currencies and did not make them public), and it obtained public commitments from the FRG and Japan to reflate their economies, along with a U.S. pledge to restrain its domestic demand growth. The Summit in effect sought to shift the burden for future balance of payments adjustment away from currency realignment to macroeconomic policy adjustment.

Just as in the 1972–74 Phase V of the preceding cycle, the execution of the Carter policy precipitated a series of developments in 1978–80 similar to those which proceeded from Nixon's August 1971 program. Inflation rose significantly in 1979/80, as it had from 1972–74, and the U.S. merchandise trade and current account balances improved in 1979, as they had in 1973.

The Bonn Summit was preceded by an expansion in developed sector money supply growth in 1977/78 caused by FRG and Japanese government (among others) intervention in the currency markets to stem the dollar's slide. This development reproduced the process which generated growth in Japanese and FRG money supplies from 1971 to early 1973.

The transition to a reflationary policy mix in the developed sector in 1978 prompted a recovery in primary commodity prices beginning late that year, and in 1979/80 primary commodity prices experienced as prolonged a recovery as they had from 1972–74.[15] Further, special circumstances—including the eruption of large CPE food deficits and political instability in West Asia—evolved in 1978–80 to accelerate food and energy price advances, as they had from 1972–74.[16]

But the market-generated components of the 1978–80 primary commodity price rise were smaller than in 1972–74 because the intensity of aggregate developed sector reflationary initiatives in Phase V of Cycle 3 were weaker than those in the same phase of Cycle 2. Absent was the strong fiscal stimulus in Western Europe, Japan, and the United States evident from 1971–73.

Another factor undermined the primary commodity price recovery: the harsh developed sector deflationary policies that began Phase VI— deflationary policies that were stronger and were introduced earlier than was the case in Phase VI of the 1968–75 cycle.

Following the boom in food prices beginning in 1978 in response to large Soviet agricultural purchases—a boom which continued into 1979—petroleum prices began their recovery. In an even more palpable fashion than in Phase V of Cycle 2, the rise of petroleum prices dominated the advance in primary commodity prices. After five straight years of decline in real oil prices, increased domestic demand in the developed sector in late 1978 incited the rise. From late 1978 to early 1980, oil prices rose from $13 a barrel to $30 a barrel—or nearly 130 percent. In 1979, other raw material prices rose strongly, though by no means as sharply as petroleum.

Unlike in 1972–74, some of the primary commodity price increase of 1979/80 resulted from speculative hoarding and defensive buying (i.e., hedging against future price rises), especially in the more vulnerable Japanese and West European economies, producing price increases more like those that accompanied the speculative buying wave at the onset of the Korean War in the second half of 1950 than the 1972–74 primary commodity price recovery.

Moreover, a hypersensitive oil market conditioned by its experience in late 1973 and 1974 reacted in a speculative fashion to the fall of the Shah of Iran in late 1978 and the outbreak of the Iran-Iraq War in 1980 to drive up oil prices.

Sensitivity to earlier primary commodity supply shocks coupled with speculative activity served to amplify the primary commodity price recovery, especially in oil, above what market conditions would have recommended.

Looking at the J-Curve Again

From the second quarter of 1978 through the third quarter of 1980 the U.S. merchandise trade balance underwent an improvement similar to that experienced in Phase V of the previous cycles. In nominal terms, the 1979/80 progress in the U.S. merchandise trade balance was only slightly larger than the 1973 gain and was smaller when measured against U.S. GNP or total U.S. merchandise exports and imports. As was the case for the advance in the 1973 merchandise trade balance, the 1979/80 improvement was accompanied by greater progress in the U.S. current account balance.

Like that of 1973, the 1979/80 gain in U.S. external accounts has often been attributed to the J-curve. But closer analysis suggests that it, like its predecessor, was less the work of the J-curve than of other factors.

Recalling the structure of the progress in U.S. external balances in 1973, import growth was vigorous in 1979. That year, when the U.S. merchandise trade deficit contracted by $6.4 billion and the U.S. current account balance improved by $14.4 billion, U.S. imports grew by a very healthy 20.5 percent, bettering the 15.7 percent growth registered in 1978.[17] In 1980, however, when the U.S. merchandise trade deficit declined by another $2.0 billion and the U.S. current account balance advanced by $2.9 billion, the U.S. import growth rate decelerated to 17.8 percent.

Hence, as in 1973, 1979 progress in U.S. external balances was not attributable to a reduced rate of growth of U.S. imports. Again, the entire gain was the result of an acceleration in exports. After growing by only 5.1 percent in 1977, U.S. exports grew by 17.6 percent in 1978, and 29.8 percent in 1979. In 1980, the export growth rate declined to 21.6 percent. Thus, in 1980—unlike in 1979 or 1973—progress in the U.S. merchandise trade balance was due to a deteriorating U.S. import growth rate.

But the gain in the U.S. merchandise trade balance in 1979 overstates the magnitude of improvement that could possibly be attributed to the J-curve. Since dollar depreciation began in earnest in 1977, the 1978 U.S. merchandise trade performance also reflected the impact of the J-curve. As in 1972, the U.S. merchandise trade balance worsened in 1978. The U.S. merchandise trade deficit grew by $2.8 billion that year, leaving a net gain of only $3.6 billion for 1978/79 (see Figure 7.1).

Also as in 1972/73, the U.S. export expansion from 1978–80 was in part the result of special circumstances—new food deficits centered in the European CPEs which bolstered world food prices. As a result, U.S. agricultural exports from 1978–80 grew at rates much greater than in 1976/77. Employing the same methodology for estimating the increment to U.S. exports precipitated by special circumstances used in the 1973 case (which, as previously explained, involves an indeterminate overestimate), for 1979, we see that U.S. agricultural exports increased by $1.7 billion over their recent historical rate, accounting for 26.0 percent of the 1979 U.S. merchandise trade balance gain (see Figure 7.1). However, Cycle 3 food deficits also influenced 1978 U.S. agricultural exports. For 1978/79, the advance of U.S. agricultural exports over recent historical rates was much greater than for 1979 as it accounted for more than twice the net gain in the U.S. merchandise trade balance in 1978/79 (see Figure 7.1).

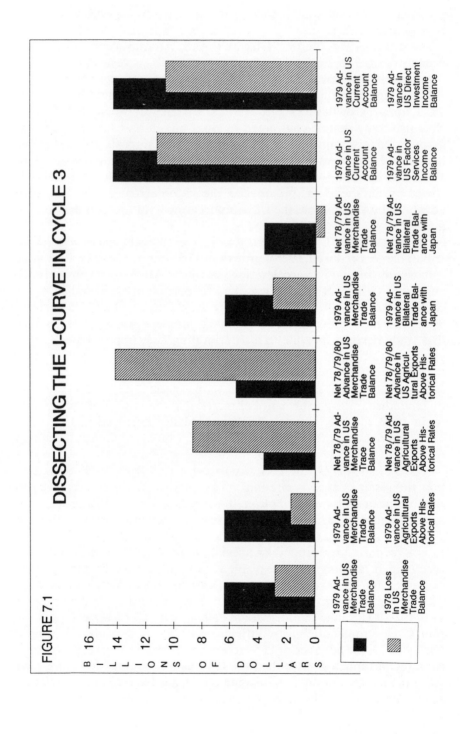

FIGURE 7.1

DISSECTING THE J-CURVE IN CYCLE 3

This latter development parallels the relationship of the advance in U.S. agricultural exports above recent historical rates to the net gain in the U.S. merchandise trade balance in 1972/73—the years in which the J-curve developed in Cycle 2.

Moreover, if we extend our examination to 1980, we see that the magnitude of the advance in U.S. agricultural exports above recent historical rates comes close to three times the size of the net 1978/79/80 gain in the U.S. merchandise trade balance (see Figure 7.1).

That the J-curve did have some impact, at least in 1978/79, is suggested (as was the case in 1972/73) by the behavior of the U.S.-Japanese merchandise trade balance, since a substantial exchange rate realignment took place between the dollar and yen from 1977 to 1978. In 1979, Japan's merchandise trade surplus with the U.S. fell by $3.0 billion, representing close to half of the gain in the U.S. merchandise trade balance (see Figure 7.1). In 1978, however, Japan's merchandise trade surplus with the U.S. grew by $3.6 billion. Hence, over the course of 1978/79 the U.S. merchandise trade deficit with Japan continued to grow (see Figure 7.1). Further, in 1980 Japan's merchandise trade balance with the U.S. grew anew, by $1.3 billion. This latter development indicates that the impact of the J-curve on U.S. external accounts was restricted to 1978/79, just as it had been contained to two years—1972/73—in the previous cycle. Therefore, in 1978/79, the years of J-curve maturation, the net improvement in the U.S.-Japan merchandise trade balance—the most important indicator of the J-curve's functioning—was negative, while the acceleration in U.S. agricultural exports above recent rates of growth towered over the net gain in the U.S. merchandise trade balance.

More than was the case in 1973, the progress in the U.S. current account balance in 1979 was determined by the recovery in the U.S. factor services income balance. The drop in the U.S. merchandise trade deficit in 1979 represented less than half of the total advance in the U.S. current account balance. The factor services income balance accounted for a larger 78.5 percent (the non-factor services trade balance change in 1979 made a negative contribution to the U.S. current account balance) (see Figure 7.1). The gain in the direct investment income balance represented 74.3 percent of the improvement in the current account balance (see Figure 7.1).

As in 1974 when U.S. external balances deteriorated, all the gains of 1979 and 1980 were offset in 1981/82.

PHASE VI—A WHIFF OF ECONOMIC DEPRESSION

Just as a more deflationary developed sector macroeconomic policy characterized the first five phases of Cycle 3 compared to the same period in the previous cycle, the economic policy response of the developed sector economies to the jump in inflation in 1979/80 took on a more deflationary character than it had in 1973/74.

Governments moved to bring the demand-side contribution to the Phase V inflationary process to a halt beginning in late 1979. The most intense deflationary macroeconomic policy initiatives were adopted in Western Europe and included concentration on reduction of government fiscal deficits and tighter monetary policies, an approach most strongly advanced by Bonn and by the Thatcher government in London. Tokyo, too, emphasized reduction of its large public deficits. In late 1979 the ruling Liberal Democratic Party resolved to make the 1980s a period in which the government deficit would be reduced as a percent of GNP.[18] Against strong domestic business and foreign pressure, especially in 1982, the Japanese government persisted in its war on the central government deficit.

Finally, in October 1979 the U.S. Federal Reserve Board embarked on a policy aimed at reducing domestic inflation.[19] In this effort it got only rhetorical help from the elected branches of government, which continued to pursue fiscal policies prioritizing recession-avoidance, policies that had ruled out raising tax rates or cutting "payments to individuals" as means of reducing the budget deficit since the 1970 recession. Soon after the 1980 election, the Fed moved forcefully to choke off credit expansion, prompting an unprecedented rise in real and nominal interest rates. Phase VI of the 1976–82 cycle had begun.

Deflationary Policies and Their Impact on Developed Sector Trade and Current Account Balances . . .

The shift to more contractionary economic policies in the developed sector had important implications for world trade and payments. Ultimately, these actions reduced the dimensions of the developed/ developing sector merchandise trade imbalance that had erupted in 1979/80 (see Table 7.2—Developed/Developing Sector Trade Balances). This reversal was sharper than that of 1975, especially in Western Europe. Just as Western Europe's response to trade and payments imbalances and inflation from 1976–78 helped fuel its decline as the center of world trade growth, harsh deflationary measures undertaken from 1980–82 in response to renewed current account imbalances and inflation accelerated the West European retreat.

Therefore, in 1981 while the U.S. merchandise trade deficit increased, Western Europe's trade deficit dropped sharply. In addition, unlike Japan whose imports rose in 1981—as did the U.S.'s—Western Europe's trade deficit reduction was due entirely to a huge decline in imports. In 1982 Western Europe's trade and current account balance improved further, and again it was the result of a decline in imports.

Japan's current account balance also underwent a radical turnaround in 1981, due, like Western Europe's, to an improved trade balance (see Table 7.2—Japan). While Japanese domestic deflationary policies slowed the growth rate of imports, the growth in Japan's trade surplus in 1981 was primarily a result of export growth, especially to oil exporters. Japan's export performance was a reflection of improved trade competitiveness resulting from superior supply-side adjustment. From 1980–84 the share of Japan's exports accounted for by machinery—the most technologically advanced component of exports—grew from 37.1 percent to 43.6 percent. No such improvement was visible in the composition of U.S. or FRG exports. In 1982, in the depth of the global recession, the Japanese merchandise trade surplus remained stable, as both imports and exports fell. However, that year Japan's exports were still above their 1980 level, while the exports of the U.S., the FRG, and all of Western Europe had fallen below 1980 levels.

The U.S. trade balance worsened in 1981 and 1982, losing the marginal gains made during the previous two years.[20]

... and on Developing Sector and CPE Trade and Current Account Behavior

The decline in total developed sector domestic demand during Phase VI had a more profound impact on primary input costs than had the recession of 1974/75. Real wage growth in the developed sector declined over the 1981/82 period as unprecedented levels of post-World War II unemployment created soft labor markets.[21]

Further, recession in the developed sector combined with the amelioration of 1978/79 CPE-centered food deficits to put considerable downward pressure on primary commodity prices, which began to fall in 1980/81—a development that continued into 1982. Petroleum prices continued to rise in 1981 as a result of the speculative momentum driven by the outbreak of the Iran-Iraq War. But in the second half of 1981 and especially in 1982, enormous downward pressure on petroleum prices began to build as petroleum export volume collapsed.

In addition to worsening terms of trade, developing sector current account balances were, during Phase VI, also damaged by rising developed sector interest rates—a development that prompted a rise in the sector's net interest deficit (see Table 7.3). For Third World debtors, factor services income balances deteriorated sharply. Only the handful of capital exporting developing countries centered in the Persian Gulf with net investment surpluses with the rest of the world experienced improvement in their factor services income balances.

Further, the momentum of the developed sector's shift to a more deflationary policy included an emphasis on adjustment in developing

TABLE 7.2

NATIONAL AND SECTORAL MERCHANDISE TRADE BALANCES AND EXPORT AND IMPORT GROWTH RATES IN PHASES V AND VI OF CYCLE 3

	Export Growth Rate (Percent)					Import Growth Rate (Percent)				
	1979	1980	1981	1982	1980-82	1979	1980	1981	1982	1980-82
Developed Sector	24.0%	17.7%	-1.2%	-6.0%	-7.1%	29.5%	19.8%	-4.0%	-6.4%	-10.2%
US	29.8%	21.6%	5.7%	-10.9%	-5.8%	20.5%	17.8%	6.1%	-6.6%	-0.8%
Japan	6.1%	25.3%	18.0%	-7.9%	8.7%	40.0%	25.4%	4.0%	-7.7%	-4.0%
Western Europe	25.5%	14.9%	-6.6%	-4.0%	-10.3%	32.3%	19.6%	-10.5%	-5.1%	-16.8%
Developing Sector	37.4%	33.8%	-1.7%	-11.4%	-12.9%	20.8%	29.3%	10.3%	-5.9%	3.8%
Oil Exporters	48.1%	41.6%	-3.4%	-17.1%	-22.5%	7.4%	27.9%	20.6%	-3.8%	16.0%
Oil Importers	26.0%	24.1%	5.0%	4.0%	0.6%	29.6%	30.0%	4.8%	-7.2%	-2.7%
Manufac. Exporters	25.4%	25.8%	13.8%	-4.9%	8.3%	35.1%	27.1%	5.4%	-8.0%	-3.1%
European CPEs*	19.6%	15.2%	1.0%	5.4%	6.1%	12.9%	15.3%	0.1%	-1.2%	-1.1%
Soviet Union*	24.1%	17.9%	3.4%	10.0%	13.7%	14.5%	18.5%	6.6%	6.6%	13.6%
China*	41.2%	33.6%	20.2%	-0.5%	19.7%	44.0%	24.8%	12.2%	-14.1%	-3.6%

Merchandise Trade Balance
($Billions)

	1979	1980	1981	1982
Developed Sector	-$42.2	-$72.3	-$33.3	-$26.3
US	-$27.5	-$25.5	-$28.0	-$36.5
Japan	$1.7	$2.1	$20.0	$18.1
Western Europe	-$26.5	-$63.1	-$26.2	-$17.6
Developing Sector	$68.1	$107.2	$50.5	$17.4
Oil Exporters	$109.2	$171.7	$117.7	$72.1
Oil Importers	-$41.1	-$64.4	-$67.2	-$54.7
Manufac. Exporters	-$15.0	-$20.3	-$11.8	-$6.8

SOURCE: US and Japan - IMF IFS Yearbook 1986; all others - UNCTAD Handbook 1987.

* Imports CIF

TABLE 7.3

THE GROWTH OF DEVELOPING SECTOR DEBT AND NET INTEREST AND THEIR EVOLVING STRUCTURE

	1970	1975	1979	1980	1981	1982
Developing Sector Outstanding Debt ($billions)	$62.7	$169.0	$385.5	$437.9	$484.5	$536.7
Percent Official (%)	71.9%	61.6%	51.6%	53.1%	52.2%	51.0%
Percent Financial Markets (%)	12.1%	26.8%	40.4%	39.9%	41.5%	43.3%
Non-Oil Exporter Outstanding Debt ($billions)	$51.8	$126.0	$272.9	$316.0	$347.7	$383.7
Developing Sector Net Interest ($billions)	-$1.8	-$7.8	-7.2	-8.5	-11.3	-27.2
Oil Importer Net Interest ($billions)	-$2.0	-$6.6	-13.7	-18.8	-28.6	-36.3

SOURCE: UNCTAD Handbook 1986.

sector economies which forced the primary focus of 1974/75—financing their current account deficits—to recede in importance.

From 1980–82 a larger proportion of developing sector current account deficits were being financed from private sources than in 1974–75 (see Table 7.3). Private creditors were, by their nature, less concerned with the global function of "recycling" than with securing profits for their institutions and thus, under certain conditions, more prone than official creditors to constrain lending to developing economies in need.

As a result of the privatization of financing of developing sector current account deficits, maturities shortened, the cost of borrowing rose, and those potential debtors deemed not creditworthy were not provided financing. Indeed, by 1979 non-oil exporting sub-Saharan African and Caribbean economies saw their private financing reduced. With insufficient official financing, these countries led the world economy into an import growth slowdown and eventual contraction.

In 1980, oil importing economies' current account deficits expanded as nonfuel primary commodity prices flattened, oil prices rose, and interest rates began to increase. As a result, developed sector private financing became more cautious, spreads widened, fees grew, and Eurodollar loans slowed.

In 1981, current account pressure on oil importers escalated as nonfuel primary commodity prices fell, oil prices continued to advance, and interest rates rose substantially. In addition, oil importing developing sector borrowers were forced to compete against increasingly more creditworthy and in some cases more profitable investment alternatives. For instance, in 1980 West European balance of payments deterioration sparked increased developed sector borrowing, and in 1981 capital importing oil exporters sought new foreign loans as their export growth rates fell. Finally, the rise in real interest rates sparked an ever-increasing volume of intra-developed sector investment in debt instruments.

The impact of these developments crescendoed in 1981 as the developing sector turned in its first negative GNP per capita growth year (apart from the late 1950s) in the post-World War II period. Debt-related balance of payments crises surfaced throughout sub-Saharan Africa and the Caribbean and spread to Latin America (i.e., Peru and Bolivia). The activity of the IMF increased again. And even in North Africa and West Asia with high concentrations of oil exporters, economic growth weakened.

In 1982 oil prices stopped rising. But stabilization of oil prices was only accomplished at the expense of a collapse in export volume. As a result, capital importing oil exporters saw their external imbalances worsen. Indeed, in August 1982 one of these economies, Mexico, brought into focus the accelerating debt-related balance of payments crisis of the developing sector. Mexico's crisis—because of the size of its debt and the dangerous exposure of developed sector banks in that debt—precipitated a Third World debt crisis, which in fact had been long in the making.[22]

The increased caution of creditors had, in the first half of 1982, caused a shortening in the maturity of new loans. The Mexican crisis turned the earlier caution to panic, as the "recycling" process which had financed developing nation current account deficits since the early 1970s crumbled. The capital markets, the banks, and the bank regulators were all swept by a wave of extreme fear when it came to new developing sector loans. As a result, by the end of 1982 a contraction in capital flows to the developing sector sparked additional debt-related balance of payments crises among large debtors, including Argentina and Brazil.

To prevent a wave of defaults, the IMF, central banks, and governments rushed into ad hoc arrangements to provide liquidity, with the proviso that debtors undertake more dramatic economic adjustments than had hitherto been the case. Ultimately, the absence of sufficient private credit induced a huge import compression in developing sector economies.

The CPEs' imports were also damaged by the decline in primary commodity prices, rising interest rates, and the shrinkage in developed sector manufactured goods markets, especially in Western Europe. Throughout the 1970s the European CPEs' development strategy of redressing insufficient productivity and economic growth through hard currency imports was financed by the rise in petroleum prices and by access to relatively cheap hard currency credits. In 1974/75 the Soviet Union's terms of trade only worsened slightly as oil prices stabilized and oil export volume sagged. From 1979–81, rising petroleum prices improved Soviet terms of trade, but in 1982 petroleum prices stabilized and oil export volume fell sharply. Soviet import growth was, in turn, affected by these developments (see Table 7.2—Soviet Import Growth).

Of more importance, East European economies had financed hard currency imports and current account deficits with hard currency debt. From the absence of hard currency debt at the beginning of the 1970s, the East European CPEs had accumulated a $18.8 billion hard currency debt by 1975, and this grew to a peak of $59.5 billion in 1981. But when East European CPE exports fell due to import compression in Western Europe and as interest rates on its hard currency debt rose, the sector's current account deficits with the West exploded. In 1981 Poland experienced a debt-related hard currency balance of payments crisis that produced a virtual default. Eastern Europe's private creditors were hit with a cold chill of caution, and this chill precipitated an enormous reduction in Eastern Europe's imports from the West in 1981/82. Over that period Poland's hard currency imports were cut in half while Romania's dropped by 40.0 percent.[23]

Another development that hampered aggregate CPE imports in 1981 and 1982 was the "Readjustment" in China launched in 1979. The "selective" trade policy associated with the "Ten Year Plan" was abandoned by newly ascendant reformers under the leadership of Deng Xiaoping, as that program's import goals were considered unaffordable.[24] As a result, China's imports, which grew forcefully in 1978 and 1979, began to tail off in 1980/81, and fell after an economic "retrenchment" in 1982 (see Table 7.2).

SLOWED GROWTH IN WORLD MARKETS AND UNEVEN EXPORT PERFORMANCE MAXIMIZE PRESSURE ON THE POSTWAR TRADE ORDER

While the rates of growth of world import and export volume and value declined in Cycle 3 compared to their performance in Cycle 2, the deceleration was not uniformly experienced in all sectors of the world economy.[25] The decline in the developed sector import growth rate (value) was greatest in Western Europe, while the decline in the world export growth rate (value) was least pronounced in Japan and among the East Asian NIEs. At the end of Cycle 2 in 1975, Western Europe accounted for 63.3 percent of developed sector imports; at the end of Cycle 3 in 1982, it accounted for only 60.2 percent of developed sector imports.[26] Also, at the end of Cycle 2 Japan accounted for 6.4 percent and the NIEs, 4.3 percent of world exports. By the end of Cycle 3 in 1982, Japan accounted for 7.6 percent and the NIEs, 6.8 percent of world exports.[27] These developments were reflected in a shift in the center of post-World War II transoceanic trade from the Atlantic to the Pacific beginning early in Cycle 3.[28]

The more deflationary developed sector economic policies of Cycle 3 acted to reduce the rates of growth of both developed sector markets and developing sector as well as CPE markets from what they had been in the preceding cycle. In Cycle 3 the developed sector import volume growth rate dropped from 6.6 percent a year in Cycle 2, to 4.0 percent, while the developing sector import volume growth rate fell from 7.8 percent a year in Cycle 2 to 5.4 percent.[29] The decelerating expansion of developing sector (and CPE) markets represented the beginning of a reversal from the acceleration in their expansion during Cycle 2—a reversal that turned into a full-scale retreat in Cycle 4. It was precipitated by weaker acceleration in primary commodity prices in Cycle 3 and by the shift in developed sector payments policy toward the developing sector and East European CPEs that erupted at the end of Cycle 3.

As a result of slower growth in developed sector markets, the less robust developing sector and CPE import expansion, and the more competitive export position of Japan and the East Asian NIEs in North American and West European markets, the process of market crowding evident in Cycle 2 intensified, infusing greater vigor into the "new protectionism." At the same time, the less robust growth of developing sector markets and especially those of oil importers gave new voice to the trade diverting planks of the New World Economic Order.

The Decline in Import Vigor

At the beginning of Cycle 3 the most visible development was the weakness in the West European import growth rate (in value) in 1976 and especially 1977, the first year of Phase III—a period in previous cycles when the West European import growth rate had accelerated to lead world import growth. Later, in Phase V of Cycle 3, the domestic demand growth rates and, consequently, the import growth rates (in value) of Japan, the FRG, and the second-tier West European economic powers did not recover as strongly as they had in Phase V of Cycle 2.[30]

Then from 1980–82 the rate of contraction in West European imports (value) was substantially greater than had been the case in 1974/75 and this led to a deeper fall in the aggregate developed sector import growth rate.

One result of the unevenness of the decline in the developed sector import growth rate in Cycle 3 was that the share of West European imports in developed sector imports fell while the share of U.S. imports grew. While Western Europe's share of developed sector imports declined from 1975 to 1982, the U.S. increased its share from 17.1 percent to 20.5 percent.[31]

Further, two developments emerged during the 1976–78 period which suggested that the robust import expansion experienced by the developing sector and the European CPEs in Cycle 2 would deteriorate in Cycle 3.

First, the relative weakness in the primary commodity price performance in Phases II and III implied eventual limits to the import capacity of primary commodity exporters. The limits to unbridled import growth were becoming clear even to oil exporters by 1978. After oil export unit value had stagnated in 1977 and began to decline in 1978, OPEC continued to increase imports at a 20 percent rate. As a result, OPEC suffered a sharp drop in its current account surplus—a drop that could not long be sustained.

And while a mini-boom in export volume helped developing sector oil importers to reduce record 1975 trade deficits in 1976 and a subsequent rise in nonfuel primary commodity prices in 1977 permitted a further drop in these deficits, the principal cause of progress in external balances was constrained import growth. In 1978, the developing sector oil importers' trade deficit rose anew as the terms of trade of nonfuel primary commodities declined in relation to manufactured goods.[32]

Second, the developing sector's import growth since 1974 had been subsidized by a rapidly growing foreign debt. By 1976 the outstanding debt of the developing sector had reached $200 billion, after starting the decade at $60 billion. In addition, a sizable portion of Eastern European hard currency imports had been financed through hard currency debt.

Developing sector debt grew rapidly in the 1974/75 recession, but in 1976 oil importers borrowed at three times the pace of the previous year. That year capital inflow to the developing sector reached $33 billion, with a greater proportion coming from private sources even in the face of growing developing sector debt/GDP and debt service ratios. In 1977, the foreign borrowing binge continued, with over 50 percent of the new money coming from private sources.

A harbinger of the future for most of the developing sector, the foreign debt burden for low income oil importers had already become over-whelming by 1977, their total debt having grown by 76 percent from 1974 to 1977 while debt service grew by 100 percent. In 1978, the Phase III decline in the developing sector trade surplus provoked further enlargement of the stock of the sector's foreign debt, but for low income oil importers, faltering external balances meant mini-balance of payments crises sufficient to prompt their virtual decoupling from the private petrodollar recycling process.

During Phase VI, balance of payments stress for the developing sector and the CPEs escalated. The weak primary commodity price recovery of 1976–78 turned into a primary commodity price rout in 1981/82, and by 1981 developed sector payments policy—which had become more cautious beginning in 1978—took a decidedly deflationary turn. But in 1979/80, the recovery in primary commodity prices and the maintenance of the petrodollar recycling process for most oil importers served to support a new expansion in aggregate developing sector/European CPE imports. And from 1980/81 developing sector oil exporter import growth assumed a larger share of world import growth than in 1974. In 1981, oil exporter imports were the most dynamic in the world.

Nevertheless, the combined developing sector/European CPE market actually contracted in 1982, a development that had not taken place in the 1974/75 recession. The collapse of oil export volume was sufficient to prompt an absolute decline in the imports of developing sector oil exporters in 1982 and a sharp deceleration in Soviet imports in 1981/82. More dramatic was the absolute drop in the imports of capital importing developing economies and the East European CPEs which suffered from a gradual shutdown of the petrodollar recycling process from 1981 to 1982 and from severe declines in nonfuel exports.

Even the oversold China market, which had been heralded in 1978/79 in the wake of the announcement of the "Ten Year Plan," withered in the 1980–82 period.

The Challenge of Japan and NIE Export Growth and the Retreat of Western Europe

In Cycle 2, the explosion in primary input costs undermined the pace of expansion of the world market that had evolved in Cycle 1. This development provoked a slowdown in the rate of growth of world trade and an intensification of market crowding.[33] In Cycle 3, the growth rate of world markets continued to decelerate, and although less vigorous, the culprit was again rising primary input costs which this time were accompanied by more austere developed sector economic policies.

While manufacturing and intra-developed sector trade recaptured their position as the leading forces in world trade from Phase I through Phase III of Cycle 3, both lost a measure of the dynamism they enjoyed over a similar span in the first two cycles. The central cause of declining intra-developed sector trade dynamism was the sizable retreat of West European trade—a retreat that was evident through the entire cycle. The decline of Western Europe's trade in Cycle 3 was the result of its collective turn to a more austere economic policy than in the remainder of the developed sector. These policies helped suffocate the most important component in West European trade since World War II: West European intra-trade. Throughout Cycle 3 West European intra-trade, including EEC and EFTA intra-trade, remained very weak, and as a result developed sector trade under "special arrangement" suffered a decline in its rate of growth. At the end of Cycle 2 in 1975 developed sector "special arrangement" trade accounted for 19.0 percent of world trade, while by the end of Cycle 3 in 1982 it had fallen to 17.9 percent.[34] Leading this retreat was EEC intra-trade, whose share of world trade declined from 16.7 percent in 1975 to 16.1 percent in 1982.

Western Europe also experienced a decline in its investment growth rate in Cycle 3 and this helped undermine West European and especially FRG export competitiveness, a phenomenon in sharp contrast to the continued export dynamism of Japan and the increasingly improved export position of the NIEs. Japan's export competitiveness had reflected itself in Phases I–III of Cycle 2 when the surge in its exports underwrote a substantial rise in its merchandise trade surplus. In Phases I–III of Cycle 3, Japan once again asserted its export prowess by more deeply penetrating U.S. and West European markets, and later Japan was the only area in the developed sector to experience an increase in exports during Phase VI.

The only other economies to increase exports during the 1981/82 recession were the developing sector manufacturing exporters. The rise in export power of the NIEs had been evolving since Cycle 1 when their share of developing sector exports grew, and this process continued through Phases I–III of Cycle 2 before being reversed by the explosion in primary commodity prices. From Phase I through Phase III in Cycle 3, the export power of the NIEs, and especially the East Asian NIEs, reasserted itself, and this became particularly apparent in 1978. In that year the East Asian NIEs enjoyed the Phase III terms of trade advantages of all manufacturing exporters and the Phase IV advantages over developed sector manufacturing exporters Japan and the FRG, whose currencies appreciated against those of the East Asian NIEs (which moved in concert with the U.S. dollar).

The retreat in West European export competitiveness relative to that of Japan and the developing sector manufacturing exporters, especially the East Asian NIEs, was reflected in changes in the share of cross-Pacific and cross-Atlantic trade in total transoceanic trade. By 1976 the Pacific share had already grown larger than that of the Atlantic.

The Takeoff of the "New Protectionism"

Deceleration in the expansion of the developing sector and CPE markets in Cycle 3, especially during the 1981/82 recession, combined with continued retreat in the expansion of developed sector markets and the growing competitive advantages of Japan and the NIEs to severely aggravate the momentum toward market crowding in the North American and West European manufactured goods markets. These pressures were worsened by the emergence of higher developed sector unemployment rates and lower capacity utilization rates. Indeed, in Western Europe unemployment rates from Phases I–III of Cycle 3 recovered little from the 1974/75 recession. Higher unemployment rates served to propel trade issues to the top of the list of concerns of the organized labor movement while the more intense competition for home markets served to heighten the importance of trade issues for the corporate community.

The resulting takeoff in the "new protectionism" caused the percentage of merchandise goods under some form of protection in the developed sector to climb. Managed trade in agriculture, textiles, and footwear spread forcefully in Phases I–III to the steel sector, where U.S. restrictions on Japanese specialty steel exports in 1976 and on EEC steel exports in 1977 were enacted. The wave of managed trade during this period extended to consumer durables, including autos and electronic equipment, and the period climaxed in 1978 with an extension and intensification of the Multi-Fibre Arrangement.

The early surge in the "new protectionism" in Cycle 3, while more vigorous, paralleled its expansion during the same phases of Cycle 2. In each cycle the first spurt of the "new protectionism" appeared in Phase I and grew through Phase III, and in each cycle its momentum moderated in Phase V. This pattern held in Cycle 3, as the early protectionist momentum retreated in 1979/80, as it had in 1972/73. However, in each Phase

VI recession, the momentum of the "new protectionism" regained force, and it is during Phase VI that it has grown most vigorously. In 1981/82, the developed sector was overcome by an avalanche of VRAs, OMAs, countervailing duties and antidumping actions.

In particular, U.S. trade pressure directed at Japan exploded in 1981/82. Economic tensions between the two countries reached a peak in the recession, and only eased as a result of the 1983 economic recovery and a more energetic Japanese effort under Prime Minister Yasuhiro Nakasone to accommodate Washington. In 1981, Japan was forced to accept a VRA on auto exports to the U.S.—a development quickly repeated in Canada and the FRG. Italy and France had already erected barriers to Japanese auto exports. The U.S. pursued a host of additional efforts to constrain Japanese consumer goods exports, including motorcycles and videotape recorders. And from 1980 through 1982, the U.S. International Trade Commission (ITC) was deluged with a massive number of complaints against Japanese exporters. The momentum for managed trade in the U.S. was not only targeted at Japan, but Western Europe as well, as the U.S. secured a VRA on EEC steel exports in 1982.

But Western Europe, too, intensified its efforts to constrain imports, taking particular aim at the NIEs by moving to limit imports of their steel and footwear. And in 1981 the MFA was further enhanced, a move that had a special negative impact on NIE exports.

When the Ministerial Meeting of GATT commenced in late 1982, the postwar system of international trade was clearly on the defensive, with GATT's MFN principle badly battered under the torrent of bilateral trade arrangements secured under duress. The meeting set a goal of rolling back the protectionist momentum that had grown in Cycle 3 through the means of a new GATT negotiating round.[35]

The counterpoint to the "new protectionism" in the developed sector during Cycle 3 was the Tokyo Round of multilateral trade negotiations under GATT, the second major GATT round in the postwar period.[36] Following up on the progress of the Kennedy Round, the Tokyo Round, concluded in 1979, secured a series of member multilateral tariff reductions.

Despite the successes in tariff reduction, the gains to the trading order won in the Tokyo Round paled in comparison to the surge in illiberal trade practices in the developed sector. Moreover, illiberal trading practices had expanded in the developing sector during Cycle 3 as OPEC's aura of power was sufficient to support the rise in oil prices in 1979–81.

The leap in petroleum prices during Cycle 2 undermined the fragile payments balances of the non-oil primary commodity exporters in the developing sector, a group representing the majority of developing sector nations. By Cycle 3, 75 percent of the developing sector economies still depended for 75 percent of their export earnings on primary commodity exports and only a small minority of those nations were oil exporters. In addition, the manufactured goods exports of the developing sector were highly concentrated in only a few nations. By 1973, 70 percent of the developing sector's manufactured exports were accounted for by just ten nations.

In Cycle 2, a movement centered among non-oil primary commodity exporters emerged to promote a regime for stabilizing world commodity prices. Interest in such a trade-diverting regime had long been in the air, especially after the collapse of primary commodity prices in the 1930s and again following the Korean War. However, alternative and more illiberal strategies for blunting the impact of large and uneven fluctuations in primary commodity prices were more easily implemented—"import substitution," because it required no agreement with external powers, and "producer cartels," which also required no developed sector blessing. (The leverage of producers did, however, generate hybrid producer-consumer commodity price arrangements typified by the International Coffee Agreement.)

Nevertheless, the extraordinary balance of payments stress experienced by developing sector non-oil primary commodity exporters in 1974/75 spurred a new movement for arrangements to stabilize primary commodity prices. While some of these balance of payments pressures were relieved by means of petrodollar recycling, low income oil importers found themselves with little chance of obtaining durable lines into the recycling process, and thus became the bedrock supporters of the revived call for a NWEO.

In part, the Tokyo Round extension of a Generalized System of Preferences (GSP) was a developed sector response to the NWEO momentum. Larger concessions were made through the aegis of the Lomé Convention (1975, expanded in 1979), involving the EEC together with most African, Caribbean, and Asian developing nations associated with the metropolitan EEC countries. With these rather unsatisfactory successes, the NWEO momentum crumbled under the weight of the more extreme balance of payments problems that erupted with the 1981/82 recession.

A REVOLUTION IN CAPITAL FLOWS: VOLUME AND DIRECTION

By the end of Cycle 3, two developments had transpired that radically altered the postwar evolution of cross-border capital flows. First, the value of capital flows as a percentage of merchandise trade grew at a more rapid pace than in Cycle 2, and second, this rise in capital flows was driven primarily by intra-developed sector flows—not North-South flows as had been the case in the preceding cycle.

Indeed, by the end of Cycle 3 in 1982, North-South (and West-East) capital flows were on the verge of collapse as developed sector payments policy to developing sector capital importers and East European CPEs turned decidedly contractionary. While dark clouds were converging over North-South (and West-East) capital flows from 1980–82, intra-developed sector flows skyrocketed, as differences in both the degree and the structure of retrenchment in macroeconomic policy among developed economies produced substantial real interest rate differentials. Further, a major wave of developed sector capital market liberalizations which commenced at the end of Cycle 3 extended into Cycle 4, facilitating enlarged capital flows. What had been the junior partner to the enormous expansion in current account imbalances in fostering the acceleration in capital flows in Cycle 2 rushed to a position of dominance at the end of Cycle 3.

Merchandise Trade Imbalances in Cycle 3

In Cycle 2 a principal objective of the postwar monetary order—stable merchandise trade and current account balances—was overwhelmed by the explosive growth in North-South and intra-developing sector trade and current account imbalances unleashed by the surge in primary commodity prices and the more radical rise in the price of oil than in the price of other primary commodities. In Cycle 3 these imbalances continued to grow, as did primary commodity prices and the divergence between oil and non-oil primary commodity prices, although the assertion of a more deflationary developed sector economic policy slowed the pace of the primary commodity price recovery and therefore the growth in North-South imbalances.

In Cycles 1 and 2, a second objective of the postwar monetary order—aligned and stable exchange rates—also faltered, as intra-developed sector macroeconomic policy and development strategy differences became more assertive in the face of rising primary input costs. In Cycle 3, following the discarding of any strategic commitment of nations to adjust macroeconomic policy to maintain stable and aligned exchange rates, both the stability and alignment of those rates withered at a more rapid pace. By the end of Cycle 3, unusual flows of capital spurred by real interest rate differentials and capital market liberalization provoked unprecedented exchange rate misalignments.

The behavior of North-South merchandise trade balances in Cycle 3 reflected the impact of more deflationary developed sector policies and a slower rise in primary input costs. While developing sector merchandise trade balances improved in Phase II (1976/77) of Cycle 3, the pace of improvement was less vigorous than in Phase V of Cycle 2 (1973/74). And the degree of deterioration in the developing sector's merchandise trade balance was slightly greater in Phase III of Cycle 3 (1978) than in Phase III of Cycle 2 (1971). This pattern continued in Phase VI (1981/82) of Cycle 3, when the deterioration in the developing sector merchandise trade balance was greater than in Phase VI (1975) of Cycle 2 despite a more pronounced contraction in developing sector imports.[37]

The distribution of merchandise trade imbalances within the developing sector in Cycle 3 followed the same pattern as that which unfolded in Cycle 2. But in Cycle 3 the pace of improvement in primary commodity exporter merchandise trade balances and the pace of deterioration in developing sector manufacturing exporter merchandise trade balances slowed due to the weaker surge in primary commodity prices and to successful supply-side adjustment strategies in the East Asian NIEs. The degree of improvement in manufacturing exporter merchandise trade balances in 1978 (Phase III) and 1981/82 (Phase VI) were notably stronger than they were at the same points in Cycle 2.

Further, the pace of deterioration in developing sector non-oil and non-food primary commodity exporters' merchandise trade balances—i.e., developing sector primary commodity exporters whose exports were not distorted by special circumstances—was greater in Cycle 3 than in Cycle 2 as non-oil and nonfood primary commodity prices recovered less vigorously in Cycle 3.

The evolution of merchandise trade balances within the developed sector in Cycle 3 reflected growing differentials in macroeconomic policy and export competitiveness as the U.S. merchandise trade balance worsened at a greater pace than it had in Cycle 2. Japan's merchandise trade balance improved at a stronger pace, and although its macroeconomic policy had taken a more deflationary course in Cycle 3, its enhanced export competitiveness played a larger role in securing the advance. The opposite was the case for Western Europe. While its merchandise trade balance deteriorated at a milder pace in Cycle 3, its export competitiveness had weakened. The entirety of the improvement in Western Europe's trade performance in Cycle 3 was the result of a lower rate of growth of imports.

Intra-Developed Sector Capital Flows Take the Lead as the Petrodollar Recycling Process Weakens

In Phase VI of Cycle 3, international capital flows experienced a series of radical transformations—transformations precipitated by the dimension and the character of the developed sector shift to a more contractionary domestic and international economic policy. During Phase VI the ratio of cross-border capital flows to merchandise trade grew at an extraordinary pace, a development to be expected under recession conditions when the magnitude of international trade weakens. But in 1980–82, the unusual rise in the ratio of the size of capital flows to trade was more the responsibility of the scale of growth in capital flows.

In addition to differences in the degree of retrenchment in national

economic policy, meaningful differences arose among leading developed
sector economies in the structure of their monetary and fiscal policy mix.
Western Europe and Japan launched contractionary fiscal and monetary
initiatives while the U.S. restricted its effort to monetary policy. This
yielded significant real and nominal interest rate differentials which
served to catalyze cross-border investment in debt instruments.[38] The dimension of growth in such flows was further enlarged by the magnitude of
the rise in developed sector interest rates, which made investment in debt
instruments more attractive than investment in goods and services.
These flows were also aided by greater liberalization of world capital markets led by Japanese actions in 1980 and by technological advances in
communications and information services which reduced man-made and
technical obstacles to cross-border capital flows.

One result of the acceleration in capital flows was a severe aggravation
of the delinkage of currency values from current account performance,
and this produced unprecedented postwar currency misalignments.
While the Japanese yen appreciated from the fourth quarter of 1980 to
the third quarter of 1982 in accord with its current account performance,
the dollar appreciated by over 25 percent from 1980–82, while its current
account balance was eroding. Also in Phase VI, the European Monetary
System currencies depreciated even though the aggregate EMS current
account balance improved.

In addition to the growth in the magnitude of international capital
flows and currency misalignments, the ratio of intra-developed sector to
North-South (and West-East) capital flows increased substantially during
Phase VI of Cycle 3, and the cause of this phenomenon was not simply
the steep rise in intra-developed sector flows. Another component of the
contractionary economic policy shift in the developed sector—the turn
to a stricter international payments policy—undermined capital flows
from the developed sector to the developing sector. While North-South
capital flows were sustained in 1980–81, they began to slow in 1982 in
concert with the crumbling of the petrodollar recycling process. By the
end of 1982 private capital flows from the developed to the developing
sector had fallen. A similar process erupted in 1981/82 (beginning with
the Polish debt crisis) to sharply reduce capital flows from the developed
sector to Eastern Europe.

The Rise in the Factor Services Income to Merchandise
Trade Ratio

The transition to a more constrictive set of economic policies in the developed sector in Cycle 3 also resulted in important changes in both the
dimensions and the character of services trade (see Table 7.4). Early indications of these changes were visible in Phase III of the cycle. While by

1978 the ratio of services trade to merchandise trade and the ratio of factor services income to non-factor services trade did not deviate from post-war patterns, the share of direct investment income in developed sector factor services income declined while the share of interest income grew. This shift reflected the growth in the stock of international debt relative to growth in direct investment and the more moderate expansion in primary commodity prices in Cycle 3 which slowed growth in direct investment income.

TABLE 7.4 **THE CHANGING DIMENSIONS AND STRUCTURE OF WORLD SERVICES TRADE (Percent)**						
	1970	*1973*	*1978*	*1980*	*1982*	*1984*
Services Trade as a % of Merchandise Trade	36.8	33.3	36.0	37.5	45.3	41.4
Non-Factor Services Trade as a % of Merchandise Trade	27.0	22.9	24.8	22.9	24.9	23.0
Factor Services Income as a % of Merchandise Trade	9.8	10.3	11.1	14.6	20.4	18.4
Interest Income as a % of Factor Services Income	53.9	57.6	71.4	77.9	88.9	86.6
SOURCE: UNCTAD Handbook 1986.						

From 1980–82, a more radical change in the dimensions of services trade emerged, reflecting the impact on services trade of the turn toward more restrictive economic policies in the developed sector. First the ratio of services to merchandise trade grew dramatically. Services trade increased from 36.0 percent to 45.5 percent of merchandise trade from 1980–82. The change was even more pronounced in the developed sector, where the ratio of services to merchandise trade grew from 40.2 percent to 51.7 percent. In the developing sector, the improvement in the ratio was less robust, advancing from 24.1 percent to 30.0 percent.

The greater sensitivity of merchandise trade to a recession suggests that the ratio of services to merchandise trade should grow under recession conditions, and indeed this had been the case in earlier postwar recessions. The 1980–82 rise in the ratio was, however, much larger than in previous recessions, and the ratio of services to merchandise trade in the subsequent cycle, while slightly lower than in the 1981/82 recession, was higher than those experienced in 1980 and earlier. Hence, in Phase VI of Cycle 3 the historically stable relationship between services and merchandise trade that had marked the postwar period was broken.

The superior performance of the developed sector on this score points to the source of the alteration in the relationship between services and merchandise trade. A larger component of developed sector trade was in factor services income than it was for the developing sector. From 1980–

82, the ratio of factor services income to non-factor services trade grew sizably—a development due entirely to an increase in interest income as the ratio of interest income to direct investment income grew at a shocking pace. The rise in interest income was the result of the adoption in the developed sector of much tighter domestic monetary policies which produced higher interest rates. The higher interest rates and the large stock of international debt accumulated during Cycles 2 and 3 produced the major increase in interest income.[39]

8

The Cycle of Disinflation—Phases I–IV: 1983–86

The first four phases of Cycle 4 unfolded from the beginning of 1983 through the first half of 1986, with Phase V commencing in the second half of 1986. Although the current cycle is not complete, important trends in world trade and payments emerged in the first four phases to clearly distinguish Cycle 4 from the earlier ones. And as in all cycles, the features distinguishing this from its predecessors can be traced to the nature of the interaction between developed sector economic policy and primary input costs as well as to the degree of divergence among developed nations' economic policies.

In Cycle 4 as in Cycle 3, aggregate developed sector economic policy has played a more proactive role while primary input costs have assumed a more reactive posture than in Cycle 2. The pivotal difference between Cycles 3 and 4 is that aggregate developed sector macroeconomic policy was more constrictive in the first three phases of the latter than during the same period in the former, and developed sector international payments policy was less accommodative.

The result has been a lower global domestic demand growth rate, which has forced a contraction in primary input costs. Looser labor and primary commodity markets produced deflation in the real prices of both. And the institutions that successfully promoted the advantageous supply/demand position of primary inputs in Cycles 2 and 3—organized labor and OPEC—have been in retreat.

The decline in primary input costs in Cycle 4 underlay the cycle's most distinctive feature, "disinflation"—but at the price of a lower global GNP growth rate.[1]

In Cycle 3, the dimensions of intra-developed sector macroeconomic policy differences widened as the magnitude of differences in government fiscal policy in particular grew more dramatic. While Western Europe and Japan assumed more deflationary fiscal policies in Phases I–III of Cycle 4, the United States adopted a more expansionary fiscal policy and this produced much larger intra-developed sector domestic demand growth rate differentials, which in turn caused greater import growth rate differentials.

Domestic demand growth rate differences in the developed sector were not the only Cycle 4 development that produced a dynamic in world trade more hostile to U.S. external balances. Plummeting primary commodity prices, a more contractionary payments policy toward the developing sector (and the European CPEs), and the retention of tighter domestic monetary policies and higher interest rates in the developed sector undermined developing sector and CPE payments balances, forcing an absolute drop in the combined imports of the two from the recession year of 1982 to 1986, the end of Phase III of Cycle 4. Hence, the domestic demand growth rate differential between the U.S. and the remainder of the world was far greater in the first three phases of Cycle 4 than it had been in the same period in Cycle 3.

The deleterious impact of this development on U.S. external balances was aggravated by unprecedented dollar appreciation. The dollar appreciation of 1980–85 was caused by the growing attractiveness of investment in dollar assets—both financial assets and direct investment. The expansionary U.S. fiscal policy and the contractionary fiscal policies in the remainder of the developed sector produced imbalances in intra-developed sector monetary and fiscal policy mixes that forced U.S. real interest rates up above the developed sector average, spawning enlarged U.S. capital inflow, while higher domestic demand growth in the U.S. produced a more encouraging environment for foreign direct investment than did the more depressed domestic demand condition of the rest of the world.

But the expanding U.S. government fiscal deficit and domestic demand growth did not yield an increase in U.S. goods and services price inflation or meaningful inflation differentials with the rest of the developed sector. Indeed, the U.S. inflation rate fell and therefore did not produce conditions in the United States hostile to either direct investment or investment in financial assets (i.e., accelerating inflation or bigger intra-developed sector inflation rate differentials). Instead, in the first three phases of Cycle 4 the U.S. successfully exported what would have been a dramatic rise in domestic goods and services price inflation to the rest of the world through the aegis of trade and current account deficits.

PHASE I–THE U.S. IMPORT EXPANSION
STANDS ALONE

Phase I (1983/84) of the current cycle began with an economic recovery in the developed sector centered in the United States and, repeating the pattern of the previous cycles, initial growth in world trade was heavily predicated on an expansion of U.S. imports. However, in 1983/84 the importance of the U.S. recovery to world trade growth was significantly greater than it had been in previous cycles.[2] Moreover, the role which West European imports played in stimulating world trade growth was smaller than it had been in 1976.

Two factors underlay these Phase I developments. First and of greatest importance, the strength of each world trade recovery since 1968 has been augmented by the expansion of developed sector public deficits. However, following the 1968–75 cycle the willingness of Western Europe and Japan to adopt more expansionary fiscal policies declined while the U.S.'s willingness increased. In Phases I–III of Cycle 3 (1976–78) the rate of growth of West European and Japanese public deficits advanced at a slower pace while that of the U.S. grew at a faster pace than during the same period in Cycle 2. Then from 1980 through 1982, Western Europe and Japan used both domestic monetary and fiscal tools to reduce inflation, while the U.S. resorted only to domestic monetary initiatives.

Western Europe, under the pressure of inflation and balance of payments stress, carried the restrictive macroeconomic policies it had adopted in 1980–82 into the 1983 recovery, and Japan held to the objective determined by the Liberal Democratic Party in 1979 of cutting the government fiscal deficit as a percent of GNP.[3] While in the U.S. real interest rates remained unprecedentedly high, one component of developed sector macroeconomic policy moved contrary to the deflationary momentum during Phase I: U.S. government fiscal policy. From a large, recession-generated deficit in FY81, the U.S. government fiscal deficit doubled in size for two consecutive years—FY82 and FY83—and hovered within a range of $175–$225 billion until FY86.[4] It was these U.S. government fiscal deficits that enlarged the magnitude of what would have otherwise been a relatively weak cyclical recovery in the U.S. The deficits also produced domestic demand growth rate differentials between the U.S. on the one hand and Japan and Western Europe on the other in 1983/84 which greatly exceeded those of 1976.[5]

Second, the dollar exchange rate misalignment in 1983/84 was greater than in 1976. The dollar had appreciated 25.9 percent in effective terms in 1981/82 and appreciated by another 14.1 percent in 1983/84.[6] In 1976, the dollar only appreciated by 5.2 percent.

The Impact on Import Growth Rates

The importance of U.S. import growth in supporting world trade in Phase I of Cycle 4 is reflected in the fact that in the first year of recovery, 1983, no other major component of the world economy except the CPEs experienced import growth (see Table 8.1). In 1983 Western Europe, including the Federal Republic of Germany, Italy, and France, suffered import contractions just as they had in the 1981/82 recession. Japan's imports also declined during 1983, while developing sector imports as a whole fell, led by the imports of oil exporters and heavily indebted developing nations. Even the NIEs experienced lower imports.

The consolidation of more austere economic policies outside of the U.S. early in Cycle 4 produced two unique developments. While in Phase I of previous cycles developing sector imports had been weak, never had they contracted as they did in 1983. And never in Phase I of previous cycles had developed sector imports outside of the U.S. declined.

Further, in 1984 when U.S. imports grew at a vigorous pace, most other sectors of the world economy had still not yet recovered to 1982 import levels (see Table 8.1). West European imports in 1984 were still below those of 1982, including those of the FRG, France, and Italy. Of Western Europe's major economies, only the United Kingdom's imports had grown—by 5.9 percent—above 1982 levels. Developing sector imports fell sharply below 1982 levels in 1984 as oil exporter imports collapsed (see Table 8.1). In the two sectors containing the largest number of troubled debtors, Latin America and sub-Saharan Africa, imports fell dramatically in 1984 from their 1982 levels.

The only sectors of the world economy aside from the United States showing improvement in imports from 1982–84 were Japan, developing sector manufacturing exporters, and the European CPEs, and the only area of the world economy whose import growth rate surpassed that of the United States from 1982–84 was China (see Table 8.1).

Changes in Developed Sector External Balances

Large import growth differentials radically accelerated the worsening of U.S. merchandise trade and current account balances (see Table 8.1). The expansion of the U.S. merchandise trade deficit in 1983 and 1984 was complemented by a reduction in the U.S. services trade surplus, causing the U.S. current account deficit to mushroom from $8.7 billion in 1982 to $107.1 billion in 1984.[7]

In 1983/84 the non-U.S. developed sector saw trade and current account balances improve markedly. Western Europe's merchandise trade deficit declined in 1983 and in 1984 it swung into surplus, underwriting improvements in the region's current account balance (see Table 8.1),

TABLE 8.1

DISTRIBUTION OF WORLD MERCHANDISE TRADE BALANCES AND EXPORT AND IMPORT GROWTH IN PHASES I-III OF CYCLE 4

	Merchandise Trade Balance ($Billions)					Export Growth Rate (FOB) (Percent)					Import Growth Rate (FOB) (Percent)				
	1982	1983	1984	1985	1986	1983	1984	1982-84	1985	1986	1983	1984	1982-84	1985	1986
US	-$36.5	-$67.1	-$112.5	-$122.2	-$144.3	-4.5%	9.0%	4.1%	-1.8%	3.9%	8.6%	23.6%	34.2%	1.7%	9.1%
Japan	$18.1	$31.5	$44.3	$56.0	$92.8	5.7%	15.7%	22.2%	3.4%	18.2%	-4.7%	8.8%	3.7%	-4.8%	-4.4%
FRG	$25.0	$21.4	$21.9	$28.6	$56.0	-3.7%	0.9%	-2.8%	7.7%	32.9%	-1.7%	0.6%	-1.1%	4.2%	20.4%
Western Europe	-$18.7	-$5.7	$3.1	$11.1	$37.5	-0.9%	2.7%	1.8%	5.1%	22.7%	-2.8%	1.4%	-1.4%	4.0%	19.4%
Developed Sector	-$27.5	-$25.4	-$50.1	-$39.4	-$3.2	-0.2%	6.5%	6.2%	3.1%	16.4%	-0.4%	8.5%	8.0%	1.9%	13.3%
Developing Sector	$17.8	$24.2	$54.2	$57.2	$19.6	-5.0%	4.9%	-0.4%	-5.3%	-9.0%	-6.6%	-1.7%	-8.2%	-6.6%	-1.0%
Oil Exporters	$72.8	$61.1	$69.5	$65.5	$21.4	-13.3%	-1.4%	-14.4%	-9.3%	-32.4%	-12.1%	-7.2%	-18.4%	-11.0%	-14.9%
Oil Importers	-$55.0	-$36.8	-$15.3	-$8.3	-$1.8	3.8%	10.5%	14.8%	-2.0%	8.4%	-3.2%	1.4%	-1.8%	-4.3%	5.8%
Manufacturing Exporters	-$6.9	$5.5	$20.0	$25.1	$28.6	7.6%	17.1%	26.0%	0.2%	11.3%	-2.6%	6.2%	3.5%	-3.6%	10.7%
Latin America	$5.4	$27.7	$34.9	$28.5	$11.1	-0.1%	3.6%	3.5%	-7.2%	-14.2%	-21.8%	-4.1%	-25.0%	-2.1%	3.4%
CMEA-6, Hard Currency						2.4%	5.4%	8.0%	-3.8%	-0.4%	-0.5%	2.1%	1.2%	5.6%	8.9%
European CPE - Total*						7.8%	-1.2%	-2.7%	-2.2%	10.5%	6.3%	-1.3%	4.9%	2.9%	10.7%
USSR - Hard Currency						1.8%	-3.0%	-1.2%	-14.8%	-6.7%	-1.3%	-3.6%	-4.8%	-2.6%	-10.5%
USSR - Total (Imports-CIF)						5.1%	0.4%	5.5%	-5.1%	11.8%	3.3%	0.4%	2.9%	2.5%	7.5%
China (Imports-CIF)						1.4%	12.2%	13.7%	9.6%	13.9%	12.7%	23.0%	38.6%	62.2%	0.2%

*USSR, CMEA-6, and Albania

SOURCE: USSR, CMEA-6 Hard Currency Import and Export Growth - PlanEcon, Sept. 17, 1987, Vol. III, Nos. 36, 37, and 38; US, Japan, FRG - IMF IFS Yearbook 1986 and Nov. 1988; All others - UNCTAD Handbook 1987.

which moved from a deficit of $3.4 billion in 1982 to a surplus of $28.2 billion in 1984. As in Cycle 3, Western Europe's merchandise trade and current account improvement was the result of import compression as its exports actually fell in 1983 before recovering in 1984, following much the same pattern as U.S. exports. From 1982–84 its imports decreased (see Table 8.1).

A leading force in West European trade, the Federal Republic symptomized the degree of decline in the region's export performance. The FRG's trade surplus stabilized from 1982 through 1984, even though its exports were still lower in 1984 than they were in 1982 because its imports over the period declined.

Like Western Europe, Japan experienced improvement in its trade and current account balances from 1982–84 (see Table 8.1). The Japanese merchandise trade surplus more than doubled and its current account surplus grew from $6.9 billion in 1982 to $35.0 billion in 1984. But unlike Western Europe, Japan's improved external balances were due to export growth rather than to import compression. While its imports did contract during 1983, they grew from 1982–84, whereas Western Europe's declined over the same period. On the other hand, Japan's exports grew in 1983 when Western Europe's fell, and from 1982–84 Japan's exports grew at a brisk pace while Western Europe's exports barely advanced and the FRG's declined.

PHASE II—AN UNEXPECTED EROSION IN PRIMARY COMMODITY PRICES

Just as the Phase I economic recovery in the developed sector precipitated primary commodity price advances in earlier cycles, it did so again in 1983. However, while the primary commodity price recovery was stronger in 1976/77 than it had been during the previous cycle in 1969/70, it was weaker in 1983/84 than in 1976/77. In 1983 nonfuel primary commodity prices enjoyed a short-lived recovery while oil prices dipped. In 1984—the peak year of the economic recovery—primary commodity prices failed to grow.[8]

There were seven reasons for the unexpectedly poor performance of primary commodity prices in Phase II of the current cycle:

- The overriding cause was a weak developed sector and global domestic demand growth rate.[9]
- The drop in oil prices in 1983/84 was in part a result of pressures produced in Phase VI of Cycle 3 whose impact had been delayed until Phase II of Cycle 4 as a result of Persian Gulf instability and the speculative character of the oil market.

- Because of higher priced primary commodities, in Cycles 2 and 3 the developed sector sought primary commodity substitutes, enhanced domestic primary commodity output, and launched efforts to constrain primary commodity use in order to reduce the burden of high priced primary commodity imports, especially petroleum.

- In a more dramatic fashion than had occurred in 1976/77, Western Europe's import growth weakened relative to that of the U.S., and since the composition of Western Europe's imports is more weighted to primary commodities than is that of the U.S., world import growth in 1983/84 put less pressure on primary commodity supplies.

- The principal developed sector importer, the United States, increasingly produced less of the merchandise it consumed, and at an accelerating pace U.S. domestic growth in 1983/84 was weighted more than in the past to services—a sector less primary commodity intensive than the goods producing sector.

- High interest rates and the negative results of carrying large primary commodity inventories built up in 1979/80 into the 1981/82 recession combined to convince the developed sector to work with leaner inventories than in the past.

- Finally, the debt problems of the developing sector forced it to increase primary commodity export volume, which had the effect of depressing unit values.

Nonfuel primary commodities enjoyed a brief price recovery in 1983 after a severe decline from 1980–82. While the price drop of nonfuel primary commodities was greater during the 1981/82 recession than it had been during the 1974/75 recession, their price advance in Phase II of Cycle 4 (1983/84) was weaker than in Phase II of Cycle 3 (1976/77). After progressing in 1983, nonfuel primary commodity price growth unexpectedly slowed in 1984, and by the end of that year the nonfuel primary commodity price index was still 13.4 percent below that of 1980.

Unlike 1976 when oil prices rose, in 1983 they fell by 10.4 percent. The soft demand for petroleum caused by the structure and the weakness of the economic recovery placed enormous downward pressure on oil prices—a pressure that was contested with partial success in March 1983 when OPEC agreed to production quotas. But despite the fact that 1984 was the first year since 1979 in which aggregate world demand for oil increased (a development partially induced by nonmarket circumstances—i.e., the advent of the British coal miners' strike), oil prices fell by 2.2 percent.[10]

As a result of price and export volume losses, oil exporter exports contracted from 1982–84, whereas from 1975–77 they had grown sizably. In addition, from 1982–84 developing sector oil importer exports grew at almost half the rate at which they advanced from 1975–77. Total developing sector exports declined by 0.4 percent from 1982–84.

While the sector's export earnings declined, interest rates remained high, causing an expansion of the developing sector's factor services income deficit. Further, since much of the developing sector foreign debt accumulated in 1981/82 was short term, principal repayments became bunched up in the 1983/84 period. And the contractionary thrust in developed sector payments policy produced a serious shrinkage in the net external borrowing of the developing sector, down from $127.2 billion in 1981 to $56.1 billion in 1984.[11] As a result, in 1983/84 the developing sector experienced severe balance of payments stress.

Capital surplus developing sector nations began liquidating foreign assets to relieve the stress.[12] And by 1984 capital deficit developing nations became, for the first time in the post-World War II period, net capital exporters to the developed sector—that is, developing sector debtors registered a net negative balance on factor services income and long-term capital accounts combined.[13] If "errors and omissions"—a category in which developing sector deficits were particularly high from 1980–84 and which reflects flight capital and unreported factor services income flows—are added, the net capital exports of these economies in 1984 were much greater than reported.[14] Under these conditions, capital importing developing economies were left with only one vehicle for balancing payments—cutting imports.

In 1983 in particular, the sudden and severe deterioration in capital account balances due to the cutback in private loans prompted a series of debt-related balance of payments crises which served to advance the momentum set in motion by the Latin America-centered balance of payments crises of late 1982. Additional ad hoc financial packages were put together to advance lines of credit in order to avoid default. A portion of the new money was squeezed from developed sector governments, the IMF, and other multilateral lending institutions, followed by small increments of private credit. In exchange for avoidance of default, debtor nations pledged to take measures to adjust external and domestic imbalances.

As revealed in the mammoth collapse of imports in Latin America and Africa in 1983/84, merchandise trade deficits of debtors were turned into surpluses by means of import compression.

The developing sector merchandise trade surplus more than doubled from 1982 to 1984, even though exports declined (see Table 8.1). The sector's current account deficit was by these means more than cut in half. Latin America, which accounted for a disproportionate share of developing sector international debt, improved its merchandise trade surplus from 1982–84 although exports from the region barely grew.

Moreover, oil exporters, who suffered an absolute drop in exports from 1982–84, managed to stabilize their trade surplus over the period by taking equally sharp cuts in imports.

The only segment of the developing sector able to increase imports from 1982–84 were the manufacturing exporters, and this was the result of their continued export dynamism as their exports grew—even faster than those of Japan.

The decline in primary commodity prices and the tougher developed sector international payments approach also undermined the import growth of the European CPEs. The deterioration in primary commodity terms of trade, especially for petroleum, weakened the purchasing power of Soviet hard currency exports, as total Soviet exports from 1982–84 rose at a slow pace and hard currency exports shrank. Reflecting the impact of weaker export growth, Soviet imports grew only marginally from 1982–84 and hard currency imports fell (see Table 8.1).

The commodity composition of trade for the CPEs of Eastern Europe is different from that of the USSR. The composition of their exports is less dominated by primary commodities, but like the USSR the bulk of their hard currency trade is with Western Europe. In 1983/84, Eastern Europe's access to hard currency capital markets was still highly constricted and its principal export market—Western Europe—remained weak. Nevertheless, from 1982–84 the region was able to increase its hard currency exports (see Table 8.1). Export growth was insufficient to offset high interest rates on hard currency debt and the absence of hard currency capital inflow from the West. As a result, this sector's total imports experienced only marginal improvement while hard currency imports grew by only 1.2 percent from 1982–84, after falling by 16.6 percent in 1982.[15]

The only market outside of the United States which grew rapidly was the very small Chinese market. China's imports advanced by 38.6 percent from 1982–84. But China's exports grew by only 13.7 percent. Thus, Beijing was rapidly running down its foreign reserves accumulated over the 1980–82 period and was beginning to borrow heavily in Western capital markets.

PHASE III—THE DESCENT OF THE WORLD IMPORT GROWTH RATE

Just as the initial surge in world output and trade growth subsided in 1977 and, especially, 1978, the output and trade growth of Cycle 4's Phase I began to subside in the second half of 1984. But the decline of world output and trade growth rates was steeper than it had been in 1977 or 1978. Output growth declined from 4.7 percent in 1984 to 2.9 percent in 1985, while world trade growth (in volume) fell from 9.0 percent in 1984 to 3.5 percent in 1985.

By 1984 the growth of the U.S. government fiscal deficit incited a process that ultimately culminated in the Gramm-Rudman federal budget deficit reduction legislation of 1985. While effective deficit reduction did not take place in FY85 or FY86, the U.S. federal government deficit did reach a plateau.[16] The absence of large new injections of government fiscal stimulus into the U.S. economy left it open to cyclical decline.

Indeed, the U.S. GNP growth rate fell by more than 50 percent in 1985 from its 1984 level.[17] As the U.S. domestic demand growth rate sank, other developed nations failed to pick up the slack.[18] As a result, the developed sector import growth rate collapsed in 1985 and the U.S. import growth rate fell even more rapidly than that of the developed sector (see Table 8.1). By 1985 the U.S. import growth rate differential with the rest of the developed sector had vanished.

While the U.S. domestic demand growth rate declined in 1985, those of Japan and Western Europe showed little improvement. Thus, convergence was a one-way street resulting solely from the slide in the U.S. domestic demand growth rate as Western Europe and Japan continued to suffer from restrictive monetary and fiscal policies.

As a result of the decline in the U.S. import growth rate, the rate of expansion in the U.S. trade and current account deficits slowed significantly (see Table 8.1). After rising by $45.4 billion in 1984, the U.S. merchandise trade deficit grew by only $9.7 billion in 1985, and after growing by $64.8 billion in 1984, the U.S. current account deficit grew by only $9.3 billion. The importance of the decline in the U.S. import growth rate in moderating the pace of deterioration in U.S. external balances was amplified by the fact that U.S. exports decreased in 1985.

The ratcheting down of the U.S. import growth rate had an immediate impact on Japan's trade performance. Japan's economy felt the slowdown in U.S. import growth from the second half of 1984, as the Japanese export growth rate slowed to a crawl (see Table 8.1). The export slowdown weakened Japan's import demand, which combined with lower world primary commodity prices in 1985 to reduce Japan's imports. The Japanese experience was duplicated for the East Asian NIEs; NIE exports actually declined slightly but imports fell at a greater pace (see Table 8.1).

The fall in the aggregate developed sector domestic demand growth rate in 1985 led to pronounced downward pressure on primary commodity prices. Although developing sector terms of trade deteriorated in 1978 (Phase III of Cycle 3), primary commodity prices did not fall. In 1985, the first year of Phase III of Cycle 4, however, the losses in terms of trade for the developing sector were deeper and primary commodity prices did drop.

In 1985 a 15.5 percent decline in food prices led a 13.0 percent retreat in nonfuel primary commodity prices.[19] Notwithstanding food deficits in sub-Saharan Africa, efforts in the 1970s to increase food self-sufficiency in the developing sector, a rural-based economic revival in China, and the absence of sectoral recessions in Soviet agriculture had advanced world food supplies, undermining those conditions that had prompted higher food prices in Cycles 2 and 3.

The cause of pressure on nonfood primary commodity prices in 1985 was the relatively low rate of developed sector import growth, leaner inventories, and the availability of alternatives for nonfood primary commodities. By the end of 1985 nonfuel primary commodity prices had sunk 24.1 percent below what they were in 1980.

Petroleum exporter exports fell in 1985 due to reduced oil export volume (see Table 8.1). A collapse of oil prices was only averted when OPEC "swing producer" Saudi Arabia reduced its production, while other OPEC members, under greater financial pressures, repeatedly exceeded new output quotas that had been negotiated at the end of 1984 in an effort to stem the price decline.

The reduction in developed sector interest rates in 1985, led by U.S. interest rates, helped moderate the burden that declining exports placed on developing sector current account balances, but since the total volume of developing sector debt grew in 1985 over 1984, this relief was in part offset. In addition, developed sector private capital flows to the developing sector shrank to a trickle and IMF net flows to that sector sank close to zero due to increased repayments on previous IMF loans.[20]

The combination of these factors produced two developments. First, it provoked a new wave of flight capital which undermined developing sector reserves and helped spark a series of new debt-related balance of payments problems starting with Mexico in the middle of 1985.[21] Second, significant downward pressure was once again placed on developing sector imports.

In addition to the developing sector's export losses, Soviet petroleum exports plummeted due to volume contraction. While total Soviet exports fell, imports continued to grow, and while Soviet hard currency exports dropped dramatically, hard currency imports retreated at a slower pace (see Table 8.1). To finance its hard currency current account deficit, Moscow turned to the Western capital markets and borrowed $5.0 billion.[22]

Aggregate East European CPE imports also grew more rapidly than exports in 1985 while hard currency imports increased, even though hard currency exports declined (see Table 8.1). As in the case of the USSR, Eastern Europe's hard currency current account deficit was financed by means of a return to the developed sector capital markets with borrowings up to $5.7 billion.[23]

Finally, in 1985 China's imports grew much more vigorously than exports. In addition to further drawing on its reserves, China moved deeper into the Western capital markets, borrowing $4.0 billion.[24]

Thus, CPE import growth in 1985, subsidized by hard currency debt, offset part of the drag on world import growth caused by the decline in developing sector imports.

PHASE IV—ENTER THE PLAZA ACCORDS AND THE BAKER PLAN

By the middle of 1985 three alarming trends had surfaced: world economic growth was weakening, U.S. external imbalances were still growing (albeit more slowly), and debt-related developing sector balance of payments crises were on the verge of erupting anew. Responding to these Phase III conditions, the U.S. government once again resorted to a set of tactical objectives similar to those pursued by Nixon on August 15, 1971, and by the Carter Administration in 1977/78, at similar points in the preceding two cycles.

Even before these initiatives were launched, from late 1984 through 1985, efforts were made to prop up economic growth by pumping additional stimulus into the U.S. economy through domestic monetary means. Nominal interest rates were permitted to fall continuously and M1 growth was allowed to surge above the Federal Reserve upper limit target.[25] As a result, U.S. private debt in the form of household and corporate debt—which had already been growing above historic rates earlier in Cycle 4—continued its dynamic expansion. Nonfinancial U.S. debt, private and public, grew relative to nominal GNP in 1985 at a faster pace than in 1983/84, which itself was above the 1970s rates.[26]

Then in September 1985, U.S. Treasury Secretary James Baker III, with the public support of the other member nations of the Group of Five (the "G-5," comprising the U.S., Japan, the FRG, France, and the U.K.), ushered in a period of dollar depreciation. The decline in the U.S. GNP growth rate in late 1984, the continued expansion of the U.S. merchandise trade deficit, and the contraction in manufacturing sector employment put new vigor into protectionist political momentum in the United States, which escalated in early 1985, taking aim at Japan. The force and momentum of the congressionally centered protectionist movement concerned the Reagan Administration and helped convince an alarmed Japan and Western Europe of the need for dollar depreciation. The G-5 agreement to depreciate the dollar came directly on the heels of initial market-induced dollar depreciation beginning in February 1985. With developed sector governments and the markets in agreement on the dollar's fate, a future depreciation was inevitable.

While the targets for dollar depreciation were unclear, equally nebulous was the nature of the commitments of the participants to coordinate their macroeconomic policies toward the end of reducing external imbalances.

Soon after the September 1985 Plaza agreement, the U.S. Treasury Secretary introduced the so-called "Baker Plan" aimed at addressing the growing liquidity needs of the developing sector.[27] In exchange for pledges to liberalize domestic economic and trade and payments policies, developing sector debtors in need of liquidity to reduce balance of payments stress would, under the Baker Plan, be able to secure financing to service their old debts from a new pool of official and private funds. The objective of the Plaza agreement and the Baker Plan was to reverse the prospects for the faltering world economic expansion, restore growth in the overindebted economies of the developing sector, and reduce U.S. external imbalances.

The Plaza Accords lasted until February 1987 when they were superseded by the Louvre Accords of the Group of Seven (now also including Canada and Italy). Over the life of the Plaza Accords, dollar depreciation against West European and Japanese currencies was greater than in 1971–73 or 1977–79. From 1971–73, the dollar depreciated 17.0 percent; in 1977–79, the dollar's effective exchange rate depreciated 11.0 percent. But from the first quarter of 1985 through the first quarter of 1987 and the Louvre Accords, the dollar depreciated 30.4 percent. Dollar depreciation against the yen, the deutsche mark, and many other West European currencies was even more substantial.

In addition, several initiatives reflecting macroeconomic coordination did unfold in 1986, especially between the U.S. and Japan, through the vehicle of coordinated interest rate reductions. Nevertheless, the G-5/ G-7 process from September 1985 to February 1987 hardly suggested agreement on critical issues among the players and it was replete with implied threats, pressure, and bluff among the three key participants, the U.S., Japan, and the FRG, with the pressure generally directed by the United States at the other two.

Both Tokyo and Bonn were increasingly fearful that the size of dollar depreciation would drive their economies—now more dependent than at any time since the mid-1960s on the U.S. market—into recession. These fears provoked huge Japanese and West European intervention into the currency markets to constrain the dollar's fall in the second and third quarters of 1986 and later that year brought forth increasing political pressure from these countries for a halt to the depreciation.

The United States was generally unsatisfied with the level of government stimulus that the FRG in particular was prepared to contribute during the life of the Plaza Accords, while the FRG and Japan were concerned about the inflationary consequences of a shift to reflationary policies at home. Thus, just below the surface of G-5/G-7 coordination lay fundamental disagreements, just as had been the case in 1971–73 and 1977/78, and the disagreements were over the same issues. The Louvre Accords were the result of Japanese and West European pressure to halt the dollar depreciation, signs of willingness, especially on the part of Japan, to reflate, and concerns emanating from the Federal Reserve and its Chairman Paul Volcker that the pace of dollar depreciation could become less controllable, a prospect that would bring counterproductive repercussions.

The G-7 agreement at the Louvre was the functional equivalent of Phase V developments in the two previous cycles—the Smithsonian Agreement of 1971 and the Bonn Summit agreement of 1978. At the Louvre, the G-7 agreed to put a halt to the fall of the dollar, to accomplish this by means of joint currency intervention if necessary, and to coordinate macroeconomic policies to reduce external imbalances.[28] It addressed the concern of Japan, the West Europeans, and the Fed by coordinating action to bring a halt to the dollar's long slide and it addressed the concern of the U.S. Administration that Tokyo and Bonn take additional reflationary steps. Soon after, Nakasone outlined a $40 billion, multiyear public works and tax cut package and Bonn pledged to move up the date for a phased $22 billion tax cut.

The Baker Plan to provide additional balance of payments financing for developing sector debtors in need made little visible headway, as private creditors balked at funding the plan. Moreover, debtor response to the plan was cool, and developed sector governments under domestic pressure to cut their own deficits were reticent to fund a World Bank component of the program.

Although there were obstacles to the Baker Plan, an eleventh-hour stabilization package worked out between Mexico and developed sector monetary authorities in 1986 and grudgingly agreed to by Mexico's private creditors represented a version of that plan. Despite implementation of the arrangement—whereby Mexico was accorded $12 billion in new loans—there was little real recovery in the Mexican economy. Economic growth was barely positive and the country continued to suffer from triple-digit inflation.

And while Mexico's finances temporarily recovered in 1987 as a result of the loan and the partial revival of oil prices from their 1986 collapse, the financial condition of most other debtors—led by Argentina and Brazil—deteriorated, and relationships with private creditors and monetary authorities became more tense.

1986: THE COMBINED IMPACT OF PHASES III AND IV ON WORLD TRADE

In 1986 the impact of dollar depreciation on world trade was overshadowed by the drop in petroleum prices, a Phase III development deferred by Saudi actions from 1985 to 1986. By the end of 1985, after oil prices inched up on a wave of speculative activity caused by an escalation in the Iran-Iraq War, world oil prices came under massive downward pressure. When speculative buying stopped, maximum pressure again fell on "swing producer" Saudi Arabia who had lost export earnings in 1985 by cutting production to prop up prices.[29] With the rest of OPEC continuing to flagrantly cheat on production quotas, making repeated use of the spot market and countertrade, the Saudi government—after several suggestive forays in 1985 involving large countertrade arrangements of its own at below-market prices—began to increase production systematically.

The weakening of OPEC burst into the open in the first months of 1986. The fall in oil prices had been delayed and the force of pent-up downward pressure, once unleashed, pushed prices down well below what most observers had anticipated.

Petroleum prices dropped by 40.7 percent in 1986, falling 20 percent below what they were in real terms in 1974, and it was not until December that OPEC was able to regather itself and establish a consensus on production quotas sufficient to generate some recovery in prices. With nonfuel primary commodity prices still declining (by 3.8 percent in 1986), real prices for primary commodities as a whole had reached a 50-year low by July.

The 1986 retreat of primary commodity prices translated into a 20 percent contraction in developing sector terms of trade. The terms of trade of individual oil exporters fell anywhere from 15 percent to 60 percent.

This Phase III primary commodity price deflation combined with dollar depreciation to produce pronounced shifts in the global distribution of merchandise trade imbalances in 1986. The oil price fall and the continued decline in nonfuel commodity prices provided the developed sector with a $94 billion terms of trade windfall, an advantage that was, however, unevenly distributed because of the different exposure of developed sector economies to imported primary commodities. The greatest terms of trade advantages accrued to Japan, followed by Western Europe and then North America.

In addition, the large appreciations of the yen and of most West European currencies against the dollar drove up the value of Japanese and West European exports to the U.S. and to economies with currencies tied to the dollar and drove down the value of their imports from the U.S., from economies with dollar-linked currencies, and from dollar-denominated commodities such as oil. Terms of trade advantages flowing from this development were of more benefit to Japan than to Western Europe because a larger portion of Japan's total trade was with the U.S. and economies with currencies tied to the dollar. Combined, these terms of trade advantages resulted in a large expansion of Japanese and FRG merchandise trade and current account surpluses, even though the volume of Japan's exports actually fell by 1.4 percent and the growth rate of the FRG's export volume declined from 6.4 percent in 1985 to 1.2 percent in 1986 (see Table 8.1). Indeed, the decline in export volume in Japan and its weak growth in the FRG and the enlarged growth of Japanese and FRG imports in volume in 1986 damaged their net export performance, and this was reflected in their GNP growth.

While Japanese and FRG GNP growth suffered, their merchandise trade and current account surpluses grew. Japan's merchandise trade surplus rose forcefully in 1986 (see Table 8.1) and its current account surplus almost doubled, rising from $49.2 billion in 1985 to $85.8 billion. The FRG's merchandise trade surplus doubled in 1986 (see Table 8.1), and its current account surplus more than doubled, growing from $15.7 billion in 1985 to $37.7 billion. The terms of trade advantage accruing to Japan and the FRG as a result of oil price collapse and dollar depreciation were most visible in their oil imports, for which the price is denominated in dollars. In 1986, it required 65–70 percent less yen or marks to buy the same volume of oil as it had in 1985.

Outside of the United States, of the major developed economies only the United Kingdom suffered an expansion in its merchandise trade deficit in 1986, as U.K. losses on petroleum exports were not outweighed by gains from dollar depreciation.

The U.S. merchandise trade deficit continued to grow in 1986 despite the terms of trade advantage rendered by falling primary commodity prices (see Table 8.1). The early J-curve effect drove up U.S. import prices in 1986 and the U.S. merchandise trade deficit rose from $122.2 billion to $144.3 billion, as imports grew more rapidly than in 1985. The size of the increase in the U.S. current account deficit in 1986 was even greater than that in the merchandise trade deficit. Declining primary commodity prices damaged the magnitude of U.S. direct investment income. The dollar depreciation did, however, ease pressure on the U.S. net investment balance as dollar-denominated assets lost value, as did the income generated from such foreign investment (most portfolio investment in the U.S. originated in economies whose currencies appreciated against the dollar in 1986).

Although by the fourth quarter of 1986 the U.S. net export deficit in constant dollars began to decline, the trade deficit in current dollars continued to rise. Hence, with some lag dollar depreciation resulted in increments to U.S. GNP growth, just as it had rendered losses to GNP growth in Japan and the FRG.

One reason why U.S. net exports in constant dollars did not respond earlier to dollar depreciation was the existence of more dynamic third force exporters in Cycle 4—those manufacturing exporters whose currencies did not appreciate against the dollar or did so only marginally. This was the case with most developing sector manufacturing exporters, who in 1986 were able to capture a disproportionate share of Japanese and West European export volume losses in the U.S. market and more deeply penetrate the Japanese and West European markets.

East Asian NIEs increased their exports to the U.S. by 24 percent, to

Japan by 12 percent, and to the EEC by 40.0 percent in 1986. Indeed, the exports of developing sector manufacturers grew by 13 percent in value in 1986 and accounted for the total increase in growth of world manufacturing trade in volume that year.[30] In 1978, the combination of Phase III terms of trade advantages for manufactured exports and the Phase IV dollar depreciation produced early signs that NIE trade improvements would be great under such conditions. In 1986, under even more favorable Phase III and IV conditions, the combined effect of growth in developing sector manufacturing exports and the contraction in oil prices made manufactured goods the developing sector's leading export for the first time. That year, manufactured exports represented 41.5 percent, fuel exports, 34.4 percent, and nonfuel primary commodity exports, 24.1 percent of developing sector exports.[31] In 1980, fuel had represented 60 percent of developing sector exports. As a result, in 1986 many NIEs, including Taiwan, South Korea, and Brazil, ran large merchandise trade surpluses.

The economies to suffer the most damage from the oil price slide and dollar depreciation were the oil exporters. Because oil prices are denominated in dollars, oil exports suffered a loss of 66.0 percent of their purchasing power in economies whose currencies significantly appreciated against the dollar, especially Japan and Western Europe. For economies like the Soviet Union, whose hard currency imports are mostly from Western Europe, the combined effect of these two developments was greater than it was for Mexico, which imported mostly from the U.S. The developing sector oil exporters were forced to accelerate import cuts in 1986, while drawing down reserves and enlarging liquidation of foreign assets.

Soviet hard currency imports fell substantially in 1986 and were only prevented from collapsing by an additional $4.4 billion of hard currency borrowing, increased sales of gold, and a large increase in export volume, mostly petroleum made affordable by a recovery in domestic oil output (see Table 8.1). Soviet hard currency exports in volume grew by 14.5 percent in 1986, while hard currency exports in value declined by 6.7 percent.[32]

In a more general sense, the financial condition of capital importing developing nations grew precarious in 1986. While interest rates continued to fall, the positive impact of this process on their current account balances was overwhelmed by the drop in primary commodity prices. And developed sector financing was even less available in 1986 than in 1985. Net external borrowing for developing sector capital importers fell to $41.2 billion in 1986 from a peak of $124.7 billion in 1982.[33] And private sector retrenchment on loans to the developing sector was not the only problem; capital flows from the IMF were a negative $2.7 billion in 1986 as repayment on past IMF loans grew.[34]

From 1982—when the debt crisis began—to 1986, the developing sector's foreign debt to GDP and debt service ratios grew and its creditworthiness deteriorated.[35]

CYCLE 4 PERTURBATIONS IN WORLD TRADE AND THE ACCELERATION OF THE "NEW PROTECTIONISM"

In Cycle 4 the emergence of a more contractionary set of developed sector economic policies and the depressed status of primary input costs as well as the much wider differences in developed sector macroeconomic policies produced a number of acute alterations in long-term trade and payments trends.

In the first three phases of Cycle 4—as in Cycle 3—the rate of growth of world import volume fell from what it had been in the first three phases of the preceding cycle.[36] And the lower rate of world import volume growth once again triggered a slowdown in the growth rate of world trade and a more severe crowding in developed sector manufactured goods markets.

But in the first three phases of Cycle 4, three developments worked to significantly aggravate the degree of market crowding which in turn produced a visible growth in the magnitude of the "new protectionist" response. On the import side, the mitigating role played by expanding developing sector and CPE hard currency markets on market crowding in Cycles 2 and 3 vanished as the aggregate imports (volume and value) of these two sectors dropped over the first three phases of Cycle 4. In addition, the degree of dependency of the rest of the world on and consequent crowding in the U.S. merchandise goods market swelled in Cycle 4 well above what it had been in preceding cycles. On the export side, the role of Japanese and East Asian NIE exports in the Cycle 4 export expansion rose above what it had been in Cycle 3, fostering growth in their market shares in North America and Western Europe.

New Alterations in the Configuration of the World Market and World Trade

As in Phase I of the previous cycles, the center of import dynamism in 1983/84 was the developed sector. But the magnitude of the contractionary turn in aggregate developed sector macroeconomic policy produced a weaker developed sector import growth rate in volume in 1983/84 than in 1976. In 1976 the developed sector import volume growth rate registered 13.5 percent while the 1983/84 average was 7.1 percent.[37] And from Phase I to Phase III of Cycle 3 (1976–78), the developed sector import growth rate (volume) averaged 7.2 percent, higher than the growth rate of 6.8 percent over the same phases in Cycle 4 (1983–86).

Despite the lower absolute growth rate of developed sector imports, the sector's share of world imports (volume) grew more sizably in the first three phases of Cycle 4 than in Cycle 3. This came as the result of a severe contraction in developing sector imports. From 1983–86 the developing sector import volume growth rate fell by an annual average of 2.8 percent, after advancing at a 7.9 percent rate from 1976–78.[38] Lower primary commodity prices, higher interest payments on foreign debt, and the reduction in capital inflow led to a decline in developing sector imports from Phase I through Phase III of Cycle 4—a trend opposite to that which evolved in Phases I–III of Cycles 2 and 3, when rising primary commodity prices, lower interest rates, and accommodative payments policies permitted developing sector imports to rise. The forces that produced a loss in developing sector imports in Cycle 4 also worked to weaken the performance of European CPE hard currency imports (although this condition was moderated in Phase III of Cycle 4 when developed sector payments policy toward Eastern Europe was relaxed and Moscow commenced heavy borrowing in the West).

Further, the share of developed sector and world import (value) growth accounted for by U.S. import growth in Phase I of Cycle 4 was much greater than in Phase I of earlier cycles.[39] And in 1985, the first year of Phase III, the U.S. import growth rate was virtually equal to that of the developed sector—a development that had not occurred during Phase III of the first two cycles. As a result, the share of world imports accounted for by the United States at the end of Phase III of Cycle 4 was much higher than it was at similar stages in the previous cycles.

Cycle 4's lower global import (volume) growth rate prompted a continuation of the inter-cyclical decline in the world merchandise trade growth rate (in volume).[40] However, in Cycle 4 the large disparity in world merchandise trade volume and value growth rates which erupted in Cycle 2 and extended into Cycle 3 narrowed in accord with the reduced inflation registered for merchandise goods.[41]

The depressed primary commodity prices of Cycle 4 produced large terms of trade advantages for manufactured exports (in value) and equally sharp disadvantages for primary commodity exports (in value), reversing the trend that asserted itself in Cycle 2 and extended through most of Cycle 3. As a result, the share of manufactured goods in world trade increased substantially, while the share of primary commodities in world trade decreased (see Table 8.2).

The performances of manufactured and primary commodity exports were paralleled by the export performances of the developed and developing sectors. Developed sector exports (in value) assumed a larger share of world trade and developing sector exports (in value), a lower share in Cycle 4 than had been the case in Cycle 3.

TABLE 8.2 **CHANGE IN SECTORAL EXPORT SHARES IN CYCLE 4 (Percent)**

	1982	1983	1984	1985	1986
Manufactured Goods	57.1	58.5	60.0	61.8	67.5
Primary Commodities	42.9	41.5	40.0	38.2	32.5
Developed Sector	63.5	64.0	64.6	66.4	69.2
Intra-Developed Sector	44.0	45.6	47.1	49.3	53.4
Developing Sector	26.0	24.7	24.4	22.9	19.3

SOURCE: Manufactured Goods and Primary Commodities, 1982-84 and 1985/86 - GATT International Trade 1985/86 and 1986/87, respectively; Developed, Intra-Developed, and Developing Sector, 1982-85 and 1986 - GATT International Trade 1985/86 and 1986/87, respectively.

And as in earlier cycles, Phase I world export growth was lead by intra-developed sector exports (see Table 8.2). However, in Phase I of Cycle 4 the leadership of intra-developed sector exports in world trade was more pronounced, even though its absolute rate of growth was lower than in the previous Phase I. The surge in importance of developed sector intra-trade at the beginning of Cycle 4 was not the result of its greater dynamism but of severe weakness in developing sector trade and in developing sector imports from the developed sector. Both developments were prompted by the faltering recovery of primary commodity prices and debt difficulties.

The decline in the intra-developed sector export growth rate in Phase I of Cycle 4 from earlier Phase I performances was led by a contraction in Western Europe's export growth rate. Particularly poor was the performance of West European intra-trade, marked by poorer EEC and EFTA intra-trade growth rates. In 1984, the peak of Phase I, EEC intra-trade declined as a share of world trade from 18.0 percent in 1983 to 17.3 percent.[42] This weakness led to a further erosion in the share of "special arrangement" trade in world trade. However, in Phase III (1985/86), with developing sector exports especially depressed and with a revitalization of West European trade (especially in 1986) due to the early effect of Phase V macroeconomic stimulation, West European trade and EEC intra-trade led the recovery in world trade. From 17.3 percent in 1984, EEC intra-trade claimed 21.3 percent of world trade by 1986.[43]

Contrary to Western Europe's export performance in Phase I of Cycle 4, Japan saw its share of world trade increase at an accelerated pace (see Table 8.1). Surpassing even Japan in export vigor were the developing sector manufacturing exporters and especially the East Asian NIEs. (This development did not positively affect the vast majority of the developing sector since the share of developing sector manufacturing exports has become even more concentrated in a few countries during the 1980s than was the case in the previous decade. By 1985, 80 percent of developing sector manufacturing exports were concentrated in ten countries, compared to 70 percent in 1973.)[44] And in 1986 Japanese and NIE exports surged anew (see Table 8.1) after weakening in 1985 in response to the decline in U.S. import growth.

An Accelerated Advance in the "New Protectionism"

The lower rate of developed sector import growth in Cycle 4 intensified the market crowding that had been evolving since Cycle 1. The strain on national trade policies caused by a lower rate of expansion in developed sector manufactured goods markets had been moderated in Cycles 2 and 3 by the emergence of more robust developing sector and European CPE markets. But in Cycle 4 these markets contracted, aggravating the stress on national trade policies. The more extreme concentration of developed sector import growth in the U.S. market during the first three phases of Cycle 4 put maximum strain on U.S. trade policy, and with the competitiveness of East Asian exports growing, trade tensions between the U.S. and its East Asian trading partners grew at an alarming pace.

Greater market crowding in the developed sector in Cycle 4 prompted a surge of the "new protectionism" in North America and Western Europe, a surge encouraged by higher unemployment and lower factory capacity utilization rates in the first three phases of Cycle 4 than in the first three phases of Cycle 3.

The growing magnitude of the "new protectionism" since the beginning of Phase VI of Cycle 3 in 1980 caused the percentage of U.S. as well as West European merchandise goods falling under some form of protection to rise from 1980–87.[45] And while the share of transoceanic trade accounted for by trans-Pacific trade grew, the percentage of world trade represented by transoceanic trade remained the same, suggesting the debilitating impact of the rise of the "new protectionism" on U.S. and West European transoceanic imports.[46]

The ascent of the U.S. economic recovery produced an easing of U.S.-Japan trade tensions from their recession level of 1981/82. The retreat in anti-Japanese trade momentum in the U.S. was also helped by more energetic Japanese efforts to open domestic markets and by Tokyo's willingness to transfer militarily applicable technologies for use in the U.S. defense sector.[47] But in 1984, trade tensions involving the U.S. escalated anew with the NIEs and Western Europe assuming the role of chief antagonists. Trade tensions between Western Europe on the one hand and Japan and the NIEs on the other also accelerated.

In the U.S. a rapidly growing trade deficit, which undermined a recovery from recession levels of manufacturing sector employment, and deteriorating export competitiveness aggravated by dollar appreciation led to election year political pressure sufficient to push Washington toward reinforcing existing trade restrictions in several areas. With 25–40 percent of Japan's exports already under some form of constraint, U.S. energies in 1984 were primarily directed at the NIEs. In September 1984, the U.S. government moved to restrict steel imports to 20 percent of domestic consumption as part of an effort to structurally adjust the domestic steel industry (the EEC was already reorganizing its steel sector through the Davignon Plan, introduced in 1982, and Japan was engaged in similar efforts). Steel exporters most damaged by the action were NIEs—South Korea, Mexico, and Brazil. Also before the 1984 election the U.S. took action to further restrict another key NIE export—textiles.[48]

Western Europe, whose imports declined in Phase I under the weight of harsh government domestic economic policies, saw its trade tensions with the U.S. rise in 1984. At the center of U.S./Western European Phase I and, later, Phase III trade disputes was agriculture; in 1984, the U.S. engaged in an agricultural export subsidy skirmish with the EEC.

With the ratchet down of the U.S. GNP growth rate in the second half of 1984, domestic political pressures swelled for a more restrictive U.S. trade policy—pressures that gained momentum in Phase III (1985/86) and helped provoke and shape the U.S. policy initiatives of Phase IV. The political surge for more restrictive trade policies did not peak until the end of 1987, and even in 1988, while U.S. trade balances recovered, the political pressure for restrictive trade action remained strong.

The year 1985 opened with lower U.S. GNP growth, climbing U.S. external imbalances, and falling U.S. manufacturing sector employment. These developments combined to incite a Congress-centered groundswell for restrictive trade action, targeted first and foremost at Japan. In the first half of the year the U.S. Congress passed a resolution condemning Japanese trade practices as an avalanche of anti-Japan trade legislation was introduced.[49]

The force of the U.S. Congress's trade wrath was exacerbated by the continued (albeit slowing) expansion of the U.S. trade deficit, and by the summer of 1985 their efforts were threatening enough to provoke an Executive Branch reaction. In the wake of a September Reagan Administration White Paper on trade, a three-pronged trade policy surfaced. First, the Administration announced its intention to pursue a new GATT round of multilateral trade negotiations aimed at liberalizing world markets in areas in which the U.S. enjoyed a comparative advantage, including services, agriculture, and high technology.[50] Second, the Administration pledged to assume a more activist approach in identifying and pursuing cases against unfair foreign trade practices. Finally, it sought to engineer dollar depreciation.

The Reagan Administration and the more aggressive congressional trade initiatives spurred a series of reactions from Tokyo over the course of Phase III. Anxious to defuse the protectionist momentum in the

United States, the Japanese government entered into a series of talks (the Market-Oriented Sector Specific, or MOSS, talks) with Washington in 1985 aimed at opening up specified sectors of the Japanese market, through which Tokyo made a number of concessions during 1985/86. The Japanese government's growing sensitivity to the repercussions of its trade policy and practices in Washington also played a role in its decision to extend the VRA on Japanese auto exports to the U.S. in 1986. Second, Tokyo joined the Reagan Administration, through the auspices of the G-5 Plaza Accords, in pursuit of dollar depreciation. And finally, in 1986 Japan first acknowledged the need and then agreed to take steps to accelerate its domestic demand growth rate. Japan joined the U.S. in a series of joint interest rate reductions and ultimately announced plans to introduce a multiyear, $40 billion fiscal stimulus package. And a longer-term Japanese commitment to move its economy toward a greater reliance on domestic demand and less on exports was issued in the 1986 Maekawa Report.[51]

At the end of October 1986, U.S. Treasury Secretary James Baker III and Japan's Finance Minister Kiichi Miyazawa reached an agreement in which Japanese pledges of macroeconomic expansionism were exchanged for a U.S. commitment to stabilize the dollar.[52] But this forerunner of the Louvre Accords collapsed in January 1987 on the news that the U.S. merchandise trade deficit had once again widened. (Later that year the Louvre Accords would meet the same fate as the Baker-Miyazawa agreement and for the same reason.)

Throughout 1986 U.S. restrictive trade actions expanded at an unprecedented post-World War II pace. The steady growth of the U.S. merchandise trade deficit in 1986 helped to consolidate international trade as a hot political issue, especially in the U.S. Congress. In the 1986 election year, the best the Reagan Administration could muster was a controlled explosion in restrictive trade actions directed at virtually all key U.S. trading partners, including Western Europe (over corn, soybeans, and wheat), Canada (over lumber), Japan (over semiconductors), and the NIEs (over a stronger MFA, secured in August 1986)—among a host of other actions.

THE EXPLOSION IN INTRA-DEVELOPED SECTOR TRADE IMBALANCES AND CURRENCY MISALIGNMENTS

In Cycles 2 and 3 the greatest source of expansion in sectoral and national merchandise trade and current account imbalances was the rise in primary commodity prices coupled with the enormous gap that opened between oil and non-oil primary commodity prices. Nevertheless, even during these two cycles, widening differences in macroeconomic policy and development strategy among developed economies produced ever wider intra-developed sector external imbalances. In Cycle 4 these imbalances soared—as economic policies among developed economies diverged further—to become the most dynamic force behind growing global trade and current account imbalances.

In Cycles 2 and 3 it was the growth in current account imbalances that prompted an unusual rise in cross-border capital flows. By Phase VI of Cycle 3 and through Cycle 4, a more pronounced acceleration in cross-border capital flows took place, prompted, like the rise in Cycle 4 merchandise trade and current account imbalances, by enlarged divergences in developed sector economic policies—divergences that have resulted in substantial fluctuations in the value of national assets—and facilitated by a period of marked capital market liberalization. These capital flows have overwhelmed the expected response of national capital account balances to current account performance, producing unprecedented postwar currency misalignments.

Thus, in the first three phases of Cycle 4 the two principal goals of the postwar international monetary order—minimal merchandise trade and current account imbalances and stable and aligned exchange rates—found themselves in a rout.

Stabilization of North-South Trade Imbalances

The more constrictive developed sector domestic and international economic policies and the fall in primary input costs generated new perturbations in the distribution and makeup of North-South, intra-developing sector, and intra-developed sector merchandise trade imbalances. In Cycle 4 the negligible recovery in primary commodity prices in Phase II and the pronounced deterioration in these prices in Phase III helped to undermine the performance of developing sector exports. Poorer merchandise exports combined with larger factor service income deficits and a major decline in capital inflow to produce immense balance of payments strains. Balance of payments stress in turn forced an absolute reduction in developing sector imports in Phases II and III. The developing sector merchandise trade balance therefore improved in 1983/84 as it had in earlier Phase II's, but the source of the improvement had been radically altered from earlier reliance on export growth to import compression (see Table 8.1). In Phase III of Cycle 4, the merchandise trade balance of the developing sector deteriorated, repeating its behavior in earlier Phase IIIs. In Phase III of previous cycles, however, the merchandise trade balance of the developing sector worsened primarily because of an expansion in imports, while in Phase III of Cycle 4, developing sector imports fell.

The terms of trade advantages for manufactured goods in Cycle 4 led to changes in the causes of merchandise trade imbalances within the developing sector (see Table 8.1). First, the magnitude of advance in developing sector manufacturing exporter merchandise trade balances during Phases II–III of Cycle 4 was greater than in the same phases in earlier cycles (see Table 8.1). But the decline in the merchandise trade surpluses of the oil exporters in the first three phases was equivalent to that in the preceding cycle. In Cycle 3 the small loss in oil exporter merchandise trade surpluses was experienced while these nations' imports were undergoing an immense expansion, whereas in Cycle 4, an equally small merchandise trade surplus decline occurred while oil exporter imports were undergoing profound compression (see Table 8.1).

The merchandise trade balance performance of the developing sector non-oil primary commodity exporters was similar to that of the oil exporters: the rise in their merchandise trade deficit over the first three phases of Cycle 4 was roughly equivalent to that in Cycle 3. But in the earlier cycle this rise was driven by growth in imports, while in Cycle 4 the expansion in the deficit took place despite a significant reduction in imports (see Table 8.1).

The Redistribution of Inflationary Forces and Capital Flows in Cycle 4

The cessation of growth in North-South and oil exporter-importer trade imbalances—imbalances that would have declined were it not for the enormous fall in primary commodity exporter imports—is a reflection of the peculiar evolution of inflationary forces in Cycle 4. The strength of inflationary forces has been reduced as a result of substantial policy adjustment which began in 1980. One result of this process has been a drop in primary input costs (e.g., primary commodity prices). However, there is another, more revealing side to the motion of inflation in Cycle 4. While inflationary forces have been suppressed, the structure of their distribution has also been altered—a development that has been facilitated by unusual changes in the behavior of cross-border capital flows.

One of the more intriguing Cycle 4 phenomena has been the evolution of U.S. goods and services price inflation. The U.S. economy experienced a disinflation in goods and services prices despite unprecedented government fiscal deficits and high domestic demand growth rates.[53] This feat was accomplished through the export of U.S. inflation to the rest of the world by means of goods and services trade deficits.

As a result of the growth in the U.S. goods and services trade deficit, unemployment rates declined and manufacturing capacity utilization rates rose in the rest of the world, relieving inflationary pressures on U.S. primary input and fixed capital supplies. The export of inflation also meant an export of GNP growth from the U.S. to the rest of the world, seen in widening U.S. net export deficits and only modest advance in U.S. nonresidential fixed investment. The rest of the world's net exports climbed and this in turn encouraged nonresidential fixed investment outside of the United States.

Also, in aggregate, the rest of the world's currencies depreciated against the dollar, assuring additional inflationary pressure on the domestic prices of merchandise goods and non-factor services from dollar imports. Indeed, U.S. disinflation was further encouraged by the reverse process: downward pressure on U.S. merchandise goods and non-factor services prices from foreign imports. Reflecting the degree of retrenchment in macroeconomic policy outside of the United States, the rest of the world sustained large goods and services trade surpluses with the U.S. in concert with currency depreciation while goods and services prices disinflated. (This was attributable to non-U.S. developed sector disinflation, since inflation continued to climb in the developing sector.)

But U.S. goods and services price disinflation in Cycle 4 was only won at the cost of gross dollar "inflation" (i.e., overvaluation). Dollar overvaluation in the first three phases of Cycle 4 was produced by dollar appreciation and a simultaneous expansion in the U.S. current account deficit. It was prompted by capital inflow to the U.S. required to finance aggregate domestic deficits led by the central government fiscal deficit—deficits which had provoked U.S. domestic demand growth rates far in excess of those experienced elsewhere in the world—and the U.S. current account deficit led by the merchandise trade deficit—a deficit which provided the means whereby the inflationary consequences of high U.S. domestic demand growth rates could be exported to the rest of the world.

Further, since primary commodity exporter merchandise trade balances could not improve in the face of declining primary commodity prices, the merchandise trade surplus of the rest of the world with the U.S. was shared by manufacturing exporters, led by Japan, the FRG, and the NIEs.

The same forces that prompted a Cycle 4 explosion in merchandise trade and current account imbalances between the U.S. and the leading manufacturing exporters—more extreme macroeconomic and, especially, government fiscal policy divergences within the developed sector —also provoked an even more vigorous expansion in intra-developed sector capital flows.

Intra-developed sector capital flows not only grew as a consequence of the financing of U.S. current account deficits. The more constrictive developed sector domestic monetary policy and high real interest rates of Cycle 4 served to extend the incentives for investment in high-yield debt instruments and the disincentives to investment in goods and services which began at the end of Cycle 3. And the striking differences in developed sector macroeconomic policies in Cycle 4 served to increase the proportion of cross-border investment in the growing volume of investment in financial assets. As a result, by the beginning of Phase III in 1985 the ratio of cross-border capital flows to goods and services trade had escalated dramatically. Capital flows reached $50 trillion that year, while goods and services trade registered only $2 trillion.

The increased differences in developed sector macroeconomic policy and the capital and trade flows they prompted sparked the greater exchange rate misalignments. Hence, from 1980 to 1985, the U.S. dollar experienced a 50.2 percent appreciation, while the U.S. merchandise trade and current account deficits underwent massive growth.[54]

The increase in capital flows during Cycle 4 also reflected a process that was working to undermine not just U.S. but global goods and services price inflation: the enlarged share of investment resources attracted to financial assets had the effect of shifting inflationary pressure to financial asset prices and away from goods and services prices. Hence, in addition to the dollar, stocks, bonds, and other debt instruments became overvalued. Until 1985, large capital flows remained rooted in debt instruments. Despite the declining nominal interest rates in 1983 and much of 1984, the United States continued to sustain real interest rate advantages. The higher U.S. domestic demand growth rates compared to the rest of the world in 1983/84 also attracted additional capital inflow in the form of direct investment. Equally important, these large cross-border movements in capital inspired follow-on waves of speculative flows seeking to profit from future fluctuations in national asset values, not the least of which were currency exchange rates.

The beginning of Phase III of Cycle 4 in the second half of 1984 prompted a prolonged decline in U.S. interest rates, which endured through the entirety of Phase III. The fall in interest rates reduced the incentive to invest in debt instruments, and because U.S. domestic demand growth was rapidly receding while domestic demand growth in the rest of the world failed to advance, there existed little incentive to shift resources to direct investment in goods and services. Instead, investment gravitated toward bonds and stocks, and cross-border capital flows followed suit.[55]

Transformations in Capital Account and Net Investment Balances

The size and structure of Cycle 4 capital flows reflected a profound transformation in the behavior of sectoral and national capital account and net investment balances—a transformation that also had the effect of swelling the ratio of intra-developed sector to North-South (and West-East) capital flows.

The capital exporting developing economies, predominantly Persian Gulf oil exporters, whose terms of trade surged ahead in Cycles 2 and 3 experienced a severe decline in terms of trade in Cycle 4. Their earlier terms of trade advantages had facilitated a large net investment surplus built on repeated current account surpluses and capital account deficits. But beginning in 1983, these economies were forced into significant foreign asset liquidation. Their capital account deficits that had provided the means for financing global current account deficits in Cycles 2 and 3 disappeared, and as a result, in Cycle 4 the net investment surplus of this sector declined.

At the same time, the deterioration in the net investment balance experienced by the developing sector capital importers during the previous two cycles slowed to a crawl in Cycle 4, a consequence of the change in developed sector payments policy toward them and a consequent slowdown in the rate of growth of developing sector foreign indebtedness (see Figure 8.1). Indeed, when the performance of factor service accounts is added to developing sector long-term capital accounts, developing sector capital importers had actually become net capital exporters by 1984.

The terms of trade advantage of manufactured goods in Cycle 4 advanced the major manufacturing exporters, Japan and the FRG, into the position occupied by developing sector capital exporters during the previous two cycles. Both have accumulated more sizable capital account deficits and larger net investment surpluses than in Cycle 3 (see Figure 8.1). At the same time, the domestic demand growth differentials in the developed sector and dollar overvaluation have combined to push the United States into the position occupied by developing sector capital importers in Cycles 2 and 3.

As a result, by the end of Phase III in 1986 the U.S. had accumulated a large net investment deficit, after enjoying its largest net investment surplus in history in 1981. While there is no question as to the deterioration in the U.S. net investment balance during Cycle 4 since large annual capital account surpluses have been accumulated over this period, there is dispute over its precise status. Because the U.S. Department of Commerce calculates U.S. foreign investment on the basis of book value and not current value, it has been argued that the absolute status of the U.S. net investment balance is much better than reported.[56] According to some studies, the degree of undervaluation of U.S. foreign assets in the Commerce Department's report is well over $300 billion—enough to have erased all of the deficit reported at the end of 1986—and this figure includes a reduction in the book value of overvalued U.S.-owned developing sector debt. It does not, however, address accumulation of a $182.0 billion surplus in "errors and omissions" by the U.S. from 1978 to 1985.

FIGURE 8.1

CHANGES IN DEVELOPED SECTOR NET INVESTMENT
BALANCES AND SIZE OF DEVELOPING SECTOR CAPITAL
IMPORTER BORROWING, 1980-87

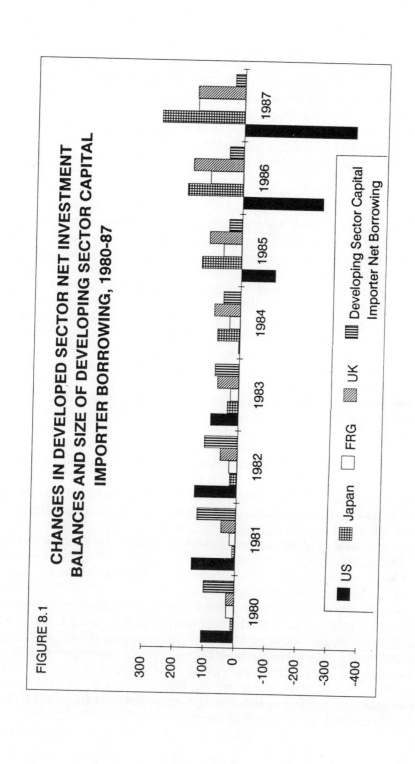

While a portion of this sum reflects unreported factor services surpluses (indicating that the deterioration in the U.S. current account balance over the 1978–85 period had been somewhat overstated), an indeterminate but no doubt large portion of it represents unreported net capital inflow. No matter, the pace of deterioration in the U.S. net investment balance in Cycle 4 has been breathtaking.

In addition to the rise in the volume of capital inflow to the U.S., the surplus in the U.S. capital account was helped by a contraction in U.S. capital outflow to the developing sector beginning in 1983 as the U.S. payments posture turned harshly contractionary. In 1983 the United States consequently experienced a net transfer of capital from the developing sector—and this despite the liquidation of dollar assets by developing sector oil exporters. By 1985 Japan accounted for one-third of the net capital inflow to the U.S., and the rest of the developed sector, one-fifth. The remainder of it was shared by offshore banks (reflecting additional developed sector net outflow to the U.S.) and the developing sector.

But in 1986 two developments hinted at possible problems in the future foreign funding of U.S. domestic and external imbalances. First, net private capital flow to the U.S. dropped for the first time in the 1980s. The $18.0 billion decline was offset by a $32.9 billion advance in net official capital inflow—the first major advance in Cycle 4.[57] The proportion of total net capital inflow to the U.S. accounted for by official inflow was 21.7 percent in 1986 as foreign governments, especially Tokyo and Bonn, tried to moderate the fall of the dollar. The decline in net private capital inflow to the U.S. and the growth in net official inflow indicated growing market recognition of the inflated value of the dollar.

Second, an expanding portion of dollar assets held by foreigners were highly liquid and easily marketable. In 1986, the net portfolio investment in the U.S. was $77 billion. Japan's net portfolio investments abroad amounted to $102 billion. These flows, which were hardly in existence at the beginning of Cycle 4, came to represent the primary vehicle for financing the U.S. twin deficits.[58]

The chemistry of market recognition of dollar overvaluation and the liquid and marketable nature of a growing majority of foreign-owned dollar assets represent vulnerabilities that could be translated into a sudden and unwanted dollar depreciation.

The change in global capital flows toward securities and away from the international bank loans that had dominated Cycles 2 and 3 reflected not only the expansion in intra-developed sector capital flows but also the contraction in North-South capital flows. By 1985, the value of international bank loans fell below the value of international bonds. And while in 1980, developed sector commercial bank loans to the developing sector accounted for 25 percent of total commercial bank lending, by 1986 that figure had fallen to only 6 percent.

The Changing Dimensions of Services Trade

The accelerated expansion of cross-border capital flows beginning in Cycle 2 combined with the turn to tighter aggregate developed sector domestic monetary policy at the end of Cycle 3 to produce visible changes in services trade patterns.

The growth in the ratios of services to merchandise trade, factor services income to non-factor services trade, and interest income to direct investment income that burst onto the scene in the 1980–82 period held in Cycle 4. In addition, significant changes had emerged in the composition of non-factor services trade since the second half of the 1970s. The ratio of traditional non-factor services trade to "other" non-factor services trade fell. Those traditional non-factor services most relevant to servicing the transport of merchandise goods—shipping and other transportation—experienced the greatest decline in share of total non-factor services trade.[59] Those "other" services experiencing rapid technological advance such as communications and information or those in higher demand such as financial services (both relevant to servicing capital flows) accounted for the largest increase in share.[60]

The growth in the ratio of factor services income to merchandise trade has also produced another modification in postwar trade and payments trends. The close relationship between merchandise trade and current account performances has been weakened as economies accumulate larger net investment imbalances. Notable on this score has been the slower improvement in capital-importing developing economies' current account balances compared to their merchandise trade balances, a development that also began to afflict the U.S. in 1987/88.

Part IV

THE CURRENT SITUATION AND BEYOND

9

Phase V of the Current Cycle: What's Happened to the J-Curve and Inflation

THE UNMISTAKABLE FINGERPRINTS OF PHASE V

By the middle of 1986, the unmistakable characteristics of Phase V of the trade and payments cycles had surfaced. In the second and third quarters, Japan and the Federal Republic of Germany moved to contain dollar depreciation through large-scale purchases of dollar assets. As a result, the United States' official capital balance turned in a large surplus—a surplus that was repeated in 1987 as the continued slide of the dollar provoked sustained foreign official acquisition of dollar assets. Aided by interest rate reductions, especially in Japan, the currency interventions of 1986/87 unleashed a discernible acceleration in money supply growth in Japan and the FRG, just as it had in Phase V of Cycles 2 and 3. In addition to a more accommodative domestic monetary policy in the non-U.S. developed sector (indeed, in the entire developed sector since a more relaxed U.S. monetary policy had supported an acceleration in the growth of the U.S. money supply in 1985/86), a more expansionist fiscal policy later emerged, almost wholly the result of initiatives taken by Tokyo.

In response to these reflationary steps, the domestic demand growth rate of the non-U.S. developed sector expanded from 1986 to 1988, peaking in the fourth quarter of 1987 and first quarter of 1988.

Since the U.S. domestic demand growth rate failed to decelerate significantly over this period, the entire developed sector domestic demand growth rate grew, sparking as it had in earlier Phase Vs a recovery in primary commodity prices. From the third quarter of 1986 to the fourth quarter of 1987 nonfuel primary commodity prices advanced by 28.7 percent, after suffering a severe setback in Phase III, while oil prices grew by 27.6 percent, after plummeting in the first three quarters of 1986.[1] Finally, in 1988 a drought placed new pressure on world food supplies and—just as had occurred in Phase V of all previous cycles—world food prices rose. Through the first three quarters of 1988 food prices increased by 25.2 percent over 1987.[2]

The recovery in primary commodity prices underwrote a revitalization in the developing sector's exports sufficient to support renewed growth in its imports. The acceleration in developing sector imports had been a critical feature of all Phase Vs and in Phase V of Cycle 4, after falling by 5.7 percent from 1984–86, developing sector imports climbed by 10.9 percent from 1986–87 and are estimated to have grown by 28 percent from 1986–88.[3]

The relaxation of macroeconomic policy and the subsequent rise in the domestic demand growth rate of the non-U.S. developed sector together with the improvement in the developing sector import growth rate are the essential conditions that have produced the two dominant features of Phase V of the trade and payments cycles: a recovery in U.S. external balances and an acceleration in goods and services price inflation.

Changes in domestic demand growth rate differentials between the United States and the rest of the world contributed as early as 1986 to changes in the U.S. economy that have characterized each Phase V:

- an acceleration in the U.S. GNP growth rate led by net exports and nonresidential fixed investment;
- increased levels of domestic resource utilization in the form of lower unemployment rates and higher manufacturing sector capacity utilization rates; and
- the elimination of the cyclical components of the U.S. twin deficits—the government fiscal deficit and merchandise trade deficit.

Through 1987 and the first half of 1988, continued change in the differential between the U.S. domestic demand growth rate and that of the rest of the world—both developed and developing—enhanced the pace of improvement in U.S. net exports (in constant dollars). This was driven by rapid growth in U.S. gross exports (in constant dollars) (see Table 9.1). And as in all earlier Phase Vs, the rise in the U.S. gross export growth rate stimulated substantial expansion in U.S. nonresidential fixed investment (see Table 9.1). In the second half of 1987 and first half of 1988, U.S. net exports and nonresidential fixed investment surged ahead, driving the

U.S. GNP growth rate in those years well above what it had registered during Phase III, in 1985 and 1986.

The pressure of enhanced demand in the form of exports and business investment on U.S. supplies of labor and fixed capital pushed the U.S. unemployment rate down and the manufacturing capacity utilization rate up in 1987 and the first half of 1988, again repeating developments in earlier Phase Vs (see Table 9.1). The advances in resource utilization prompted accelerated growth in U.S. government revenues and moderated outlay growth in the form of "payments to individuals," producing a recovery in the U.S. government fiscal balance in FY87 (the $71 billion decline in the deficit was also aided by the positive impact on revenues of the first year of tax reform). Indeed, in all earlier Phase Vs, the substantial improvement in the rate of resource utilization driven by exports and business investment had eliminated the cyclical component of the U.S. government fiscal deficit as the unemployment rate was driven below the mark associated with budgetary full employment, leaving only the structural, or policy-determined, component of the fiscal deficit (see Table 9.1).

In Phase V the United States has not only experienced the elimination of the cyclical segment of the U.S. government fiscal deficit, but the elimination of the cyclical segment of its merchandise trade deficit as well (in Cycle 1 the U.S. still enjoyed a merchandise trade surplus, and thus in Phase V of that cycle the cyclical suppression of the U.S. merchandise trade surplus was eliminated) (see Table 9.1). Two factors—domestic demand growth rate differentials with the rest of the world most advantageous to the U.S. merchandise trade balance of any phase in the trade and payments cycle and the cyclical nadir of the U.S. dollar's effective exchange rate (in Cycles 2–4)—underlay Phase V advances in the U.S. merchandise trade balance.[4] In the first half of 1988, those conditions again contributed to the improvement in U.S. external balances. And the increase in U.S. and developed sector resource utilization levels combined with the advance in the U.S. merchandise trade balance to moderate the momentum of the "new protectionism" in 1988, as in all Phase Vs.

The acceleration of the world domestic demand growth rate from 1986–88 also produced the second dominant Phase V phenomenon— growth in goods and services price inflation. Compelling this price rise has been a rise in primary input costs, especially primary commodity prices, as well as increased demand pressures on supplies of fixed capital.

Despite these similarities with Phase V of earlier cycles, the performance of world trade and payments in Phase V of Cycle 4 is clearly distinguishable: both the recovery in U.S. external balances and goods and services price inflation have been noticeably weaker.

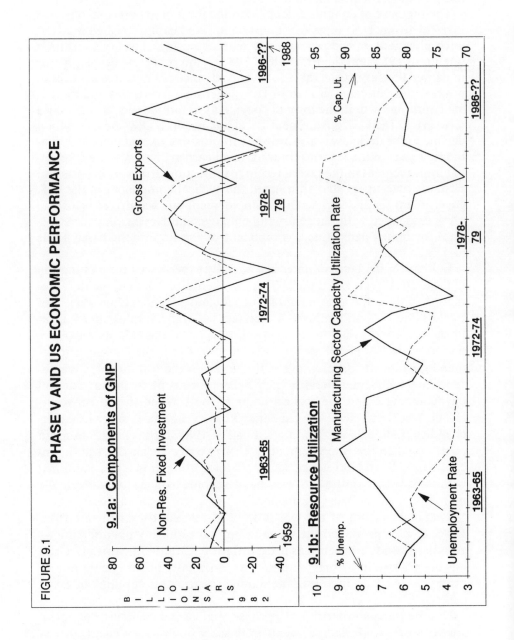

FIGURE 9.1

PHASE V AND US ECONOMIC PERFORMANCE

9.1a: Components of GNP

9.1b: Resource Utilization

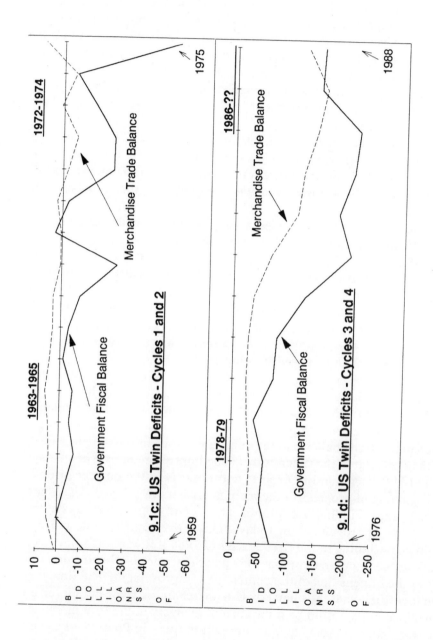

9.1c: US Twin Deficits - Cycles 1 and 2

9.1d: US Twin Deficits - Cycles 3 and 4

The J-Curve: A Delayed and Incomplete Maturation

Perhaps the most disturbing feature of Phase V of Cycle 4 has been the delayed appearance and lack of vitality in the maturation of the J-curve. In Cycles 2 and 3, the J-curve began to mature (that is, the U.S. merchandise trade balance began to improve) only four quarters and three quarters, respectively, from the initiation of dollar depreciation. In Cycle 2, the Smithsonian devaluation of the dollar was launched in December 1971 and improvement in the U.S. merchandise trade balance began in the fourth quarter of 1972, while in Cycle 3 dollar depreciation commenced in earnest in the third quarter of 1977 and the trade balance began to improve in the second quarter of 1978. But in Phase V of Cycle 4, the U.S. merchandise trade balance began to improve in the first quarter of 1988—eleven quarters after dollar depreciation began in early 1985.

Although the U.S. experienced a sharp recovery in its merchandise trade balance in the first half of 1988, continued improvement in the second half and beyond promises to be far more difficult. From the fourth quarter of 1987 to the second quarter of 1988, the quarterly U.S. merchandise trade deficit (annualized) dropped from $164.8 billion to $120.8 billion, or by $44.0 billion. But in the third quarter, progress slowed significantly as the deficit only fell another $6.8 billion, to $114.0 billion. (Indeed, the preliminary report on the fourth quarter U.S. merchandise trade deficit showed it rising anew.)

In Table 9.1 we compare the strength of the 1988 merchandise trade recovery with those of earlier Phase Vs. In each case we have determined the size of the advance in the U.S. merchandise trade balance from the quarter prior to the beginning of the Phase V rebound in the merchandise trade balance to the quarter in which improvement ended. We then calculated the magnitude of the improvement as a percentage of total U.S. merchandise exports and imports in the quarter prior to the beginning of progress in the merchandise trade balance. These percentages appear in the first column. The second column shows what the size of the improvement in today's U.S. merchandise trade balance would be beginning in the first quarter of 1988 if it were the same magnitude as the improvement that took place in Cycles I–III and compares that to the dimensions of the actual 1988 improvement. The final column identifies what the quarterly U.S. merchandise trade deficit (on an annualized basis) would be if the current recovery in the U.S. merchandise trade balance were equal in strength to those in Phase V of Cycles I–III and compares that to the actual U.S. quarterly trade deficit at present (the third quarter of 1988).

TABLE 9.1

COMPARING US MERCHANDISE TRADE BALANCE RECOVERIES IN PHASE V

	Deficit Reduction as % of Merchandise Exports and Imports in Quarter Preceding Deficit Reduction (Percent)	Size of Deficit Reduction in 1988 Terms ($Billions)	Merchandise Trade Deficit Trough in 1988 Terms ($Billions)
CYCLE 1:			
IQ63-IQ64	9.71%	$68.8	-$96.0
CYCLE 2:			
IVQ72-IVQ73	10.56%	$74.9	-$89.9
CYCLE 3:			
IIQ78-IQ79	7.50%	$55.7	-$109.1
CYCLE 4:			
IQ88-IIIQ88	7.17%	$50.8	-$114.0

SOURCE: Cycles 2-3 - National Income and Product Accounts; Cycle 4 - Merchandise Trade: Third Quarter 1988-Balance of Payments Basis, US Department of Commerce, Nov. 28, 1988.

What these comparisons reveal is that the Phase V 1972/73 U.S. trade recovery was the strongest one up to this point. And the differences between the magnitude of that recovery and the current one when considered in light of the limited prospects for continued improvement in the U.S. merchandise trade balance within existing policy parameters suggests that the 1972/73 advance will wind up being superior to that of the current cycle. This raises immense questions regarding the relative importance of the J-curve in Phase V U.S. trade recoveries—questions already noted in Chapters 6 and 7—especially since in effective terms the U.S. dollar depreciation in 1986/87 was nearly two times the size of the 1971–73 depreciation (and more than three times the size of the 1971 depreciation).

These questions take on even greater dimension when we turn to the improvement of the U.S. merchandise trade balance in Phase V of Cycle 1, a period in which no dollar depreciation took place and, therefore, no J-curve phenomenon was at work. In this case, too, the size of the improvement in the U.S. merchandise trade balance surpassed that which has taken place thus far in Phase V of the current cycle, and from its present pace, it seems unlikely that today's recovery will match that of Phase V of Cycle 1.

Perhaps the Phase V merchandise trade recovery that will prove to be most like that of Cycle 4 was the one that took place in Cycle 3. But this too raises doubts about the clout of the J-curve; the 1977–79 dollar depreciation was one-third the size of the 1986/87 depreciation.

Even more demonstrative of the weakness in the maturation of the J-curve in Phase V of Cycle 4 has been the failure of the U.S. merchandise trade deficit to fall below the deficit that existed when dollar depreciation began (see Figure 9.2). In Phase V of Cycles 2 and 3, a J-curve in the U.S. merchandise trade balance performance clearly emerged. After deteriorating from the second half of 1971—the half prior to the onset of dollar depreciation—to the first half of 1972, the U.S. merchandise trade balance reached the peak of its advance in the second half of 1973. The U.S. merchandise trade balance in the second half of 1973 represented a large improvement over that of the second half of 1971. And in the next cycle, following a deterioration in the fourth quarter of 1977 and the first quarter of 1978 from the half just prior to severe dollar depreciation (the second and third quarters of 1977), the U.S. merchandise trade balance rebounded in the fourth quarter of 1978 and first quarter of 1979 to produce a deficit smaller than that of the second and third quarters of 1977.

In the current trade and payments cycle, the J-curve has not fully matured and it remains uncertain whether the U.S. trade recovery has enough strength to make that happen. From the fourth quarter of 1984 and first quarter of 1985—the half just prior to dollar depreciation—the U.S. merchandise trade balance worsened until the second half of 1987. The recovery in the U.S. merchandise trade balance by the second and third quarters of 1988 was not sufficient to push the deficit below the level that existed prior to the beginning of dollar depreciation (see Figure 9.2).

The delay in improvement in the U.S. merchandise trade balance and the failure of the J-curve to fully mature during Phase V of Cycle 4 (up to this point) as it had in the two previous cycles raises several interesting questions that are made even more intriguing by the fact that the depreciation of the dollar has been far greater in Cycle 4 than in Cycles 2 and 3. From the second quarter of 1985 through the fourth quarter of 1987 (the quarter prior to the beginning of improvement in the U.S. merchandise trade balance), the dollar's effective exchange rate depreciated by 35.3 percent, compared to 17.0 percent from 1971–73 and 11.0 percent from 1977–79.

In addition to the absence of a full recovery in the U.S. merchandise trade balance in Phase V of Cycle 4, another development has surfaced to further damage the magnitude of progress in the U.S. current account balance. In Phase V of Cycles 2 and 3, the U.S. current account balance improvement was noticeably larger than that of the merchandise trade balance due to an expansion in the U.S. factor services income surplus. In Phase V of Cycle 4, the U.S. current account balance recovery has not matched that of the merchandise trade balance because the U.S. factor services income surplus contracted.

WHY THE J-CURVE IS WEAK IN CYCLE 4

The cause of the difficulties in J-curve maturation and the cause of the changed relationship between the U.S. merchandise trade and current ac-

FIGURE 9.2

THE J-CURVE IN PHASE V OF THE LAST THREE TRADE AND PAYMENTS CYCLES

(Amounts are average merchandise trade balances over the two quarters listed)

SOURCE: Cycles 2 and 3 - The National Income and Product Accounts of the US, 1929-82, US Department of Commerce, Sept. 1986; Cycle 4 - The Economic Report of the President, Feb. 1988, and US Merchandise Trade: Third Quarter 1988-Balance of Payments Basis,
US Department of Commerce, Nov. 28, 1988

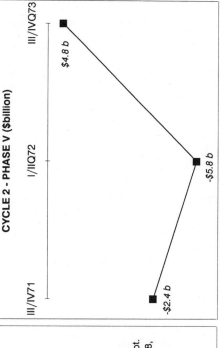

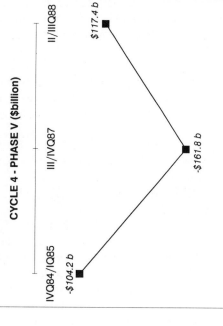

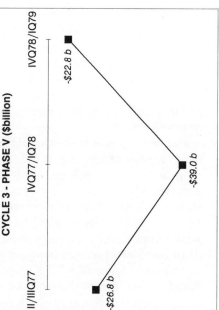

count balances are one and the same: both developments have resulted from the particular relationship that evolved during the cycle between aggregate developed sector macroeconomic and international payments policy and the behavior of primary input costs, as well as growing intra-developed sector macroeconomic policy differences.

The combination of these forces has produced changes in the performance of non-U.S. developed sector domestic demand growth, developing sector import growth, and U.S. competitiveness in Phase V of Cycle 4 compared to Phase V of Cycles 2 and 3 sufficient to depress the pace of improvement in the U.S. merchandise trade balance. These developments have forced U.S. exports to grow at a slower pace in Cycle 4 than in the preceding two cycles. And relative U.S. export weakness has been exacerbated in Phase V of Cycle 4 by a smaller recovery in U.S. agricultural exports.

The turn toward a more austere macroeconomic policy in the developed sector outside of the U.S. in the first three phases of Cycle 4 was carried into Phase V. The smaller increment of aggregate non-U.S. developed sector fiscal and monetary stimulus introduced in Phase V of this compared to previous cycles has produced a smaller recovery in the non-U.S. developed sector domestic demand growth rate.

The less vigorous recovery in the non-U.S. developed sector's domestic demand growth rate has not only slowed the recovery in its import growth rate; it has fueled a less forceful advance in primary commodity prices and a slower recovery in developing sector export earnings than occurred in Phase V of the previous two cycles. In addition, the highly constrictive early Cycle 4 developed sector payments policy toward the developing sector was sustained in Phase V, whereas during Phase V of the previous two cycles, the developed sector payments posture toward the developing sector was highly accommodative. These factors left the developing sector's import recovery in 1987/88 weaker than it had been in 1972–74 and 1978–80.

Further, the slower developing sector import recovery of 1987/88 damaged the pace of advance in U.S. exports more than it did exports of the remainder of the developed sector. The percentage of total U.S. exports accounted for by exports to the developing sector is significantly greater than for Western Europe, especially the FRG, and the percentage of U.S. exports represented by exports to Latin America and Africa (the two areas whose import recoveries were most damaged by the strict payments policies of the developed sector) is higher than Japan's or Western Europe's.

The rate of growth of U.S. exports in Phase V of Cycle 4 was also hindered by the late arrival and the small size of global food deficits, especially when compared to 1963/64 and 1972/73.

Finally, Cycle 4 economic conditions have produced a number of forces damaging to U.S. competitiveness in home and foreign markets.

The unusual macroeconomic policy and domestic demand growth rate differentials between the U.S. and the rest of the world throughout the early phases of Cycle 4 created higher levels of dependence on U.S. markets in the rest of the world for export earnings and GNP growth (i.e., net export volume and related nonresidential fixed investment) than was the case in earlier cycles. Private exporters and their governments have therefore been more willing to fight the challenge of dollar depreciation to their market share by accepting smaller profits.

The dollar misalignment in Phases I–III of Cycle 4 was extraordinary, greater than in earlier cycles, as exchange rates responded to the exacerbated differences in national macroeconomic policies within the developed sector. The larger and more prolonged dollar misalignment produced greater structural distortions in the U.S. economy. The contraction in size or even elimination of some sectors of the U.S. economy under this strain made it more difficult for the U.S. to win back lost domestic and foreign markets in Phase V.

U.S. competitiveness relative to the rest of the developed sector during Phase V of Cycle 4 has been undermined by the superior performance of manufactured goods terms of trade compared to Phase V of Cycles 2 and 3, when the terms of trade of primary commodities made enormous strides. The U.S. has a larger share of its exports in primary commodities and a larger share of its imports in manufactured goods than the non-U.S. developed sector. Further, the pace of supply-side adjustment in the U.S. manufacturing sector continued to lag behind that of Japan and the East Asian NIEs, giving the latter two greater competitive advantages.

The stunning reversal in the relationship between merchandise trade and current account behavior in Phase V of Cycle 4 was provoked by the deterioration in the U.S. net investment balance during earlier phases, a development absent from previous cycles. The slide in the U.S. net investment balance was spawned by Cycle 4's large U.S. current account deficits, in turn driven by the enormous intra-developed sector macroeconomic policy differences and faltering developing sector import growth. The reduction in U.S. capital outflow to the developing sector in response to the retrenchment in payments policy has also contributed to the fall in the U.S. net investment balance. Moreover, the large improvement in U.S. direct investment income which underwrote the advances in U.S. current account balances in 1973 and 1979 did not materialize in Phase V of Cycle 4, due to the weaker recovery in primary commodity prices.

Domestic Demand Growth Rates in the Developed Sector

One of the crucial differences between Phase V of Cycle 4 and Phase V of the preceding two cycles is that U.S. trading partners in the developed

sector have been less willing to increase public debt for fear of the inflationary consequences of such actions and of the deflationary ramifications of larger stocks of debt in the next recession.

Therefore, in 1986–88—years equivalent to 1972/73 in Cycle 2 and
1978/79 in Cycle 3—the average improvement in domestic demand
growth rates of the U.S.'s leading developed sector trading partners from
the year preceding Phase V was smaller than it had been at the same stage
in the two previous cycles (see Table 9.2).

In addition, the absolute average annual rate of domestic demand
growth in Phase V of Cycle 4 has been lower than in Phase V of Cycles 2
and 3 among the most important U.S. developed sector trading partners
(see Table 9.2).

One of the important contributing factors to the poorer domestic demand growth rate performance of major U.S. developed sector trading
partners has been their reduced willingness to resort to central government fiscal deficits to prop up domestic demand growth rates (see Table
9.2). Only one of the leading developed sector economies—the FRG—
saw its average central government fiscal deficit grow as a percentage of
GNP from 1985 to 1986/87. In Phase V of Cycles 2 and 3, the average of
the Japanese and FRG government fiscal deficits as a percentage of GNP
increased above the Phase III level, as was also the case for the average of
the British, French, and Italian government fiscal deficits as a percentage
of GNP.

The reduced willingness of leading developed sector economies to increase their government fiscal deficits in Phase V of Cycle 4 is underestimated in Table 9.2. In Cycle 4, GNP growth in these economies has been
lower than in Cycles 2 or 3. Hence, the rate of growth of their fiscal deficits has been substantially lower than in Phase V of the previous two
cycles.

Nevertheless, because of large-scale intervention in the currency markets to slow the descent of the dollar in 1986/87, the money supplies of
the FRG and Japan (in particular) have grown at a pace equivalent to that
of the 1972/73 period and at an even greater pace than in 1978/79.

Despite the absence of the degree of acceleration in non-U.S. developed sector domestic demand growth rates in Phase V of Cycle 4 that was
present in Cycles 2 and 3, as early as 1987 indications arose from U.S.
trading partners that there was little left in terms of additional
macroeconomic adjustment they were prepared to undergo. In May
1987, key FRG monetary aggregates began to exceed the upper limit of
government-set targets. A June 1987 Bundesbank annual report keynoted
a growing mood within FRG financial circles that the consequences of
overshooting government monetary targets would be to risk renewed inflation. After coaching caution in private sector lending practices, Bonn

TABLE 9.2

FISCAL STIMULUS AND DOMESTIC DEMAND
GROWTH IN THE NON-US DEVELOPED SECTOR
IN PHASE V OF CYCLES 2-4

	Japan / FRG (Average)			
	Cycle 2: *1972/73 Avg.* *Minus 1971*	*Cycle 3 :* *1978/79 Avg.* *Minus 1977*	*Cycle 4:* *1986/87 Avg.* *Minus 1985*	*Add* *1988 Estimate* *Minus 1985*
Change in Total Do- *mestic Demand Growth* *Rate (Percentage Points)*	3.0	2.0	1.5	1.9
Change in Central Govern- *ment Fiscal Deficit as %* *of GNP (Percentage Points)* *	-0.4	-0.2	+0.3	+0.2
	Cycle 2: *1972/73 Avg.*	*Cycle 3:* *1978/79 Avg.*	*Cycle 4:* *1986/87 Avg.*	*Add* *1988 Estimate*
Domestic Demand Growth *Rate (Percent Growth)*	6.8	5.5	4.0	4.3

	Second-Tier West European Economies (UK, France, Italy - Average)			
	Cycle 2: *1972/73 Avg.* *Minus 1971*	*Cycle 3:* *1978/79 Avg.* *Minus 1977*	*Cycle 4:* *1986/87 Avg.* *Minus 1985*	*Add* *1988 Estimate* *Minus 1985*
Change in Total Do- *mestic Demand Growth* *Rate (Percentage Points)*	3.1	3.0	0.9	1.0
Change in Central Govern- *ment Fiscal Deficit as %* *of GNP (Percentage Points)* *	-0.7	-1.1	+0.8	+0.9
	Cycle 2: *1972/73 Avg.*	*Cycle 3:* *1978/79 Avg.*	*Cycle 4:* *1986/87 Avg.*	*Add* *1988 Estimate*
Domestic Demand Growth *Rate (Percent Growth)*	6.1	3.8	3.7	3.8

SOURCE: OECD Economic Outlook, June 1988; 1988 Estimates - Author's.

* - = expansion of deficit as percent of GNP; + = decline of deficit as percent of GNP.

financial authorities began to nudge up interest rates from July to September 1987.[5]

By the summer of 1987 it had become clear that the FRG had surpassed the upper limits of tolerable domestic monetary reflation, despite the fact that such reflation was insisted upon by the spirit if not the letter of the Louvre Accords. Bonn's effective break with the spirit of the agreement helped bring forth the conditions—the rise in developed sector interest rates and the collapse of world equity markets—which caused the demise of the Louvre Accords soon after the October stock market collapse.

The U.S.'s subsequent decision not to stabilize the dollar by resort to higher interest rates opened the door for renewed downward pressure on the dollar. Encouraged by a substantial rise in the U.S. merchandise trade deficit in October 1987 (announced in December), the U.S. dollar fell intermittently until early January.

Even under the pressure of precipitous dollar depreciation, FRG authorities made only marginal concessions on monetary and fiscal policy. In 1988 the reversal in U.S. merchandise trade performance and higher U.S. interest rates in response to increased inflation fears provoked dollar appreciation and deutsche mark depreciation, providing Bonn with sufficient maneuvering room to respond to its own inflation concerns by tightening monetary policy.[6] When the dollar began to show renewed signs of weakness in October 1988, the FRG, unlike the majority of the G-7 countries, showed little interest in adjusting its monetary policy to contest the dollar's slide.[7] With renewal of inflation fears in the U.S. in late 1988 and early 1989 and with a subsequent rise in U.S. interest rates, Bonn once again tightened its domestic monetary policy, and in 1989 the initial phase of Bonn's tax reform effort will make its fiscal policy mix more contractionary than it was in 1988.[8]

In addition, as has been the case in previous Phase Vs, second-tier and weaker West European economies have experienced balance of payments stress, although because of their more moderate domestic demand growth rate recoveries and the slower advance of primary commodity prices, the degree of stress has been less severe than in earlier Phase Vs. Nevertheless, in 1987 and with alarming speed in 1988, the United Kingdom's external balances worsened, while in 1988 the aggregate non-FRG West European external balance also faltered, placing pressure on the U.K. and, to a lesser degree, on other West European economies to adopt less accommodative macroeconomic policies in 1989.[9] These pressures have been exacerbated by concern over inflation, especially in the U.K.

Tokyo's currency interventions in 1986–87, like those of Bonn, pushed up its rate of domestic money supply growth. The large Japanese monetary expansion helped to finance a boom in the Tokyo stock market and an improvement in personal income growth, and by the spring of 1987, a recovery in the Japanese domestic demand growth rate was under way. In late 1987 and 1988, the rate of growth of Japan's domestic demand was further enhanced by the beginning of a multiyear, $40 billion Japanese government fiscal stimulus package.

Like the Bundesbank, the Bank of Japan became sufficiently concerned over inflation in the summer of 1987 to begin lobbying Japanese commercial banks to exert caution in their lending practices.[10] But Japan conducts a larger proportion of its trade with the U.S. and owns a larger stock of dollar assets than does the FRG. As a result, dollar depreciation has a greater negative impact on Japan's net export volume (and nonresidential fixed investment) and GNP growth, on its resource utilization levels and government fiscal balance, and on its merchandise trade, factor services income, and net investment balances than it does for the FRG. Hence, Tokyo has followed a more accommodative monetary policy path than has Bonn.

When the dollar and U.S. interest rates began to rise in 1988, Tokyo did not respond—as Bonn did—by pushing up interest rates, and when the dollar began to depreciate anew in October 1988, the government of Japan led the intervention in the currency markets to contain the dollar's decline.[11]

Nevertheless, it appears that Japan has little room remaining for additional monetary and fiscal stimulus above that to which it has already committed itself.

Domestic demand growth rates are almost certain to contract in 1989 from their 1988 levels for all major developed sector economies.[12] The years of full J-curve maturation—1973 and 1979—marked the point in previous cycles at which the improvement in Phase V domestic demand growth rates among the U.S.'s leading developed sector trading partners had peaked. In Phase V of Cycle 4, the peak for U.S. developed sector trading partner domestic demand growth rates was 1988. Indeed, the aggregate non-U.S. developed sector domestic demand growth rate reached its apex in the first quarter of that year. It declined in the second quarter and was lower in the second half of 1988 than in the first. The domestic demand growth rate average of the FRG and Japan will have topped off in 1988 at an estimated 5.0 percent. The average of the second-tier West European economy domestic demand growth rates peaked in 1988, reaching an estimated 3.9 percent.

Falling West European/Japanese domestic demand growth rates do not bode well for the full maturation of the J-curve. They suggest that one very crucial variable—non-U.S. developed sector domestic demand growth rates—will not support a continued acceleration of the U.S. export growth rate. And even though the U.S. domestic demand growth rate will decline in 1989, its differential with the rest of the developed sector will not increase significantly unless new expansionary fiscal/monetary packages are introduced outside of the U.S.—a development that seems extremely unlikely, especially in Western Europe—or the United States moves toward a more contractionary macroeconomic policy—a development whose prospects remain unclear (if the U.S. government were to take action to subdue domestic demand, the resulting improvement in the U.S. merchandise trade deficit would not come from export acceleration, the traditional Phase V means, but from a lower import growth rate).

Depressed Developing Sector Markets

Equally detrimental to the maturation of the J-curve in Phase V of Cycle 4 has been the marginal recovery of the developing sector import growth rate. In Phase V of Cycles 2 and 3, the developing sector import growth rate was not only higher than in Phase V of Cycle 4; its degree of recovery from Phase III levels was greater.

The absolute weakness of the developing sector import growth rate in Phase V of Cycle 4 is further revealed when we examine the expansion of developing sector imports from the recession year of 1970 to 1973, the year of J-curve maturation, and from the recession year 1975 to 1979, the next year of J-curve maturation (see Table 9.3). Developing sector imports showed enormous improvement in both cases. On the other hand, when we turn to developing sector imports in 1987, we find them to be barely higher than in the recession year of 1982. And the magnitude of developing sector imports estimated for 1988—the year of anticipated full J-curve maturation—while greater than in 1982, represents a much smaller improvement than the 1973 and 1979 advances from preceding recessions.

The cause of the weakness in developing sector import growth in Cycle 4 has been twofold. First, overindebted developing sector economies have been virtually cut off from private financing—which was not the case in Cycles 2 and 3—and developing sector capital importers have therefore seen their imports drop sharply. The majority of the heavily indebted capital importers are located in the developing economies of the Americas and Africa and it could be anticipated that the import growth rate in Cycle 4 in these regions would be worse than that for the developing sector as a whole. Indeed, the imports in these areas from 1982, a recession year, to 1987 or 1988 (estimated) dropped (see Table 9.3).

A second cause of the collapse of the developing sector import growth rate in Cycle 4 has been the weakness in primary commodity exports.

TABLE 9.3

IMPORT GROWTH IN THE DEVELOPING SECTOR
FROM PRECEDING RECESSION TO PHASE V (Percent Growth)

	CYCLE 2: 1970-73	CYCLE 3: 1975-79	CYCLE IV: 1982-87	1982-88(est.)
Developing Sector	75.3	75.9	1.4	12.5
Developing Sector of the Americas	63.2	62.4	-16.2	-11.8
Africa	52.9	45.1	-35.2*	-31.8
Oil Exporters	107.3	92.5	-44.2**	-38.0

* Based on African imports in the first half of 1987 annualized.
** Based on oil exporter imports in first three quarters of 1987 annualized.

SOURCE: IMF IFS Supplement to Trade Statistics, Supplement Series No. 15, 1988.

Leading the decline in primary commodity exports has been petroleum. In response, developing sector oil exporters' imports have fallen dramatically, and this contrasts to the vigor with which they expanded during the previous two cycles.

Oil exporter import growth rates led those of the developing sector in Cycles 2 and 3, and in Phase V of those cycles, they accelerated rapidly from preceding recession levels. Thus far in Phase V of Cycle 4, oil exporter imports have not surpassed 1982 levels.

The anemic developing sector import recovery in Phase V of Cycle 4 (especially when compared to the robust import recoveries in the two preceding Phase Vs) has served to depress the advance in the export growth rate of the developed sector. But the impact of the developing sector's poor import performance seems to fall especially heavily upon the U.S. compared to the FRG and, to some extent, Japan. In the mid-1970s, the percentage of U.S. exports accounted for by exports to the developing sector was higher than the FRG's.[13] At that time, exports to the developing sector accounted for 35.9 percent of all U.S. exports and only 19.1 percent of FRG exports. As a result, the acceleration in developing sector imports in Phase V of Cycles 2 and 3 benefited U.S. external balances more. Now, in Phase V of Cycle 4, the tables have turned. In the mid-1980s, the percentage of U.S. exports accounted for by exports to the developing sector has only dropped marginally, to 32.3 percent, while the FRG's has dropped much more, to 12.8 percent. Hence, the weakness of the developing sector import growth rate in Phase V of Cycle 4 has hurt U.S. external balances more than those of the FRG.

The percentage of Japanese exports accounted for by exports to the developing sector in the mid-1970s was higher than that of the U.S.—48.4 percent. Therefore, in Phase V of Cycles 2 and 3, Japan's external balances benefited more from the rise in the developing sector import growth rate. But by the mid-1980s, the share of Japan's exports accounted for by exports to the developing sector had dropped severely, to 32.2 percent, just below that of the U.S. Hence, in Phase V of Cycle 4 Japan's external balances have not been damaged more than those of the U.S. as a result of the weakness in developing sector imports.

Moreover, a greater proportion of U.S. than FRG or Japanese exports to the developing sector is to areas whose imports have been particularly depressed in Cycle 4—OPEC and developing countries of the Americas and Africa.[14] In 1985 U.S. exports to these sectors accounted for 22.7 percent of all U.S. exports; for Japan, this percentage was 13.9, and for the FRG, only 9.5. This has meant that the low developing sector import growth rate in Phase V of Cycle 4 has been more damaging to U.S. export performance than to that of the FRG or Japan.

A small decline in the developing sector import growth rate in 1989 from what it is estimated to be in 1988 will compound the negative effect of declining non-U.S. developed sector domestic demand growth rates on the U.S. export growth rate.

Food Deficit: Timing and Magnitude

Interestingly, in all trade and payments cycles the initiation of recovery in the U.S. merchandise trade balance during Phase V coincided with an acceleration in U.S. agricultural exports due to global food deficits. In Cycle 1, both the improvement in the U.S. merchandise trade balance and an acceleration in U.S. agricultural exports began in the fourth quarter of 1962. In Cycle 2, these improvements began in the fourth quarter of 1972, in Cycle 3 the same two developments emerged in the second quarter of 1978, and in Cycle 4 they erupted in the first quarter of 1988. The dynamic relationship between U.S. merchandise trade balance recoveries and the rise in U.S. agricultural exports caused by sudden stress on global food supplies points to one reason for the late arrival of the U.S. trade balance recovery in Phase V of Cycle 4.

Of equal importance, the dimensions of U.S. merchandise trade balance gains have been strongly influenced by differences in the absolute size of U.S. agricultural export expansions in the various Phase Vs. Both in absolute magnitude and in its effect on the U.S. merchandise trade balance, the Cycle 4 Phase V U.S. agricultural export expansion has been noticeably weaker than those in Phase V of the previous two cycles. To measure these differences we have employed a methodology similar to that used to identify the possible role of global food deficits in fostering improvement in U.S. external balances in 1973 and 1979. In the Cycle 4 case, because the acceleration in U.S. agricultural exports has only evolved through three quarters (as of this writing)—the first three quarters of 1988—we compare this period with the first three quarters of agricultural export expansions that occurred in Phase V of Cycle 2 (the fourth quarter of 1972 and first two quarters of 1973) and of Cycle 3 (the second through fourth quarters of 1978). To do this we first determined the growth rate of U.S. agricultural exports for these two three-quarter periods in Cycles 2 and 3 relative to the three-quarter periods preceding them. Then we subtracted from these growth rates the average growth rate of U.S. agricultural exports for the two three-quarter periods immediately prior to each of them—periods that reflected the U.S. agricultural export growth rate when global food deficits were absent.

On this basis the degree of acceleration in the U.S. agricultural export growth rate from the fourth quarter of 1972 through the second quarter of 1973 and from the second through fourth quarter of 1978 was substantially greater than in the first three quarters of 1988 (see Table 9.4). In addition, agricultural export growth in the three-quarter periods in Cycles 2 and 3 played a much larger role in total U.S. merchandise export growth than it did in the Cycle 4 three-quarter period, and represented a larger percentage of the merchandise trade balance improvement (see Table 9.4).

Again, as with the case of our estimate of the impact of food deficits on U.S. external balances in 1973 and 1979, some of the improvement in the U.S. agricultural export growth rate above recent historical rates was due to dollar depreciation. Nevertheless, the differences in agricultural export growth rates and their influence on the U.S. export growth rate and on the recovery in the U.S. merchandise trade balance between Cycles 2 and 3 on the one hand and Cycle 4 on the other is sizable enough to offer a reason for the failure of the J-curve to mature fully in Cycle 4.

Other Forces Impacting U.S. Trade Competitiveness

In addition to these developments, other factors, detrimental to U.S. competitiveness in home and foreign markets, have asserted themselves in Phase V of Cycle 4.

Two of the most dramatic developments differentiating Cycle 4 from earlier cycles—the unparalleled proportion of world import growth accounted for by the U.S. and the long and unprecedented currency misalignments—have contributed to weakening U.S. trade competitiveness in Phase V. The dependence of the rest of the world for export earnings and GNP growth (i.e., net export volume and related business investment) on the U.S. market reached staggering proportions in Phases I–III of Cycle 4 as the percentage of world import growth accounted for by U.S. import growth dwarfed those in Phases I–III of earlier cycles, while at the same time the world GDP growth rate was lower than in all previous Phases I–III. In Cycle 2, from Phase I–III (1968–71) the U.S.

TABLE 9.4

US AGRICULTURAL EXPORTS IN PHASE V AND THEIR IMPACT ON US EXPORTS AND MERCHANDISE TRADE BALANCE (Percent)

	Rate of Growth of US Agricultural Exports Above Recent Historical Rate	Growth of US Agricultural Exports Above Recent Historical Rate As Percentage of Growth In US Merchandise Exports	Growth of US Agricultural Exports Above Recent Historical Rate As Percentage of Improvement In US Merchandise Trade Balance
IVQ72 - IIQ-73	55.4	34.8	140.0
IIQ78 - IVQ78	28.0	25.1	104.7
IQ-88 - IIIQ88	19.5	10.1	15.7

SOURCE: IVQ72-IIQ73 and IIQ78-IVQ78 - National Income and Product Accounts of the US, 1929-82-Statistical Tables, US Department of Commerce; IQ-IIIQ88 - Merchandise Trade: Third Quarter 1988, US Department of Commerce, Nov. 28, 1988, and Economic Report of the President, Feb. 1988.

accounted for 13.5 percent of world import growth, and over the same phases in Cycle 3 (1976–78), the U.S. accounted for 18.4 percent. But in Cycle 4, from Phase I–III (1983–85) the U.S. accounted for 93.5 percent of world import growth.[15] At the same time the average annual world GDP growth rate in Phase I–III of Cycle 4 declined from 4.1 percent and 4.4 percent over the same phases in Cycles 2 and 3, respectively, to 3.7 percent.[16]

With unusual levels of dependence on U.S. imports for export and GDP growth in the rest of the world, exporters to the U.S. have been less willing to yield market share. A greater number of exporters accounting for a larger portion of exports to the U.S. than in earlier Phase Vs have been prepared to deter the impact of dollar depreciation on their market share by accepting lower profits.

Further, a successful reduction in U.S. import growth in Cycle 4 would have a bigger negative impact on U.S. exports than in previous cycles since a greater proportion of non-U.S. export earnings and domestic demand growth is linked to the vitality of exports to the U.S.

A second factor damaging to U.S. competitiveness has been the larger dollar misalignment preceding Phase V of Cycle 4. In Cycle 2, Phase V was not preceded by dollar appreciation. In Cycle 3, Phase V was not only preceded by dollar appreciation of 5.2 percent (in 1976) but by a larger deterioration in U.S. external balances than had occurred in Phases I–III of Cycle 2. Hence, dollar overvaluation prior to Phase V of Cycle 3 had been greater than in Cycle 2. But prior to Phase V of Cycle 4, the dollar had experienced a mammoth five-year appreciation of 50.2 percent while the dimensions of the deterioration in U.S. external balances were far greater than those in Cycle 3. This caused dollar overvaluation of unprecedented proportions.

One result of currency appreciation during periods of merchandise trade and current account balance losses is an inefficient purge of real and potential plant and equipment, labor skills, and R&D—a process that runs counter to successful supply-side adjustment. Although supply-side improvements are rendered as a result of enterprise response to competitive pressures exacerbated by advantages granted imports, these fail to outweigh the supply-side distortions precipitated by currency overvaluation.[17]

While the U.S. economy suffered from distortion of its supply-side adjustment, the East Asian NIEs and Japan sustained effective supply-side adjustment, enhancing the relative trade competitiveness of both versus the United States and helping to undermine the recovery in the U.S. merchandise trade balance.[18] Since the East Asian NIEs and Japan have a high proportion of their exports in manufactured goods and a high proportion of their imports in primary commodities, their competitive advantages have been advanced in Phase V of Cycle 4 more forcefully than in earlier Phase Vs as a result of the superior terms of trade performance of manufactured goods to primary commodities in 1986–88 compared to 1972–74 and 1978–80. Indeed, among the world's manufacturing exporters, the United States (along with Canada and Australia) has seen its competitiveness suffer relative to other manufacturing exporters in Phase V of Cycle 4 because of the comparatively high proportion of primary commodities in its exports and high percentage of manufactured goods in its imports.

Factor Services Income

Equal in importance to the progress in the U.S. merchandise trade balance in producing improvement in the U.S. current account balance in Phase V of Cycles 2 and 3 was the growth in U.S. factor service income surpluses. Indeed, in Phase V of Cycle 3 it was the jump in the U.S. factor services income surplus that was responsible for the majority of the current account gain. But in Phase V of Cycle 4, at the same time the U.S. merchandise trade balance began to recover, the factor services income balance faltered. As a consequence, the recovery in the U.S. current account balance in the first half of 1988 was only one-half the size of the recovery in the merchandise trade balance, while in 1973 and 1979 the advance in the current account balance was on average twice the size of that of the merchandise trade balance.

The two causes of this important turn of events were the worsening in the U.S. net investment balance during Cycle 4 and the weakness in the advance of U.S. direct investment income in Phase V of Cycle 4 (see Table 9.5).

Despite a dispute over the absolute size of the U.S. net investment balance, there is no argument over the degree of deterioration in that balance since 1981, when the U.S. achieved its largest net investment surplus. The decline in the U.S. net investment balance from 1981 to the end of 1987 was $509.4 billion. This dramatic turnaround in the U.S. net investment balance has fueled a decline in the U.S. factor services income surplus, and this decline has made it more difficult to reduce the current account deficit. Indeed, in the first half of 1988 the U.S. factor services income balance fell from sizable, albeit declining, surpluses in 1986 and 1987 to a small deficit.

When the U.S. factor services income balance improved in 1973 and 1979, the principal cause was a rise in direct investment income which in turn led to an improvement in U.S. net investment income.

The U.S.'s strong investment position in the overseas extractive sector, especially petroleum, led to soaring growth in U.S. direct investment income in 1973 and 1979, when primary commodity prices ascended. The size of growth in U.S. direct investment income and the advance in U.S.

TABLE 9.5

THE US NET INVESTMENT BALANCE AND THE US DIRECT INVESTMENT AND FACTOR SERVICES INCOME BALANCE IMPACT ON IMPROVEMENT IN THE US CURRENT ACCOUNT BALANCE IN PHASE V

	1973	1979	1st Half 1988 (estimate)
US Net Investment Balance ($Billions)	$61.9	$94.5	-$434.6
US Direct Investment Income Change as a Percentage of Improvement in the Current Account Balance	55.0%	88.2%	-50.7%
US Direct Investment Income Balance Change as a Percentage of Current Account Improvement	40.3%	74.3%	-116.2%
US Factor Services Income Balance Change as a Percentage of Current Account Improvement	31.0%	78.5%	-66.2%

SOURCE: US Net Investment: 1973 - Survey of Current Business, US Department of Commerce, June 1977; 1979 - Economic Report of the President 1988; 1988 first half estimate - author's; all others - 1973 - Survey of Current Business, June 1981; 1979 - Survey of Current Business, June 1986; 1988 first half estimates - Summary of US International Transactions-Second Quarter 1988, US Department of Commerce, Sept. 13, 1988.

net investment income in 1973 and 1979 represented large percentages of the improvement in the U.S. current account balance (see Table 9.5). In the first half of 1988, with only a meager rise in primary commodity prices, U.S. direct investment income fell (some of the movement from 1987's substantial advance to the drop in 1988 had to do with the volatility of the dollar), and the U.S. factor services income balance has worsened. As a result, unlike 1973 and 1979 both have made large negative contributions to the change in the U.S. current account balance (see Table 9.5).

Whither Inflation?

Symptoms of the second development that has characterized Phase V of the trade and payments cycles—goods and services price inflation—began to surface in 1986. A more expansive aggregate developed sector macroeconomic (predominantly monetary) policy precipitated by Phase IV initiatives began to unfold in 1985 with a steady retreat in U.S. interest rates, followed in 1986 by accelerated non-U.S. developed sector monetary growth. Aggregate developed sector monetary expansion boosted the sector's domestic demand growth rates from 1986–88 and the enlarged developed sector domestic demand growth rate exerted pressure on primary input supplies—especially primary commodities, whose prices began to rise.

But for the same reason that the maturation of the J-curve was muted in Phase V of Cycle 4, so was the rise in goods and services price inflation. The less accommodative developed sector macroeconomic policy and smaller domestic demand growth rate recoveries provoked a less severe rise in primary input costs. In addition, a higher proportion of the economic stimulus produced by the expansionist developed sector macroeconomic policy was siphoned off into financial assets than in earlier cycles.

The revival of goods and services price inflation in Phase V of Cycle 4 has therefore been less severe when compared to the surge in world inflation in Phase V of the past two cycles. While world inflation has been weaker than in the past two cycles, the magnitude of developed sector inflation has been dramatically lower (see Table 9.6). Developing sector inflation has been higher in Phase V of Cycle 4 and virtually all of this is the result of much greater inflation in Latin America—itself due to the combined inflation among the three largest developing sector foreign debtors, Brazil, Mexico, and Argentina.[19] Thus, the higher developing sector inflation rate in 1987 compared to 1973/74 and 1979/80 is in part a result of the more deflationary developed sector payments posture which has served to constrain developing sector imports, thereby putting greater pressure on goods and services supply in those economies.

TABLE 9.6

CONSUMER PRICE INFLATION IN PHASE V OF THE LAST THREE TRADE AND PAYMENTS CYCLES

Sectoral Inflation Performance in Phase V of Last Three Cycles (Percent Growth)

	CYCLE 2: 1973/74	CYCLE 3: 1979	CYCLE 4: 1987
World Consumer Price Inflation Rate	12.3	12.4	11.2
Developed Sector	10.5	9.1	2.9
Developing Sector	21.1	23.4	40.8
Western Hemisphere	28.3	50.5	119.5

Dimensions of Change in Consumer Price Inflation Rate in Phases III and V (Percentage Point Change)

	Phase III 1968-71	Phase V* 1972-73	Phase III 1977-78	Phase V* 1978-79	Phase III 1984-86	Phase V* 1986-87
Changes in World Consumer Price Inflation	1.3	3.7	-1.7	2.8	-5.1	2.4

SOURCE: Cycles 2 and 3 - IMF IFS Yearbook 1986; Cycle 4 - IFS Nov. 1988.

* First Year

The decided weakness of world goods and services price inflation in Phase V of Cycle 4 reflects the general evolution of inflation in Cycle 4 compared to Cycles 2 and 3. In Cycle 4, the Phase III contraction in world consumer price inflation was greater than in Phase III of the previous two cycles (see Table 9.6), and the advance of world consumer price inflation in Phase V from its nadir in Phase III has been far weaker than was the case in Cycles 2 and 3.

Behind the weakness of inflation in Phase V of Cycle 4 has been the poor recovery of primary commodity prices, especially in comparison to their performance in the previous two Phase Vs.[20] In addition, labor costs in the developed sector failed to increase as they had in Phase V of earlier Cycles.

The prospects for an acceleration of world inflation in the remainder of Phase V appear quite slim. A close look at the evolution of prices in Phase V of Cycle 4 reveals that the principal force driving inflation in previous Phase Vs—the rise in primary commodity prices—has already peaked. The pace of acceleration in oil prices began to slow after the first quarter of 1987, when they grew by 22.9 percent, and in the first three quarters of 1988 oil prices slumped. A belated OPEC production quota agreement at the end of 1988 prompted a price recovery, but one that will be difficult to sustain in the face of declining developed sector domestic demand growth rates. The quarterly rate of growth in nonfuel primary commodity prices reached a peak in the fourth quarter of 1987 when they grew by 13.5 percent, but in the third quarter of 1988 nonfuel primary commodity prices began to drop.[21]

PHASE V PERTURBATIONS IN CYCLE 4

The nature of the interaction between aggregate developed sector macroeconomic policy and primary input costs in Phase V of the current cycle has not only helped to foster a weak recovery in U.S. external balances and in world goods and services price inflation; it has also extended the duration of Phase V beyond what it was in Cycles 2 and 3. Both the recovery in U.S. external balances and the period of peak growth in primary commodity prices in Phase V of Cycles 2 and 3 occurred within five quarters of the launching of Phase IV initiatives. In Phase V of Cycle 4 it has taken twice as long for these developments to emerge. Second, the Phase V spike in primary commodity and goods and services prices was much sharper in Cycles 2 and 3, causing an earlier and more severe contractionary turn in aggregate developed sector macroeconomic policy and thus an earlier onset of Phase VI. In Cycle 4, the weaker inflationary spike resulted in adjustments in developed sector economic policy in 1988 insufficient to produce an early onset of Phase VI.

In length, Phase V of Cycle 4 resembles more Phase V of Cycle 1 than those of the interim cycles. In Phase V of both Cycles 1 and 4, the early expansion in developed sector macroeconomic policy, the inflationary spike, and the subsequent adjustments in macroeconomic policy were noticeably weaker than in Cycles 2 and 3. Phase V of Cycle 1 lasted over three years, while in Cycles 2 and 3 it lasted about two years. Phase V of Cycle 4 turned two years of age in mid-1988.

But there are two crucial differences between Phase V of Cycle 1 and of Cycle 4. First, the elements comprising the third factor that has caused the trade and payments cycles—intra-developed sector macroeconomic policy differences and resulting intra-developed sector merchandise trade and current account imbalances—are larger in the later cycle, both in absolute terms and as a percentage of GNP.[22] Indeed, Cycle 4 intra-developed sector external imbalances are much larger than those of Cycles 2 and 3 as well. As a result, in Cycle 4 the United States has traded goods and services price inflation through the vehicle of external deficits for another kind of inflation, dollar overvaluation—a degree of dollar overvaluation and intra-developed sector currency misalignment unimaginable in the first cycle.

Second, while developed sector macroeconomic policy turned more contractionary in Cycle 4, a larger portion of the monetary and fiscal stimulus introduced found its way into financial assets as opposed to goods and services than in earlier cycles. This development tended to increase the magnitude of overvaluation in the world stock of financial assets, again to a degree unimaginable in Cycle 1.

The future duration of Phase V, the depth and length of the next recession (Phase VI), and the structure and substance of the next trade and payments cycle will in large part be determined by whether and at what pace the reduction in the dollar's overvaluation is managed. Administration of this process will represent the greatest test of the commitment of nations to the postwar objective of a liberalized and internationally coordinated trade and payments order. And failure to effectively manage this process could expose the inflated value of a more vulnerable stock of financial assets to shocking contraction à la October 1987.

The Dollar and Financial Asset Prices in the Evolution of Phase V of Cycle 4

The history of Phase V of Cycle 4 reveals the growing importance of the relationship of the dollar and financial asset prices to the evolution of the three variables that have determined the trade and payments cycles and their differences.

The transition from Phase III to Phase V in Cycle 4 (1985 to 1986) was distinguished from transitions in Cycles 2 and 3 in two ways. First, the decline in primary input costs in Phase III of Cycle 4 was much deeper and the recovery in these costs early in Phase V was noticeably weaker.[23] Second, despite more forceful dollar depreciation, U.S. external deficits continued to expand well beyond the time frame experienced in Cycles 2 and 3.

The Phase IV policy response during the transition from Phase III to Phase V fell less upon macroeconomic and payments policy adjustment than in Cycles 2 and 3. Unlike in Cycle 3, the United States—fearing the recessionary implications of the more pronounced Phase III economic slide—failed to constrain its domestic monetary policy. As a result, the U.S. domestic demand growth rate failed to contract in 1986–88 as much as it did in Phase V of Cycle 3. On the other hand, concerned with the consequences of reflationary policy for goods and services price inflation and for government fiscal overindebtedness, the remainder of the developed sector responded with a weaker macroeconomic policy adjustment than was the case in Cycles 2 and 3 and the acceleration of the non-U.S. developed sector domestic demand growth rate was therefore not as strong in 1986–88 as it had been in the previous two Phase Vs. Finally, the recovery of the developing sector import growth rate was impaired by the maintenance of a restrictive developed sector payments posture—a development absent from earlier Phase Vs.

Intra-developed sector macroeconomic (Plaza Accords) and international payments (Baker Plan) policy initiatives were thus insufficient to support a reduction in U.S. external deficits, and this in turn put maximum pressure on dollar depreciation.

Further, because the U.S. was restrained by law and by the market reaction from using fiscal policy to stimulate higher growth and because Japan and Western Europe prioritized containment of government fiscal overindebtedness, a larger portion of the expansion in aggregate developed sector macroeconomic policy fell to monetary policy than in the past. The 1985/86 decline in developed sector interest rates, combined with the failure of primary commodity prices and world domestic demand growth to induce direct investment in goods and services, fostered a dramatic growth in the prices of bonds and stocks.

The second stage in the evolution of Phase V of Cycle 4 began with the Louvre Accords in February 1987. Representing a consensus of the leading developed sector economies, the Louvre Accords sought to redress the earlier imbalance between macroeconomic policy adjustment and dollar depreciation in the collective effort to reduce dollar overvaluation. It sought to halt the decline of the dollar while enhancing national government commitments to macroeconomic policy adjustment. Tokyo and Bonn affirmed government fiscal policy initiatives while Washington restated its commitment to constraining domestic demand. The latter pledge was to be assured through a new U.S. willingness to adjust its domestic monetary policy (i.e., raise interest rates) in order to stabilize the dollar.

The Louvre Accords turned out to be a miscalculation, and by the fall of 1987 Bonn and Washington had effectively rescinded their promises. Of less import was the FRG's retreat from its pledge of a more expansionist macroeconomic policy. As in Phase V of Cycles 1 and 2, Bonn was the first major OECD government to adopt a less accommodative domestic monetary policy in response to the initial signs of Phase V goods and services price inflation. Unfolding later in Phase V than had been the case in earlier cycles, developments associated with goods and services price inflation, especially accelerated growth of FRG and Japanese domestic money supplies, led Bonn to take steps to constrain money growth in the summer of 1987 by nudging up interest rates.

While the FRG's deflationary policy tilt put new pressure on the dollar, much more important was the failure of the J-curve to mature. A spike in the monthly U.S. merchandise trade deficit in June, reported in August 1987, threatened the dollar. But honoring its Louvre pledge, the United States tightened domestic monetary policy, leading to a marginal increase in interest rates. When the August merchandise trade deficit, reported in October, rose unexpectedly, the financial markets reacted with anticipation of further U.S. domestic monetary tightening. The end of the 1985/86 decline in U.S. interest rates in 1987 following the Louvre Accords had already sparked an enormous contraction in the U.S. bond market, and financial market concern over rising interest rates in October unleashed a collapse in the U.S. equity markets, a collapse copied around the globe. The sudden decline in bond and stock prices—a decline which almost wiped out the 1985/86 accretion in the prices of these assets—forced the U.S. to withdraw its commitment to the Louvre Accords. Hence, when the October 1987 U.S. merchandise trade deficit was reported in December to have reached an all-time high, the dollar was left to fall, and fall rapidly, despite G-7 rhetorical efforts and public commitments to intervene to prevent further dollar depreciation.[24]

The stage in the evolution of Phase V that began with the Louvre Accords ended in January/February 1988 when developed sector domestic demand growth outside of the U.S. peaked, finally producing a contraction in the U.S. merchandise trade deficit. Both the November and December 1987 U.S. merchandise trade balances (reported in January and February 1988) showed the beginning of the long-awaited J-curve maturation. The continued fall in the U.S. merchandise trade deficit through the first half of 1988 not only stabilized the dollar, but eventually helped spark a small dollar rally.[25]

In FY87, the revitalization of U.S. resource utilization associated with Phase V eliminated the cyclical component of the U.S. government fiscal deficit, and in 1988 the changes in the 1987 U.S. export volume performance spilled over to export value, fostering a sharp reduction in the cyclical component of the U.S. merchandise trade deficit. While the turn in the fortunes of the U.S. trade balance led to dollar stability, the superior levels of U.S. resource utilization, once joined with rising primary commodity prices, created inflationary pressures and, by the spring of 1988, a tighter U.S. domestic monetary policy. Because inflationary pressures were greatest in the United States, the rise in U.S. interest rates led those in the remainder of the developed sector (aside from Japan, whose interest rates did not change), and the small interest rate differentials produced through this process were sufficient to place additional upward pressure on the dollar.

Peak domestic demand growth rates in the developed sector were reached in the fourth quarter of 1987 and first quarter of 1988. Their deceleration in the second quarter was followed in the third by a decline in gold, oil, and nonfuel primary commodity prices, as well as a slowdown in U.S. economic performance (i.e., lower net exports and nonresidential fixed investment growth and a lower GNP growth rate). These conditions marked the beginning of a process of deceleration in Phase V.

In the last two Phase Vs the process of deceleration was quite short, as more forceful contractionary economic policies brought about Phase VI. While goods and services price inflation in Phase V of Cycle 4 has been too weak to prompt a policy reaction capable of forcing a rapid slide into Phase VI, this does not necessarily mean that there will be a slow descent into the next phase. As inflationary pressures began to wither in the third quarter of 1988, the pace of decline in the U.S. merchandise trade deficit also slowed, and these two developments incited a new round of dollar depreciation beginning in October. Maturation of these trends and the growing pressure against the dollar it would engender could prompt a response in U.S. interest rates sufficient to plunge the world economy into Phase VI.

Despite a short-term recovery in U.S. net exports and merchandise trade balance in the first quarter of 1989, two trends surfaced by the end of 1988 to suggest that the process of deceleration in Phase V had commenced. First, the U.S. merchandise trade recovery, which had slowed to a crawl in the third quarter of 1988, stumbled in the fourth quarter as the U.S. merchandise trade deficit expanded anew.[26] Second, the advance in U.S. net exports and related non-residential fixed investment came to a halt as both combined made no contribution to U.S. GNP growth in the second half of 1988.[27]

With non-U.S. developed sector domestic demand growth rates anticipated to fall in 1989/90 and with the dollar having appreciated in 1988 and early 1989, it is difficult to see how the U.S. export growth rate will not retreat in the future. And a withering U.S. export recovery bodes ill for further improvement in both the U.S. merchandise trade and net export balances (as well as for the component of nonresidential fixed investment driven by the expansion of U.S. exports).

Indeed, by the first quarter of 1989, further evidence indicating a process of deceleration had emerged as the U.S. domestic demand growth rate (discounting the one-time change in agricultural inventories) sank. While this development will work to offset pressures for further deterioration in U.S. external balances caused by a declining export growth rate and thereby shield the dollar exchange rate, it will also serve to remove a prop that has facilitated a transitory appreciation in the dollar exchange rate during Phase V.

Rising U.S. interest rates and widening of interest rate differentials favorable to the dollar supported a dollar rally during 1988 and early 1989, as the markets and the U.S. Federal Reserve Board were impressed with the continuous rise in U.S. resource utilization rates and an early 1989 jump in inflation, largely in response to short-term advances in fuel and food prices (the former prompted by the late 1988 OPEC agreement on production quotas, and the latter, by a jump in non-grain food prices resulting from the 1988 drought).

As long as investor concerns are focused on U.S. goods and services price inflation, the dollar will remain under the protection of favorable interest rate differentials. When these concerns will recede remains uncertain. But the short-term nature of early 1989 spikes in fuel and food prices, the slowdown in U.S. domestic demand growth, and the contraction in non-U.S. developed sector domestic demand growth suggest that the prospects for inflation-induced interest rate differentials favorable to the dollar will dim.

Despite the protestations of some observers that the dollar was no longer overvalued at the end of 1988, the dollar will once again become vulnerable when inflation fears ease.

10

Conclusion: Meeting The Challenge

In the remainder of the current trade and payments cycle and during the next, the already battered postwar trade and payments order will confront its stiffest challenge. Since 1968, internationally coordinated balance of payments adjustment has been severely weakened first by the collapse of the Bretton Woods and Smithsonian fixed exchange rate regimes and then by the fleeting staying power of looser exchange rate regimes such as those associated with the Plaza and Louvre Accords. At the same time, national government commitments to trade liberalism in the form of tariff reductions and trade symmetry forged around the GATT's Most Favored Nation principle have been increasingly undercut through the expansion of nontariff barriers and the "new protectionism's" penchant for bilaterally managed trade.

In the remainder of Cycle 4 and through the next, the trade and payments system will be rocked by forces inciting even greater exchange rate volatility and trade protectionism. Enormous social, political, and economic limitations to the magnitude and pace of developed sector macroeconomic policy adjustment and to the flexibility in developed sector payments policies toward the developing sector suggest that the future size and speed of U.S. merchandise trade and current account deficit contraction will not be sufficient to appreciably reduce dollar overvaluation. If so, this means that the principal burden for reducing currency misalignment will fall to the mechanism of market-induced dollar depreciation.

One result of the reduction in the dollar's overvaluation—no matter how it unfolds—will be a decline in the U.S. import growth rate which, because of the limits placed on the non-U.S. import growth rate by over-indebtedness, will lead to a decline in the world import growth rate. Smaller U.S. and world import growth means more intense market crowding and greater pressure for unilateral national actions to secure markets.

In these looming challenges to the world trade and payments order lies a deeper threat: the possibility that market-induced dollar depreciation may overwhelm the joint capacity of the Group of Seven governments to manage it. Joint G-7 currency intervention aimed at containing market momentum remains a useful tool in managing developed sector exchange rates, but failure to produce real and sustainable change in underlying merchandise trade and current account imbalances will at some point undermine the effectiveness of such actions, and in addition central banks—like all banks—must be concerned with the decline in the value of and income produced from their dollar assets, a concern that will become a further disincentive to coordinated intervention.

Indeed, there is no guarantee of G-7 effectiveness in managing the dollar exchange rate outside of a long-term program to reduce intra-developed sector external imbalances—a program that, to work, must focus on meaningful changes in the economic policies of the United States, the Federal Republic of Germany, and Japan. But historical trends in the economic policy behavior of the three from Cycle 2 to Cycle 4—trends that reveal emphatic commitments to historical economic and commercial biases—offer little basis for optimism regarding the sustained economic adjustment needed to reduce external imbalances. Further, the growing inter-cyclical improvement in the current account and net investment surpluses of Japan and the FRG and the U.S.'s ever larger inter-cyclical current account deficits and new net investment deficit create additional incentives for each to abide by its national macroeconomic policy biases toward goods and services price inflation vs. unemployment.

The magnitude of the political, social, and economic dislocations implied in needed long-term economic adjustment only appears manageable when measured against the risks of avoiding it. Unmanaged dollar depreciation would force either U.S. resort to a tighter domestic monetary policy in support of higher interest rates in order to sustain capital inflow and dollar stability—as it did in the summer of 1987—or worse, acceptance of the dollar's plunge, a plunge that would unleash severe inflationary and eventually recessionary forces generated by a sharp rise in U.S. import prices and a steep reduction in U.S. import volume (it was the immense increase in U.S. import volume in Cycle 4 that allowed the U.S. economic expansion to evolve without an acceleration in goods and services price inflation).

But rising U.S. interest rates would expose the pronounced vulnerabilities in the world economy that have evolved from Cycle 2 to Cycle 4: the U.S. twin (government fiscal and trade) deficits, developing sector and CPE foreign debt, and, more recently, overpriced bonds and stocks. By reducing economic output growth, higher interest rates would widen the U.S. government fiscal deficit while at the same time aggravating the cost of the twin deficits through enlarged government interest outlays and a more rapidly deteriorating factor services income balance. Higher interest rates would also drive up developing sector and CPE current account deficits by exacerbating factor services income deficits. Developing sector current account balances would be further undermined by reduced export volume growth and lower primary commodity prices. Finally, higher interest rates would, as they did in 1987, provoke a contraction in inflated bond and stock prices.

The Test in the Remainder of Phase V: Securing G-7 Credibility

The G-7 governments' ability to pursue an effective program for reducing intra-developed sector trade imbalances—one that would guarantee G-7 credibility in managing exchange rates and thereby avoid higher interest rates—is complicated by another factor: the stage of the trade and payments cycle we are currently in.

The period of peak economic performance in the developed sector climaxed in the first half of 1988. Since the second quarter of 1988 the GNP and domestic demand growth rates of the developed sector have been decelerating, and future deceleration will be exacerbated by the impact of rising developed sector interest rates. This process will produce larger obstacles to further macroeconomic policy adjustment. Future lower GNP growth and resource utilization rates in the U.S. will spark concern that any meaningful fiscal retrenchment might provoke what U.S. economic bias fears most—a recession. The passing of the peak of Phase V economic performance also means that the cyclical component of developed sector government fiscal deficits will once again grow, inciting more alarm in Western Europe and Japan over central government overindebtedness.

In addition to this deterrent to a more expansive non-U.S. developed sector macroeconomic policy, second-tier and smaller West European economies led by Britain began to experience traditional Phase V balance of payments stress in 1988, a development that will curtail any effort, especially on London's part, to adopt an even more accommodative domestic economic approach. When a more constrictive FRG 1989 fiscal policy is added to U.K. balance of payments problems, it is likely that the pace of deceleration in the West European domestic demand growth rate will be aggravated in 1989/90. Japan has already made relatively large contributions of domestic monetary and fiscal stimulus during Phase V of Cycle 4, and it is difficult to see Tokyo advancing any new expansionary economic packages beyond those already planned.

Failure to recognize where we are in the trade and payments cycle can lead to unrealistic proposals for balance of payments adjustment. For example, current Phase V conditions make it very unlikely that two essential features of American economist C. Fred Bergsten's proposal for eliminating U.S. external deficits in four years can be realized.[1] Bergsten has argued for U.S. initiatives to eliminate the structural component of the federal government fiscal deficit (about $150 billion) in four years as mandated in the Gramm-Rudman legislation's deficit reduction targets. But lower U.S. economic growth than that enjoyed during the Phase V peak in 1987/88 will increase political resistance to deficit reduction, making elimination of the structural component of the budget deficit a near impossible task while the cyclical segment of the deficit will reemerge, pushing Gramm-Rudman targets well out of reach. Bergsten also argues for Japanese and West European policy adjustments sufficient to secure 5.0% and 3.0% annual GNP growth, respectively. These rates marginally surpass even those that both were able to achieve in the peak performance year of Phase V, 1988, and with the process of economic deceleration already under way—and with constraints on macroeconomic policy accommodation being reinforced, especially in Western Europe—these growth targets are inaccessible over a long period.

This is not to say that significant and immediate developed sector macroeconomic policy adjustment is not desirable; it is essential. But it is to say that there is no quick fix to intra-developed sector external imbalances, that the process of adjustment will evoke substantial cultural, social, and economic pain and therefore resistance, and that emerging economic conditions will be less conducive to such adjustment. Instead of accomplishing elimination of intra-developed sector merchandise trade and current account imbalances in the short term, realistic and feasible changes in developed sector domestic economic policies could guarantee an interim goal—G-7 ability to effectively manage the dollar exchange rate.

Securing this latter objective will be crucial in controlling damage to the trade and payments order during the remainder of Cycle 4. To the extent that G-7 management of the dollar's exchange rate is successful, it will serve to enhance the G-7's credibility in what is likely to be the sterner test for the dollar and world trade and payments system in Phase VI.

Maximization of the contraction in U.S. and expansion in Japanese and West European macroeconomic policies to the extent feasible within the cultural, political, and economic limitations likely to persist during the remainder of Phase V would produce several important results. It would moderate any market pressures on the dollar by causing some additional reduction in merchandise trade and current account imbalances and by demonstrating the commitment of developed sector governments to such adjustment. This would enhance the G-7's ability to manage the dollar's exchange rate, thereby relieving pressure on U.S. interest rates and extending the duration of Phase V. On the other hand, minimal contraction in U.S. and expansion in Japanese and West European macroeconomic policies would maximize pressure on the dollar by yielding no additional reduction in developed sector merchandise trade and current account imbalances through economic policy adjustment and by signaling the unwillingness of developed sector governments to make such adjustments. This would cripple the G-7's credibility and undermine its ability to manage the dollar's exchange rate, thereby transferring the pressure for adjustment to U.S. domestic monetary policy. Higher U.S. interest rates would bring—as did tighter developed sector domestic monetary policy in response to goods and services price inflation in previous Phase Vs—the early onset of Phase VI.

It is probable that the maximal range of developed sector economic adjustment will not be reached in Phase V, and if not, the credibility of the G-7 governments' ability to manage the reduction of external imbalances will suffer and pressure on the dollar will grow. Nevertheless, the threat of early entry into Phase VI inspired by the failure of the developed sector to undertake adequate economic adjustment is likely to spur at least some degree of adjustment among the G-7 economies.

In Phase V of Cycles 2 through 4, changes in developed sector merchandise trade and current account balances came as a result of a more rapid rise in the U.S. export growth rate than in its import growth rate while other developed nations went through the opposite process as import growth rates rose faster than export growth rates. These Phase V trends were provoked by a particular mix of economic policy in which the non-U.S. developed sector's macroeconomic policy became more expansionist while the U.S.'s experienced little change. Indeed, it was this set of policy conditions that produced the changes in developed sector economy external balances in Phase V of the current trade and payments cycle.

An extension of this economic policy adjustment mix into the remainder of Phase V would be less impressive to the financial markets than one in which the U.S. adopted a more constrictive fiscal policy even if the non-U.S. developed sector's fiscal and monetary policy were to go unchanged. What investors have not seen thus far is a clear demonstration on the part of the U.S. that it intends to adjust, and such a demonstration will be crucial to G-7 efforts to contain future dollar bearishness. A more constrictive U.S. domestic economic policy would also relieve pressure on goods and services price inflation, thereby helping to further moderate pressure on U.S. interest rates. A more expansionist developed sector economic adjustment policy would not only be less convincing to investors and therefore more troublesome for the dollar, it would fail to moderate the threat of goods and services price inflation and thus also the pressure on developed sector interest rates.

The Challenge of Phase VI: Avoiding Financial Chaos

Maximum developed sector economic adjustment in Phase V—or, at minimum, serious U.S. efforts to constrain its fiscal deficit and import growth—will be essential if the Group of Seven is to have authority and credibility, the attributes it will require to manage developed sector exchange rates in what promises to be the tougher challenge of Phase VI. The ability of the G-7 to avoid excessive pressure on the dollar and subsequent higher U.S. interest rates will be the pivotal factor determining the depth and duration of Phase VI.

But weighing against successful G-7 management of the dollar in Phase VI will be the unprecedented dimensions of developed sector domestic and external imbalances both in absolute terms and relative to GNP entering this phase. The U.S. government fiscal deficit is likely to range between $100–$150 billion (depending on the degree of U.S. economic adjustment implemented during the remainder of Phase V), while U.S. corporate debt/earnings and consumer debt/income ratios will be unusually high. The U.S. merchandise trade deficit will range between $90–$110 billion, depending on the nature of the adjustment process, and the U.S. current account deficit, between $100–$120 billion. The U.S. current account deficit will have fallen at a slower pace than the U.S. merchandise trade deficit, due to continued worsening of the U.S. factor services income balance. And the official U.S. net investment deficit will range between $600–$750 billion. Finally, favorable interest differentials, which bolstered the dollar in 1988/89, will have receded as developed sector interest rates converge.

While the interaction of inflation and aggregate developed sector macroeconomic policy in Phase V of the current cycle resembles that of Phase V of Cycle 1 and thus is likely to produce a descent in global domestic demand growth rates similar to that of 1967—that is, a growth recession—failure of the Group of Seven to enhance its credibility through invigorated intra-developed sector macroeconomic policy adjustment keeps ajar a window of vulnerability for a "hard landing" in Phase VI, a "landing" closer to those of 1974/75 and 1981/82 than to that of 1967. Higher U.S. interest rates, this time provoked by pronounced dollar weakness, could bring a deeper Phase VI recession—as did tighter developed sector domestic monetary policy in response to inflation in Phase V of Cycles 2 and 3. Further, while the United States will inherit large and expanding financial deficits going into Phase VI, those deficits—the fiscal, current account, and net investment deficits—are almost certain to worsen during Phase VI, serving to aggravate pressure on the dollar.

Higher U.S. interest rates in response to the dollar's predicament would deepen and extend the Phase VI economic recession, and by doing so further expose the major economic problems which have plagued the global economy in the 1980s—the U.S. twin deficits, Third World debt, and other overpriced financial assets.

A deep and long Phase VI economic recession would exacerbate the decline in U.S. government revenues (as well as state and local revenues, corporate earnings, and personal income), driving up the federal budget deficit (as well as other public and private deficits). In addition, legally mandated enlargement of "payments to individuals" would accelerate U.S. government outlays and the U.S. government fiscal deficit would be still further exacerbated by higher net interest outlays directly prompted by higher interest rates. Higher U.S. interest rates would also worsen the U.S. interest income balance and thereby the current account balance. So the twin deficits would grow at a faster pace.

Higher U.S. and developed sector interest rates in Phase VI would devastate the developing sector current account balance, which will have already been damaged by the effect of recession on its export growth. A larger economic recession would aggravate the decline in the developing sector merchandise trade balance by further weakening export volume and primary commodity prices. Higher interest rates would also widen the developing sector's interest income deficit and consequently its current account deficit.

Finally, higher interest rates would provoke an exodus from stocks and bonds, producing a fall in their prices.

A sustained rise in U.S. interest rates in Phase VI of Cycle 4 would unleash such forces of financial chaos as to threaten to shatter the credibility and cohesiveness of the Group of Seven as well as national allegiances to the postwar trade and payments order. To avoid the possibility of a severe financial crisis borne of potential deflationary pressure on dollar, Third World foreign debt, and stock and bond prices (and other developed sector debt), the G-7 requires a feasible long-term plan for eliminating developed sector external imbalances. Such a plan would give the G-7 an edge in containing the dollar bearishness likely to increase in Phase VI and would produce a mechanism for an early exit from Phase VI into a new cycle—one whose Phase I take-off would otherwise be compromised by the U.S.'s inability to lead it as it had in earlier Phase Is.

The Coming "Cycle of Adjustment"

If the coming Cycle of Adjustment is to provide the foundation for an acceleration in world output and trade growth in the subsequent cycle, it must be predicated upon four crucial policy steps:

1. A more contractionary U.S. macroeconomic policy resulting in lower U.S. domestic demand and import growth rates and a more expansionary Japanese and West European macroeconomic policy producing higher domestic demand and import growth rates than in Cycle 4. Having the latter in place during Phase VI would serve to quicken the pace of exit from that phrase.

2. A shift in the resource allocation mix by developed sector economic powers— the United States, Japan, and Western Europe. The U.S. must deprioritize current operating expenses, especially those associated with social peace accounts (as well as national defense) and divert a portion of these savings into economic investment. This means the U.S. will be forced to confront its historical government spending bias toward social peace/personal consumption accounts, especially those embedded in "payments to individuals" outlays. Growth in such outlays will have to be slowed while new government taxes should be directed at personal consumption. With meager U.S. domestic demand growth, the supply-side adjustment process in the U.S. will have to be driven by exports. To support this, Japan will have to shift resource distribution emphasis away from investment—especially in export-related sectors— towards current operating expenses, i.e., personal consumption and, where feasible, national defense. The enlargement in West European domestic demand and import growth in the Cycle of Adjustment will have to come from its surplus economies, led by the FRG, but all West European economies, including that of the FRG, will have to prioritize accounts associated with economic investment at the expense of social peace accounts. Where feasible, Western Europe should also increase the priority of its national defense accounts. Supply-side adjustment in Western Europe will not be driven by extra-European trade but by domestic demand and intra-West European trade, which should be facilitated by the further integration of the EEC market.

3. Improvement in U.S. external balances should also be advanced by a reversal in the combined performance of developing sector and CPE hard currency imports from what it has been in Cycle 4. Central to revitalizing developing sector imports is a reduction in the size of their factor services income and, as a result, current account deficits. This can only be accomplished by reducing the foreign interest debit of the developing sector. Efforts to support developing sector imports through a non-market induced expansion in developed sector capital flows to the developing sector may offer short-term relief, but only at the expense of more deterioration in the creditworthiness of the developing sector (that is, larger foreign debt to GDP and interest to export ratios). Instead, what is required is the kind of debt relief that relaxes immediate balance of payments stress followed by relief that seeks to improve the sector's creditworthiness by reducing the stock of its foreign debt.

   In addition to debt relief induced improvement in developing sector import growth, greater CPE hard currency import growth should also be fostered. The slow integration of the CPEs into the free world trade and payments order should continue and steps should be taken cautiously to encourage it. Such efforts, however, will directly impact U.S. external balances little, since the majority of European CPE hard currency trade is conducted with Western Europe and the plurality of China's, with Japan.[2]

4. Finally, concerted efforts to expand the sectoral menu of the GATT, a rollback in the "new protectionism," and enhancement of trade-creating "special trade arrangements" such as the U.S.-Canada Free Trade Agreement and planned 1992 intra-EEC trade liberalization should be pursued.[3]

This adjustment program would have a profound impact on the internal structure and overall character of the next trade and payments cycle, producing several radical alterations in the nature of the cycle itself. In Phase I of the Cycle of Adjustment there would be an immediate and dramatic change from past patterns. While developed sector import growth would accelerate—as has happened in all previous cycles—and would be driven to do so by an advance in developed sector domestic demand, the U.S. import and domestic demand growth rates would not lead this process. Instead, Japan and Western Europe would take the lead. Hence, the Phase I intra-developed sector import growth rate differentials which caused an early deterioration in the U.S. merchandise trade balance in the first four cycles would not appear. Indeed, the process would be reversed, and U.S. external balances would improve in Phase I.

In addition, because the combined gain in the domestic demand and import growth rates in the non-U.S. developed sector as well as the developing sector (the latter brought about by a change in developed sector payments policy) will be insufficient to offset the loss in U.S. domestic demand and import growth, the world domestic demand and import growth rates will advance at a weaker pace than in Phase I of Cycle 4. As a result, the primary input cost and primary commodity price recovery of Phase II will be small, as will the rise in goods and services price inflation.

Improved intra-developed sector external balances and low goods and services price inflation will work to mitigate and perhaps to alter the evolution of the next trade and payments cycle from Phases III–V. Low goods and services price inflation will lessen and possibly even eliminate the necessity for a contractionary tilt in aggregate developed sector macroeconomic policy, thereby altering the traditional evolutionary path of the cycle into Phase III. Improving U.S. external balances in Phases I–III and the absence of a decided deterioration in global economic growth in Phase III would reduce the need for Phase IV U.S. policy initiatives, and in the absence of these initiatives their effects, which have characterized previous Phase Vs, will not appear.

There are, however, immense obstacles to the implementation of the four-point adjustment program identified above and therefore to this scenario for the structural evolution of the Cycle of Adjustment. Most formidable among these obstacles are:

1. Central government fiscal overindebtedness in Japan and Western Europe which, along with historical macroeconomic policy biases (especially in the surplus countries of Western Europe), promises to curb severely the commitment of the non-U.S. developed nations to a more expansionist macroeconomic policy despite the fact that they will enjoy relatively more macroeconomic policy flexibility than the U.S. going into the next cycle as a result of their less rapid buildup of domestic debt and their superior external balance performance in Cycle 4.

2. Immense resistance will erupt in the United States, Japan, and Western Europe to the resource priority adjustments identified above, especially in the austere fiscal and low economic growth environment envisioned for the U.S. in the next cycle. U.S. historical hostility to recession and unemployment will make it inordinately difficult to deprioritize social peace/personal consumption accounts in order to support supply-side adjustment. Japan's historical fears of isolation from access to foreign sources of raw materials and foreign markets, post-World War II hostility toward rearmament, and its cultural affinity for individual frugality will work to slow any transfer of resources from export-oriented investment to personal consumption and national defense. Led by the FRG, surplus West European economies' historical fear of inflation will work to constrain the magnitude of macroeconomic policy expansion, while the high cost of social peace driven by more rigid class distinctions and more powerful organized labor movements than in the U.S. or Japan will result in an enormous resistance to a shift of resources from social peace accounts to economic investment and national defense.

3. The lower world domestic demand growth rate in the next cycle will limit any improvement in developing sector imports by undermining developing sector export earnings. At the same time, the developing sector's creditors will resist the international payments adjustment we have identified because it will damage their profits. And any CPE advance in hard currency imports will be tempered by East European CPE overindebtedness, soft primary commodity prices, and nagging CPE fears over a relative loss of independence as well as Western fears of indirect support for CPE defense efforts.

4. An expansion of GATT's sectoral purview and a rollback of the "new protectionism" will run up against a prolonged intensification of market crowding due to a slowdown in the world import growth rate and lower economic growth in the United States. Under such economic conditions, the trade-creating potential of reinvigorated "special trade arrangements" could transmute into trade-diverting protectionist blocs.

Notes

INTRODUCTION

1. "J-curve" refers to the expected brief rise and subsequent decline in a nation's trade deficit following depreciation of its currency. When fully matured, the J-curve produces a trade balance improved from the one inherited just prior to currency depreciation.

2. Estimation of the "equilibrium exchange rate" and its derivation for a particular currency are largely a subjective matter. However, the severe escalation of U.S. external imbalances during the course of the 1980s combined with the enormous rise in the dollar's effective exchange rate has removed virtually all controversy as to the dollar's "overvaluation," i.e., a price in excess of that associated with the equilibrium exchange rate or real value, for most of the 1980s. For a discussion of the concepts of "equilibrium exchange rate" and "undervaluation" and "overvaluation," see C. Fred Bergsten and John Williamson, "Exchange Rates and Trade Policy," in William R. Cline, ed., *Trade Policy in the 1980s* (Washington, DC: Institute for International Economics, 1983), pp. 103–106.

3. For examination of the dimension of contraction in world equity markets in October 1987, see IMF, *World Economic Outlook,* April 1988, Supplementary Note: "Implications of the Recent Decline in Equity Prices," pp. 41–52. For a review of the magnitude of the Third World debt crisis and North American primary commodity-based debt difficulties of the 1980s, see Darrell Delamaide, *Debt Shock* (Garden City, NY: Doubleday and Co., Inc., 1984).

4. The Group of Seven is comprised of the governments of the United States, Japan, the Federal Republic of Germany, the United Kingdom, France, Italy, and Canada (it was known as the G-5 before the last two member governments joined).

CHAPTER 1

1. See Roger Benjamin, Robert T. Kudrle, and Jennifer McCoy, "The Dynamics of Economic Change in the Pacific Basin," in Roger Benjamin and Robert T. Kudrle, eds., *The Industrial Future of the Pacific Basin* (Boulder, Co.: Westview Press, 1984), pp. 5 and 8. A "crowding effect" emerges when a market niche is saturated.

2. Wilfred Ethier, *Modern International Economics* (New York: W.W. Norton & Co., 1983), pp. 221–26.

3. W.M. Scammell, *The International Economy Since 1945,* Second Edition (London: The MacMillan Press Ltd, 1983), pp. 14–18; C. Fred Bergsten, *The Dilemmas of the Dollar* (New York: New York University Press, 1975), pp. 62–65.

4. See J.W.M. Chapman, R. Drifte, I.T.M. Gow, *Japan's Quest for Comprehensive Security,* (New York: St. Martin's Press, 1982), pp. 20–36, for a discussion of the dimensions of the postwar transformation in Japan's military effort. See John Lewis Gaddis, *The United States and the Origins of the Cold War, 1941–47* (New York: Columbia University Press, 1972), p. 338, for a discussion of the allied debate over the nature of postwar German disarmament.

5. See Tatsuro Uchino, *Japan's Postwar Economy: An Insider's View of Its History and Its Future,* (Tokyo and New York: Kodansha International Ltd, 1983), pp. 17–18, for a discussion of the dimension of Japanese economic losses due to the dismemberment of its empire. See Gaddis, *The United States and the Origins of the Cold War,* pp. 95–173, for a discussion of the allied debate over the postwar constraints on the German economy.

6. UN, *World Economic Survey, 1956,* pp. 17–24.

7. The abundance or scarcity of primary factor inputs is a principal force in the evolution of economic performance. The change from relative abundance to scarcity of primary inputs produces economic and productivity growth changes in an economy or a group of highly integrated economies that, when plotted, defines an economic long cycle–that is, an extended period of high or accelerating growth rates followed by a prolonged period of low or decelerating growth rates. The postwar economic growth performances of the United States, the OECD economies as a whole, the Soviet Union, and the CMEA economies as a whole all define such long cycles. Whether and to what extent economies suffer the downward trajectory of a long cycle may be influenced by the degree of improvement in the third factor of production, capital. Supply-side adjustment reflected in the quantitative and qualitative advance of capital can offset or overcome the effect of contracting supplies of primary inputs by reducing the volume of input required per unit of output. Capital is the repository of technology (and is associated with a skill level of labor). Ultimately, it is a technological regime that defines what is a primary input by determining the boundaries of primary commodities and "raw labor."

8. Combined U.S. private nonresidential fixed investment and U.S. government outlays for major public physical capital investment rose from $80.1 billion in 1940 to $372.6 billion (in 1982 constant dollars) in 1945, or by four and one-half times. At the same time, the U.S. economy nearly doubled in size. Virtually all of the advance in investment was on the U.S. government account. After the war U.S. government investment dropped dramatically while private nonresiden-

tial investment grew, offsetting some of the loss. For an analysis of the 1950s German investment boom, see Klaus Hinrich Hennings, "West Germany," Section II: Export Led Growth, 1950–60, in Andrea Boltho, ed., *The European Economy: Growth and Crisis* (Oxford and New York: Oxford University Press, 1982), and Uchino, *Japan's Postwar Economy,* especially "The Jimmu Boom," pp. 95–108, and "The Iwato Boom," pp. 121–141.

9. See Franco Bernabe, "The Labour Market and Unemployment," in Boltho, *The European Economy,* pp. 161–169.

10. From 1945 to 1959 the world economy labored under the threat of a "dollar gap"—a situation in which the U.S. current account surplus was unequaled by U.S. capital account deficits. The reality of the dollar gap surfaced with intensity during the immediate postwar period, in 1945–48. From 1948–52, the gap was financed by special U.S. government outflows in the form of grants and aid. At the same time, the size of the U.S. current account surplus fell. From 1952–58 the U.S. current account surplus dropped close to zero while the special mechanisms for financing the gap from 1948–52 were abandoned.

11. Powerful institutions arose just prior to, during, and after World War II in leading developed sector economies to address economic shocks—institutions that, as they expanded in influence in the postwar period, gave vent to national economic biases. Hence, in the U.S. and U.K.—both overwhelmed by the prolonged high unemployment of the Great Depression—the New Deal in the U.S. and the "Beveridge System" in the U.K. gave birth to large government transfer payment mechanisms for those in need that in the postwar period have come to dominate not only the central government outlays of these two economies but of most West European economies as well. In the FRG, whose inflation phobia was forcefully exacerbated in the immediate aftermath of World War II, the postwar period saw the emergence of a powerful central bank, the Bundesbank, dedicated to war on inflation. And in Japan in the 1950s, overcoming postwar losses of protected markets and raw material resources fell to Japan's ability to export. This prompted early industrial policies guided by the Ministry of International Trade and Industry (MITI) targeted at increasing exports.

12. Werner Baer, "The Economics of Prebisch and ECLA," in Charles T. Nisbet, ed., *Latin America: Problems in Economic Development* (New York: The Free Press, 1969), pp. 211–214.

13. Albert O. Hirschman, "The Political Economy of Import-Substituting Industrialization in Latin America," in Nisbet, *Latin America: Problems,* pp. 237–266.

14. Cheng Chu-yuan, *China's Economic Development: Growth and Structural Change* (Boulder, Co.: Westview Press, 1982), pp. 265–68 and 270–74.

15. Cheng, *China's Economic Development,* pp. 451–53, and Paul R. Gregory and Robert C. Stuart, *Soviet Economic Structure and Performance* (New York: Harper and Row, 1986), pp. 303–06.

16. John P. Hardt and Jean F. Boone, "The Soviet Union's Trade Policy," *Current History,* Vol. 87, No. 531, Oct. 1988, pp. 329–332.

17. Scammell, *The International Economy,* pp. 14–18.

18. Scammell, *The International Economy,* pp. 41–46.

19. Bernabe, "The Labor Market and Unemployment," in Boltho, *The European Economy,* pp. 169–184.

20. Abel Aganbegyan, *The Economic Challenge of Perestroika* (Bloomington and Indianapolis: Indiana University Press, 1988), pp. 1–15. Aganbegyan, a close adviser to Soviet President Mikhail Gorbachev, reports on the dramatic deceleration in Soviet NMP (national material product, i.e., GNP minus services) produced since the end of the 1960s. He suggests that the pace of decline is greater and the depth of decline steeper than Soviet official reports indicate (as well as most Western accounts which derive their estimates of Soviet economic growth from Soviet data) because Soviet estimates of real growth have underestimated the increase of inflation. For estimates of a similar deterioration in the performance of other East European economies, see *PlanEcon Report,* Vol.2, Nos. 50–52, Dec. 31, 1986.

21. In the 1952–58 period and in Cycle 1 the rate of growth of world trade volume exceeded that of world trade value. From 1952–58, world trade volume grew at a 6.3 percent annual pace—better than world trade value, which registered 4.1 percent. In Cycle 1, world trade volume grew at an 8.7 percent yearly pace, while world trade value advanced at an 8.3 percent rate. These patterns were radically reversed in Cycle 2: while world trade volume grew at a 7.2 percent annual rate, world trade value advanced at a 19.9 percent rate. Data source: GATT, *International Trade, 1985/86.*

22. After more than doubling in Cycle 2 over Cycle 1, consumer price inflation continued to accelerate in Cycle 3, but at a slower pace. After averaging 3.7 percent annual increases in Cycle 1, consumer price inflation grew at an average 8.1 percent rate in Cycle 2. In Cycle 3, inflation averaged 12.3 percent a year. At the same time, while the world GDP growth rate fell from 5.4 percent to 4.7 percent a year from Cycle 1 to Cycle 2, the pace of deceleration in world GDP growth increased in Cycle 3, as the world GDP growth rate declined to 3.0 percent. Data Source: IMF, *International Financial Statistics Yearbook, 1986.*

23. From its 12.3 percent average in Cycle 3, world consumer price inflation has leveled off, averaging 12.2 percent in the first three phases of Cycle 4. Further, the average world consumer price increase in the first half of Cycle 4 was decidedly lower than in the second half of Cycle 3 (1979–82), when it registered 13.6 percent a year. Data Source: IMF, *International Financial Statistics Yearbook, 1986* and *International Financial Statistics,* Nov. 1988.

24. The reintegration of the European CPEs into the world economy was the result of a CPE policy response to the severe rise of factor input costs and parallel retreat in the CPE output growth rate beginning in the first half of the 1960s.

CHAPTER 2

1. The average annual U.S. current account balance in the immediate postwar period points to the magnitude of the dollar gap. From 1930–39, the average annual U.S. current account surplus was just $0.6 billion but because of special circumstances precipitated by the war, the average U.S. current account surplus rose to $7.2 billion from 1946–49. Data source: UN, *World Economic Survey, 1955.*

2. While world inflation rose substantially in the postwar period, its distribution was uneven. In areas untouched by military devastation—including the

U.S., Canada, and Australia—inflation was only 30–45 percent higher than in 1938 and 1939. But in the economies of the Axis powers, inflation rose dramatically. In Japan, postwar inflation rose tenfold, in Italy, 25-fold, and in Germany the currency collapsed and monetary control was absent until the 1948 currency reform. On these points, see W.M. Scammell, *The International Economy Since 1945*, Second Edition (London: The Macmillan Press Ltd, 1983), pp. 21–23.

3. The changes in West European/North American trade flows rendered by postwar West European shortages caused a huge advance in the share of world trade accounted for by North American exports to Western Europe. In 1938 the share of world trade accounted for by these exports was 10 percent; by 1948, it had risen to 15 percent. At the same time, the percent of world trade accounted for by West European exports to North America did not change. In 1938, this percentage was 5, as it was as well in 1948. Data source: UN, *World Economic Survey, 1955*.

4. The U.S. merchandise trade surplus rose to an average of $6.9 billion a year from 1946–49, well above prewar averages.

5. The U.S. had run substantial merchandise trade surpluses since the late 1870s and by 1900 began to run trade surpluses on manufactured exports. Until 1914, merchandise trade surpluses plus capital inflow financed large service and remittance deficits. After World War I the U.S. became a net creditor. Its trade surplus in manufactured goods shot up substantially while it also began to run a deficit on its raw material trade balance (the latter in contrast to pre-World War I patterns). In addition, the U.S. began to experience a rise in foreign investment income. From 1929–32 the first taste of a dollar shortage emerged as U.S. imports collapsed and U.S. private capital outflow contracted, provoking a series of balance of payments crises. But this forced the rest of the world to cut imports, which in turn prompted a drop in U.S. exports sharper than that which U.S. imports were experiencing. After a subsequent dollar depreciation and stabilization, gold sales to the U.S. rose sharply. And this helped finance dollar current account deficits in the remainder of the 1930s. For the data on these points, see UN, *World Economic Survey, 1955*.

6. Fred L. Block, *The Origins of the International Economic Disorder* (Berkeley and Los Angeles: University of California Press, 1977), pp. 86–99. From 1946–49 to 1950–54, average annual U.S. government disbursements to the rest of the world declined and the share of nonmilitary international transfers fell in favor of military expenditures. Data source: UN, *World Economic Survey, 1955*.

7. UN, *World Economic Survey, 1956*, pp. 20–22.

8. Scammell, *The International Economy*, pp. 33–34, and Block, *Origins*, pp. 99–102.

9. By the end of the period of reconstruction, the restoration of European productive capacity and the vitality of European intra-trade had already taken a large bite out of the role of U.S. exports to Western Europe in world trade. In 1948 U.S. trade with the EPU accounted for 15 percent of world trade, but by 1952 it had dropped to just 8 percent. Meanwhile, EPU intra-trade rose from 35 percent of world trade in 1948 to 39 percent in 1952. Western Europe also began to claim a larger portion of the U.S. market as EPU exports to the U.S., which accounted

for only 5 percent of world trade in 1948, rose to 7 percent in 1952. Data source: UN, *World Economic Survey, 1955.*

10. UN, *World Economic Survey, 1956,* p. 25.

11. FRG machinery exports during the first phase of the Korean War surged ahead, growing by 100 percent in 1951 over 1950, while U.S. machinery exports only grew by 15.6 percent and U.K. machinery exports by only 13.6 percent. Data Source: UN, *World Economic Report, 1951/52.*

12. By the end of the first half of 1952, the FRG had reversed its chronic post-war current account deficits. From a $296 million current account deficit in the first half of 1950 the FRG current account swung close to balance in the first half of 1951 before posting a surplus in the next two halves. Meanwhile, the U.K. and French current account deficits grew. The U.K.'s $151 million deficit in the first half of 1950 became a huge $1,103 million deficit by the second half of 1951, and France's $101 million deficit in the first half of 1950 became a $548 million deficit by the second half of 1951. Data source: UN, *World Economic Report, 1951/52.*

13. Tatsuro Uchino, *Japan's Postwar Economy: An Insider's View of Its History and Its Future* (Tokyo and New York: Kodansha International Ltd, 1983), pp. 55–62.

14. From 1937 to 1945, world gold reserves and dollar holdings rose by $5.7 billion, from $15.1 billion to $20.8 billion. Of that, Latin America, which ran trade surpluses with North America during the war, accounted for half of the increase. Its reserves rose from $1.0 billion in 1937 to $3.8 billion in 1945. Aside from Latin America, the remainder of the developing sector saw reserves rise from $1.0 billion in 1937 to $1.5 billion after the war. Thus, close to 75 percent of the increase in reserves during the war years was accounted for by the developing sector. Data source: UN, *World Economic Survey, 1956,* p. 18.

15. Data Source: UN, *World Economic Report, 1950/51* and UN, *World Economic Report, 1951/52.*

16. Data Source: UN, *World Economic Report, 1950/51* and UN, *World Economic Report, 1951/52.*

17. Latin America and the sterling area accounted for over half of the deterioration in the developing sector merchandise trade balance in the second half of 1951 and the first half of 1952. In the second half of 1951, after running a large surplus in the first half of the year ($1.71 billion), Latin America and the sterling area combined ran a merchandise trade deficit of $1.33 billion. In the first half of 1952, the Latin American and sterling area deficit combined was $1.55 billion. Data source: UN, *World Economic Report, 1951/52.*

18. The rise in CPE intra-trade during the Korean War period caused its role in world trade to advance at a remarkable pace. In 1948, CPE intra-trade only represented 3 percent of world trade. By 1953 it accounted for 8 percent of world trade. At the same time CPE trade with the rest of the world contracted sharply as a percent of world trade, falling from 7 percent in 1948 to 4 percent in 1953. Data source: UN, *World Economic Survey, 1955.*

19. Paul Marer, "The Political Economy of Soviet Relations With Eastern Europe," in Sarah Meiklejohn Terry, ed., *Soviet Policy in Eastern Europe* (New Haven, Ct.: Yale University Press, 1984), p. 156.

20. Marer, "Political Economy of Soviet Relations," in Terry, *Soviet Policy,* pp. 156–60.

CHAPTER 3

1. Most of the damage to the developing sector trade balance in 1954 was due to faltering trade balances in the non-dollar Latin American economies and parts of the sterling area. See UN, *World Economic Report, 1953/54,* p. 142.

2. UN, *World Economic Report, 1953/54,* pp. 142–144.

3. The posted price of petroleum (Saudi Arabia-Ras Tanura) remained unchanged in 1956, while on average agricultural raw material prices declined and metal prices rose. Data source: IMF, *International Financial Statistics Supplement on Trade Statistics, 1982.*

4. The posted price of petroleum (Saudi Arabia-Ras Tanura) dropped in 1957, as did a number of key metal prices including copper and lead. Agricultural raw material prices on average also fell. Data source: IMF, *International Financial Statistics Supplement on International Trade Statistics, 1982.*

5. The Soviet Union joined by Czechoslovakia began a new military/economic aid effort in the Third World beginning in 1955 with arms shipments to Egypt. After the Suez crisis of 1956/57, Moscow became a heavy arms supplier of Egypt. Following Egypt, Yemen (1956) and Indonesia (1957/58) became recipients of Soviet aid. See Stephen T. Hosmer and Thomas W. Wolfe, *Soviet Policy and Practice Toward Third World Conflicts* (Lexington, Ma.: Lexington Books, 1983), pp. 11–12.

6. UN, *World Economic Survey, 1958,* p. 3.

7. While CPE exports to and imports from non-CPE sectors grew faster than world trade from 1953–58 (exports rose from $1.4 billion in 1953 to $3.0 billion in 1958 and imports from $1.3 billion in 1953 to $3.2 billion in 1958), the share of each in world exports and imports was miniscule and still well below 1948 levels. Data source: GATT, *International Trade Statistics, 1957/58.*

8. George W. Breslauer, *Khrushchev and Brezhnev as Leaders: Building Authority in Soviet Politics* (Boston: George Allen and Unwin, 1982), pp. 23–27.

9. From 1950 to 1954 China's trade with the European CPEs grew dramatically. China's trade with the Soviet Union had grown fivefold over the period, and with East Germany, where trade had been tiny in 1950, by 30-fold. See UN, *World Economic Survey, 1955,* pp. 114–116.

10. U.S. defense expenditures fell in the aftermath of the Korean War and they were followed by a slower paced reduction in military expenditures in the rest of the developed sector. In real terms, U.S. national defense outlays fell by 26.9 percent from their peak in FY53 to FY56. In addition, the wartime burden of high tax rates was relieved. From FY50–53, U.S. individual income and corporate income tax revenues rose by 100 percent. In FY55, revenue from these sources was down by 8.6 percent from FY53 levels. Data source: *Historical Tables—Budget of the United States, FY1989.*

11. In the early 1950s, prior to extensive West European trade liberalization with the rest of the world, there was a distinct trend toward regionalization in the

evolution of developed sector intra-trade. See GATT, *International Trade, 1953,* pp. 14–23.

12. U.S. import dependency grew steadily during the Period of Transition. In 1953, the ratio of U.S. imports to output was 4.48 percent. By 1957, it had climbed to 4.75 percent. Data source: UN, *World Economic Survey, 1957.*

13. UN, *World Economic Survey, 1957,* p. 149.

14. From 1950–58 OECD Europe ran an average annual current account surplus of $1.4 billion and the FRG was responsible for 55.6 percent of it. From 1955–58 the FRG's share of OECD Europe's current account surplus was even higher—73.5 percent.

15. From 1950–58, the FRG averaged the highest investment to GNP ratio and annual output growth rate of the major European and North American trading powers. The FRG investment to GNP ratio of this period averaged 20.8 percent, the U.K.'s only 14.0 percent, France's 17.2 percent, and that of the U.S., 14.2 percent. The FRG's average annual output growth rate was 7.4 percent, the U.K.'s 2.2 percent, France's 4.3 percent, and the U.S.'s 3.3 percent. Data source: UN, *World Economic Survey, 1959.*

16. Klaus Hinrich Hennings, "West Germany," in Andrea Boltho, ed., *The European Economy: Growth and Crisis* (Oxford and New York: Oxford University Press, 1982), pp. 483–485.

17. Japan's average annual investment/GNP ratio and output growth rates from 1950–58 surpassed those of all major European and North American trading powers. Japan's investment to GNP ratio averaged 21.7 percent, higher than the FRG's (20.8 percent), and its output growth rate of 7.9 percent also exceeded the FRG rate of 7.4 percent. Data source: UN, *World Economic Survey, 1959.*

18. Tatsuro Uchino, *Japan's Postwar Economy: An Insider's View of Its History and Its Future* (Tokyo and New York: Kodansha International Ltd, 1983), pp. 79–83.

19. Chalmers Johnson, *MITI and the Japanese Miracle: The Growth of Industrial Policy, 1925–75* (Stanford: Stanford University Press, 1982), pp. 198–241.

CHAPTER 4

1. After growing at an annual rate of 6.3 percent from 1952–58, world trade volume grew at an 8.7 percent rate in Cycle 1. But from 1959–73 the average growth rate of world trade volume was a remarkable 9.2 percent. Data source: GATT, *International Trade, 1985/86.*

2. See Figure 1.1b in Chapter 1.

3. The 1964 spike in developed sector fixed investment would be repeated at the same point in subsequent trade and payments cycles. It was prompted by the expansion in global demand fostered by an acceleration in the developed sector domestic demand growth rate due to a more expansionary aggregate macroeconomic policy and in the developing sector due to a rise in primary commodity prices.

4. Taturso Uchino, *Japan's Postwar Economy: An Insider's View of Its History and Its Future* (Tokyo and New York: Kodansha International Ltd, 1983), pp. 151–169.

5. Michael Davenport, "The Economic Impact of the EEC," in Andrea Boltho, ed., *The European Economy: Growth and Crisis* (Oxford and New York: Oxford University Press, 1982), pp. 225–226.

6. Davenport, "Economic Impact," in Boltho, *The European Economy,* pp. 226–232.

7. Data Source: UNCTAD, *Handbook of International Trade and Development Statistics, 1972.*

8. Data Source: UNCTAD, *Handbook of International Trade and Development Statistics, 1972.*

9. Data Source: UNCTAD, *Handbook of International Trade and Development Statistics, 1972.*

10. Data Source: UNCTAD, *Handbook of International Trade and Development Statistics, 1972.*

11. Fred L. Block, *The Origins of International Economic Disorder* (Berkeley and Los Angeles: University of California Press, 1977), pp. 174–77, and W.M. Scammell, *The International Economy Since 1945,* Second Edition (London: The Macmillan Press Ltd, 1983), pp. 169–74.

12. See Dale E. Hathaway, "Agricultural Trade Policy for the 1980s," in William R. Cline, ed., *Trade Policy In the 1980s* (Washington, DC: Institute for International Economics, 1983), pp. 435–453, for a discussion of GATT's relationship to trade in agricultural goods.

13. Block, *Origins,* pp. 174–177.

14. UN, *World Economic Survey, 1964,* p. 145.

15. Wilfred Ethier, *Modern International Economics* (New York: W.W. Norton & Co., 1983), p. 70. The European Community instituted a preferential tariff system in 1971, Canada followed suit in 1974, and the US, in 1976.

16. Albert L. Danielsen, *The Evolution of OPEC* (New York: Harcourt Brace Jovanovich, 1982), pp. 143–54.

17. Data Source: UNCTAD, *Handbook of International Trade and Development Statistics, 1983.*

18. Data Source: UNCTAD, *Handbook of International Trade and Development Statistics, 1986.*

19. Data Source: UNCTAD, *Handbook of International Trade and Development Statistics, 1986.*

20. The deterioration in Soviet economic performance was clearly visible in the 1961–65 period. The average annual growth of NMP (national material product, equivalent to GNP minus services) dropped from 9.2 percent a year from 1956–60 to 6.5 percent a year. The agricultural production growth rate plummeted from 5.9 percent a year in the 1956–60 period to 2.4 percent from 1961–65, as did gross investment, moving from 13.0 percent a year from 1956–60 to 6.2 percent a year from 1961–65. Data source: *PlanEcon Report,* Vol.2, No. 7, February 17, 1986.

21. Data Source: UNCTAD, *Handbook of International Trade and Development Statistics, 1972.*

22. Data Source: UNCTAD, *Handbook of International Trade and Development Statistics, 1972.*

23. Klaus Hinrich Hennings, "West Germany," in Boltho, *The European Economy,* p. 487.

24. Scammell, *The International Economy,* pp. 24–25.

25. GATT, *International Trade, 1960,* p. 11. While U.S. and U.K. exports in value had only doubled from 1948–60, the FRG's and Japan's combined were fifteen and one-half times as large in 1960 as in 1948. And while the industrial production of the U.S. and the U.K. was around 60 percent larger in 1960 compared to 1948, the FRG's and Japan's combined industrial production was close to five times its 1948 size in 1960.

26. Uchino, *Japan's Postwar Economy,* pp. 42–51.

CHAPTER 5

1. For dollar overvaluation in the period covering 1968, 1976, and the beginning of Phase I of Cycle 4 (1983), see C. Fred Bergsten and John Williamson, "Exchange Rates and Trade Policy," in William R. Cline, ed., *Trade policy in the 1980s* (Washington, DC: Institute for International Economics, 1983), pp. 109–115. The severe decline in the U.S. merchandise trade and current account surpluses in 1958/59 in the absence of the special circumstances that propped them up in 1957 plus the large balance of payments deficits accumulated by the U.S. in 1958/59 suggest that the dollar had first become overvalued in Phase I of Cycle 1, a development that prompted a negative market reaction from 1959–61.

2. Derived from data in *Economic Report of the President, 1988.*

3. Tatsuro Uchino, *Japan's Postwar Economy: An Insider's View of Its History and Its Future* (Tokyo and New York: Kodansha International Ltd, 1983), pp. 205–212.

4. Klaus Hinrich Hennings, "West Germany," in Andrea Boltho, ed., *The European Economy: Growth and Crisis* (Oxford and New York: Oxford University Press, 1982), p. 490.

5. Perhaps the two most glaring examples of overindebtedness since Cycle 2 are government overindebtedness in the developed sector and foreign overindebtedness in the developing sector. The behavior of the U.S. government's fiscal deficit over the four cycles provides a clear-cut example of government fiscal overindebtedness. In Cycle 1 the U.S. government fiscal deficit as a percent of GNP was 0.8 percent. It grew to 1.5 percent of GNP in Cycle 2, 2.9 percent in Cycle 3, and 4.9 percent in Cycle 4 (1983–87). As a consequence, one of the symptoms of acute overindebtedness has surfaced: the net interest outlays of the U.S. government have increased from cycle to cycle as a percent of GNP. In Cycle 1 the average net interest outlay as a percent of GNP was 1.2 percent, in Cycle 2 it rose to 1.4 percent, in Cycle 3, to 2.2 percent, and in Cycle 4 it reached 3.0 percent. Data source: *Historical Tables—Budget of the U.S. Government, FY89.*

6. From early in Cycle 1 (1960) to the end of Cycle 3 (1982), government expenditures as a percent of GNP grew forcefully throughout the developed sector. Over this period the advance in the U.S. was 7.8 percentage points, in the FRG, 17.7 percentage points, in the EEC, 18.7 percentage points, and in Japan, 14.1 percentage points. Outside of Japan the largest contribution to the rise in the

growth of government expenditures are transfer payments to individuals. For instance, in the U.S. payments to individuals grew from 4.8 percent of GNP in 1960 to 11.4 percent in 1982. Sources: Michel Albert and James Ball, *Toward European Economic Recovery in the 1980s: Report to the European Parliament* (New York: Praeger, 1984), and *Historical tables—Budget of the United States Government, FY89.*

7. From Cycle 1 (1960–67) to Cycle 2 (1968–75), the average annual ratio of world investment to GDP increased from 23.0 percent to 23.8 percent. But because the rate of growth of world GDP contracted more sharply from Cycle 1 to Cycle 2—down from an annual average of 5.0 percent from 1960–67 to 3.8 percent from 1968–75—the average rate of growth of world investment declined in Cycle 2 from its postwar peak in Cycle 1. In Cycle 3 (1976–82) the average world GDP growth rate declined still further, to 3.0 percent. In addition, the ratio of world investment to world GDP fell to 23.1 percent. Hence, in Cycle 3 the rate of growth of world investment declined from its performance in Cycle 2. Data source: IMF, *International Financial Statistics Yearbook, 1986.*

8. The large transfer of resources from developed to developing sector in Cycles 2 and 3 and, in particular, to OPEC reflected a shift in investment emphasis from manufacturing to extractive sectors. Such a process unfolded within the developed sector as well. One example of this was the enormous investment effort to exploit developed sector oil reserves. The U.S. investment profile over the two cycles also pointed to a shift in emphasis toward extractive sector investment. From 1967 (the end of Cycle 1) to 1975 (the end of Cycle 2) business investment in the U.S. manufacturing sector grew by 66.4 percent, but investment in the U.S. mining sector grew by 343.6 percent. From 1975 to 1982 (the end of Cycle 3) business investment in the U.S. manufacturing sector grew by 124.9 percent, while investment in the U.S. mining sector grew by 227.6 percent. From 1952–67 business investment in the U.S. manufacturing sector rose by 191.3 percent, while business investment in the mining sector only grew by 24.3 percent. Data source: *Economic Report of the President, 1988.*

9. The U.S. Central Intelligence Agency estimated that Soviet factor productivity turned in a negative performance from 1976–85. This meant that larger volumes of factor inputs were required to produce the same volume of output. Data source: "The Soviet Economy Under a New Leader," Central Intelligence Agency and Defense Intelligence Agency submission to the Subcommittee on National Security Economics of the Joint Economic Committee of the U.S. Congress (March 19, 1986). There are varying estimates of Soviet defense spending performance, both official and private. All agree, however, that from 1959–63 and especially from 1966–75 Soviet defense spending as a percent of GNP grew at a rapid pace. Since then, Soviet defense spending as a percent of GNP has leveled off.

10. Richard Cohen and Peter A. Wilson, "Superpowers in Decline? Economic Performance and National Security," in *Comparative Strategy,* Vol. 7, No. 2, Spring 1988, p. 107.

11. For the decline of non-U.S. developed sector central government deficits as a percent of GNP in Cycle 4, see OECD, *Economic Outlook,* June 1988, p. 23. For the decline of capital importing developing sector current account deficits as a percent of GDP, see IMF, *World Economic Outlook,* April 1988, pp. 116 and

146. From 1982 to 1987 the current account deficit of the developing sector capital importers swung from a deficit of $94.2 billion to a surplus of $3.0 billion, while their GDP growth advanced at an annual rate of 3.9 percent.

12. See footnote 4, Chapter 5 above, regarding U.S. fiscal overindebtedness. At the same time the U.S. government was experiencing growing overindebtedness, the U.S. economy was suffering from the emergence of foreign overindebtedness. From Cycle 1 to Cycle 2, the average U.S. merchandise trade balance deteriorated as a percent of GNP, moving from a surplus of 0.7 percent to zero. And in Cycle 3 this ratio averaged -1.1 percent before declining anew in Cycle 4 (1983–87) to -3.0 percent. As a result, average U.S. net factor services income which had increased from a surplus of 0.7 percent of GNP in Cycle 1 to 1.4 percent of GNP in Cycle 2 declined in Cycle 3 to a surplus of 1.0 percent of GNP and 0.6 percent of GNP in Cycle 4 (1983–87). Data source: *Economic Report of the President, 1988*.

13. The U.S. personal savings rate has tumbled in Cycle 4 from 6.8 percent in 1982 to 3.9 percent in 1987. In 1983, U.S. nonresidential fixed investment fell while personal consumption boomed. Data source: *Economic Report of the President, 1988*.

14. From 5.9 percent of GNP in 1982, U.S. national defense spending rose to 6.4 percent of GNP in 1987. Data source: *Historical Tables—Budget of the U.S. Government, FY89*.

15. By 1976 the ratio of government transfer payments to government expenditures was far higher in the FRG—49.9 percent—than in the U.S.—36.1 percent —and, especially, than in Japan—8.4 percent. Data source: Roy Hofheinz, Jr. and Kent E. Calder, *The Eastasia Edge* (New York: Basic Books, 1982), p. 35.

16. See footnote 15, Chapter 5 above, for a comparison of the ratio of transfer payments to government outlays in Japan, the U.S., and the FRG. Also, in Cycle 4 Japan's personal savings rate has continued to far outpace that of the U.S. and the FRG; from 1983–87 Japan's savings rate averaged 16.3 percent, the FRG's, 11.6 percent, and the U.S.'s, 4.9 percent. Data source: OECD, *Economic Outlook*, June 1988.

17. "Effective exchange rate" refers to rates derived from the IMF's Multilateral Exchange Rate Model (MERM). See IMF, *International Financial Statistics Yearbook, 1986*, p. 5.

18. The developing sector export unit value growth rate declined from 1.6 percent in 1960 (the end of Phase II of Cycle 1) to 0.0 percent in 1961 (the beginning of Phase III of Cycle 1). It rose from 2.3 percent in 1969 (the end of Phase II of Cycle 2) to 3.1 percent in 1970 (the beginning of Phase III of Cycle 2). It declined from 11.7 percent in 1977 (the end of Phase II of Cycle 3) to 1.8 percent in 1978 (the beginning of Phase III of Cycle 3) and it declined from -1.3 percent in 1984 (the end of Phase II of Cycle 4) to -4.4 percent in 1985 (the beginning of Phase III of Cycle 4). Data Source: UNCTAD, *Handbook of International Trade and Development Statistics, 1973* (for Cycles 1 and 2) and *Handbook of International Trade and Development Statistics, 1987* (for Cycles 3 and 4).

19. After declining by 0.3 percent in Phase III of Cycle 1, nonfuel primary commodity prices rose in Phase III of Cycles 2 and 3 by 2.5 percent and 1.5 percent, respectively. Then in Phase III of Cycle 4, nonfuel primary commodity

prices fell by 16.4 percent. Similarly, oil prices declined by 3.8 percent in Phase III of Cycle 1 and advanced in Phase III of Cycles 2 and 3 by 28.9 percent and 2.3 percent, respectively. Then in Phase III of Cycle 4 oil prices fell by 35.4 percent. See IMF, *International Financial Statistics Yearbook 1986* and *International Financial Statistics,* Feb. 1988 (for nonfuel primary commodity prices and oil prices [Saudi Arabia-Ras Tanura] in Cycles 1–3), and OECD, *Economic Outlook,* June 1988 (for spot prices in Cycle 4).

20. In the first three quarters of 1988, food output shortages centered in North America did spark a rise in food prices similar to those which erupted in Phase V of earlier cycles. Food prices grew by 25.2 percent in the first three quarters of 1988 above their 1987 level. Data source: IMF, *International Financial Statistics,* Nov. 1988.

21. In Phase V of Cycle 1 the developed sector merchandise trade balance worsened from a deficit of $2.5 billion in 1962 to a deficit of $3.3 billion in 1963. In Cycle 2 the deterioration was more forceful: from a surplus of $7.2 billion in 1971 the developed sector suffered a merchandise trade deficit of $32.2 billion in 1974. In Cycle 3 the Phase V collapse of the developed sector merchandise trade balance was as substantial as it was in Cycle 2. From a surplus of $0.1 billion in 1978 the developed sector merchandise trade balance hit a deficit of $76.9 billion in 1980. In Cycle 4 the deterioration has been less severe. From a deficit of $0.9 billion in 1986 the developed sector merchandise trade balance fell to a deficit of $14.9 billion in 1987. In 1988 it is projected to recover somewhat. Data source: IMF, *International Financial Statistics Yearbook,* various years (for Cycle 1), UNCTAD, *Handbook of International Trade and Development Statistics, 1983* (for Cycles 2 and 3), and IMF, *World Economic Outlook, 1988* (for Cycle 4). The data for the cycles are not directly comparable due to different data bases, but the patterns hold.

22. In Phase V of Cycle 2 the FRG's merchandise trade balance improved from a surplus of $6.7 billion in 1971 to a surplus of $20.6 billion in 1974. At the same time Japan's merchandise trade surplus dropped from $7.8 billion in 1971 to $1.4 billion in 1974. Data source: IMF, *International Financial Statistics Yearbook, 1986.*

23. In Phase V of Cycle 3 the FRG's merchandise trade surplus shrank from $24.6 billion in 1978 to $16.8 billion in 1979. Japan's also fell, from $24.3 billion in 1978 to $1.7 billion the following year. Data source: IMF, *International Financial Statistics Yearbook, 1986.*

24. After growing from $92.8 billion in 1986 to $96.5 billion in 1987, Japan's merchandise trade surplus in the first quarter of 1988 grew at an annual $84.0 billion rate. The FRG's merchandise trade surplus advanced more strongly than that of Japan in 1987; from $55.7 billion in 1986 it jumped to $70.0 billion in 1987. And in the first half of 1988 the FRG's merchandise trade surplus expanded at a $72.0 billion annual rate. Data source: IMF, *International Financial Statistics,* Nov. 1988.

25. In Phase V of Cycle 1 it was Italy and France that experienced balance of payments stress. Italy's merchandise trade balance fell from a deficit of $0.9 billion in 1962 to $1.9 billion in 1963, and France's dropped from a deficit of $0.1 billion in 1962 to a deficit of $1.1 billion in 1964. In Phase V of Cycle 2 the mer-

chandise trade balances of the U.K., Italy, and France collapsed. From a surplus of $0.5 billion in 1971, the U.K.'s balance slipped to a deficit of $12.5 billion in 1974, while Italy's fell from a surplus of $0.6 billion in 1971 to a deficit of $8.5 billion in 1974, and France's faltered from a surplus of $0.9 billion in 1971 to a deficit of $4.8 billion in 1974. In Phase V of Cycle 3 it was primarily Italy and France that suffered severe merchandise trade balance losses. From a surplus of $2.9 billion in 1978 Italy's merchandise trade balance swung to a deficit of $16.4 billion in 1980, and from a surplus of $0.1 billion in 1978, France's merchandise trade balance dipped to a deficit of $13.4 billion in 1980. Data source: IMF, *International Financial Statistics Yearbook, 1986*.

26. See Figure 1.2a in Chapter 1.

CHAPTER 6

1. In Cycle 1 the world export growth rate in volume averaged 8.7 percent, while the world export growth rate in value trailed at 8.3 percent. But in Cycle 2 the world export growth rate in volume fell to 7.2 percent while the world export growth rate in value jumped to 19.9 percent. Data source: GATT, *International Trade, 1985/86*.

2. The U.S. government fiscal deficit rose from $8.6 billion in FY67 to $25.2 billion in FY68, or from 1.1 percent of GNP to 3.0 percent. Data source: *Historical Tables—Budget of the U.S. Government, FY89*.

3. Klaus Hinrich Hennings, "West Germany," in Andrea Boltho, ed., *The European Economy: Growth and Crisis* (Oxford and New York: Oxford University Press, 1982), pp. 490–91.

4. See Table 5.1 in Chapter 5.

5. See Table 5.2 in Chapter 5.

6. UN, *World Economic Survey, 1968*, pp. 106, 109–110.

7. See Figure 5.2 in Chapter 5.

8. Data Source: UNCTAD, *Handbook of International Trade and Development, 1987*.

9. Data source: GATT, *International Trade, 1985/86*.

10. The European wage explosion was ushered in during the middle of 1968 by a three-week general strike in France. Similar developments erupted in Italy and the FRG in 1969, leading to a sizable jump in real wages in continental Europe during this period. See Franco Bernabe, "The Labor Market and Unemployment," in Boltho, pp. 174–75.

11. Hennings, "West Germany," in Boltho, *The European Economy*, pp. 490–91.

12. See Table 5.2 in Chapter 5.

13. Fred L. Block, *The Origins of International Economic Disorder* (Berkeley and Los Angeles: University of California Press, 1977), pp. 93–96.

14. See UN, *World Economic Survey, 1968*, pp. 109–110, for a discussion of events leading up to the deutsche mark revaluation of 1969.

15. Unlike the 1960 recession when U.S. imports fell by 3.3 percent, they rose by 11.5 percent in the 1970 recession. Data source: IMF, *International Financial Statistics Yearbook, 1986*.

16. See Table 5.2 in Chapter 5.

17. While nonfuel primary commodity prices averaged a loss of 0.2 percent in

1960/61, they averaged a 1.3 percent advance in 1970/71, and while petroleum prices (Saudi Arabia-Ras Tanura) declined by an average 2.3 percent in 1960/61, they averaged a 14.4 percent gain in 1970/71. Data source: IMF, *International Financial Statistics Yearbook, 1986.*

18. See Table 5.3 in Chapter 5.

19. Riccardo Parboni, *The Dollar and Its Rivals,* (London: Verso, 1981), pp. 83–84.

20. Tatsuro Uchino, *Japan's Postwar Economy: An Insider's View of Its History and Its Future* (Tokyo and New York: Kodansha International Ltd, 1983), pp. 189–196.

21. See Table 5.7 in Chapter 5.

22. UN, *World Economic Survey, 1972,* pp. I–5—I–6 and I–12—I–13.

23. The Teheran Agreement of Feb. 14, 1971, involved the Persian Gulf oil producers and oil companies and resulted in a 46 percent increase in the region's oil prices. Another 20-cent per barrel increase was included in the agreement scheduled to take place in 1975. The Teheran Agreement was paralleled by the Tripoli Agreement of April 2, 1971, involving the North African oil producers and the oil companies. See Albert L. Danielsen, *The Evolution of OPEC* (New York: Harcourt Brace Jovanovich, 1982), p. 189.

24. Data source: *Economic Report of the President, 1988.*

25. The competitive advantage of FRG exports in 1973/74 was based on intra-developed sector inflation differentials; while the FRG's export prices rose 17.0 percent, the average for developed sector exports was 26 percent over that period. In 1974 the FRG's merchandise trade balance improved despite the deutsche mark's appreciation against the dollar in 1973 and the rise of primary commodity prices in 1974 based upon a substantial jump of 12 percent in the FRG's export volume and a 2 percent drop in the FRG's import volume. UN, *World Economic Survey, 1974,* pp. 63–64.

26. Data source: *Economic Report of the President, 1988.*

27. World consumer price inflation doubled in Phases V and VI (1972–75) compared to Phases I–III (1968–71). From 1968–71 world consumer prices rose an average 5.4 percent a year, while from 1972–75 they rose by 10.9 percent a year. Data source: IMF, *International Financial Statistics Yearbook, 1986.*

28. Hennings, "West Germany," in Boltho, *The European Economy,* pp. 493–96.

29. See Figure 1.1a in Chapter 1.

30. Ed. A. Hewett, "Foreign Economic Relations," in Abram Bergson and Herbert S. Levine, eds., *The Soviet Economy: Toward the Year 2000* (London and Boston: George Allen and Unwin, 1983), pp. 176–78.

31. Hennings, "West Germany," in Boltho, *The European Economy,* pp. 485–86, 497.

32. From 1970 to 1975 total private lending to the developing sector had grown four-fold, from $17.6 billion to $70.0 billion. Data source: UNCTAD, *Handbook of International Trade and Development Statistics, 1986.*

33. From 1970 to 1975 public lending to the developing sector had more than doubled, advancing from $45.1 billion in 1970 to $104.0 billion in 1975. Data source: UNCTAD, *Handbook of International Trade and Development Statistics, 1986.*

CHAPTER 7

1. From Cycle 1 to Cycle 2 the average advance in consumer price inflation more than doubled, growing from 3.7 percent to 8.1 percent. At the same time GDP growth fell from 5.0 percent to 3.8 percent. In Cycle 3 the pace of acceleration in consumer price inflation was slowed. The Cycle 3 inflation rate advanced by about 50 percent over the Cycle 2 rate, growing from 8.1 percent to 12.3 percent. The slowdown in the acceleration of inflation was accomplished at the expense of GDP growth, which fell in Cycle 3 to 3.0 percent a year. Data source: IMF, *International Financial Statistics Yearbook, 1986.*

2. From Cycle 2 to Cycle 3 there was a decline in the ratio of world investment to GDP. In Cycle 2 the ratio was 23.8 percent; in Cycle 3, it dropped to 23.1 percent. Because the average GDP growth rate from Cycle 2 to Cycle 3 fell precipitously, the average annual growth rate of investment in Cycle 3 not only declined from its performance in Cycle 2—it declined at a more rapid pace than the GDP growth rate. Data source: IMF, *International Financial Statistics Yearbook, 1986.*

3. Gertrude E. Schroeder, "The Soviet Economy," *Current History,* Vol. 84, No. 504, October 1985, pp. 309–312.

4. Some estimates suggest that in the 1970s (1971–80) when primary commodity prices rose forcefully, eventually pushing up the price of Soviet exports to Eastern Europe, the net transfer of resources from the Soviet Union to Eastern Europe was close to $80 billion. See Paul Marer, "The Political Economy of Soviet Relations With Eastern Europe," in Sarah Meiklejohn Terry, ed., *Soviet Policy in Eastern Europe* (New Haven, Ct.: Yale University Press, 1984), pp. 175–180.

5. In Cycle 3 Japan averaged a 4.9 percent growth rate in its gross private nonresidential fixed investment, while the U.S. averaged 4.1 percent and the FRG, only 3.2 percent. Data source: OECD, *Economic Outlook,* June 1988.

6. Total OECD inflation stood at 11.3 percent in 1975 compared to only 3.1 percent in 1967. Data source: OECD, *Economic Outlook,* June 1985.

7. See Table 5.1 in Chapter 5.

8. See Figure 5.2 and Table 5.7 in Chapter 5.

9. See Table 5.3 in Chapter 5.

10. From March to October 1977 U.S. oil inventories were built up by 249 million barrels, well above the historical seasonal level. Data source: Albert L. Danielsen, *The Evolution of OPEC* (New York: Harcourt Brace Jovanovich, 1982), p. 177.

11. See Figure 5.3b in Chapter 5.

12. Far Eastern Economic Review, *Asia Yearbook 1978* (Hong Kong: Far Eastern Economic Review Ltd, 1979), p. 211–213.

13. See Table 5.3 in Chapter 5.

14. UN, *World Economic Survey, 1979–80,* p. 11.

15. See Table 5.7 in Chapter 5.

16. Food prices rose by 13.2 percent in 1978 after declining by 2.8 percent in 1977 as new food deficits opened up. And again as in 1972/73, the deficits were centered in the Soviet Union. In response to aggravated food shortages Soviet imports of agricultural goods rose in 1978, helping to push the volume of imports of the CPEs up 8.2 percent in 1978 after they had grown by only 3.9 percent in 1977.

Food prices rose by another 16.7 percent in 1979. Data source: IMF, *International Financial Statistics Yearbook, 1986* (for food prices) and UN, *World Economic Survey, 1979/80* (for CPE import volume).

17. Data source: *Economic Report of the President, 1988.*

18. Far Eastern Economic Review, *Asia Yearbook 1980,* p. 202, and *Asia Yearbook 1981,* p. 165 (Hong Kong: Far Eastern Economic Review Ltd, 1981 and 1982, respectively).

19. Maxwell Newton, *The Fed: Inside the Federal Reserve, the Secret Power Center that Controls the American Economy* (New York: Times Books, 1983), pp. 99–101 and 217–222.

20. Important changes took place in the U.S. current account balance in 1981: the U.S. current account surplus grew by $6.4 billion even while the U.S. merchandise trade deficit worsened, while in 1982 the U.S. current account swung into a deficit of $8.0 billion—a deterioration greater than the expansion in the merchandise trade deficit. This phenomenon emerged in response to large changes in the U.S. services trade balance that occurred principally in the area of factor services income. In 1981, the gain in the services trade account was due to a $6.6 billion advance in net interest income in response to a rise in interest rates, a gain partially offset by a $2.8 billion loss in net direct investment income resulting from a slowdown in the performance of overseas extractive sectors, especially petroleum. The decline in overseas oil earnings in 1982 forced U.S. net investment income to fall by $8.4 billion, a decline only partially offset by a smaller $2.0 billion advance in net interest income. Data Source: UNCTAD, *Handbook of International Trade and Development Statistics, 1986.*

21. Indirect labor costs in the form of payments to individuals did not decline in the 1981/82 recession. Indeed, soaring unemployment pushed government outlays for countercyclical income insurance programs up, especially in the U.S. and Western Europe, at the very point that revenues were declining, placing immense pressure on government fiscal balances.

22. Norman A. Bailey and Richard Cohen, *The Mexican Time Bomb,* A Twentieth Century Fund Paper, (New York: Priority Press, 1987), pp. 16–30.

23. Data source: *PlanEcon Report,* Vol. 3, Nos. 36, 37 and 38, Sept. 17, 1987.

24. Cheng Chu-yuan, *China's Economic Development: Growth and Structural Change* (Boulder: Westview Press, 1982), pp. 278–81.

25. See Figure 1.1a, Chapter 1.

26. Data Source: UNCTAD, *Handbook of International Trade and Development Statistics, 1987.*

27. Data Source: UNCTAD, *Handbook of International Trade and Development Statistics, 1987.*

28. GATT, *International Trade, 1984/85,* pp. 13–16.

29. Data Source: UNCTAD, *Handbook of International Trade and Development Statistics, 1987.*

30. See Table 5.6 in Chapter 5.

31. Data Source: UNCTAD, *Handbook of International Trade and Development Statistics, 1987.*

32. Nonfuel primary commodity prices grew by only 1.3 percent and petro-

leum prices (Saudi Arabia-Ras Tanura) grew by just 2.3 percent in 1978. Data source: IMF, *International Financial Statistics Yearbook, 1986.*

33. See Figure 1.1b in Chapter 1.

34. Data Source: UNCTAD, *Handbook of International Trade and Development Statistics, 1986.*

35. C. Fred Bergsten and William R. Cline, "Conclusion and Policy Implications," in William R. Cline, ed., *Trade Policy in the 1980s* (Washington, DC: Institute for International Economics, 1983), pp. 760–767.

36. For a list of agreements produced by the Tokyo Round, see John H. Jackson, "GATT Machinery and Tokyo Round Agreements," in Cline, *Trade Policy,* p. 165.

37. See Table 5.3 in Chapter 5.

38. Stephen Marris, *Deficits and the Dollar: The World Economy at Risk* (Washington, DC: Institute for International Economics, 1985), pp. 19–21, and UN, *World Economic Survey, 1981/82,* pp. 78–79.

39. Data Source: UNCTAD, *Handbook of International Trade and Development Statistics, 1987.* The evolution of U.S. and U.K. services accounts during Phase VI demonstrates the dimensions of the changes in international services trade. The U.S. services to merchandise trade ratio rose from 54.9 percent to 65.2 percent and the factor services income share of services trade grew from 54.2 percent to 60.1 percent from 1980–82. The share of interest income to total services trade rose from 21.5 percent to 45.2 percent while direct investment income's share fell from 32.7 percent to 15.5 percent over the same period. The U.K.'s services to merchandise trade ratio surged ahead from 67.4 percent to 110.3 percent from 1980–82, and factor services income's share of total services trade rose from 47.4 percent to 71.5 percent. (The greater U.K. improvement in the latter two ratios compared to the U.S. reflects the larger share of portfolio investment in British foreign assets.) The share of services trade represented by interest income advanced from 33.7 to 63.6 percent while direct investment income fell from 12.9 percent to 7.9 percent.

CHAPTER 8

1. While the average advance in the world consumer inflation rate for the first three phases of Cycle 4—12.3 percent—is equal to that of Cycle 3 and is slightly higher when the two years—1987/88—of Phase V are added, the average rate of inflation for the developed sector is substantially lower in Cycle 4. From an annual average of 8.9 percent in Cycle 3, developed sector consumer price inflation has slowed to just 3.9 percent a year from 1983–87. Data source: IMF, *International Financial Statistics Yearbook, 1986* and *International Financial Statistics,* Nov. 1988.

2. See Figure 5.1 in Chapter 5.

3. Japan's central government budget deficit dropped from 5.2 percent of GNP in 1982 to 4.9 percent in 1983 and 4.0 percent in 1984. The FRG's deficit also dropped, from 2.1 percent of GNP in 1982 to 1.6 percent in 1983 and 1.3 percent in 1984. At the same time, the U.S. central government budget deficit rose from 4.6 percent of GNP in 1982 to 5.2 percent in 1983 before retreat-

ing to 4.5 percent in 1984. Data source: OECD, *Economic Outlook,* June 1988, p. 23.

4. The U.S. government budget deficit rose from $78.9 billion in FY81 to $127.9 billion in FY82 and again to $207.8 billion in FY83 before temporarily declining to $185.3 billion in 1984. Data source: *Historical Tables—Budget of the U.S. Government, FY89.*

5. See Table 5.1 in Chapter 5.

6. Exchange rate as measured by the IMF's Multilateral Exchange Rate Model. IMF, *International Financial Statistics Yearbook, 1986,* p. 5.

7. The U.S. services trade balance deteriorated in 1983 and 1984 by $6.1 billion and $12.2 billion, respectively. In 1983, $4.4 billion of the $6.1 billion decline took place in the factor services income balance, with net direct investment income responsible for $3.2 billion of the contraction—reflecting the weak recovery in primary commodity prices and weaker GNP growth outside of the U.S. The following year the factor services income balance accounted for about half of the decline in the services trade balance. In 1983/84 dollar appreciation and relatively poor foreign domestic demand were clearly damaging the U.S. non-factor services trade balance as well. Data source: UNCTAD, *Handbook of International Trade and Development Statistics, 1986.*

8. In 1983 nonfuel primary commodity prices rose by 6.2 percent while the spot price of petroleum declined by 10.4 percent. In 1984 nonfuel primary commodity prices only advanced by 2.1 percent while the spot price of petroleum sank again by 2.2 percent. Data source: IMF, *International Financial Statistics,* Dec. 1987 (for nonfuel prices) and OECD, *Economic Outlook,* June 1988 (for petroleum prices).

9. The import growth rate (volume) of the developed sector in 1976 was 13.5 percent, while the average for 1983/84 was 7.1 percent. Data Source: UNCTAD, *Handbook of International Trade and Development Statistics, 1987.*

10. The 1984 British coal miners' strike added 450,000–500,000 barrels a day to world oil demand that year.

11. Data source: IMF, *World Economic Outlook,* October 1988.

12. OPEC's net investment surplus fell by over 20 percent from 1981–84. See Richard Cohen, "The Future of OPEC and World Oil Prices Under conditions of Global Disinflation," *Washington/World Intelligence Focus,* Vol. 2, No. 3, March 15, 1985, p. 17.

13. UN, *World Economic Survey, 1986,* p. 73.

14. From 1980–84 the developing sector registered an aggregate loss of $63.5 billion in "errors and omissions." Data Source: UNCTAD, *Handbook of International Trade and Development Statistics, 1986.*

15. Data source: *PlanEcon Report,* Vol. 3, Nos. 36, 37, and 38, Sept. 17, 1987.

16. The FY85 U.S. government fiscal deficit surged to $212.3 billion from $185.3 billion in 1984 before peaking in 1986 at $221.2 billion. Data source: *Historical Tables—Budget of the U.S. Government, FY89.*

17. The U.S. GNP growth rate fell from 6.8 percent in 1984 to 3.0 percent in 1985.

18. See Table 5.4 in Chapter 5.

19. Data source: IMF, *International Financial Statistics,* Nov. 1988.

20. Data source: IMF, *World Economic Outlook,* April 1988.

21. Norman A. Bailey and Richard Cohen, *The Mexican Time Bomb,* A Twentieth Century Fund Paper, (New York: Priority Press, 1987), pp. 35–38.

22. Net Soviet hard currency debt rose from $10.8 billion in 1984 to $15.8 billion in 1985. *PlanEcon Report,* Vol. 3, Nos. 36, 37, and 38, Sept. 17, 1987.

23. Net hard currency debt of the East European economies (Poland, Romania, Hungary, Bulgaria, East Germany, and Czechoslovakia) rose from $48.7 billion in 1984 to $54.5 billion in 1985. *PlanEcon Report,* Vol. 3, Nos. 36, 37, and 38, Sept. 17, 1987.

24. From 1983–85 China's foreign debt doubled, growing from $9.6 billion in 1983 to $20.0 billion in 1985. Louise do Rosario, "Trade—A Policy Marked by Erratic Twists and Turns," in "China '87: The Door Shuts," *Far Eastern Economic Review,* Vol. 135, No. 12, March 19, 1987, p. 80.

25. Interest rates on 3-month U.S. Treasury bills fell from 10.49 percent in August 1984 to 7.07 percent by December 1985. They kept falling, reaching a low of 5.19 percent by October 1986. Hence, over a little more than two years, interest rates were halved. After growing by only 5.8 percent in 1984, U.S. M1 grew by 12.5 percent in 1985 and 16.5 percent in 1986. Data source: *Economic Report of the President, 1988.*

26. From 1980–85 total U.S. debt rose at a nominal rate of 11.75 percent a year, surpassing the pace of nominal GNP growth, which averaged 8.07 percent. But in 1985 the difference between the nominal growth of U.S. debt and GNP widened substantially. Total debt grew at a 15.23 percent rate while nominal GNP advanced at a 5.67 percent rate. Data source: Henry Kaufman, "Debt: The Threat To Economic and Financial Stability," speech delivered at a symposium of the Federal Reserve Bank of Kansas City, August 27–29, 1986.

27. Bailey and Cohen, *Mexican Time Bomb,* pp. 39–40.

28. Hobart Rowen, "Paris Talks Restored Cooperation," *The Washington Post,* February 25, 1987.

29. Richard Cohen, "How Far Will Oil Prices Fall?" *Washington/World Intelligence Focus,* Vol. 3, No. 1, Jan. 15, 1986.

30. GATT Press Communique, March 23, 1987, p. ii.

31. GATT Press Communique, March 23, 1987, pp. 12–13.

32. Data source: *PlanEcon Report,* Vol. 3, Nos. 36, 37, and 38, Sept. 17, 1987.

33. IMF, *World Economic Outlook,* April 1988, p. 161.

34. IMF, *World Economic Outlook,* April 1988, p. 161.

35. The developing sector debt to GDP ratio rose from 119.8 percent in 1982 to 167.8 percent in 1986 while the developing sector debt service ratio rose from 18.9 percent in 1982 to 21.9 percent in 1986. Data source: IMF, *World Economic Outlook,* April 1988, p. 180 (for debt to GDP ratio) and p. 182 (for debt service ratio).

36. See Figure 1.1a in Chapter 1.

37. Data Source: UNCTAD, *Handbook of International Trade and Development Statistics, 1987.*

38. Data Source: UNCTAD, *Handbook of International Trade and Development Statistics, 1987.*

39. See Figure 5.1 in Chapter 5.

40. See Figure 1.1b in Chapter 1.

41. The world trade volume growth rate in the first three phases of Cycle 4 declined from 6.9 percent in the first three phases of Cycle 3 to 4.6 percent. But the growth rate of world trade value also declined, from 10.8 percent to 3.6 percent, in the same period. Data source: GATT, *International Trade, 1985/86* and *International Trade 1986/87.*

42. Data Source: UNCTAD, *Handbook of International Trade and Development Statistics, 1987.*

43. Data Source: UNCTAD, *Handbook of International Trade and Development Statistics, 1987.*

44. GATT, *International Trade, 1985/86,* p. 16. The top five developing sector manufacturing exporters—Taiwan, South Korea, Hong Kong, Brazil, and Singapore—saw their share of developing sector manufactured exports rise from 57.3 percent in 1973 to 64.0 percent in 1985.

45. C. Fred Bergsten, *America In the World Economy: A Strategy for the 1990s* (Washington, DC: Institute for International Economics, 1988), pp. 71–72.

46. GATT, *International Trade, 1984/85,* pp. 14–17.

47. See Japan Economic Institute of America, *Yearbook of U.S.-Japan Economic Relations in 1983* (Washington, DC: Japan Economic Institute of America, 1984), p. 63, for a discussion of the process leading to agreement on exchange of military technology.

48. Robert Manning, "The Unkindest Cut," *Far Eastern Economic Review,* Vol. 125, No. 33, August 16, 1984, pp. 55–57.

49. Jean Seaberry, "Hill Skeptics Doubt Japan's Sincerity," *The Washington Post,* July 31, 1985, and Robert Manning, "Retreat From Reason," *Far Eastern Economic Review,* Vol. 129, No. 35, Sept. 5, 1985, pp. 52–53.

50. Paul Lewis, "GATT, Backing U.S., Votes to Prepare New Trade Round," *The New York Times,* November 29, 1985.

51. "Premier Has High Hopes for Private Panel's Report," *Japan Times Weekly,* March 22, 1986.

52. Hobart Rowen, "Paris Talks Restored Cooperation," *The Washington Post,* Feb. 25, 1987.

53. U.S. consumer prices in the first three phases of Cycle 4 were down from the first three phases of Cycle 3. From 1983–86 U.S. consumer inflation averaged 3.7 percent a year, down from the 6.7 percent a year it averaged from 1976–78. U.S. consumer inflation from 1983–86 dropped dramatically from that experienced in the last two phases of Cycle 3—1979–82—of 9.6 percent. Data source: IMF, *International Financial Statistics Yearbook, 1986.*

54. IMF, *International Financial Statistics Yearbook, 1986,* p. 5. "Effective exchange rate" refers to rates derived from the IMF's Multilateral Exchange Rate Model.

55. IMF, *World Economic Outlook,* April 1988, pp. 41–52.

56. Sarah A. Hooker, "The International Investment Position of the United States," a study produced by the Rand National Defense Research Institute, Santa Monica, Ca., Oct. 1988.

57. Data source: *Economic Report of the President, 1988.*

58. Net portfolio investment in the U.S. rose from $4.7 billion at the beginning

of Cycle 4 in 1983 to $77.0 billion in 1986; Japan's net portfolio investment abroad rose from $2.9 billion in 1983 to $102.0 billion in 1986. Data source: IMF, *International Financial Statistics,* Dec. 1987.

59. In 1975 the share of non-factor services trade accounted for by traditional shipping and other transport was 35.8 percent. By 1985 the share had fallen to 29.4 percent. Data source: UN, *World Economic Survey, 1986.*

60. Data Source: UN, *World Economic Survey, 1986.* "Other" services' share of non-factor services trade rose from 31.1 percent in 1975 to 33.3 percent in 1985.

CHAPTER 9

1. Data source: IMF, *International Financial Statistics,* Nov. 1988 (for nonfuel primary commodity prices) and OECD, *Economic Outlook,* June 1988 (for oil prices).

2. Data source: IMF, *International Financial Statistics,* Nov. 1988 (for food prices).

3. Estimates are the author's own. They differ little from those of the IMF and OECD.

4. By distinguishing the four trade and payments cycles beginning in 1959, we are able to determine—as is the case with government fiscal balances—a structural and cyclical component to merchandise trade balances. For the U.S. the absence of the cyclical feature of the merchandise trade deficit occurred in Phase V during the last three cycles when the differential between the U.S. domestic demand growth rate and that of the rest of the world was most favorable to the U.S. balance and the dollar's effective exchange rate was at its cyclical low.

5. OECD, *Economic Outlook,* Dec. 1987., p. 96.

6. OECE, *Economic Outlook,* Dec. 1987, p. 96, and OECD, *Economic Outlook,* June 1988, p. 91–92.

7. Michael R. Sesit and Walter S. Mossberg, "Intervention Helps Dollar," *The Wall Street Journal,* November 18, 1988. This article notes that, "The Fed and Bank of Japan have repeatedly intervened during the dollar's slide over the past couple of weeks but the Bundesbank—the key European central bank—has been noticeably absent."

8. The OECD reports that, "Faced with rising government deficits, the Government announced measures in January 1988 to raise revenues and to reduce spending in 1989 by DM 10 billion via increases in excise taxes (tobacco and heating oil) and cuts in subsidies. Earlier, the Government made known its intention to introduce in 1989 a 10 percent withholding tax on interest income as an advanced part of a financing package to recover about half of the revenue losses likely to occur on an annual basis as a consequence of the 1990 Tax Reform. The planned reduction of expenditure and the increase in taxation would reduce the general government deficit by one-half percentage point to 2 percent of GNP in 1989, implying a switch of stance of fiscal policy towards restriction." OECD, *Economic Outlook,* June 1988, p. 91.

9. The U.K.'s merchandise trade balance fell from a deficit of $2.7 billion in 1985 to $12.8 billion in 1986 and plunged anew in 1987 to a deficit of $16.7 billion. In the first half of 1988 the U.K.'s merchandise trade deficit expanded, ris-

ing forcefully to $33.8 billion on an annualized basis. At the same time the U.K.'s current account swung into a $0.3 billion deficit in 1986 after enjoying a surplus of $4.7 billion in 1985. In 1987 the U.K.'s current account balance collapsed anew as the deficit rose to $4.3 billion, and in the first half of 1988 the current account deficit exploded to $24.0 billion on an annualized basis. Data source: IMF, *International Financial Statistics,* Nov. 1988.

10. OECD, *Economic Outlook,* Dec. 1987, p. 89. This report notes the concern over the rise in money supply in 1987.

11. See Marcus W. Brauchli, "Japan Begins to Ease Credit as Dollar Falls," *The Wall Street Journal,* October 20, 1988, for a discussion of Japan's interest rate policy in 1988.

12. The OECD forecasts that Japan's domestic demand growth rate will fall from 5.50 percent in 1988 to 4.25 percent in 1989 and that the EEC's domestic demand growth rate will decline from 3.25 percent in 1988 to 2.50 percent in 1989. OECD, *Economic Outlook,* June 1988, p. 5.

13. Data Source: UNCTAD, *Handbook of International Trade and Development Statistics, 1986.*

14. Data Source: UNCTAD, *Handbook of International Trade and Development Statistics, 1986.*

15. Data Source: UNCTAD, *Handbook of International Trade and Development Statistics, 1987.*

16. Data source: IMF, *International Financial Statistics Yearbook, 1986* and *International Financial Statistics,* Nov. 1988.

17. Many observers have noted the degree of improvement in U.S. manufacturing sector productivity in Cycle 4. Manufacturing sector productivity averaged a 4.7 percent growth rate from 1983–87, far better than the 1.2 percent average advance from 1978–82. The pressure generated on the U.S. manufacturing sector as a result of severe dollar overvaluation played a critical role in bringing about this result. However, it produced another development detrimental to U.S. market share: the price of higher productivity in this case was a contraction in the size of the U.S. manufacturing sector. From an average of 20.2 million employees from 1978–82, the U.S. manufacturing sector dropped to an average 19.0 million employees from 1983–87. Data source: U.S. Department of Labor, Bureau of Labor Statistics, "Productivity and Costs—Fourth Quarter and Annual Averages 1987," Feb. 4, 1988 (for productivity), and Economic Report of the President, 1988 (for employment).

18. The U.S. savings rate, which has declined during Cycle 4 from what it was in earlier cycles, averaged only 5.0 percent a year from 1983–87, compared to 16.3 percent for Japan (1983–87), 35.0 percent for Taiwan (1983–86), and 30.0 percent for South Korea (1983–87). The average growth rate in gross nonresidential fixed investment was only 4.3 percent a year, compared to Japan's 8.3 percent. Data source: OECD, *Economic Outlook,* June 1988 (for U.S. and Japanese savings rates and gross nonresidential fixed investment), and IMF, *World Economic Outlook,* April 1988 (for Taiwan and South Korean savings rates).

19. In Phase V of Cycle 2 (1972–74) the average annual inflation rate of Argentina, Brazil, and Mexico combined was 80.7 percent. In Phase V of Cycle 3 (1978–80), it rose to 224.1 percent. In Phase V of Cycle 4 (1987), it jumped to

492.9 percent, and it continued to rise in 1988. Data source: IMF, *International Financial Statistics Yearbook, 1986* and Nov. 1988.

20. See Table 5.7 in Chapter 5.

21. In the third quarter of 1988 nonfuel primary commodity prices fell by 2.0 percent, and this occurred despite another 9.5 percent jump in food prices. Data source: IMF, *International Financial Statistics,* Nov. 1988.

22. See Figure 1.2b in Chapter 1.

23. In Phase III of Cycle 3 (1978) nonfuel primary commodity prices rose by 1.2 percent, while in Phase III of Cycle 4 (1985/86) they fell by 16.4 percent. Also in Phase III of Cycle 3 oil prices (Saudi Arabia-Ras Tanura) rose by 2.3 percent while in Phase III of Cycle 4 oil prices (spot average) declined by 35.4 percent. While in Phase V of Cycle 4 (1987/first three quarters of 1988) nonfuel primary commodity prices rose by 32.3 percent, slightly better than in Phase V of Cycle 3 (1979/80) when they rose by 28.9 percent, the recovery in oil prices has been much weaker, with prices rising by 12.6 percent (1987 spot prices) whereas in Cycle 3 they rose by 156.0 percent (Saudi Arabia-Ras Tanura). Data source: IMF, *International Financial Statistics Yearbook, 1986* and *International Financial Statistics,* Nov. 1988 (for nonfuel primary commodity prices and Ras Tanura oil prices), and OECD, *Economic Outlook,* June 1988 (for oil spot prices).

24. Walter S. Mossberg, "Group of Seven Declares the Dollar Dropped Enough, May Intervene," *The Wall Street Journal,* December 23, 1987.

25. The dollar's effective exchange rate rose by 7.4 percent from April to August 1988. Data source: IMF, *International Financial Statistics,* Nov. 1988.

26. After falling from a quarterly peak of $164.8 billion (annualized) in the fourth quarter of 1987 to $120.8 billion in the second quarter of 1988, the U.S. merchandise trade deficit fell to only $116.8 billion in the third quarter before jumping to $128.0 billion in the fourth quarter.

27. After accounting for 97.6 percent of GNP growth in the first half of 1988, net exports and nonresidential fixed investment combined made no contribution to GNP growth in the second half of 1988.

28. The appreciation of the dollar in 1988 and early 1989 has led some observers to believe that the pressure on the dollar which persisted from 1985–87 has come to an end and that the dollar's overvaluation has been eliminated.

Examination of the causes of the dollar recovery in Phase V of Cycle 4 suggests a quite different conclusion. At first, the dollar's advance in 1988 was provoked by a recovery in the U.S. trade balance. This development was to be anticipated since similar trade recoveries in Phase V of Cycle 2 (1973) and of Cycle 3 (1979) prompted small, transitory dollar appreciations in 1974 and 1980, respectively. But while the size of the dollar appreciation in 1988/early 1989 has been marginally greater than in 1974 and 1980, the dollar's recovery in Phase V of the current cycle was supported by another factor that was absent in Phase V of the previous two cycles. In 1988/early 1989, U.S. interest rates advanced at a healthy pace, surpassing the rise in inflation. In 1973/74 and 1979/80, U.S. interest rates rose even more sharply than in Phase V of the current cycle, but they still trailed the more dramatic rise in inflation. In Phase V of the current cycle the dollar has been boosted by the opening of real interest rate differentials favorable to it, while in the earlier Phase Vs this was not the case.

A review of the dollar's behavior and the causes of it in Phase VI of Cycle 2 (1975) and Cycle 3 (1981/82) offers insight into the dollar's prospects in the remainder of Phase V of the current cycle. In 1975 the dollar depreciated in response to the 1974 deterioration in the U.S. trade balance, and this persisted despite a sizable recovery in 1975 in U.S. external balances. In addition, in 1975 the dollar was not helped by real interest rate differentials. In 1981/82 the dollar appreciated dramatically despite a deterioration in U.S. external balances. The dollar's forceful rise resulted from a huge advance in U.S. real interest rates as U.S. interest rates remained extremely high while inflation plummeted. The rise in U.S. real interest rates generated interest rate differentials favorable to the dollar.

In the remainder of Phase V of Cycle 4, the dollar is unlikely to receive support from a recovery in U.S. external balances, as in 1975, or from growing real interest rate differentials, as in 1981/82. There appears little room for visible improvement in the U.S. merchandise trade balance, while it is certain that the U.S. services trade balance driven by the U.S. factor services income balance will deteriorate, prompting a worsening in the U.S. current account balance. In 1975 the United States ran a current account surplus, while in 1989/90, the huge U.S. current account deficits will add one quarter of a trillion dollars to the U.S. net investment deficit.

While the pressure on the U.S. dollar derivative of U.S. external balances in the remainder of Phase V of Cycle 4 will dwarf those of 1975, the real interest rate differentials which inspired the appreciation of the dollar in 1981/82 are unlikely to reappear. Inflationary pressures in Phase V of Cycle 4 are far weaker than in Phase V of Cycle 3. At the same time, U.S. monetary policy has been more aggressive in its effort to preempt inflation.

With inflationary forces weaker and with preemptive anti-inflationary actions stronger than in earlier Phase Vs, inflation is likely to increase at a much slower pace and is likely to weaken sooner than was the case in earlier cycles. When this occurs, interest rates will be likely to follow inflation down, thereby removing the protection afforded the dollar in 1988/early 1989.

CHAPTER 10

1. C. Fred Bergsten, *America in the World Economy: A Strategy for the 1990s* (Washington, DC: Institute for International Economics, 1988), pp. 103–104.

2. In 1984, 26.0 percent of the Soviet Union's imports came from the developed sector and 19.2 percent from the developed sector of Western Europe. In 1984, 68.0 percent of China's imports came from the developed sector and 31.3 percent from Japan. In 1984, only 4.1 percent of the Soviet Union's imports came from the U.S. and Canada, while 18.8 percent of China's imports came from the U.S. and Canada. Data Source: UNCTAD, *Handbook of International Trade and Development Statistics, 1986.*

3. See U.S. Department of State, "The European Community Prepares to Complete a Single Market by 1992," July 5, 1988, and "Canadian Trade Policy: The Anatomy of a Trade Deal," *The Economist,* Oct. 22, 1988, pp. 77–78.

Figure Sources

Figure 1.1
Data Source: Imports—1952–80: International Monetary Fund, *International Financial Statistics Supplement on Trade Statistics, 1982;* 1981–87—IMF data; Exports and GDP—1952–85: General Agreement on Tariffs and Trade, *International Trade, 1985/86;* 1986–87; GATT, *International Trade, 1988.*

Figure 1.2
Data Source: Sectoral—1952–69; IMF, *IFS Supplement on Trade Statistics, 1982;* 1970–85; IMF, *IFS Yearbook 1986;* Developed Sector—1959–83: IMF, *IFS Yearbook, 1986;* 1984–87: IMF, *IFS,* November 1988. (Data not directly comparable, but trends hold.)

Figure 2.1
Data Source: U.S. Department of Commerce, Bureau of Economic Analysis, *The National Income and Product Accounts of the United States, 1929–82—Statistical Tables.*

Figure 4.1
Data Source: Developed Sector Trade and Intra-Trade—1958–59: GATT, *International Trade, 1963;* 1960–67: GATT, *International Trade, 1969;* Manufactured Goods—GATT, *International Trade, 1985/86.*

Figure 5.1
Data Source: Cycle 1—United Nations Conference on Trade and Development, *Handbook of International Trade and Development Statistics, 1972;* Cycles 2 and 3—UNCTAD, *Handbook, 1983;* Cycle 4—UNCTAD, *Handbook, 1986.*

Figure 5.2
Data Source: Export Volume and Unit Value—Cycles 1 and 2: UNCTAD, *Handbook, 1972;* Cycles 3 and 4: UNCTAD, *Handbook, 1986;* Non-Fuel Primary Commodity Prices and Oil Prices—IMF, *IFS Yearbook, 1986;* Export Value—Cycle 1: UNCTAD, *Handbook, 1972;* Cycles 2 and 3: UNCTAD, *Handbook, 1983;* Cycle 4: UNCTAD, *Handbook, 1986.*

Figure 5.3
Data Source: Cycle 1—UNCTAD, *Handbook, 1972/73;* Cycles 2 and 3—UNCTAD, *Handbook, 1983;* Cycle 4—UNCTAD, *Handbook, 1987.*

Figure 5.4
Data Source: U.S.—Executive Office of the President, *Economic Report of the President, 1988;* FRG and Japan—Cycles 1–3: Organization for Economic Cooperation and Development, *National Accounts Statistics, 1986;* Cycle 4: OECD, *National Accounts Statistics, 1986,* and OECD, *Economic Outlook,* December 1987.

Figure 6.1
Data Source: Merchandise Trade Balance, Current Account Balance, Agricultural Exports, Factor Services Income—*Economic Report of the President, 1988;* Direct Investment Income—U.S. Department of Commerce, *Survey of Current Business,* June 1986; U.S.-Japan Bilateral Balance—*Survey of Current Business,* data cited in Daniel I. Okimoto, ed., *Japan's Economy: Coping With Change in the International Environment* (Boulder: Westview, 1982), p. 132.

Figure 7.1
Data Source: Merchandise Trade Balance, Current Account Balance, Agricultural Exports, Factor Services Income—*Economic Report of the President, 1988;* Direct Investment Income—*Survey of Current Business,* June 1986; U.S.-Japan Bilateral Balance—*Survey of Current Business,* data cited in Daniel I. Okimoto, *Japan's Economy.*

Figure 8.1
Data Source: IMF, *World Economic Outlook,* April 1988.

Figure 9.1
Data Source: 1959–86—*Economic Report of the President, 1988;* 1987/88—White House Council of Economic Advisers, Economic Indicators, November 1988.

Figure 9.2
Data Source: Cycles 2 and 3—*The National Income and Product Accounts of the United States, 1929–82;* Cycle 4—*The Economic Report of the President, 1988,* and U.S. Department of Commerce, U.S. Merchandise Trade: Third Quarter 1988—Balance of Payments Basis, November 28, 1988.

Select Bibliography

DATA SOURCES

U.S. Government

Executive Office of the President. *Economic Report of the President, Transmitted to Congress February 1988.* Washington, DC: U.S. Government Printing Office, 1988.

Executive Office of the President. Office of Management and Budget. *Historical Tables—Budget of the United States Government, Fiscal Year 1989.* Washington, DC: U.S. Government Printing Office, 1988.

U.S. Department of Commerce. Bureau of Economic Analysis. *National Income and Product Accounts of the United States, 1929–82—Statistical Tables.* Washington, DC: U.S. Government Printing Office, September 1986.

U.S. Department of Labor. Bureau of Labor Statistics. "Productivity and Costs—Fourth Quarter and Annual Averages, 1987." Washington, DC: U.S. Department of Labor, February 4, 1988.

United Nations (UN)

United Nations. United Nations Conference on Trade and Development (UNCTAD). *Handbook of International Trade and Development Statistics* (Handbook). New York: UN, published annually the year following the title date.

United Nations. *World Economic Survey.* New York: UN, published annually the year following the title date (called *World Economic Report* prior to 1955).

International Monetary Fund (IMF)

International Monetary Fund. *International Financial Statistics Yearbook* and *International Financial Statistics* monthly reports (IFS). Washington, DC: IMF, Yearbooks published the year of the title date.
International Monetary Fund. *World Economic Outlook.* Washington, DC: IMF, published biannually in April and October.

Organization for Economic Cooperations and Development (OECD)

Organization for Economic Cooperation and Development. *OECD Economic Outlook.* Paris: OECD, published annually the year of the title date.

General Agreement on Tariffs and Trade (GATT)

General Agreement on Tariffs and Trade. *International Trade.* Geneva: GATT, published annually the year following the title date.

Non-Governmental

PlanEcon, Inc. *PlanEcon Report.* Washington, DC: PlanEcon, Inc., various issues.

GENERAL SOURCES

Aganbegyan, Abel. *The Economic Challenge of Perestroika.* Bloomington and Indianapolis: Indiana University Press, 1988.
Albert, Michel, and James Ball. *Toward European Economic Recovery in the 1980s: Report to the European Parliament.* New York: Praeger, 1984.
Aliber, Robert Z. *The International Money Game.* New York: Basic Books, 1979.
Andors, Stephen. *China's Industrial Revolution: Politics, Planning and Management, 1949 To the Present.* New York: Pantheon, 1977.
Baer, Werner. "The Economics of Prebisch and ECLA." In *Latin America: Problems in Economic Development,* edited by Charles T. Nisbet. New York: The Free Press, 1969.
Bailey, Norman A., and Richard Cohen. *The Mexican Time Bomb.* A Twentieth Century Fund Paper. New York: Priority Press, 1987.
Baldwin, Robert E., and J. David Richardson, eds. *Current U.S. Trade Policy: Analysis, Agenda, and Administration.* Cambridge, Ma.: National Bureau of Economic Research, 1986.
Benjamin, Roger, and Robert T. Kudrle, eds. *The Industrial Future of the Pacific Basin.* Boulder, Co.: Westview Press, 1984.
Benjamin, Roger, Robert T. Kudrle, and Jennifer McCoy. "The Dynamics of Eco-

nomic Change in the Pacific Basin." In *The Industrial Future of the Pacific Basin,* edited by Roger Benjamin and Robert T. Kudrle. Boulder, Co.: Westview Press, 1984.

Bergson, Abram, and Herbert S. Levine, eds. *The Soviet Economy: Toward the Year 2000.* London and Boston: George Allen and Unwin, 1983.

Bergsten, C. Fred. *America In the World Economy: A Strategy for the 1990s.* Washington, DC: Institute for International Economics, 1988.

Bergsten, C. Fred. *The Dilemmas of the Dollar.* A Council on Foreign Relations Book. New York: New York University Press, 1975.

Bergsten, C. Fred, and John Williamson. "Exchange Rates and Trade Policy." In *Trade Policy In the 1980s,* edited by William R. Cline. Washington, DC: Institute for International Economics, 1983.

Bergsten, C. Fred, and William R. Cline. "Conclusion and Policy Implications." In *Trade Policy In the 1980s,* edited by William R. Cline. Washington, DC: Institute for International Economics, 1983.

Bernabe, Franco. "The Labour Market and Unemployment." In *The European Economy: Growth and Crisis,* edited by Andrea Boltho. Oxford and New York: Oxford University Press, 1982.

Blackwell, William L. *The Industrialization of Russia: An Historical Perspective.* New York: Thomas Y. Crowell, 1970.

Block, Fred L. *The Origins of International Economic Disorder.* Berkeley and Los Angeles: University of California Press, 1977.

Boltho, Andrea, ed. *The European Economy: Growth and Crisis.* Oxford and New York: Oxford University Press, 1982.

Breslauer, George W. *Khrushchev and Brezhnev As Leaders: Building Authority In Soviet Politics.* Boston: George Allen and Unwin, 1982.

Calleo, David P. *The Imperious Economy.* Cambridge: Harvard University Press, 1982.

Central Intelligence Agency and Defense Intelligence Agency. "The Soviet Economy Under a New Leader." Submission to the Subcommittee on National Security Economics of the Joint Economic Committee of the U.S. Congress. Washington, DC: Central Intelligence Agency, March 19, 1986.

Chapmen, J.W.M., R. Drifte, and I.T.M. Gow. *Japan's Quest for Comprehensive Security.* New York: St. Martin's Press, 1982.

Cheng Chu-yuan. *China's Economic Development: Growth and Structural Change.* Boulder, Co.: Westview Press, 1982.

Cline, William R. *International Debt: Systemic Risk and Policy Responses.* Washington, DC: Institute for International Economics, 1984.

Cline, William R., ed. *Trade Policy In the 1980s.* Washington, DC: Institute for International Economics, 1983.

Cohen, Richard. "The Future of OPEC and World Oil Prices Under Conditions of Global Disinflation." *Washington/World Intelligence Focus,* Vol. 2, No. 3 (March 15, 1985): 1–21.

Cohen, Richard. "Will There Be A Second International Debt Crisis in the 1980s?" *Washington/World Intelligence Focus,* Vol. 2, No. 4 (April 15, 1985): 1–28.

Cohen, Richard, and Peter A. Wilson. "Superpowers in Decline? Economic Performance and National Security." *Comparative Strategy,* Vol. 7, No. 2 (Spring 1988): 99–132.

Danielsen, Albert L. *The Evolution of OPEC.* New York: Harcourt Brace Jovanovich, 1982.

Davenport, Michael. "The Economic impact of the EEC." In *The European Economy: Growth and Crisis,* edited by Andrea Boltho. Oxford and New York: Oxford University Press, 1982.

Delamaide, Darrell. *Debt Shock: The Full Story of the World Credit Crisis.* Garden City, N.Y.: Doubleday, 1984.

Destler, I.M. *American Trade Politics: System Under Stress.* Washington, DC: Institute for International Economics, 1986.

Dimancescu, Dan. *Deferred Future: Corporate and World Debt and Bankruptcy.* Cambridge, Ma.: Ballinger, 1983.

Enders, Thomas O., and Richard P. Mattione. *Latin America: The Crisis of Debt and Growth.* Washington, DC: The Brookings Institution, 1984.

Ethier, Wilfred. *Modern International Economics.* New York: W.W. Norton, 1983.

Far Eastern Economic Review. *Asia Yearbook.* Hong Kong: Far Eastern Economic Review Ltd. Published annually the year following the title date.

Gaddis, John Lewis. *The United States and the Origins of the Cold War, 1941–47.* New York: Columbia University Press, 1972.

Gregory, Paul R., and Robert C. Stuart. *Soviet Economic Structure and Performance.* New York: Harper and Row, 1986.

Hardt, John P., and Jean F. Boone. "The Soviet Union's Trade Policy." *Current History,* Vol. 87, No. 531 (October 1988): 329–332, 341–343.

Hathaway, Dale E. "Agricultural Trade Policy For the 1980s." In *Trade Policy in the 1980s,* edited by William R. Cline. Washington, DC: Institute for International Economics, 1983.

Hennings, Klaus Hinrich. "West Germany." In *The European Economy: Growth and Crisis,* edited by Andrea Boltho. Oxford and New York: Oxford University Press, 1982.

Hewett, Ed. A. "Foreign Economic Relations." In *The Soviet Economy: Toward the Year 2000,* edited by Abram Bergson and Herbert S. Levine. London and Boston: George Allen and Unwin, 1983.

Hirschman, Albert O. "The Political Economy of Import-Substituting Industrialization In Latin America." In *Latin America: Problems In Economic Development,* edited by Charles T. Nisbet. New York: The Free Press, 1969.

Hofheinz, Roy, Jr., and Kent E. Calder. *The Eastasia Edge.* New York: Basic Books, 1982.

Hohmann, Hans-Hermann, Alec Nove, and Heinrich Vogel. *Economics and Politics in the USSR: Problems of Interdependence.* Boulder, Co.: Westview Press, 1986.

Hooker, Sarah A. "The International Investment Position of the United States." A study produced by the Rand National Defense Research Institute. Santa Monica, Ca. October 1988.

Hosmer, Stephen T., and Thomas W. Wolfe. *Soviet Policy and Practice Toward Third World Conflicts.* Lexington, Ma.: Lexington Books: 1983.

Jackson, John H. "GATT Machinery and the Tokyo Round Agreements." In

Trade Policy In the 1980s, edited by William R. Cline. Washington, DC: Institute for International Economics, 1983.

Japan Economic Institute of America. *Yearbook of U.S.-Japan Economic Relations In 1983.* Washington, DC: Japan Economic Institute of America, 1984.

Johnson, Chalmers. *MITI and the Japanese Miracle: The Growth of Industrial Policy, 1925–75.* Stanford, Ca.: Stanford University Press, 1982.

Kaufman, Henry. "Debt: The Threat To Economic and Financial Stability." *In Debt, Financial Stability and Public Policy.* Kansas City: The Federal Reserve Bank of Kansas City, 1986.

Kushnirsky, Fyodor. "The Limits of Soviet Economic Reform." *Problems of Communism,* Vol. 33 (July–August 1984): 33–43.

Leddy, John M., ed. *The Uruguay Round of Multilateral Negotiations Under GATT.* Report of the Atlantic Council's Advisory Trade Panel. Washington, DC: The Atlantic Council of the United States, 1987.

Marer, Paul. "The Political Economy of Soviet Relations With Eastern Europe." In *Soviet Policy in Eastern Europe,* edited by Sarah Meiklejohn Terry. New Haven, Ct.: Yale University Press, 1984.

Marris, Stephen. *Deficits and the Dollar: The World Economy At Risk.* Washington, DC: Institute for International Economics, 1985.

Newton, Maxwell. *The Fed: Inside the Federal Reserve, the Secret Power Center That Controls the American Economy.* New York: Times Books, 1983.

Nisbet, Charles T., ed. *Latin America: Problems In Economic Development.* New York: The Free Press, 1969.

Nove, Alec. *An Economic History of the USSR.* New York: Penguin, 1969.

Okimoto, Daniel I., ed. *Japan's Economy: Coping With Change In the International Environment.* Boulder, Co.: Westview Press, 1982.

Parboni, Riccardo. *The Dollar and Its Rivals: Recession, Inflation, and International Finance.* London: Verso, 1981.

Patrick, Hugh, and Henry Rosovsky. *Asia's New Giant: How the Japanese Economy Works.* Washington, DC: The Brookings Institution, 1976.

Rumer, Boris. "Structural Imbalance In the Soviet Economy." *Problems of Communism,* Vol. 33 (July–August 1984): 24–32.

Scammell, W.M. *The International Economy Since 1945.* Second Edition. London: The MacMillan Press, 1983.

Schroeder, Gertrude E. "The Soviet Economy." *Current History,* Vol. 84, No. 504 (October 1985): 309–312, 340.

Stone, Charles F., and Isabel V. Sawhill. *Economic Policy in the Reagan Years.* Washington, DC: The Urban Institute, 1984.

Terry, Sarah Meiklejohn, ed. *Soviet Policy in Eastern Europe.* New Haven, Ct.: Yale University Press, 1984.

Uchino, Tatsuro. *Japan's Post-War Economy: An Insider's View of Its History and Its Future.* Tokyo and New York: Kodansha International Ltd., 1983.

United States Congress. Congressional Research Service. Economics Division and Foreign Affairs and National Defense Division. "Economic Changes in the Asian Pacific Rim: Policy Prospectus." A Staff Paper. Washington, DC: U.S. Congress, Congressional Research Service, August 1986.

United States Congress. Joint Economic Committee. Staff. "Restoring International Balance: Japan's Trade and Investment Patterns." A Staff Paper. Washington, DC: U.S. Congress, Joint Economic Committee, July 1, 1988.

United States Congress. Joint Economic Committee. Democratic Staff. "Trade Deficits, Foreign Debt and Sagging Growth: An Analysis of the Cause and Effects of America's Trade Problem." A Staff Paper. Washington, DC: U.S. Congress, Joint Economic Committee, September 1988.

United States Department of State. "The European Community Prepares to Complete a Single Market by 1992." Washington, DC: U.S. Department of State, July 5, 1988.

United States Department of the Treasury. "Report to the Congress on International Economic and Exchange Rate Policy." Washington, DC: U.S. Department of the Treasury, October 15, 1988.

Watkins, Alfred J. *Till Debt Do Us Part: Who Wins, Who Loses, and Who Pays for the International Debt Crisis.* Lanham, Md.: University Press of America, 1986.

Index

adjustable peg, 7
adjustment, macroeconomic, xviii–xx, xxi–xxii, 151–52, 258
Africa, sub-Saharan, 66, 169; developed sector exports to, 234; food deficit, 192; import decline, early 1980s, 186, 190
Aganbegyan, Abel, 262 n.20
agriculture, 16, 61; managed trade in, 175; U.S.-EEC clash over, 204; U.S. exports, 134–36, 138, 161–63, 234–35. *See also* food deficits
Anglo-American Loan Agreement, 74
antidumping actions, 176
Argentina, 170, 196, 240
Atlantic Charter, 6, 7
Australia, 238
Austria, 129

Baker, James, III, 194, 205
Baker Plan, 194–95, 196, 244
Bank of Japan, 231
Bergsten, C. Fred, 252
Beveridge System, 261 n.11

biases, national economic, 4, 5, 11–12, 15, 19, 261 n.11; as cause of cycles, 88; FRG and Japan, 12, 94–95; incentives to continue, 250; as obstacles to future adjustment, 258; U.S., 11–12, 94–95, 129, 251, 256; U.S. challenge to FRG and Japanese, 130
Black Monday, xvii
Bolivia, 169
Bonn Summit Agreement, 87, 131, 159, 196
Brazil, 45, 63; debt crisis, 170, 196; export performance in 1986, 199; inflation, 240; steel Voluntary Restraint Agreement (VRA), 204
Bretton Woods Monetary System, xx, 3–15 passim; challenges to, 75, 124, 128; effect of demise, 249; Nixon abandonment of, 85; unraveling of, 58, 67, 129
Bundesbank, 136, 137, 140, 149, 261 n.11; reaction to inflation, 154, 228

Canada, 30, 61, 71, 132, 137; in

G–7, 195; commodity composition of trade, 238; Free Trade Agreement, 257; U.S.-Canada Automotive Pact, 15, 57, 60

capital, flight, 35, 63, 190, 193–96

capital flows, cross border, 8–9, 11, 23, 26; East-West, 39, 177; FRG, to, 132; increase in 1980s, 206–12; relationship to trade flows, 179–80, 209; rise of, 145–50, 158; U.K., from, 75; U.S., from, 51, 68–69, 71, 72, 129; U.S., to, 208; Western Europe, within, 54

Caribbean, 169

Carter Administration, 85, 130, 158, 194

Centrally Planned Economies (CPEs), 4–17 passim; 39–41, 43, 44, 47–48, 92, 152, 262 n.24; commodity composition of trade, 191; external debt, 143, 170, 173, 193, 251, 278 n.23; import growth in 1980s, 186, 191, 193; import growth required in future, 257; trade and payments, different approaches to, 13; trade from 1959–67, 66–67. *See also* food deficits: China, USSR and European CPEs; intra-trade, regional: CPE

Chile, 45

China, 11, 13, 39–41, 48, 66; agricultural revival, 192; borrowing from West, 193; Cultural Revolution, 13; food deficits, 132, 134; Great Leap Forward, 13, 67; import decline, 173; import growth in early 1980s, 186, 191; "Readjustment," 67, 170–71; Ten-Year Plan, 13, 171; USSR relations rupture, 67

Common Agricultural Policy (CAP), 61

countertrade, 197

countervailing duties, 176

Cuba, 66

Cultural Revolution, 13

current account convertibility, 14, 16, 49, 61, 74

Czechoslovakia, 47, 66

debt, domestic, 17; developed sector, 154, 258; public, 228; U.S. private, 194, 254, 278 n.26

debt, external, 17, 140; Africa, sub-Saharan, 169; Argentina, 170, 196; Bolivia, 169; Brazil, 170, 196; Caribbean, 169; China, 193, 278 n.24; CPE, 143, 170, 173, 193, 199, 251, 278 n.23; developing sector, 63, 140, 143, 169–70, 172–73, 189, 190, 193, 199–200, 212, 251, 255, 273 nn.32, 33, 278 n.35 (*see also* Baker Plan); Mexico, 169, 170, 193, 196; Peru, 169; Poland, 170; relief, need for, 256; U.S., 210–11. *See also* International Monetary Fund: role in debt crisis; overindebtedness

developing sector, 11, 87, 101–3, 125, 128, 138–40, 146; differentiation among, 57, 63, 65, 133, 146, 174, 179, 190–91, 202; export weakness, 62; import decline in 1980s, 186, 201; imports' effect on developed sector, 233; markets, 11; in 1950s, 44–47; trade, early postwar, 38–39; trade from 1959–67, 62–65. *See also* debt, external: developing sector; import substitution

Davignon Plan, 204

Deng Xiaoping, 171

"dollar gap," 10, 14, 16, 29–37, 44, 262 n.1; defined, 261 n.10; evaporation of, 58, 67

"dollar overhang," 26, 44, 49, 58, 67–72

dollar overvaluation: in 1950s, 268 n.1; in early 1960s, 90; 1968, 126; in 1976/77, 158; in 1980s, 208–9, 212, 237, 243, 259 n.2, 281 n.17; dollar devaluation in 1971 and 1973, 132; in each Phase I, 81, 98; in future, 247, 249–50, 282 n.28; Nixon attempt to eliminate, 130

effective exchange rate, 98

Eisenhower Administration, 53
equilibrium exchange rate, 259 n.2
"errors and omissions," 149, 190,
    210, 277 n.14
Eurodollar market, 126, 149
European Economic Community
    (EEC), 15, 57, 63; creation of, 60;
    intra-trade, 144, 202; intra-trade
    liberalization in 1992, 256, 257;
    joint currency float, 132; U.S.,
    clash with over agriculture, 204
European Free Trade Association
    (EFTA), 15, 57, 60, 174, 202
European Monetary System (EMS),
    180
European Payments Union (EPU),
    14, 35, 37, 54, 55, 263 n.9

Federal Republic of Germany (FRG),
    8, 12, 14; commodity composition
    of trade, 147; deutsche mark un-
    dervaluation, 58, 73–74; domestic
    demand growth, 96, 125, 228; ex-
    ports and competitiveness, 37, 54–
    55, 73, 152, 174, 188, 197; govern-
    ment fiscal deficit, 126, 154, 185,
    228, 244; import decline, early
    1980s, 186, 188; inflation differen-
    tial, 127; investment boom, 48, 51,
    60; J-curve, 136–37; Louvre Ac-
    cords, break with, 230; macroeco-
    nomic conservatism, 68, 72, 73,
    91, 137–38, 157; monetary expan-
    sion, 86, 111, 116–18; pressure on
    to reflate, 130–31, 195–96, 230;
    revaluations in 1961, 69, 130; stag-
    flation in, 152; terms of trade ad-
    vantage, 197–98; trade dominance
    in Western Europe, 73–76;
    underinvestment, response to, 95.
    See also Bundesbank
Federal Reserve Board, 71, 72, 91,
    164, 194, 195, 247
flight capital, 35, 63, 190, 193–96
food deficits, 16, 113, 234–35; Af-
    rica, sub-Saharan, 192; China, 132,
    134; Eurasia, 76; India, 134; U.S.

in 1988, 218, 226, 271 n.20; USSR
    and European CPEs, 47, 65, 66,
    71, 86, 142, 134, 159, 161; West-
    ern Europe, 51
foreign direct investment, 39, 45, 51,
    184, 209, 238
France, 12, 16, 36; early 1980s im-
    port decline, 186; franc devalua-
    tion, 55, 73, 98; inflation, 127;
    1973 balance of payments pressure,
    137; relative decline, 54–55

General Agreement on Tariffs and
    Trade (GATT), 3, 10, 15, 16; future
    expansion needed, 257; Kennedy
    Round, 61; Most-Favored Nation
    principle, 7, 60, 176, 249; "new
    protectionism" challenge to, 145,
    249; obstacles to expansion, 258;
    Reagan Administration pursues
    new round, 204; Tokyo Round, 176
Generalized System of Preferences
    (GSP), 62, 177
gold, 6, 15, 30, 31, 53; creation of
    two-tiered price structure, 127; end
    dollar convertibility to, 129–30;
    price decline in 1988, 246; Soviet
    exports of, 143, 199; world reserves
    in 1945, 264 n.14
Gorbachev, Mikhail, 13, 262 n.20
Gramm-Rudman Act, 191, 252
Great Depression, 11, 12, 262 n.11
"Great Leap Forward," 13, 67
Great Society, 72, 124, 126
Group of Five (G-5), 194, 205, 259 n.4
Group of Seven (G-7), xxii, 195–96,
    245, 250; defined, 259 n.4; future
    credibility of, 251–55

Hong Kong, 63. See also Newly In-
    dustrializing Economies
Hungary, 66. See also Centrally
    Planned Economies

"import substitution," 9, 12–13, 30,
    38, 177
India, 132, 134

inflation / unemployment trade-off, 88, 91–94, 124, 250
"interest equalization tax," 71, 72
International Coffee Agreement, 177
International Monetary Fund (IMF), 3, 7, 47, 65, 71, 75; role in debt crisis, 170, 190, 193, 199
International Trade Commission (ITC), 176
International Trade Organization (ITO), 7, 16
intra-trade, regional: CPE, 41, 47, 66–67, 264 n.18; developed sector, 49, 57, 58, 60–61, 144, 174, 202; EEC, 144, 202; Eurasia, 39–41; North America, 61; North-South, 144 Western Europe, 15, 35, 44, 49, 85, 174, 202, 256, 263 n.9
Iran-Iraq War, 113, 120, 160, 165, 196
Italy, 12, 132; balance of payments pressure in 1973, 137; G-7 role, 195; import decline in early 1980s, 186; inflation, 127; lira, speculation against, 140; relative decline, 54

Japan, 8, 11, 12, 15, 32–33, 39–41; commodity composition of trade, 147, 197, 237; domestic demand growth, 96, 125, 228; export dynamism and competitiveness, 37, 54–56, 78, 127, 148, 152, 153, 165, 174, 188, 197; government fiscal deficit, 154, 185, 228, 244; import performance, early 1980s, 186, 188, 192; investment boom, 48, 60; J-curve, 136 (*see also* J-curve); "Jimmu boom," 56; liberalization, trade and payments, 61; merchandise trade surpluses, rise of, 73, 77–78, 127; MITI, 56, 261 n.11; monetary expansion, 86, 111; monetary policy in 1987/88, 231 "procurement boom," 37, 55; protectionism, as target of, 145, 176, 194, 203–5; reflate, pressure to, 130–31, 195–96, 205, 217, 230; supply-side adjustment, 152, 227, 237; terms

of trade advantage, 197–98; trade with U.S. in 1968, 61; underinvestment response to, 95; "window guidance," 55, 56. *See also* J-curve
J-curve, *xvii, xx*, 86, 115–16, 131, 132; defined, 259 n.1; in 1972/73, 133–37, 222, 223, 224, 231; in 1978–80, 133, 160–63, 222, 224, 231, 232; in 1986–89, 198, 222–26, 231, 232–35, 240, 245
"Jimmu boom," 56

Kennedy Administration, 61, 69–71, 85, 90
Kennedy Round, 15, 61, 176
Khrushchev, Nikita, 66
Korea, North, 39, 41, 66
Korea, South, 63, 199, 204. *See also* Newly Industrializing Economies
Korean War: effect on dollar gap, 35–36; effect on trade and investment, 10–11, 38–39, 43, 48

labor, organized, 22, 175, 183, 258
Latin America, 30, 33, 38, 45, 47, 72; debt crisis, 169, 190; developed sector exports to, 234; import decline in early 1980s, 186; inflation in, 240
Latin American Free Trade Association (LAFTA), 60
Lend-Lease, 74
Liberal Democratic Party (Japan), 164, 185
Lomé Convention, 177
long cycle, 260 n.7
Long-Term Agreement on Cotton, 16, 61
Louvre Accords, 87, 131, 195–96, 205, 249; causes of demise, 230, 244–45

Maekawa Report, 205
Market-Oriented Sector Specific talks (MOSS), 205
markets, developed sector, crowding in, 22, 61, 141, 144, 171, 175, 200, 203, 250, 258

Marshall Plan, 31, 74
Mexico, 45, 63, 199; debt crisis, 169–
    70, 193, 196; inflation, 240; steel
    Voluntary Restraint Agreement
    (VRA), 204
Ministry of International Trade and
    Industry (MITI), 56, 261 n.11
Miyazawa, Kiichi, 205
Most-Favored Nation principle
    (MFN), 7, 60, 176, 249. *See also*
    General Agreement on Tariffs and
    Trade
Multi-Fibre Arrangement (MFA), 62,
    145, 175–76, 205
Mutual Aid Agreement, U.S.-U.K., 6,
    7, 74

Nakasone, Yasuhiro, 176, 196
Netherlands, The, 54, 129
Neutrality Act, 74
New Deal, 126, 261 n.11
Newly Industrializing Economies
    (NIEs), 57; comparative advantage
    of, 227, 237; export performance
    in 1987, 198–99, 202–3; import
    decline in early 1980s, 192; "new
    protectionism" target, 145, 203–4;
    rise of, 63, 174–75
"new protectionism," *xx*, 16, 19, 22,
    62, 141; challenge to GATT, 145,
    249; increase in 1980s, 171, 175–
    77, 200, 203–5; moderation of in
    1988, 219; obstacles to roll-back,
    258; roll-back needed, 257; U.S.,
    145, 176, 194, 203–5
New World Economic Order
    (NWEO), 62, 172, 177
Nixon, Richard, 129, 158
Nixon Administration, 85, 194
Non-Tariff Barriers (NTBs), *xx*, 19,
    249. *See also* "new protectionism"
North Sea oil, 157

Oil Facility, IMF, 140, 149
Orderly Marketing Agreements
    (OMAs), 145, 176
Organization for Economic Coopera-

tion and Development (OECD),
    127
Organization for European Economic
    Cooperation (OEEC), 35
Organization of Petroleum Exporting
    Countries (OPEC), *xx*, 22, 62, 63,
    113, 120; decline of, 172, 183, 197;
    developed sector exports to, 234;
    oil price rise in 1971–74, 133; oil
    price rise in 1979/80, 176; produc-
    tion quota agreements, 189, 193,
    197, 242, 247; recycling of petro-
    dollars, 149; rise of, 141, 145
overcapacity, primary commodity,
    16, 29, 37–39, 43–45. *See also*
    supply-demand mismatch
overindebtedness, 91, 93, 118, 244,
    250, 251, 258; of U.S. government,
    268 n.5; U.S. foreign, 270 n.12

Peru, 169
petrodollar recycling process, 149,
    173, 177, 179–80
Plaza Accords, 85, 130, 194–95, 205,
    244, 249
Poland, 170
"procurement boom," Japanese,
    37, 55
producer cartel, 12–13, 133, 141,
    177. *See also* Organization of Pe-
    troleum Exporting Countries
protectionism. *See* "new
    protectionism"

"Readjustment," 67, 170–71
Reagan Administration, 85, 130, 204,
    205
recession: in 1949, 33; in 1958, 47;
    in 1960 (U.S.), 63, 69, 89; in 1965
    (Japan), 78; in 1967 (U.S. growth),
    72; in 1967 (FRG), 76; in 1969/70
    (U.S.), 126, 128; in 1974/75 (devel-
    oped sector), *xxi*, 124, 137–40,
    145, 165; in 1981/82 (developed
    sector), 165, 174, 181, 275 n.21; in
    future, 255
Romania, 170

Roosevelt, Franklin D., 5

Sato, Hideo, 131
Saudi Arabia, 140, 149, 193, 196–98
services trade, 22, 31, 180–82, 213,
    276 n.39
Shah of Iran, fall of, 113, 160
Singapore, 63. *See also* Newly Indus-
    trializing Economies
Smithsonian Agreement, 87, 130–31,
    134, 196; contrasted to Bonn Sum-
    mit Agreement, 159; effect of de-
    mise, 249; unraveling, 131–32, 150
Smoot-Hawley Act, 5
Social Democratic Party (FRG), 126,
    131
Soviet Union, 8, 13, 39, 47–48, 152;
    borrowing from West, 193, 199,
    201; China, rupture with, 67; com-
    modity composition of trade, 191;
    decline, economic, 262 n.20, 267
    n.20; defense spending, 269 n.9;
    export decline in 1986, 199; factor
    productivity, 269 n.9; food price
    rise, 274 n.16; gold exports, 143,
    199; hard currency earnings, 143;
    import performance, 170, 191;
    Khrushchev and Brezhnev periods,
    66; primitivization, economic, 92.
    See also Centrally Planned Econo-
    mies; food deficits, USSR and Eu-
    ropean CPEs; intra-trade, Regional:
    CPE
"special trade arrangements," *xx*, 8,
    12, 15, 16, 57, 60–61, 144; decline,
    174, 202; expansion needed, 257;
    potential for trade diversion, 258
spot market, petroleum, 197
Stalinist economic model, 48
Suez crisis, 53, 54
supply-demand mismatch, 30, 89,
    113, 132
"surplus disposal program," 51, 53
Switzerland, 129, 132

Taiwan, 63, 199. *See also* Newly In-
    dustrializing Economies

Tanaka, Kakuei, 131
Teheran Agreement, 133, 273 n.23
Ten-Year Plan, Chinese, 13, 171
textile trade, 22, 62, 175; U.S. action
    on, 145, 204. *See also* Multi-Fibre
    Arrangement
Tokyo Round, 176, 177
Trade Agreements Act, 5
Trade Expansion Act, 61
Treaty of Rome, 60

underinvestment, 91–93, 94, 152
United Kingdom, 6, 8, 12, 14, 15,
    16, 36; Beveridge System, 261
    n.11; coal miners strike, 189; exter-
    nal balance weakening in 1987/88,
    230; inflation, 127; Oil Facility
    borrowing, 140; pound sterling,
    pressure on, 74–77, 98, 132, 137;
    relative weakness, 54–55, 74–75;
    sterling area trade, 75, 264 n.17;
    trade deficit in 1986, 198
United Nations Conference on
    Trade and Development
    (UNCTAD), 62
United States, 12, 14, 15, 32–33, 48–
    49, 126–28, 138–40; August 1971
    initiatives, 129–30; biases, eco-
    nomic, 129, 251, 256; "Carter
    shock," 158–60; commodity com-
    position of trade, 147, 238; debt,
    domestic private 194, 254, 278
    n.26; deficit, fiscal, 184, 191, 219;
    deficit, net investment, 210–212,
    238; domestic demand growth, 96–
    98, 124–25, 184, 217–18, 247; ex-
    ternal imbalance improvement, 86,
    111; "Nixon shocks," 129–30; pro-
    tectionism, 145, 176, 194, 203–5;
    stagflation, 152; underinvestment,
    response to, 94–95. *See also* agri-
    culture: U.S. exports; Baker Plan;
    capital flows; dollar gap; dollar
    overhang; dollar overvaluation;
    J-curve
U.S.-Canada Automotive Pact, 15,
    57, 60

U.S.-Canada Free Trade Agreement,
  257

Volcker, Paul, 195
Voluntary Restraint Agreements
  (VRAs), 145, 176, 205

"wage explosion," West European,
  126
wage and price controls, 129–30
"window guidance," Japanese, 55, 56
World Bank, 3, 7, 47, 196

ABOUT THE AUTHOR

RICHARD COHEN directs his own consulting firm, Washington/ World Analysts, and writes a monthly review and forecast of U.S. economic developments. He also serves as the economic analyst for the Washington Defense Research Group, and has previously served as senior analyst for Colby-Bailey Associates. Mr. Cohen has produced in depth studies of U.S. defense spending patterns, the U.S. government budget, and the U.S., Soviet, Japanese, and Chinese economies, and is coauthor (with Norman Bailey) of *The Mexican Time Bomb*. Mr. Cohen was born in New York City and received his B.A. from Queens College in New York.